The Syntax of German

What do you know, if you know that a language has 'Object Verb' (OV) structure rather than 'Verb Object' (VO)? Answering this question and many others, this book provides an essential guide to the syntactic structure of German. It examines the systematic differences between German and English, which follow from this basic difference in sentence structure, and presents the main results of syntactic research on German. Topics covered include the strict word order in VO vs word order variation in OV, verb clustering, clause union effects, obligatory functional subject position, and subject–object asymmetries for extractions. Through this, a cross-model and cross-linguistic comparison evolves, highlighting the immediate implications for non-Germanic OV languages, and creating a detailed and comprehensive description of the syntactic differences that immediately follow from an OV type in contrast with a VO type like English. It will be of value to all those interested in syntax and Germanic languages.

HUBERT HAIDER is Professor in Linguistics at the University of Salzburg. He has worked in Germany, the USA, Norway, Sweden, Japan and Morocco, and his previous publications include *Deutsche Syntax, Generativ – Vorstudien zur Theorie einer projektiven Grammatik* (1993).

CAMBRIDGE SYNTAX GUIDES

General editors:
P. Austin B. Comrie J. Bresnan D. Lightfoot I. Roberts N.V. Smith

Responding to the increasing interest in comparative syntax, the goal of the Cambridge Syntax Guides is to make available to all linguists major findings, both descriptive and theoretical, which have emerged from the study of particular languages. The series is not committed to working in any particular framework, but rather seeks to make language-specific research available to theoreticians and practitioners of all persuasions.

Written by leading figures in the field, these guides will each include an overview of the grammatical structures of the language concerned. For the descriptivist, the books will provide an accessible introduction to the methods and results of the theoretical literature; for the theoretician, they will show how constructions that have achieved theoretical notoriety fit into the structure of the language as a whole; for everyone, they will promote cross-theoretical and cross-linguistic comparison with respect to a well-defined body of data.

Other books available in this series

O. Fischer *et al*:	*The Syntax of Early English*
K. Zagona:	*The Syntax of Spanish*
K. Kiss:	*The Syntax of Hungarian*
S. Mchombo:	*The Syntax of Chichewa*
H. Thrainsson:	*The Syntax of Icelandic*
P. Rowlett:	*The Syntax of French*
R. D. Borsley *et al*:	*The Syntax of Welsh*
C.-T. J. Huang *et al*:	*The Syntax of Chinese*
J. Aoun *et al*:	*The Syntax of Arabic*

The Syntax of German

HUBERT HAIDER
University of Salzburg

CAMBRIDGE UNIVERSITY PRESS
Cambridge, New York, Melbourne, Madrid, Cape Town, Singapore,
São Paulo, Delhi, Dubai, Tokyo

Cambridge University Press
The Edinburgh Building, Cambridge CB2 8RU, UK

Published in the United States of America by Cambridge University Press, New York

www.cambridge.org
Information on this title: www.cambridge.org/9780521865258

First published 2010

Printed in the United Kingdom at the University Press, Cambridge

A catalogue record for this publication is available from the British Library

Library of Congress Cataloguing in Publication data
Haider, Hubert.
    The syntax of German / Hubert Haider.
        p.   cm. – (Cambridge syntax guides)
    Includes bibliographical references.
    ISBN 978-0-521-86525-8 (hardback)
    1. German language–Syntax.   I. Title.   II. Series.
    PF3361.H35 2009
    435–dc22   2009031397

ISBN 978-0-521-86525-8 Hardback

Contents

Tables and figure

Foreword

In general we look for a new law by the following process. First we guess it. Then we compute the consequences of the guess to see what would be implied if this law that we guessed is right. Then we compare the result of the computation to nature, with experiment or experience, compare it directly with observation, to see if it works. If it disagrees with experiment it is wrong. In that simple statement is the key to science.

It does not make any difference how beautiful your guess is. It does not make any difference how smart you are, who made the guess, or what his name is – if it disagrees with experiment it is wrong.   Richard Feynman, from a lecture he gave in 1964

What you read, when you read this book, is inspired by the desire to live up to Feynman's standard in the field of grammar research. (Un)fortunately, this very desire made it inevitable for me to leave the well-trodden mainstream paths more often than not, for a simple reason. The paths lead to reasonable accounts for VO languages, but to questionable analyses of OV languages. I must admit though that I am not sure whether I have put to test my own pet ideas as squarely as I dealt with most of the competing hypotheses. Falsification is just labour, creativity is gift. You will have to find out.

Here is the point of departure: German is a verb-final Germanic language. Germanic languages are V-'movement' languages. This means that in a declarative clause, the finite verb is placed at a position following a single, clause-initial constituent. This is the syntactic hallmark of Germanic languages, viz. the so-called *verb second* property. These two properties – the head-final VP and the 'movability' of (finite) verbs – are the core properties that trigger a cascade of implications within a universal grammar framework. It is the major concern of this book to demonstrate in detail how this minimal set of initial conditions is sufficient for a deeper understanding of the major syntactic properties not only of German and its Germanic kin, but also of the systematic contrasts between an OV organisation of sentence structure vis-à-vis a VO organization of sentence structure.

The background understanding of universal grammar (UG) in the domain of syntax endorsed here is this: UG is the mental instantiation of a system of principles and properties that constitutes and guides (the acquisition of) a uniquely human mental capacity, viz. the language faculty. This capacity enables us to efficiently and effectively compute the string-to-structure mapping, and conversely, the structure-to-string mapping in language processing.

Syntax is (in part) an algorithm that projects at least two-dimensional structures on one-dimensional arrays of terminals and compresses two-dimensional structures to one-dimensional strings of terminals. It thereby bridges a dimension gap. It enables the mapping of the one-dimensional representations (strings) of phonetic/phonological structure to the at least two-dimensional hierarchical box-in-box structure of semantic representations, back and forth. The dimension mismatch is an unavoidable consequence of the respective interfaces. Sound structures are organized along the time axis (linear organisation), conceptual representations are timeless, hierarchically organized complex structures (hierarchical, box-in-box organisation).

You should be aware that it is the persuasion of the author that the cognitive capacities underlying the grammar faculty are characterized best in terms of capacities for computing syntactic *patterns* (as a complex 'geometric' capacity, that is, as *pattern matching* capacity) rather than in terms of computing syntactic *derivations* (as a complex 'algebraic' capacity, that is, *pattern construction and derivation* capacity). A theory of UG may justly be formulated in terms of principles and rules, but the mentally implemented (core) grammar of a given language as the model of the linguistic capacities of the speaker/listener is not a derivational machinery for tree structures; it is a pattern matching capacity.

This conviction is bolstered by findings in other cognitive domains. Human vision is the solution for a dimension management problem, too. Three-dimensional relations must be reliably projected (i.e. mentally reconstructed) from two-dimensional retinal reception patterns (Hoffmann 1998). The UG of vision as a system of rules and principles for 3D-projections is not the blueprint for a derivational system. It characterizes a system that is applied instantaneously, not sequentially.

Be that as it may, the general approach in this book is a representational, and not a derivational, one. A convergent syntactic representation for an array of terminal elements is seen as nothing else but the well-formed syntactic structure of the given array, and not, in addition, as the endpoint of a cascade of derivations (that are even taken to bifurcate into a spell-out structure and a hidden post-spell-out representation). Derivational terminology (e.g. 'movement') is used without restraint, though, in this book, just for expository and familiarity reasons, without ontological commitments.

The agreed objective for me as a contributor to the Cambridge Syntax Guides series has been to produce a comprehensive survey of German syntax while keeping a low profile on the technical apparatus, but nevertheless following a theory-inspired road map. The focus will be on data and argumentation at a primarily descriptive level. If you nevertheless come to think that there are still too many technical details in some chapter, and not enough data in another, blame it on the author.

Acknowledgements

Any substantive piece of work of a researcher is much like a mushroom. It looks like an individually grown thing, but in fact it is just the surface appearance of the activity of a huge underground mycelium which the researcher is but a part of. By the way, mycelia love trees, and so do some syntacticians.

It is impossible for me to figure out a complete inventory of all my influential co-mycelians. So I apologize to those who fed my mushroom but have fallen victim to my mediocre source memory. After all, my concern with OV and VO took shape in the early nineties, presented first at the 1991 Utrecht conference, whose proceedings took their time (Haider 1992, in Coopmans, Everaert and Grimshaw 2000).

My mushroom cultivating award for German surely goes to at least the following eminent grammarians who readily come to my mind: Klaus Abels, Werner Abraham, Josef Bayer, Manfred Bierwisch, Daniel Büring, Gisbert Fanselow, Werner Frey, Günther Grewendorf, Tilman Höhle, Joachim Jacobs, Angelika Kratzer, Gereon Müller, Stefan Müller, Marga Reis, Inger Rosengren, Arnim von Stechow, Wolfgang Sternefeld, Sten Vikner, Angelika Wöllstein, Ellen Woolford, Susi Wurmbrand, Ilse Zimmermann.

My reminiscence gratefully retrieves that valuable input came from the audiences that were willing to pay attention to my ideas. Thanks to the syntax class at the 2002 DGfS summer school in Düsseldorf and to Dieter Stein for inviting me. Thanks to the 2004 syntax seminar group at U.Mass, Amherst, and to Ellen Woolford, Lisa Selkirk and Angelika Kratzer for the invitation to South College. Thanks to Masayuki Oishi for providing me with an interested audience in the syntax seminar at Sendai's Tohoku Gakuin in 2005.

Marga Reis and Gisbert Fanselow invested time and effort in reading (parts of) an earlier version and not only pointed out deficits and problems but supplied highly valuable suggestions, due scepticism and welcome encouragement. My special gratitude goes to them. Whatever blunders are still lurking for you in the present version are to be exclusively blamed on the author, of course.

The Cambridge University Press team, whose persistence got tested over the years between the first delivery deadline and the actual one, I thank for their endurance and continuous support.

Finally, the readability of the text has benefited enormously from my companion-in-life's untiring efforts in hunting relentlessly for typos, inconsistencies and barely understandable formulations during several metamorphotic stages of this book. In general, the extent to which it has gained a more butterfly-like than larva-shaped appearance is definitely thanks to her. Hartelijk bedankt, lieveke!

This book, I dedicate to the memory of my beloved younger brother Martin, whose brilliant brain happened to be fatally devastated by bacteria at the time I was finishing this book.

Abbreviations

AC	absolute cartography
ACC	accusative
ANS	*Algemene Nederlandse Spraakkunst* ('grammar of standard Dutch'); abbreviation for the title of Geerts *et al.* (1984)
ARB	arbitrary (PRO_{ARB})
BBC	basic branching constraint
BG	Burzio's generalization
CC	copy construction
CED	condition on extraction domains
CL	clitic
CS	convergent structuring
CUS	clause union syndrome
DAT	dative
DIR	directive
DO	direct object
ECM	exceptional case marking
ECP	Empty Category Principle
EPP	extended projection principle $=_{def.}$ *'clauses have subjects'* (Chomsky 1982: 9–10)
fem	feminine
FF	focus fronting
FIN	finite
GEN	genitive
INF	infinite
INTRANS	intransitive
IO	indirect object
IPP	*infinitivus pro participio*, Latin for 'infinitive instead of participle', in German: *Ersatzinfinitiv*
IS	information structure
LD	left-dislocation
LF	logical form

LFG	Lexical Functional Grammar
LOC	locative
MAC	minimal argument complex
masc	masculine
MLC	Minimal Link Condition
neut	neutrum, neuter
NOM	nominative
OBJ	object
OV	type of language with head-final VP, that is, 'object–verb' order
P&P	Principles & Parameter Model (Chomsky 1981)
Part	Participle
PASS	passive
PDI	Principle of Directional Identification
PF	phonetic form
pg	parasitic gap
PRO	silent subject in clausal infinitival constructions
PRT	particle
REFL	reflexive
SUBJ	subject
TP	tense phrase
TRANS	transitive
UG	Universal Grammar
VC	verb cluster
VO	type of language with head-initial VP, that is, 'verb–object' order
WC	*was* (what) construction
XP	phrase of an arbitrary category (*x* serves as a variable for the head category)
<	Read 'A < B' as 'A precedes B'

1

A comparative survey: German – V2 and partially OV

1.1 The V2 property of Germanic languages

A common feature of all Germanic languages,[1] except English, is the so-called *V2 property*: the *finite* verb is the *second* constituent (whence 'V2'), following an *arbitrary, single, clause-initial constituent*. Pattern (1) is the general V2 pattern. Unless XP is a wh-phrase, the instantiations of (1) yield a declarative clause. If XP is a wh-phrase, the clause is interrogative.

(1) $[XP_{(i)} [V_{fin} [\dots (e_i) \dots]]]$

The XP constituent in the V2 structure (1) of a declarative may be any phrase that is available for fronting into the XP position in the given language (see 2). As an alternative to fronting a constituent, the XP slot in (1) may be filled with an expletive (see 3). Just for this reason, the subscript 'i' on the XP and the trace 'e_i' are in brackets in the structure (1).

(2)   a. [*Eine Maus*$_i$ [hat [heute e_i den Käse verschmäht]]]
           [a mouse [has [today the cheese disdained]]]
        b. [*Den Käse*$_i$ [hat [heute eine Maus e_i verschmäht]]]
        c. [*Heute*$_i$ [hat [e_i eine Maus den Käse verschmäht]]]
        d. [*Verschmäht*$_i$ [hat [heute eine Maus den Käse e_i]]]
        e. [[*Den Käse verschmäht*]$_i$ [hat [heute eine Maus e_i]]]

---

[1] Present-day Germanic standardized languages: Afrikaans, Danish, Dutch, English, Faroese, Frisian, German, Icelandic, Norwegian, Swedish. English, a language of Germanic origin, is exceptional. It does not share the typical Germanic clause structure property, viz. V2. Note that this list of languages names just the 'official' languages. There are numerous so-called Germanic dialects, each of which is a language in itself.

(3)   [*Es* [hat [heute jede Maus den Käse verschmäht]]][2]
        [it [has [today every mouse the cheese disdained]]]

In (2d), a single non-finite verb is the first constituent. It represents a verbal projection, though. In (2e), the fronted constituent is a verb phrase. The XP slot is a slot for phrasal constituents; the V_{fin} slot, however, is open only for *atomic* finite verbal elements.

Clauses with a particle verb provide a minimal pair context for illustrating this difference. In German, the particle + verb combination[3] is split when the *finite* verb is placed into the fronted position. In this case, the particle is obligatorily stranded. In (4a), the finite verb strands the particle in the clause-final verb position as a consequence of fronting the *atomic* verbal element. The particle must be stranded (see 4c), because only an *atomic* verbal element is accepted in the fronted position of the finite verb. In (4b), an infinitival particle verb is 'topicalized', that is, fronted to the XP position. In this case, the particle must not be stranded (4d). The atomic verb is obviously not qualified for the XP as this is a position for a *phrasal* category. The XP slot is a phrasal one. Particle stranding is the result of splitting off the atomic verbal partner of the particle verb combination.

(4)   a.   [Er [*stand*$_i$ [nicht *auf*-e$_i$]]]
               he stood not up

        b.   [*Auf*stehen$_j$ [würde$_i$ [er nicht e$_j$ e$_i$]]]
               up-stand would he not

        c. * Er *auf*stand nicht

        d. * Stehen würde er nicht *auf*

The only context in which the initial XP in (1) may be preceded by another constituent is that of *left dislocation* (5a). The left-dislocated phrase precedes the XP position, is pre-adjoined to the clause, and is obligatorily associated with a resumptive element (R) that agrees with the left-dislocated constituent. The resumptive is a demonstrative pronoun. The resumptive appears in the spec position (5a,c)

---

[2] Note that German does not show a definiteness effect in this construction. Compare this with English:

(i)   There is a /*the /*every mouse in the kitchen

A definiteness effect is operative only in topicalized VPs that contain the subject, as noted by Kratzer (1984).

(ii)   [Ein /*der /*dieser /*jeder Generativist unterrichtet]$_{VP}$ hat hier noch nie
        [a / the / this / every generativist taught] has here not ever

[3] Note that in OV languages, the particle of particle verbs precedes the verb; in VO languages it follows.

unless this position is unavailable (5b). In this case, the resumptive occurs in its clause-internal (base) position (5d,e). In (5d), the wh-word occupies the spec C position, and in (5e), the position is unavailable, since yes-no questions require a structure with a phonetically empty spec C.

(5) a. $[_{FP}$ XP^j $[_{FP}$ R$_i^j$ $[V_{fin}$ [... e$_i$ ...]]]]^4

   b. $[_{FP}$ XP^j $[_{FP}$ YP$_{wh}$ $[V_{fin}$ [... R^j ...]]]]?

   c. (Den Käse^i), *den^i* hat die Maus gefressen
      (the-ACC cheese) that-ACC has the mouse eaten

   d. (Den Käse^i), *wann* hat die Maus *den^i* gefressen?
      (the-ACC cheese) when has the mouse that-ACC eaten

   e. (Den Käse^i), hat die Maus *den^i* gefressen?
      (the-ACC cheese) has the mouse that-ACC eaten

The contrast between English and German illustrated in (6) is one between a V2 clause and a clause without the V2 property (6a). The grammatical V2 variants for (6b) are given in (7).

(6) a. Today, the mouse has disdained the cheese

   b. * Heute, die Maus hat den Käse verschmäht
      today the mouse has the cheese disdained

(6b) is ungrammatical. The two elements preceding the finite verb, namely *heute* and *die Maus* do not form a constituent. Hence only one of them yields a well-formed option for the XP position. What (6b) shows is that fronting an additional phrase to a position either preceding or immediately following the XP is not permitted in German.

The regular V2 variant with *heute* in the XP position is given under (7a). (7b) is the left-dislocation construction, with the resumptive *da* in the XP position.

(7) a. Heute hat die Maus den Käse verschmäht
      today has the mouse the cheese disdained

   b. Heute^i, da^i hat die Maus den Käse verschmäht
      today there has the mouse the cheese disdained

You may try on your own to estimate whether the V2 variant could be derived as a reduced left-dislocation (LD) variant (as was once suggested in the literature). Compare the examples in (8), and you will see easily how (un)successful this account would be.

---

^{4} Note the convention on sub- and superscripting applied in this book: a *subscripted index* is used for co-indexing a moved constituent with its trace(s); a *superscripted index* is used for co-indexing in binding or agreement relations.

(8)   a. Den Käse, (den) hat die Maus verschmäht
            the-ACC cheese (that-ACC) has the mouse disdained

        b. *Käse* (*den) hat die Maus fast *keinen* verschmäht
            cheese (that-ACC) has the mouse almost none-ACC disdained

        c. [*Käse* verschmäht] (*das) hat die Maus *nur meinen*
            cheese disdained (that-ACC) has the mouse only my-one-ACC

        d. Den Käse, (*den) hat die Maus verschmäht, mit dem ich sie lockte
            the-ACC cheese (that-ACC) has the mouse disdained with which I her
            baited

        e. Nichts (*das) hat die Maus verschmäht
            nothing (that-ACC) has the mouse disdained

        f. Jeder, *(der den Witz nicht kannte), *der* hat gelacht
            everybody (who the joke not knew) this-one has laughed

First, split-NP constructions as in (8b,c) are ungrammatical for LD constructions. Interestingly, the split-NP construction is compatible with VP topicalization (8c). This is a hard nut for those who would like to analyse NP splitting in terms of movement plus stranding. Second, relative clause extraposition is incompatible with LD (8d). Third, quantifiers are no target for LD (8e), unless they are restricted (8f). For more data coverage see Haider (1990).

The V2 pattern alternates with the embedded C°-introduced clause pattern for the complements of a class of verbs and nouns. Keep in mind, however, that V2 is never allowed within C°-introduced clauses in German (9c,f) or Dutch, contrasting with Scandinavian languages, as in (10).

(9)   a. wenn du glaubst, [*dass* er sich geirrt *habe*]
            if you believe [that he REFL erred has]

        b. wenn du glaubst, [er *habe* sich geirrt]
            if you believe [he has REFL erred]

        c. * wenn du glaubst, [*dass* er *habe* sich *geirrt*]

        d. die Annahme, [*dass* er sich geirrt *habe*]
            the assumption [that he REFL erred has]

        e. die Annahme, [er *habe* sich geirrt]
            the assumption [he has REFL erred]

        f. * die Annahme [*dass* er *habe* sich *geirrt*]

Note that the class of verbs that allows a V2 complement in German in place of a *dass*-CP is virtually identical with the verb class that allows the dropping of *that* for complements in English. For complements of N, however, English forbids dropping the complementizer in the complement clause in general, while German allows the V2 variant (9e). The reason for this difference is unknown. After all, the NP is head initial in both languages.

CP-internal V2, however, is compatible with the Germanic V2 property (see Vikner 1995), as exemplified in the Scandinavian languages (10b, Danish). CP-internal V2 is strictly ruled out in German and Dutch. In English, you can observe CP-internal V2, but only with the type of topicalization that triggers auxiliary inversion. Note that in this case, *that* must not drop in English (10a).

(10)   a. He said *(that) [never before] *has* he read such a good article

     b. Han sagde *(at) [aldrig før] *havde* han læst sådan en god artikel

Danish

he said (that) [never before] had he read such a good article

     c. Er sagte, (*dass) [nie zuvor] habe er so einen guten Artikel gelesen

German

he said (that) [never before] had he such a good article read

The class of verbs that allows the CP-internal V2 variant in place of the standard CP variant in Danish (and other Scandinavian languages) is identical with the class that allows the V2 variant in place of the CP variant in German.[5]

1.2   The linearization of heads and complements: lexically OV and functionally VO

In terms of the familiar Greenbergian OV vs VO categorization, German (like Afrikaans, Dutch and Frisian) is classified as OV. But neither German nor the other languages mentioned above are 'strict' OV languages. They are OV only in the *narrow* construal of OV. It is OV in the literal reading, insofar as this refers to the structure of the verb phrase: the *verb* as the head of the VP follows its nominal complements.

Strict OV languages are languages in which *any* phrasal head is a phrase-final one. Japanese, but not German, would qualify as a strict OV language. In strict VO languages, on the other hand, any head is head initial. English and the Scandinavian Germanic languages are strict VO languages.

In the Germanic OV languages, only V° and A° (plus a handful of exceptional postpositions) are head final; all other heads, lexical as well as functional ones (to be shown in chapter 2 on clause structure) are head initial.

---

[5] Note the nice theoretical puzzle posed by this verb class restriction: what is it that enables a matrix verb to look deeply enough into the complement clause to allow/forbid V2 in the domain of the complements C°? In this case, the matrix verb has to be able to control a structure beyond the edge of the complement clause, inside the domain of the C° head. This is a challenge for present-day assumptions on category selection.

As for the VP, in a VO language like English and the North Germanic languages, the verb precedes its nominal complements (1a); in an OV language like German, the verb follows its nominal complements (1b).

(1)   a. [*ask* someone something]$_{VP}$

    b. [jemanden etwas *fragen*]$_{VP}$
       someone something ask

As for the other major lexical categories, phrases headed by A° are *head final*, but the other phrases are *head initial* in German.

(2)   head-*final* (V°, A°)

    a.   [jemandem etwas *zeigen*$_V$°]$_{VP}$
          someone something show

    b.   * [*zeigen* jemandem etwas]

    c.   [den Kindern / uns *unangenehm*$_A$°]$_{AP}$
          (for) the children-DAT / us-DAT unpleasant

    d.   * [*unangenehm* uns / den Kindern]

The two other major lexical categories (N°, P°) form head-*initial* phrases, namely NP (3a) and PP (3b–e), just as in English. Prepositions[6] typically select noun phrases as complements (3b). There are only a small number of prepositions that may alternatively select a PP (see the preposition *bis* in 3c), or a clause (3d,e).

(3)   head-*initial* (N°, P°)

    a.   [$_{NP}$ *Nachrichten*$_N$° von mir an dich]
          messages from me to you

    b.   [$_{PP}$ *in*$_P$° [das Haus]]
          in the house

    c.   [$_{PP}$ *bis*$_P$° [$_{PP}$ *in*$_P$° [das Haus]]]
          till (= up-to) into the house

    d.   [$_{PP}$ *ohne*$_P$° [dass sie es bemerkte]]
          without that she it noticed
          'without her noticing it'

    e.   [$_{PP}$ *ohne*$_P$° [es bemerkt zu haben]]
          without it noticed to have
          'without having noticed it'

---

[6] There is a very small number of prepositions that alternatively may be used as postpositions, that is, as relation particles that *follow* their complements: *entlang* – along, *wegen* – because of, *zufolge* – according to, *gegenüber* – as against. Only *zufolge* is exclusively postpositional. The others may be used as post- or as prepositions.

1.3   German in comparison with other Germanic languages

The Germanic languages provide a well-structured space of parameter settings of grammars within a single language family. Table 1.1 lists some easily identifiable parametric differences for a sample of Germanic family members, namely, the so-called Germanic standard languages. Other Germanic languages are usually referred to as 'dialects', but this is a sociolinguistic rather than a grammar-based distinction. There is no grammar-theoretic basis for this distinction.[7] A complete list would require entries for isolated varieties of German, for instance 'Pennsylvania Dutch' or the linguistic islands in Northern Italy (e.g. the 'Dodici commune' = the twelve communities). But there are many more German

Table 1.1 *Some conspicuous (morpho-)syntactic differences among Germanic languages*

Germanic languages	V2 declaratives	OV [−OV] = [+VO]	morphological case paradigm for NP	subject–verb agreement paradigm
English	−	−	−	−/+
Afrikaans	+	+	−	−
Dutch	+	+	−	+
Frisian	+	+	−	+
German	+	+	+	+
Faroese	+	−	+	+
Icelandic	+	−	+	+
Danish	+	−	−	−
Norwegian	+	−	−	−
Swedish	+	−	−	−
Yiddish[8]	+	+ (flexible)	+	+

[7] The grammar-based differences between Norwegian and Swedish, for instance, are minimal compared to the differences between standard German and a Swiss German 'dialect'. The former varieties are acknowledged as different languages, the latter are filed as dialects. Similarly, standard Dutch and standard German are taken to be different 'languages', but 'Plattdeutsch' (literally: 'flat German'; varieties spoken in North-West Germany) is called a dialect of German although it is much closer to Dutch than to standard German in its grammar.

[8] Yiddish has conserved a property that all Germanic languages had in their historical ancestors' grammars: they were neither strictly OV nor strictly VO. The position of the verb was 'flexible', not rigid, as in all modern Germanic languages. 'Flexible' means that the verb could be placed in the head-final position, or, alternatively, in intermediate positions, or, in the head-initial position. The underspecification of the directionality feature produces this flexibility (see Haider 2005b) that allows OV and VO patterns, plus VP-internal positions. For a detailed discussion of the OV/VO property of Yiddish see Vikner (2001).

speaking minorities, for instance in Eastern Europe, some of which still use a present-day version of the variety of German their ancestors spoke when they emigrated to the East in the eighteenth century (e.g. the Alemannian variety of the Donauschwaben = Danubian Swabians; in Romania, Hungary and Serbia). So, the table should just be taken as a representative sample of Germanic languages. All Germanic languages, except for English, share the V2 property.[9] Outside the Germanic family, this property is presently confirmed only for Kashmiri (Wali and Koul 1997; Bhatt 1999).

A conspicuous but still not fully understood feature of the Germanic language family is its diachronic 'dialect split' into a VO group (North Germanic) and an OV group (West Germanic: Afrikaans,[10] Dutch, Frisian, German). Contrary to popular wisdom, it clearly does not correlate with the 'decay' of the morphological paradigms for the nominal and verbal inflections. In both groups there are on the one hand languages with rich morphological inventories for case marking and verbal inflection for agreement, tense and mood, and on the other hand languages without or with just minimal and deficient inventories.

In the OV group, Afrikaans is the extreme case of lack of morphology (no case morphology, no verbal inflection for agreement), in contrast to German with a rich morphological case paradigm (notably for articles and pronouns).

In the VO group, the continental Scandinavian languages are morphologically poor, without any subject–verb agreement on the finite verb, whereas the insular Scandinavian languages (Icelandic, Faroese) are morphologically rich. Nevertheless, the OV vs VO characteristics are robust and persistent. What this tells us is that morphological change cannot have been a trigger for the syntactic changes that lead to the OV/VO distinction. In chapter 2, the dialect split that led to the OV/VO is argued to be a split in the development from a language with a *flexible* directionality (all Old Germanic varieties and present-day Yiddish) to languages with *rigid* directionality. The switch from 'flexible' to 'rigid' opened exactly two possible, alternative implementations for 'rigid', namely head-final or head-initial order. The choice of the parametric value apparently was a matter of chance. One dialect (group) ended up with the value 'head initial'. This is the VO group. The other group is one that developed from a mother dialect with the directionality 'head final' for the V-projections. As for nouns, particles and (lexical) functional heads (complementizers, articles), all Germanic languages share the head-initial value.[11]

---

[9] English employs the V2 pattern only for wh-clauses and a special type of clause with fronted negative quantifiers: 'With no job *would* he be happy.' Contrast this with the English declarative pattern: 'With no job, he would be happy.'

[10] Language of Dutch origin, spoken in South Africa.

[11] As an alternative to the article, Scandinavian languages employ a definiteness marker as suffix of the noun. The alternation between article and definiteness marker is not free, though.

As for English, it is *the* exceptional language, not only within the Germanic language family. It is V2, but only for main clause wh-constructions (and topicalized negative operators). It requires V-to-'I' for the finite verb, but it allows this only for auxiliaries. So, it needs to employ an expletive auxiliary ('do-support') to compensate for the immobility of a finite main verb. It does not allow passivizing an intransitive verb because of the lack of a suitable subject expletive. It has a set of quasi-auxiliaries (modals) that cannot partake in infinitival constructions because they lack the finite vs infinitive distinction. It does not provide an infinitive morphology for the verb but uses the stem only. It has person + number agreement, but only in a highly deficient paradigm (only third person singular, in present tense, except for auxiliaries). Nevertheless, English still serves as *the* model language for grammar theory. This is not detrimental as long as the exceptional qualities of English are recognized and not mistaken as a model of a universal grammar.

1.4   The OV properties of German in contrast to VO properties of English

What do we know, if we know that a language is VO, or if we know it is OV, without knowing details about this language? In other words, what are reliable correlations between the OV vs VO organization of a clause and its grammatical properties? Present-day theorizing focuses primarily on a universal model of clause structure and emphasizes the *shared* properties. The ubiquitous differences between languages are disruptive rather than constitutive elements in this universal grammar account.

In the author's view, languages do not necessarily share a universal clause structure. What they share is a universal set of principles and processes that determine the organization of the grammar of a human language. Because of parameterization, two grammars might be minimally different, differing maybe only in a single parameter value. But if this parameterized principle interacts with enough other principles of grammar and triggers a cascade of effects, the two languages these two grammars account for may appear to be strongly different, depending on the parameter value. Here, we shall briefly analyse the grammatical properties that seem to correlate directly with a single parameter setting, namely the headedness value (head initial, head final), construed as a *directionality* factor of licensing a phrase by a phrasal head. Two premises, you are asked to grant. The rest will follow.

- The *first premise* (P1): positions in the projection of a phrasal head need to be licensed under the *canonical directionality* of the head. Canonical directionality is the basic parametric factor that produces head-final or head-initial structures, respectively.[12]

• The *second premise* (P2): the structural build-up ('merger') of phrases is *asymmetric*. It is universally *right branching*:

If a phrase α is merged[13] to a phrase β, the resulting structure is [β^n α β]. Hence, merger produces *right-branching structures only*. Left-branching merger structures *[β^n β α] are universally ruled out.[14] This generalization on phrase structuring was originally suggested in Haider (1992/2000).

a. **right**-branching   b. **left**-branching (ruled out)

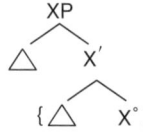 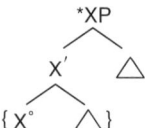

The curled brackets in the bottom line of the structures above are to signify that the branching restriction is independent of the order of head and complement, that is, head-final or head-initial order, or, as will be discussed later, in phrases with adjustable head positioning.

In combination, the premises P1 and P2 produce a set of corollaries that are characteristic of OV vs VO properties of clause structure. In the next subsection, the respective data are presented. Their relation to the premises above will be derived and discussed in the subsequent subsection.

1.4.1 The OV 'fingerprints' of German

The observations listed below are taken to be immediate effects of head-final vs head-initial phrase structure in combination with premise P2. Remember that the German NP is head initial. This provides a handy testing ground for some of the properties under discussion below, since it is easy to derive a deverbal noun: the infinitive can be used as a noun. So, we can inspect the head-initial vs head-final effects in a minimal pair setting within a single language, once we contrast a clause with the deverbal infinitival noun phrase. The following eight observations will be first described and then derived in section 1.4.2.

---

[12] The idea that directionality is a relevant parametric factor is not a new one. It has been under discussion since the advent of the Principles & Parameter model, for instance in the early work of Hilda Koopman.

[13] 'merge α with β' =$_{def.}$ combine α with β into a phrase structure [$_γ$ α β], where γ is a projection of either α or β.

[14] This premise applies to merger. It remains silent on the question as to whether there could be a transformational source of left-branching structures, as for instance, adjunction by movement to the right.

- Observation 1   Head-initial phrases are *compact*, head-final ones are not.
- Observation 2   Head-initial phrases are *strictly serialized*, head-final ones allow word order *variation* (scrambling).
- Observation 3   The *relative order* of the dependent phrases (i.e. arguments or selected adverbials) is *identical* in head-initial and in head-final phrases.
- Observation 4   Particle placement with particle verbs:
    - 4a The *particle* of particle verbs *precedes* the verb in the clause-internal position in OV, but it *follows* in VO.
    - 4b In VO, the *particle* of a particle verb may *intervene* between the objects of a double object construction, if the given language allows particle stranding. In OV, the particle is always in the clause-final, $V°$-*adjacent* position.
- Observation 5   In an OV clause structure, *verbs cluster* with clause union effects. In VO, verbs do not cluster.
- Observation 6   In a VO clause structure, the *subject position* must be lexicalized. In the absence of a subject argument, an expletive subject is mandatory (modulo[15] pro-drop or topic-drop). In OV, structural subject expletives[16] are not mandatory and do not occur, independently of pro-drop.
- Observation 7   A language with a VO clause structure and non-positional nominative checking may allow *quirky subjects*. In OV, quirky subject constructions cannot arise.
- Observation 8   *Subject–object asymmetries* widely attested in VO are absent in OV:
    - (i) no asymmetry for extraction out of subjects vs objects in OV,
    - (ii) no structure-triggered asymmetry for wh-in-situ in OV.

---

[15] Pro-drop is a parametric property for unstressed *subject* pronouns. In cliticizing languages, the subject clitic is not lexically represented in the clause since the target of cliticization, the finite verb, already specifies the person–number matrix represented by the subject clitic. In topic-drop languages, a pronominal *topic* is not lexically represented in the clause. Topic-drop is not restricted to subjects, but applies to objects as well.

[16] Structural expletives are elements that lexicalize the obligatory structural subject position in the absence of a subject argument. This function of an expletive must not be confused with the expletive argument function, that is, the function of a quasi argument. German has quasi-argument subjects, but not structurally expletive subjects. See the discussion of observation 6 below.

German and English differ in these respects. But this is not a peculiarity of German or English. In fact, the properties listed above are (just a subset of systematic) differences between an OV and a VO organization of clause structure. They all follow from a single structural difference in the organization of clause structure, namely the head position of V° in the VP.

Observation 1 – compactness

Compactness refers to a well-known property of head-*initial* phrases. They provide no room for adjuncts in between the head and the nominal arguments of the head (1a,b). This property is absent in head-final phrases (1c,d).

(1)   a. They will [investigate$_{V}$° (*thoroughly*) this phenomenon /something]
        b. They have [told their students (*enthusiastically*) boring stories]
        c. Sie werden dieses Phänomen / (et)was (*gründlich*) untersuchen
            they will this phenomenon / something (thoroughly) investigate
        d. Sie haben ihren Studenten (*begeistert*) langweilige Geschichten erzählt
            they have their students (enthusiastically) boring stories told

Compactness is a robust property of English VPs. Adverbials must not intervene between the verb and its nominal complement (1a) or between the nominal objects in a double object construction (1b). In German, this restriction does not apply. You might immediately feel tempted to heckle 'Scrambling!'. But note, there are noun phrases that precede the adverbial in (1b) that do not partake in scrambling as for instance the indefinite pronoun *was* (something) or the indefinite noun *etwas* (something) in (1c). Second, German does obey the compactness restriction, but only in head-*initial* phrases, namely NPs, as expected.

The noun phrases in (2) are the nominal counterparts of the verbal heads in (1). German noun phrases are head initial and they are as compact as English VPs or NPs, with difference in the selectable complements.

In German, the direct object of the verb corresponds to the genitive complement of the noun. In many cases, the genitive DP may be replaced by a PP headed by *von* (of), as in (2d–f). In English this is the only option. This is a fairly direct correspondence to the English nominal complementation. Compactness shows in (2c). (2d, e) are not fully parallel to (1d) because the dative of the double object construction (1d) cannot be transferred into the NP since NPs allow only complements with structural case and this case is spelled out as genitive. Lexical case – in German, dative is a lexical case – cannot be converted and so dative arguments cannot be integrated. In (2d–f), the dative argument is replaced by a goal PP. As a PP it may be extraposed. This is the reason why (2e) is acceptable and why the compactness of double object constructions cannot be tested with NP complements. NPs do not allow double object complements. Note, however, that the object PP *von Geschichten* in (2d–f) is subject to compactness, too, just like the genitive DP. The intervening adverbial *im Syntaxunterricht* makes the order ungrammatical.

(2) a. [_{VP} das Problem gründlich untersuchen_V°]
         the problem thoroughly investigate

    b. das [Untersuchen des Problems *mit geeigneten Mitteln*]
        the [investigat(ing) (of) the problem-GEN with suitable means]

    c. * das [Untersuchen *mit geeigneten Mitteln* des Problems]
        the [investigat(ing) with suitable means (of) the problem-GEN]

    d. das Erzählen [von Geschichten] an Studenten *im Syntaxunterricht*
        the telling [of stories] to students in-the syntax-class

    e. das Erzählen [von Geschichten] *im Syntaxunterricht* an Studenten
        the telling [of stories] in-the syntax-class to students

    f. * das Erzählen *im Syntaxunterricht* [von Geschichten] an Studenten
        the telling in-the syntax-class [of stories] to students

In sum, head-initial projections are compact. In English, this applies to VPs as well as NPs, since English is uniformly head initial. In German, NPs are compact, VPs are not. This correlates with the fact that the NP is head initial while the VP is head final.

Observation 2 – strict word order in head-initial phrases, variable word order in head-final phrases.

Note that this property is a subinstance of observation 1. If variable word order is a consequence of scrambling, the scrambled item should be regarded as an intervener (3b,d) just as an adverbial is an intervener (3c).

(3) a. He [showed some students this problem]
    b. * He [showed *this problem_i* some students e_i]
    c. * He [showed *enthusiastically* some students this problem]
    d. * He [showed to some students_i this problem e_i]

The scrambling structure (3b) is ruled out by whatever principle enforces compactness and the very same constraint rules out (3c). The deviance of (3b) is of a general nature and is not limited to DP objects. PP objects do not scramble either (3d).

In German, compactness obviously does not hold for the VP since adverbials may intervene (4a), and consequently scrambling is allowed, just as in (4c) and (5d). In NPs, scrambling is ruled out, as expected (5b).

(4) a. Er hat dieses Problem einigen Studenten *begeistert* erklärt   *German*
         he has this problem some students enthusiastically explained

   b.   Er hat einigen Studenten dieses Problem erklärt
        he has some students this problem explained

   c.   Er hat *dieses Problem*ᵢ einigen Studenten eᵢ erklärt
        he has this problem some students explained

(5)   a.   das [NP Verteilen_N° von / der Decken an Obdachlose]   *German*
           the distribut(ing) of / the-GEN blankets to homeless

      b.   * das [NP Verteilen_N° *an Obdachlose*ᵢ von / der Decken eᵢ]
           the distributing to homeless of / the blankets

      c.   Man hat [VP Decken an Obdachlose verteilt]
           one has blankets to homeless distributed

      d.   Man hat [VP *an Obdachlose*ᵢ Decken eᵢ verteilt]
           one has to homeless blankets distributed

      e.   * Toen hebben de autoriteiten *het kind*ᵢ de moeder eᵢ teruggegeven
                                                                              Dutch
           then have the authorities the child the mother back-given

      f.   Toen hebben de autoriteiten het kind *aan de moeder* teruggegeven
           then have the authorities the child to the mother back-given

      g.   Toen hebben de autoriteiten *aan de moeder*ᵢ het kind eᵢ
           teruggegeven
           then have the authorities to the mother the child back-given

The order in (5b) is ruled out since there is no way to derive it. Scrambling does not apply, nor does PP extraposition apply to the object PP *von Decken*. Note that the compactness restriction is stricter than the distinctness requirement that forbids scrambling of objects in Dutch. Dutch DPs are not distinguishable in terms of case since Dutch does not provide morphological case marking. This seems to be responsible for the restriction against scrambling DPs (5e). But, crucially, scrambling is allowed for PP objects in Dutch (5g) (Geerts *et al.* 1984: 989f.).

Neither in English VPs nor in German NPs, is a PP object allowed to scramble. What this shows is that compactness is a genuine property of head-initial structures and that scrambling is dependent on the head-final organization of the scrambling domain.

Observation 3 – *The relative order* of arguments in OV and VO is identical, and the *relative embedding* is identical, too (see quantifier-variable binding data in examples (7) in this section).

In Haider (1992/2000) a fact has been highlighted that had gone unremarked until then: the relative order of arguments in head-final and head-initial VPs is identical. This is clear counterevidence for head-initial/head-final as a symmetric property. The symmetry hypothesis would predict that in head-initial phrases merger applies to the right, producing left-branching phrases (6a), while in head-final structures, merger applies to the left, producing right-branching structures (6b). If this symmetric organization modulo head position existed, the order of arguments in a head-final phrase would have to be linearized as the mirror image of the order in a head-initial phrase. However, (6a) does not exist in natural languages.

(6)   a. [[[h° A_1] A_2] A_3]   head-*initial* phrase with three arguments merged to the right

   b. [A_3 [A_2 [A_1 h°]]]   head-*final* phrase with three arguments merged to the left

Here are some examples of the uniform relative order in OV and in VO. The uniform relative order for a four-place verb like *send* is <subject – indirect object – direct object – directional PP>, corresponding to the semantic ranking of <agent – recipient – theme – goal>. German and Dutch represent the OV pattern; English and Danish are representative for VO. The obvious question is why left-branching VO structures (= merger to the right) are ruled out.

(7)   a. dass sie *jedem^i ein Paket an seine^i Privatadresse* schicken werden

   that they everybody a parcel to his private address send will

   b. omdat *ze iedereen^i een pakje naar zijn^i privaatadres* zullen opsturen

   Dutch

   that they everybody a parcel to his private address will send

   c. that they will send *everybody^i a parcel to his^i home address*

   d. at de forklarede *hver deltager^i problemet på hans^i eget sprog*

   Danish

   that they explained every participant problem-DEF in his own language

The fact that the relative order of arguments is identical in (7) follows immediately from the assumption that, both in OV and VO, the ranking of the arguments in the lexical argument structure is identical. This ranking determines the order of merger and since both in OV and VO the resulting structure is right-branching, the relative order of the arguments is necessarily identical.

Observation 4a – The position of verb particles relative to the verb in OV and VO: preverbal particle in OV, postverbal particle in VO (see Vikner 2001).

Germanic languages abound in 'particle + verb' combinations. The structure of the particle plus verb unit seems to be a head-to-head adjunction structure (see Wunderlich 1983; Stiebels and Wunderlich 1994). In all Germanic V2 languages, a particle is stranded when the particle verb is the finite verb fronted to the V2 position. Additionally, in some Germanic OV languages, a particle may be stranded in a VP-internal position (see chapter 7.2 and 7.5.3, for stranding in the verbal cluster).

(8)   a.   Er wickelt es *ein*
               he wraps it in

        b.   *Ein*wickeln wird er es nicht
               in-wrap will he it not

        c.   * Er *ein*wickelt es
               he in-wraps it

        d.   * Wickeln wird er es nicht *ein*
               wrap will he it not in

        e.   dass er es *ein*wickelt
               that he it in-wraps

        f.   * dass er es *ein* gut wickelt
               that he it *in* well wraps

The particle is obligatorily stranded, when the finite verb is fronted (8a,c). The particle obligatorily precedes, and is adjacent to the verb in the non-fronted position (8e,f). Topicalization of the verb must not strand the particle (8b,d), however.

The particle position follows immediately from the canonical licensing direction. The particle is selected by the verbal head. Hence it is merged to the left. In VO, the verb obligatorily moves to the left within the shell structure (see below), hence the particle ends up postverbally. In VO it is preverbal, unless the verb is moved to the left (as in V2).

Observation 4b – Particle stranding in between two objects in VO.

Germanic VO languages provide evidence for yet another source of stranding. In English, but also in Norwegian (and other Scandinavian varieties), particles may be serialized in several variants (Haider 1997d). One variant is the V-adjacent variant. In this variant, and in all other variants (including the stranding variant by V2) the particle follows. This is a robust difference between OV and VO. In OV, the particle precedes and is adjacent to the verb (except the stranding variant by V2). The second robust difference is the fact that there are VO languages with non-adjacent particle positions in the VP (9), but that there is no OV language with a particle position that is not adjacent (8f) to the base position of the verb.

(9)   a. The secretary sent the stockholders *out* a notice   (Jacobson 1987: 32)
        b. Valerie packed her daughter *up* a lunch   (Dehé 2002: 3)
        c. Susan poured the man *out* a drink

The intermediate particle position in (9) is a stranding position, that is, the position is a position of the verbal head whose surface position is higher up. It is immediate evidence for the shell structure of a head-initial VP.

A satisfactory account must cover the following generalizations: first, the cross-linguistic generalizations that particles precede in OV but follow in VO, and that only in VO may particles intervene between objects (9). Second, unlike adverbials, particles do not violate the compactness requirement of head-initial phrases. Unlike adverbials, they intervene between objects (9). However, they are themselves apparently not subject to compactness in the sense that no adjunct may intervene between an object and the particle that follows.[17] Third, in double object constructions, a particle must not be clause final although it may be clause final in a simple transitive construction.

Observation 5 – In an OV clause structure, auxiliaries and semi-auxiliaries *cluster obligatorily*. In German, even verbs that select sentential infinitival complements may optionally cluster, with clause union effects.

In VO, each verb heads a VP, so there are as many VPs as there are verbs, and each VP is a possible site for adverbial modification, as illustrated in (10a). For OV, the situation is radically different. Any non-verbal item in '*' positions in (10) is ungrammatical. First, the sequence of verbs in (10b) is a *compact* unit, indicated by '*'. Second, even if we do not expect the kind of adverbials we see in (10a) in these positions, since they avoid post-VP positions, there are post-VP elements that should be able to appear in these positions. But, they are strictly excluded.

(10)   a. The new law [*certainly* [may [*possibly* [have [*indeed* [been [*badly* formulated]]]]]]]

(Quirk *et al.* 1985: § 8.20, 495)

b. dass das neue Gesetz *wohl wirklich schlecht* formuliert (*) worden (*) sein (*) mag
that the new law *possibly indeed badly* formulated been have may
'that presumably the new law indeed may have been badly formulated'

Extraposition targets the right edge of the VP, as can be easily verified if there is a VP in a topicalized position, as in (11a). As noted in Haider (1990), topicalized VPs may have a structure that is incompatible with their alleged base position. If the topicalized VP in (11a) or (11d) is put back into its alleged site of extraction,

---

[17] An example like '*He poured the whisky *slowly* out' (Dehé 2002: 38) is misleading, however. As shown in (i), *out* can function like a PP pro-form, since it may be modified by *right*. The example in (ii) supports the correlation: if what looks like a particle can be modified, it is not treated as particle but as a PP pro-form. If, on the other hand, it cannot be modified, it must be a particle and then a compactness effect shows in (ii).

(i)   I poured it right out.
(ii)   The strike was called (*right/*finally) off

the resulting structures (11b) and (11e), respectively, are ungrammatical.[18] The only grammatical extraposition variant is (11c).

(11)   a.   [Gesprochen [$_{PP}$ mit ihr]]$_j$ kann$_i$ er nicht e$_j$ haben e$_i$
                [spoken [with her]] can he not have

        b.   * dass er nicht [gesprochen [mit ihr]] haben kann
                that he not [spoken [with her]] have can

        c.   dass er nicht gesprochen haben kann [mit ihr]

        d.   [Gesprochen haben mit ihr] kann er nicht
                [spoken have with her] can he not

        e.   * dass er nicht gesprochen haben [mit ihr] kann
                that he not spoken have [with her] can

This is not only a problem for a naive movement account of VP topicalization, it is evidence that the structure of the right edge of the clause is not simply a counterpart of English VP stacking. Why should extraposition that stops at a lower VP be excluded, if there is a higher VP available as target? English clearly shows that stacked VPs are VPs with all the privileges of VPs. (11b) and (11e), however, seem to be ruled out because there is no lower VP. The reason is this: the verbs are parts of a cluster in a *single* VP.

Compactness is just one out of several indicators of a structural difference between a VO and an OV organization. The second property is the *variable verb order* in all Germanic OV languages in the sequence of clause-final verbs. There is no VO language with a similar variation in the order of auxiliaries and semiauxiliaries. In other words, if these verbs may optionally serialize in different orders, the language is an OV language.

(12)   a. dass er mit ihr sprechen müssen *wird*   *German*
           that he with her speak must will
           'that he will have to speak with her'

        b. dass er mit ihr sprechen *wird* müssen

        c. dass er mit ihr *wird* sprechen müssen

        d. dass er mit ihr *würde haben* sprechen müssen
           that he with her would have speak must
           'that he would have had to speak with her'

The principles that govern the distribution of the verbs in the verbal cluster will be discussed in chapter 7. Note that German and Dutch differ with respect to the

---

[18] For a copy-theory of movement the problem is evident, too. The moved phrase is clearly not identical with the alleged copy.

variant patterns. In German, the order (13b,d) is not available. On the other hand, the order (12a) is ungrammatical in Dutch.

(13)   a. dat hij met haar gesproken *heeft*   *Dutch*
            that he with her spoken has

        b. dat hij met haar *heeft* gesproken
            that he with her has spoken

        c. dat hij met haar gesproken *zou* hebben

        d. dat hij met haar *zou* hebben gesproken

One of the clause union properties was first noticed by Gunnar Bech (1955). He pointed out that the scope of negation is ambiguous if the infinitival complement is not extraposed ('coherent infinitive' in his terminology). An example is given in (14a). For non-extraposed infinitival complements (of a class) of control verbs – *versuchen* (try) is a member of this verb class – two alternative constructions are available. One construction is the familiar clausal complement (14d), the other construction is the verb cluster construction. This construction is monoclausal, that is, a clause union construction (14e). One of many differences between the biclausal and the monoclausal structure shows in the scope of sentence negation. Since the scope of sentence negation is clause bound, the scope in (14d) is the complement clause. In (14e), the scope is the simple clause. (14a) is ambiguous since it may be structured as (14d) or (14e), with the reading of (14c) or (14b), respectively. The extraposed infinitival clause (14b) is a variant of (14d), and hence the scope is unambiguously determined. Analogously, the scope of negation in (14c) is clearly identifiable as the matrix clause. (14f) illustrates that the cluster constituent is a syntactic unit and therefore it may be topicalized.

(14)   a. Sie hat ihn *nicht* zu beunruhigen versucht   *ambiguous scope of*
                                                               negation
            she has him not to alarm tried
            'She has not tried to alarm him'/'She has tried not to alarm him'

        b. Sie hat versucht, [$_{clause}$ ihn *nicht* zu beunruhigen]   *unambiguous*
            'She has tried not to alarm him'   *scope*

        c. Sie hat *nicht* versucht, [$_{clause}$ ihn zu beunruhigen]   *unambiguous*
            'She has not tried to alarm him'   *matrix scope*

        d. Sie hat [$_{clause}$ ihn *nicht* zu beunruhigen] versucht

        e. Sie hat ihn *nicht* [$_{cluster}$ zu beunruhigen versucht]

        f. [$_{cluster}$ Zu beunruhigen versucht] hat sie ihn *nicht*

A particularly clear case of a clause union effect was first noticed by Höhle (1978). Passivizing the matrix verb may turn the object of the complement verb into the passive subject. Object-to-subject conversion in passive is clause bound in German. The nominative DP in (15a) is the very same DP that is the nominative DP of the clause-union variant (15c). The accusative (as alternative to the nominative) in (15a) is the standard accusative object of the embedded infinitival clause (15b). If the clustering variant is forced by topicalizing the cluster, nominative is the only option (15d).

(15)   a. Vergeblich wurde der / den Hund zu beruhigen versucht
        in-vain was the-NOM / the dog-ACC to calm-down tried
        'In vain, it was tried to calm down the dog'

    b. dass [$_{clause}$ den Hund zu beruhigen] vergeblich versucht wurde
       that [the dog-ACC to calm down] in-vain tried was

    c. dass *der* Hund vergeblich [$_{cluster}$ zu beruhigen versucht wurde]
       that the dog-NOM in-vain [to calm-down tried was]

    d. [$_{cluster}$ Zu beruhigen versucht] wurde der-NOM /*den-ACC Hund vergeblich
       [to calm down tried] was the dog in vain

The optional choice of case in (15a) appears to be bizarre, at first glance, but it becomes fully understandable once you recognize the structural difference between a clausal infinitival complement and a clustering construction. In chapter 7, more evidence for the clause union nature will be presented. A comparison with transparency phenomena in VO infinitival complementation will show a crucial difference: compact verb clusters are an OV phenomenon.

Observation 6 – *Obligatory structural* subject position only in VO (EPP property), but not in OV. Generalization: OV languages do not require/allow structural subject expletives.

In SVO languages, as suggested already by the acronym S-V-O, the position of the subject is structurally unique. It is the only argument that precedes the verbal head, while all other arguments follow. In clause structure, the subject position is the spec of a functional head. The subject phrase is raised from its VP-internal base position into the obligatory surface position. The position is both an *obligatory structural position* and a position that is *obligatorily lexicalized*. In Generative terminology, this is referred to as the EPP property (EPP = extended projection principle =$_{def.}$ clauses have (overt/covert) subjects) (Chomsky 1982: 9–10).

A good indicator of a syntactically mandatory position is the obligatoriness of an expletive. An expletive is semantically void. Its presence is owed to syntactic requirements only. The Scandinavian languages are good models for this property. If an intransitive verb is used in the passive construction, the subject position is obligatorily lexicalized with an expletive.[19]

(16) a. Ofte vart *det* telefonert   *Norwegian*
          often was *it* telephoned

      b. Ofte telefoneres *det*
          often telephones-PASS *it*

      c. Oft wurde (**es*) telephoniert   *German*
          often was (*it*) telephoned

      d. *Es* wurde oft telephoniert

(16a,b) illustrate the two syntactic options for passive in Scandinavian languages. One option is the familiar one, namely the combination of a participle plus a *be*-type auxiliary. The other option is a passive affix (namely -*s*). This developed from a middle construction with a cliticized reflexive. In both cases (16a,b), the subject position is obligatorily lexicalized with the expletive. The subject expletive in Scandinavian languages is a cognate of either the English *there* or *it*.

German, however, does not allow a clause-internal expletive in intransitive passives (16c), although it employs an expletive for the clause-initial functional spec position in those instances of declaratives in which no phrase is fronted (16d). The clause-initial position is an obligatory functional spec position, so it provides room for an expletive. However, there is no room for an expletive in what would be the clause-internal structural subject position. There is no room because there is no position that needs to be lexically filled.

Another case for an expletive in the functional subject position is the *there*-construction (17a). Faroese is representative for a Scandinavian language in this respect, with an expletive corresponding to the *there* in (17a). In Faroese, the expletive is mandatory (17b). German, however, does not allow a subject expletive in this construction (17c).

(17) a. Today, *there* has arrived a boy

      b. Í dag er *(*Það*) komin ein drongur   *Faroese*
          today is (*there*) arrived a boy

      c. Heute ist (**es*) ein Junge gekommen   *German*
          today is (*there*) a boy arrived

---

[19] English, once more, is an exception. It does not allow a passive of an intransitive simply because English lacks a syntactically adequate expletive. *There* is always associated with a postverbal nominative.

As a critical reader you may be prepared to object. Could it be that (17c) contains an expletive subject after all, but only in a covert form? The answer is: highly unlikely.

First, German is just a well-behaved OV language in this respect. There is no strict OV language that requires subject expletives. Second, if there existed a covert variant of *es*, it should optionally show, as in other constructions (18). For instance, the 'place holder' for an extraposed clausal subject (18a) or object (18b) is principally optional. In passives and in the *there*-construction, an overt expletive is always ungrammatical in German.

(18) a. Mich hat (es) nicht überrascht, dass das so ist
         me has (it) not wondered that this so is
         'It has not surprised me that this is so'

      b. Ich habe (es) geahnt, dass das so ist
         I have (it) sensed that this so is
         'I have sensed that this is so'

In Dutch, the behaviour of *er* is intriguing. In a clause without an argument, the *er* is optional if the verbs in the cluster are ordered in the 'OV style' (19a), that is, the dependent one preceding the governing one. However, it is obligatory if the cluster is serialized in the 'VO style', namely, with the governing verb preceding the dependent verb (19b), according to Richards and Biberauer (2005: 142), who credit Hans Bennis for this observation.

(19) a. Ik weet, dat (er) gedanst *wordt*   *Dutch*
         I know that (there) danced is
      b. Ik weet dat *(er)[20] *wordt* gedanst

Why is there not the slightest evidence for an expletive subject in German? And why is this a general property of OV languages? A satisfactory grammar model should provide a straightforward account (see chapter 2). An account in terms of a language-specific null-subject expletive is both ad hoc and too weak.

Observation 7 – VO languages, but not OV ones, with non-positional (i.e. relational) nominative checking allow for quirky subjects.

---

[20] *Er* becomes optional even in this context once there is an adverbial, e.g. a locative adverbial.

(i)   dat (er) in deze hoek werd gedanst
        that (there) in this corner was danced

Note that this is similar to the English locative-inversion construction (ii). But, in English, locative inversion is not licit for intransitive passive (iii).

(ii)   that on this spot (there) will stand a huge tower
(iii)   * that on this spot (there) must not be danced

In Icelandic, just as in German, a nominative argument may stay in a VP-internal position. Nominative checking is not a function of a unique structural position but a *relational* property, namely agreement. In Icelandic, in passive, or for unaccusative verbs, the nominative argument may stay in situ, and the higher-ranked oblique argument is raised to the functional subject position and thereby turned into a 'quirky subject'. Note that this shows that there is a structural subject position, that it must be lexicalized, but that it is not exclusively reserved for the nominative. In the following example, the quirky subject is a dative.

(20) a. að *henni/stelpunum* líkuðu hestarnir   *Icelandic*
          that *her*-DAT / *girls-the*-DAT liked-3.PL horses-the-NOM
          'that she/the girls liked the horses'   (Sigurðsson 2004)

      b. dass *ihr/den Mädchen* die Pferde gefielen   *German*
          that *her*-DAT / *the*-DAT *girls* the horses pleased
          'that the horses pleased her / the girls'

How do we know that the preverbal dative in (20a) is a subject? A dative in the functional subject position displays clear subject properties. First, the word order indicates that the dative in (20a) is not in an object position but in the preverbal position reserved for the subject. Second, the dative partakes in many of the subject-specific grammatical alternations. For instance, a quirky subject of a finite clause is regularly turned into a PRO subject in the infinitival variant of the clause.[21]

(21)   Ég vonast til að [PRO líka hestarnir]   *Icelandic*
          I hope for to [PRO-DAT please-INF horses-the-NOM]
          'I hope that the horses will please me'

For German in particular, and for OV language in general, quirky subject constructions have not been attested, for principled reasons (Zaenen *et al.* 1985; Haider 2005b), as will be discussed in section 1.4.2.

Observation 8 – Subject–object asymmetries (opacity for extraction out of phrases in the functional subject position or out of fronted phrases; wh-in-situ) in VO but not in OV.

The sentences in (22) illustrate the aforesaid contrasts between English and German. The source of the ungrammaticality in English is clearly a structural one: a phrase in a (preverbal) functional subject position is opaque for extraction.

---

[21] Note that this is in conflict with the 'PRO-theorem' that postulates that the subject of an infinitive cannot be lexicalized because of the lack of case. This restricts PRO to potential nominative subject. The quirky subject in (20a) and (21) is not nominative. It is dative, in both constructions.

The German examples are grammatical, hence the structural source that rules out the English examples must be absent in German.

(22)   a.   Mit wem$_i$ hätte denn [e$_i$ speisen zu dürfen] dich mehr gefreut?
            with whom had PRT [dine to be-allowed] you-ACC more pleased

        b.   * Whom$_i$ would [to have dinner with e$_i$] please you more?

        c.   Whom$_i$ would it please you more [to have dinner with e$_i$]?

The contrast between (22a) and the ungrammatical English construction (22b) is sharp and detrimental for analyses that situate the infinitival subject clause in German in a pre-VP functional spec position. A clause in a functional spec position corresponding to the English subject position, or in a higher one, is opaque for extraction. The straightforward alternative is a subject-in-situ analysis. The infinitival clause in (22b) has not left its VP-internal position and extraction is unproblematic. The contrast between (22b) and (22c) is one between a clausal subject in a preverbal functional phrase and one in a VP-internal position, respectively.

   Given that the subject position is a functional spec position, a phrase preceding this position is either in a functional spec position as well, or it is adjoined to a functional phrase. In each case, the result is ungrammatical, as English testifies (23b). German puts no restriction on extraction in the corresponding clauses (24).

(23)   a.   He said that [eating eels] he dislikes
        b.   * What$_i$ did he say that [eating e$_i$] he dislikes?
        c.   What$_i$ did he say that he dislikes eating e$_i$?

In (24a), the extraction site is in a fronted (i.e. scrambled) object clause. In (24b), the object clause is clearly sandwiched by the fronted reflexive and the subject and it remains transparent for extraction.

(24)   a.   Wen$_i$ hat [damit e$_i$ zu konfrontieren] keiner versucht?
            whom has [it-with to confront] nobody tried

        b.   Was$_i$ hat sich [ihr e$_i$ zu schenken] Fritz denn vorgenommen?
            what has himself [her to present] Fritz PRT decided
            'What did Fritz decide to present to her?'

Examples such as the above are robust evidence for a systematic difference between a VO and an OV structure. The 'subject condition' was studied in great detail for English from the 1980s to 1990s (key term: ECP). The source of the restriction is clear, even though it tends to be ignored in the present-day models of grammar: phrases in spec positions are domains that block extraction. In the following section, the source of the OV–VO contrast will be ascribed to a principled difference of clause structure that directly relates to the directionality property of the verbal head.

Wh-in-situ patterns are another reliable source of VO–OV contrasts. For a detailed discussion see chapter 3. Here, it is sufficient to point to the contrast in (25) and to emphasize that this contrast is representative for VO and OV languages in general. The generalization that covers this data is this: in VO, wh-subjects are ungrammatical if dependent on a higher wh-element. This generalization calls for a principled explanation.

(25)   a. * Whom did *what* impress?

       b. * It is unclear whom *what* impressed

       c. * *Who* said that *what* impressed her?

       d. Wen hat *was* beeindruckt?
           whom has what impressed

       e. Es ist unklar wen *was* beeindruckt hat
           it is unclear whom what impressed has

       f. *Wer* hat gesagt, dass mich *was* beeindruckt hat?
           who has said that me what impressed has

If *what* in (25a–c) is in a functional spec position, and *was* (what) in (25d–f) is in a functional spec position as well, why are the German examples grammatical but not the English ones? The solution will be simple: their structural position is not identical, for principled reasons. The German subject stays in its VP-internal position, hence the absence of a structural subject–object asymmetry. The English subject moves to a functional spec position. The principled reason for this contrast will be discussed in the following section.

1.4.2   *The structural source of the OV–VO contrasts*

In the previous section, the following properties have been presented, together with a claim.

* compactness of head-initial phrases
* rigid serialization vs scrambling
* uniform relative order of arguments
* order and distribution of verbal particles
* verb clusters with verb order variation and clause union effects
* mandatory functional subject position; obligatory subject expletives in VO.
* quirky subjects only in VO but not in OV
* (missing) subject–object asymmetries (opacity of extraction domains)

The claim is this: these properties directly correlate with the OV vs VO organization of a clause. These properties follow from just two premises:

> *Premise 1*: universal right-branching merger. In other words, merger operates in a directionally restricted manner. The merged phrase *precedes* rather than follows its host.
>
> *Premise 2*: the merged phrase is licensed under the (parameterized) *canonical directionality* by the (projection of the) head.

Let us reflect briefly on the plausibility of the premises. The advantage of right-branching merger structures becomes evident once we take into consideration the fact that structures need to be processed (first, in the acquisition process, and second, in each and every instance of speaking/listening) and that processing is bidirectional, namely input-driven (reception) or output-driven (production). Moreover, production involves simultaneous self-reception (self-monitoring).

The *input* is a one-dimensional array, namely a sound chain that strongly corresponds to a chain of morphemes. The fact that we are able to represent speech in lines on a sheet of paper is a reflex of this one-dimensional organization. Grammar is an algorithm for mapping these one-dimensional arrays on hierarchically organized box-in-box structures. These are at least *two*-dimensional structures, and syntacticians therefore employ phrase structure graphs for representing the properties of linear order in a hierarchy.

The input-driven aspect is the mapping of the one-dimensional array on a two-dimensional hierarchical structure. The output-driven aspect is the converse: the *two*-dimensional phrase structures are 'compressed', that is, mapped on the *one*-dimensional arrays. In other words, they are *linearized* in a sequence of terminals.

Which of these two aspects is more economy-driven? Obviously, it is the processing of the input. My limited resource as a listener is the processing time I need. For generating the output, I can reserve as much time as I need, but the input must be processed as fast as it arrives otherwise an overflow of my working memory buffer will cut off my online processing activity before I have succeeded.

What does this imply for the processing strategy and the data structures? Evidently, processing should start immediately and not be delayed. That implies that I have to guess the final structure of the phrase I am processing before I have reached the end of the phrase. Otherwise I would be unable to integrate the incoming elements of the phrases.

So, the best type of structure is one that allows an optimal fit between top-down information (i.e. knowledge-driven, by the application of grammar knowledge) and bottom-up information (i.e. data-driven, by the incoming data). With this in mind, let us compare two simple structures, namely a right-branching one and a left-branching one.

(1)   a. [[[h° A] B] C]   left-branching (= merger to the right)
       b. [A [B [C h°]]]   right-branching (= merger to the left)

The representation as bracketed strings best reveals the crucial difference. When the processor meets the first element in a structure like (1a), it is unable to predict how deeply embedded the element is, or, in other words, how many brackets it needs to open. In a structure like (1b), however, the first element will inevitably be the highest one, that is, it will be dominated by the root of the phrase. So, independent of the complexity of the phrase, the root is always the first bracket. Complexity is a matter of the number of closing brackets. But at this point, all elements already have been processes. For (1a), on the other hand, the root bracket must be guessed and revised, with backtracking.

The parser prefers early commitment and little to no revision of decisions. So, (1b) clearly is more parser-friendly than (1a). However, (1a) has a valuable feature, too. The head of the phrase is presented early, and the head contains information on the structure since it contains the information on arguments and their grammatically selected properties (category, case, semantic relations). So, in the best of all worlds, we would like to combine the 'early head' advantage of (1a) and the 'who is first is higher' property of (1b).

But there is a problem that we have to solve before we can successfully combine the two properties. It is the endocentricity property. Phrases contain a head, and since merger starts with the head, the head is in the most deeply embedded position. This seems to make it impossible to add to (1b) the 'early head' property. Grammars have found a way out, though. Here it is:

(2)   a. [V° C]   *read letters*
       b. [V° [B [V° C]]]   [*send_i* [*friends* [*e_i letters*]]]
       c. [A [V° [B [V° C]]]]   *(make)* [*her* [*send_i* [*friends* [*e_i letters*]]]]

The solution to the apparently incompatible desires (have the head first and have a right-branching = left-merging structure) is the shell structure of complex head-initial phrases. The head is instantiated in each shell and lexicalized ultimately in the highest position. The lower positions are empty heads, co-indexed with the lexical head. The structure is a structure with a head chain.

(2b) and (2c) is the SVO solution for complex VPs. All arguments follow the head, except for the highest one. This one is local to the head, but it precedes. If all arguments were to follow the head, the structure would be that of a VSO language. Please keep in mind this exceptional property of the highest element. It is the seed of the exceptional property of the subject in comparison to the objects.

Let us recapitulate briefly. First, *premise 1* is the description of a property of Universal Grammar. It guarantees parser-friendly phrase structures. A phrase structure is parser friendly if it allows the immediate combination of top-down (= grammar-driven) and bottom-up (= data-driven) information. This is the case in right-branching (= left-merging) structures since the active node in bottom-up processing is at the same time the highest node in the processed subtree.

Second, head-initial phrases require a more complex structure than head-final ones, since the head cannot simultaneously be in the lowest position and precede the dependent elements with the phrase as a right-branching structure. The solution for combining the two apparently incompatible requirements (head first, head in lowest position) provided by UG is the shell structure of head-initial VPs, with a V chain that relates the initial V position to the foot position.

Where does *directionality* come into play? The directionality value (progressive/regressive = right/left = forward/backward = $\Leftarrow$ / $\Rightarrow$) is the grammatical feature that governs the application of merger. Let me illustrate this with a three place verb, and three arguments (XP, YP, ZP) with the ranking of the arguments indicated in (3a).

(3)   a. {h°; XP > YP > ZP}

		$\Leftarrow$	$\Rightarrow$
Step 1:	b.	[ZP h°]	b'. [h° ZP]
Step 2	c.	[YP [ZP h°]]	c'. [YP [h° ZP]]
Step 3	d.	[YP [ZP h°]]	d'. [h° [YP [h° ZP]]]
Step 4	e.	[XP [YP [ZP h°]]]	e'. [XP [h° [YP [h° ZP]]]]

First, the head is merged with the lowest-ranked argument, according to the directionality requirement. This is step 1. Then the next argument is merged, according to the universal restriction on merger, that is, it is merged as a *left* sister. This is step 2. Here, the crucial difference between OV and VO becomes visible. The YP in (3c') is not in the directionality domain of h°. So, the structure is merged again with h°. This is step 3 and the result is a VP-shell structure. Note that for (3c), in contrast with (3c'), this problem does not arise. Each left sister is in the directionality domain of h° or a projection thereof. In step 4, finally, the highest-ranked argument is merged (3e'). It ends up in a VP-internal position, but this position is once more not in the directionality domain. Here the 'SVO measure' applies. It is treated as the subject and eventually receives its directionality-dependent licence from a *preceding* functional head. This is the very head that attracts the verb that agrees with the subject. In OV, the need for a functional licenser does not arise. Like all other arguments, the highest argument in (3e) is in the same directionality domain as all the other arguments.

The structures in (4) are the result of the building steps in (3). The arrows indicate the directional licensing relation. The notation for the shells in (4a) just follows the notational convention in the Generative literature, with a 'VP' as the complement of a 'little v'. However, it should be clear that 'vP' and 'VP' are just two instantiations of projecting a VP. You should bear in mind that the need for having two VPs in (4a) is a purely structural one, following from the two universal requirements (directional licensing, right-branching merger). There are no inherent semantic features associated with the distinction between V° and v°. The vP is just the re-application of building up a VP.

(4)   a. head-*initial* VP: .....   b. head-*final* VP: .....

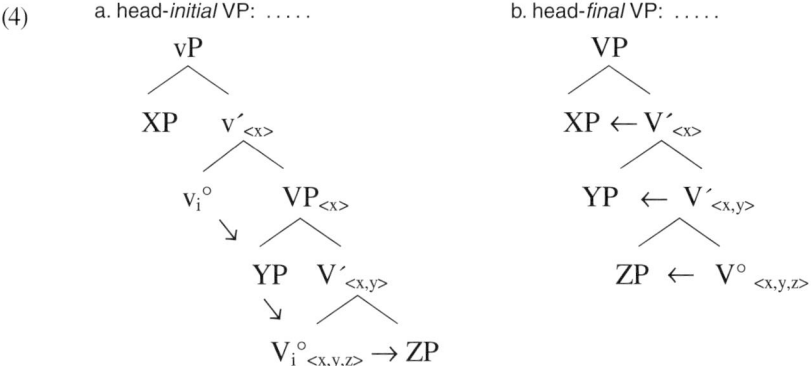

Now, we are in the position to derive an essential differentiating property of head-final and head-initial structures, namely the *compactness* property of head-initial structures. The source of this property is a *locality* condition on directional licensing that applies universally.

The merged phrases must be in a local relation to the head in order to be identified by the head. This locality relation is defined as the *Principle of Directional Identification* (PDI):

Principle of Directional Identification (PDI): A merged phrase P must be properly identified.

A merged phrase P is properly identified by the head of the host phrase h° iff

(i)   P is in the directionality domain of h°, and
(ii)   P and an extension of h° *minimally, mutually c-command* each other. (extension of h° =$_{def.}$ h° or a projection of h°)

Let us check (4b) for its PDI obedience. First, each of the three phrases (XP, YP, ZP) precedes V°, hence each one is in the proper canonical directionality domain for a head-final structure. Second, each one of the three complement phrases is in a sister position of V° or an extension of V° (namely V´). Since sister nodes minimally and mutually c-command each other, the condition (ii) of the PDI is fulfilled.

How does (4a) meet the PDI? ZP is a sister of, and follows, the verbal head. Hence PDI is clearly fulfilled. The position for YP is not in the directionality domain of the lowest V°-position, but it is in the directionality domain of the higher V-position in the shell structure. Since the two V-positions are links in a VP-internal V-chain, the YP is in the canonical directionality domain of a link of this chain. Hence, each of the two phrases is in the directionality domain of at least one chain link. Finally, we have to consider the XP in (4a). It is not in the directionality domain of a verbal, VP-internal head. Its identification domain is vP-external. The identifying head is a functional head.

Second, how is minimal, mutual c-command fulfilled in (4a)? V° and ZP are sisters, so condition (ii) of PDI is met for ZP, but what about YP? YP c-commands V°, and v° c-commands YP, and there is no phrase that intervenes between either v° and YP, or between YP and V°. So v° minimally c-commands YP and YP minimally c-commands V°. 'Mutuality' is a chain effect. Since YP c-commands V°, it c-commands a link of the V-chain. v° on the other hand c-commands YP. Hence YP c-commands, and is c-commanded by, a chain link of the V-chain. Taken together, this satisfies the *mutual* c-command requirement.

Now, we have all ingredients at our disposal for deriving **compactness**: note first that in VO, the mutual c-command requirement in the VP shell structure needs to be defined relative to the V-chain. Second, the *minimality* requirement is the crucial source for the *compactness* property of head-initial structures because interveners destroy minimality and thus destroy the identification relation. Let us compare the two cases:

(5)   a. . . . . .   b. . . . . .

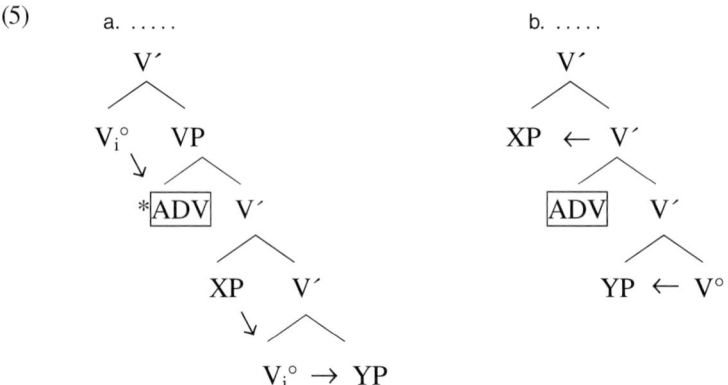

Note that the compactness property of head-initial structures like (5a) follows immediately from the requirement of *minimal, mutual, directional* c-command in a universally right-branching merger structure. In the head-initial VP (5a), the verb cannot c-command its arguments unless it is re-instantiated in a VP-shell structure. In (5a), an intervener like the boxed adverbial 'ADV' would break minimality and therefore destroy the minimality relation between V° and XP. V° would minimally c-command 'ADV', but not the XP. Analogously, a scrambled intervener between XP and the lower $V°$ would block the minimality relation between XP and the lower empty $V°$ position since XP would be unable to *minimally* c-command $V°$. It would minimally c-command the intervener, but not the $V°$ head.

In (5b), however, interveners like the boxed adverbial 'ADV' do not affect the identification relation of either XP or YP since both have their identifier in the sister position, namely a projection of the verb on the right-hand side, that matches the directionality requirement. The corresponding sister positions in (5a), on the other hand, are unable to function as identifiers because of the directionality mismatch. So, for head-initial phrases, identification rests exclusively on the head chain in the shell structure.

In sum, compactness is a VO effect (5a), because only in head-initial structures is the identification relation a matter of the head positions in the shell structure of a complex head-initial phrase. Compactness is not at issue for OV (5b), on the other hand, since here, identification employs the sister positions because these are projections of the head and positions in the required directionality. Note that the German NP is head initial and compact. The VP is head final and is not subject to compactness. This shows that 'OV' is not a global property but a property of the headedness of phrases. If there is a unique directionality value, you perceive a strict OV or a strict VO language. If it is not unique, you see a 'mixed' system like in German or Dutch.

Rigid serialization in VO vs variable word order (*scrambling*) in OV is just another instance of the compactness property. In (5a), the boxed 'ADV' could be an adjunct or it could be a scrambled object. Imagine a situation where YP is scrambled in front of XP, as in the examples in (6):

(6)   a. * [$_{VP}$ show *the picture$_i$* children e$_i$]
        b.   [$_{VP}$ das *Bild$_i$* Kindern e$_i$ zeigen]
             the picture children show
             'show children the picture'

In (6), the position of the scrambled direct object intervenes between the position of the verb and the position of the indirect object. This blocks the identification relation between the verb and the indirect object in (6a), just as an intervening adjunct would do. Note that this explanation of the absence of scrambling in head-initial phrases presupposes that scrambling is the result of re-merging a phrase and thereby generating a chain between its base position and the scrambling position. The object *the picture* is theta identified[22] in its base position.

---

[22] Theta-identification is the identification of a phrase by the head as the argument of the head, according to its status in the lexical argument grid.

The **uniform relative order of arguments** in OV and VO is a straightforward consequence of the fact that both in the VO structure as well as in the OV structure, merger operates on a right-branching structure. So the element merged 'earlier' will be lower and will follow the element merged 'later' because the lower one necessarily follows the higher one. If merger, contrary to empirical evidence, were to follow directionality, head-initial phrases would merge to the right and head-final phrases would merge to the left, and the result would be mirror image orders.

Order and distribution of verbal particles is a valuable source of evidence for the identification of chain links in the shell structure in languages with particle stranding. The stranding position is a verb position. So, a stranded particle signals a verb position. The shell structure of a head-initial phrase is a structure with *more than one* verb position (7a). The head-final structure, on the other hand, is a structure with a *single* verb position within the V-projection, hence there is only a single particle position, namely the position adjacent to the head (7b).

Second, the position of the particle relative to the verb is an indicator of the directionality. The particle is selected by the head in the canonical directionality. In OV, without exception, the particle immediately precedes the verb, and in VO, the particle follows.[23]

Why is there no clause-final particle position in English for double object constructions? The answer seems to be simple: there is no clause-final verb position and hence no stranding position in (7c).[24] Things get complicated, however, by the fact that a clause-final position for the particle of intransitive constructions, as in (7d), is grammatical.

(7)   a. The secretary [sent$_i$ [the stockholders [e$_i$ *out* a notice]]]
       b. dass der Sekretär den Aktionären eine Mitteilung *aus*händigte
          that the secretary the stockholders a notice out-handed ('handed over')

---

[23] Note that in nominalizations of particle verbs, the particle order of OV is congruent with the order in compounds, namely head-final. In German, the particle order is identical for verbs as well as for nominalizations. In English, however, there are two patterns for nominalized particle verbs. One is the verb + particle pattern, as in (i), and the other is the compounding pattern (the modifier precedes the head of the compound), as in (ii).

(i)   the make up, the fall out, the sit in, the count down, …
(ii)   the uprising, the output, the income, the downpour, …

The examples in (i) are nominalized verb + particle structures; the examples in (ii) are regular compounds.

[24] Johnson (1991) assumes that clause-final particles in double object constructions are acceptable if and only if both objects are weak pronouns. Den Dikken (1992: 163) claims that the adequate generalization is that clause-final particles are possible only if they are predicative.

(i)   Gary poured me some out
(ii)   Will you sew me a new one on?

    c. * The secretary sent$_i$ the stockholders e$_i$ a notice e$_i$ *out*
    d.   The secretary sent$_i$ a notice / it e$_i$ *out*
    e.   The secretary sent *out* a notice /*it

If what has been assumed above is correct, the absolute clause-final position in VO is not a base position for a transitive verb. The base position of the object would follow and the stranded particle would precede the object. Therefore, in (7d), the object must have moved to the left, as indicated in (8). Pronouns move obligatorily (7e).

(8)   sent$_i$ [a notice$_j$ [e$_i$ out e$_j$]]

Note that the structure in (8) is the structure normally found with double object construction. It seems as if the object of the transitive verb may alternatively use either position of the objects in a double object construction.[25] For weak pronouns, the fronted position is the only licit position (7d) because in all Germanic languages, weak pronouns are fronted to the left edge of their domain (see chapter 4.1).

Verb clustering is an OV phenomenon. Verb clusters are by no means a peculiarity of Germanic OV languages. Sells (1990) discusses clustering properties for Japanese and McCawley and Momoi (1986) for Korean. Han *et al.* (2007) discuss transparency phenomena in Korean that are typical of the clause union effect that correlates with V-clustering. The peculiarity of Germanic OV languages is the fact that clustering is accompanied by verb order variation in the cluster.[26] Why should UG provide or require clustering in OV grammars, but not in VO ones?[27]

The UG 'motive' for granting clustering to OV becomes evident once we look at the structures from the point of view of their processing implications. OV complementation produces *centre-embedding* structures, as in (9a); VO complementation does not (9b). Centre-embedding is a processing obstacle. This becomes evident if you look at the labelled bracketing structure in (9). In (9a), the parser has to guess how many brackets to open in order to instantiate the root VP node.

[25] For a different analysis see den Dikken (1992) or Johnson (1991). They argue for an analysis in which the particle is the head of a phrase selected by the verb, namely a 'small clause'.

[26] A correlating feature of this difference seems to be the following: all Germanic languages, except English, are V-movement languages (V2), with V-movement to a head-initial functional head. Japanese and Korean do not move verbs and they do not have overt head-initial functional heads. All Germanic OV languages show verb order variation in the cluster; Japanese and Korean do not. We may conclude that verb order variation in the cluster is absent if the verbs are immobile in the given language. This distinguishes strict OV from the Germanic OV languages.

[27] Apparent counterevidence – namely Romance restructuring – will be discussed at the end of this subsection.

In (9b), each of the VP complements is introduced by the head and immediately dominated by its phrase node. For the structure in (9b), the *least* embedded element *comes first*. In (9a), the *most deeply* embedded element comes first, followed in turn by the elements with a more shallow embedding.

(9)   a. [[[[… diese Strukturen verarbeiten]$_{VP}$ können]$_{VP}$ müssen]$_{VP}$ würde]$_{VP}$
          these structures process be-able-to have-to would
          'would have to be able to process these structures'

       b. [$_{VP}$ could [$_{VP}$ have [$_{VP}$ been [$_{VP}$ processing these structures]]]]

By admitting clustering, UG provides grammatical means for circumventing this obstacle. Instead of projecting a cascade of centre-embedded VPs, a single VP is projected and the verbs are clustered (10a). The cluster is a syntactic structure resulting from head-to-head merger. It is the (complex) head of the VP. The structure above the cluster in (10a) is identical with the structure of a VP with a simple head (10b). Clustering avoids phrasal centre embedding and reduces the centre-embedding property to the strictly local area of the complex head, that is, the verb cluster. The clustering structure groups the verbs into a single, compact, head-to-head adjoined structure (10c).

Dutch grammar goes one step further. It allows the full elimination of centre embedding and also the structuring of the cluster in a right-branching manner. The result is a mirror image order for Dutch (10d) compared to German (10c). As will be shown in detail in the chapter on infinitival complementation (chapter 7), (10d) is a cluster. It is as compact as the German cluster (10c).

(10)   a. [… diese Strukturen ['$_{V^{\circ}\text{-cluster}}$' verarbeiten können müssen
          würde]$_{V^{\circ}}$]$_{VP}$
          these structures process be-able-to have-to would
          'would have to be able to process these structures'

       b. [. … diese Strukturen [verarbeiten]$_{V^{\circ}}$]$_{VP}$
          these structures process
          'process these structures'

       c. [[[verarbeiten können]$_{V^{\circ}}$ müssen]$_{V^{\circ}}$ würde]$_{V^{\circ}}$
          process be-able-to have-to would
          'would have to be able to process'

       d. [zou [moeten [kunnen verwerken]$_{V^{\circ}}$]$_{V^{\circ}}$]$_{V^{\circ}}$ *Dutch*
          would have-to be-able-to process

Compactness is a key property of clustering. So-called restructuring constructions in Romance (especially in Italian) show transparency phenomena like the Germanic clustering constructions, but the verbs are not clustered. This becomes evident from

the fact that adverbials may freely intervene.[28] This shows that the verbs are projecting their own VP and are not partners in a cluster. The transparency phenomena in
Romance are explicable in terms of alternative subcategorizations: an infinitival
complement may either be a VP, and thus monoclausal, or an infinitival clause, and
thus bi-clausal (see Roberts (1997) and Cinque (2004), for a technical implementation in terms of the 'lexical' vs 'functional' category of verbs).

A **mandatory** *functional* **subject position,** that is, an obligatorily lexicalized
functional spec position exclusively reserved for the subject (EPP property),[29] is an
SVO effect. An immediate effect of this requirement is the need of a subject expletive
in order to avoid an empty spec position. SVO languages require subject expletives,
while OV languages, Dutch notwithstanding, do not. They not only do not require
them but they arguably do not allow them. This is a generalization that needs to be
captured by an empirically adequate model of human grammar systems.

What is special about SVO in comparison to SOV with respect to the subject? It
is the argument position of the subject in the structure of the VP. In OV, all arguments of the verb are merged within the same directionality domain (11b). If the
subject argument of an unergative verb is merged in the highest possible argument
position, this position precedes the *verbal* head, both in VO and of course in OV.
In VO, however, this position is not within the directionality domain of the head. In
(11a), this is exemplified by a VP in an ECM construction with a non-nominative
subject. The subject of the VP precedes the verbal head *precede*, the object follows. In an OV structure, both the subject and the object precede the head.[30]

(11)   a. (let→) [$_{VP}$ the subject [$_{V'}$→ precede$_{V°}$ the object]]
        b.   [$_{VP}$ das Subjekt [←$_{V'}$ dem Objekt vorangehen$_{V}$°]] (←lassen)[31]

---

[28] In Italian, but not in German or Dutch, the verbs in the 'restructuring' construction may
sandwich 'cluster-foreign' material (Monachesi 1999), as for instance adverbials. The
clitic *lo* in (a.) is the object of *comprare* and raised to the position of the matrix finite verb.
This is one of the transparency effects characteristic of the restructuring construction:

a.   Anna lo vuole (*immediatamente*) poter (*immediatamente*) comprare
      Anna-clit-acc wants (immediately) be-able-to (immediately) buy
b.   dass es Anna kaufen (*aus Jux /*sofort) wollte
      that it Anna buy (for fun / immediately) wanted

[29] In Chomsky's view, the EPP (= extended projection principle) is a universally valid principle that requires a clause to have a subject (Chomsky 1982: 9–10). When the P&P model
was in vogue (1981: 40), Chomsky was cautious enough to restrict the EPP to 'English
and similar languages'. Later, it got extended to universal validity. See Alexiadou and
Anagnostopoulou (1998) for a differentiation in terms of feature-checking routines.

[30] Note that the 'directionality defect' of the VP-internal subject position is a property of
SVO. SOV and VSO systems do not have this 'defect'. In each case, the subject is *within*
the directionality domain for the arguments.

[31] Be aware: German obligatorily applies verb clustering instead of VP complementation
(see chapter 7). The structure is given here just for expository purposes.

Given the first premise[32] introduced in section 1.4, the VP-internal subject position in an SVO clause is not in the canonical directionality domain of the head of the VP, but is nevertheless in need of a licensing head with the *canonical licensing directionality*. This head is a functional head.[33] So, there must be a functional projection that selects the VP as a complement and satisfies the directional licensing requirement.

(12) $[_{FP} ... [_{F'} F° \rightarrow [_{VP} DP [V° ...]]]]$

Why does the subject raise to the functional spec position? Note that the subject DP in an SVO structure (12) is within the directionality domain of the functional head F°, but it is not its sister. So, the functional head and the subject do not mutually c-command each other. This is fulfilled only if the subject raises to the functional spec position: the functional head c-commands the VP-internal subject position and the raised subject c-commands the functional head.[34]

In sum, the functional subject position of SVO languages is a direct consequence of the directionality 'defect' of the VP-internal subject position in SVO. An SOV clause structure does not have this defect, hence it arguably does not employ an obligatory functional subject position. If this is correct, UG does not require clauses to have a functional subject position in general but only if the clause structure is an SVO structure.

What is the grammar-theoretic rationale behind the lexicalization requirement for the functional spec position or, in Chomsky's terminology, the EPP *property* (see 13)? In other words, what triggers the need for an expletive subject if there is no subject argument available?

Evidently, the functional layer above the VP is not a 'just-on-demand' structure but a standard requirement for a VO clause structure. It is not merely triggered by the presence of a subject argument in need of licensing. It is an integral part of the clausal architecture of an SVO clause. The grammar principally provides the structural context for directionally licensing the preverbal, VP-internal subject position. Being a mandatory part of the structure, it must be 'interpreted', that

---

[32] The *first premise*: positions in the projection of a phrasal head need to be licensed under the *canonical directionality* of the head.

[33] Except for ECM constructions. In (11a), the lower subject is licensed by the ECM verb.

[34] If nominative checking is not exclusively constrained to spec-head agreement but implemented in terms of an overt agreement relation, the raising requirement affects whatever is the highest argument in the V-projection. If this argument is not the nominative one, the result is a so-called *quirky subject construction* (see below), as in Icelandic. Note, that this shows that the primary trigger of raising a subject is not nominative-checking, but the minimal, mutual c-command requirement. This seems to be the grammatical source of the EPP property of non-pro-drop VO languages.

is, receive a status in the derivation. Leaving it radically empty, both in the head and the spec position, would be to ignore the structure. The expletive is a way of syntactically interpreting the structure.

In a Germanic VO language, like Norwegian (13a, a') or Faroese (13b), expletive subjects typically occur in the passive of intransitive verbs (13a, a') or in the counterpart of the English *there*-construction (13b). In German, an expletive would make each of these constructions ungrammatical (13c,d).

(13) a. Ofte vart *det* telefonert   a'. Ofte telefoneres *det*   *Norwegian*
         often was it telephoned   often telephones-PASS it

      b. Í dag er *(*Það*) komin ein drongur   *Faroese*
         today is there arrived a boy

      c. Oft wurde *(*es)* telephoniert   (= 13a)   *German*

      d. Heute ist *(*es)* ein Junge gekommen   (= 13b)
         today is (there) a boy arrived

In Dutch, the data are less clear-cut. The cognate of English *there*, namely *er*, may indeed occur in these constructions. But, arguably, the grammatical properties of *er* are not exactly the properties of a *subject* expletive (see Neeleman and Weerman 1999: 210–13). First, the alleged subject expletive *er* is not obligatory in a canonical SOV structure; see observation 6 in section 1.4.1 and example (14a). Second, as observed already by den Besten (1985), an expletive does not occur in the passive of double object constructions (14c), with the passive subject in the direct object position.

(14)   a. Ik weet, dat (er) gedanst wordt
          I know that (there) danced is

       b. Ik weet dat *(er) wordt gedanst
          I know that (there) is danced

       c. dat (*er) hem / een man (*er) deze boeken niet werden getoond
          that (there) him / a man (there) these books-PL not were-3.PL shown

The case (14c) is the prototypical case for an expletive subject, unless the indirect object can be shown to be a quirky subject (see the next but one paragraph). A proof for the latter case would be that the dative is replaced by a PRO-subject in a clausal infinitive construction. This is the proof of subjecthood and Icelandic quirky subjects match this expectation; the indirect object in Dutch does not.[35]

---

[35] In all Germanic V2 languages (VO as well as OV), an expletive is used in declarative clauses for the clause-initial position if no element has been fronted to this position. This is another instance of 'making visible/audible' an otherwise radically empty

Quirky subjects, as known from Icelandic, are an immediate by-product of an SVO clause structure in a specific setting of case checking. What is a quirky subject? It is a DP in the functional subject position that is not a nominative subject. In other words, it is a DP in subject position that does not agree with the finite verb (15a). A particularly clear indicator for a quirky subject is the fact that the functional subject, that is, the phrase in the functional spec position for the subject, alternates with a PRO subject in case the clause is infinitival (15b). The fact that quirky subjects alternate with PRO is instructive for yet another reason. It shows that PRO is not necessarily the caseless counterpart of a nominative subject.

Quirky subjects are admissible in grammar settings in which case checking of nominative is not positionally constrained, that is, not constrained to a spec-head configuration reserved for the subject. This is so in Icelandic. An immediate indicator of this property is the grammaticality of a postverbal nominative (15a). In Icelandic, subjects of unaccusative verbs and passive subjects may remain in their VP-internal, postverbal argument position.

(15) a. Þá hefur henni líklega leiðst bókin   (Sigurðsson 2004: 142)
          then has her-DAT probably bored book-the-NOM
          'Then, she has probably got bored by the book'

      b. Hún vonast til [að PRO leiðast ekki bókin]
          she hopes for [to PRO-DAT bore not book-the-NOM]
          'She hopes not to be bored by the book'

      c. Dann hat ihr / der Frau das Buch gefallen   *German*
          then has her-DAT / the woman-DAT the book-NOM pleased
          'Then, the book has pleased her /the woman'

      d. * Sie hoffte [PRO das Buch zu gefallen]
          She hoped [PRO-DAT the book to please]

Note that in (15a,b), the nominative DP is postverbal, and the nominative checking is not affected by the finite/non-finite context if there is a quirky subject in the latter context in Icelandic. The corresponding property of the corresponding German verbs is the object before subject order (15c). In German, however, there is no evidence for quirky subjects. The diagnostic criteria discussed in Sigurðsson (2004) show that German does not qualify as a quirky subject language.

Crucial differences between German and Icelandic on empirical grounds have already been highlighted in Zaenen *et al.* (1985), who concluded that German

position. Without an expletive, the clause would be (mis)interpreted as a V1 interrogative clause (see Önnerfors 1997).

(i)   *Es* hat niemand angerufen
        it has nobody phoned

does not have quirky subjects. Sigurðsson (1989: 204–5) discusses in detail a wide range of contrasts (reflexivization, PRO subjects, conjunction reduction, subject position in ECM infinitives, raising) and re-emphasized this conclusion. Fanselow (2002) and Bayer (2003) analyse the corresponding data in German and confirm the conclusion that German does not show quirky subject effects.

What makes Icelandic a quirky subject language, but not English? Icelandic is an SVO language, and, crucially, nominative checking is not structurally constrained. It is relational. The nominative DP does not need to be raised to the spec position of the head that accommodates the agreement feature. This is the essential difference between Icelandic on the one hand, and English and the continental Scandinavian Germanic languages on the other hand.

German and Icelandic share *three* of *four* crucial preconditions for quirky subjects (*i.* morphological nominative, with *ii.* relational licensing; *iii.* verbs whose highest ranked argument is not the nominative candidate), but differ in a single factor, namely the licensing *directionality* of the verb. In German, all arguments are directionally licensed already in their VP-internal positions. Hence there is no grammatical trigger for moving a particular argument, which is not properly identified directionally, to a functional spec position.

In Icelandic, there is a functional projection for the subject whose spec needs to be lexicalized. Since the spec position is not the unique location for licensing a nominative it is open for non-nominative candidates, too. So, either the DP the verb agrees with is raised, or the highest DP in the VP is. In most cases, this singles out the same DP. Only if the nominative is a lower ranked DP (as in passive or with unaccusative verbs), may the higher ranked DP be a DP with an oblique case. If this DP is raised, the result is a non-nominative DP in a structural subject position. This is the quirky subject. In German, the subject is not raised since there is no need for a functional subject position, so there is no source for a quirky subject, that is, a non-nominative DP in a functional subject position.

(Missing) subject–object asymmetries constitute the final piece of evidence in confirmation of the principal structural difference with respect to the position of the subject in a VO and in an OV clause, respectively. For at least two decades, conditions constraining syntactic movement operations have been a main focus of interest, beginning as early as Ross (1967) and continuing till Chomsky (1986). Diverse and robust evidence was accumulated and analysed. Two contexts turned out to be robust opaque domains[36] for extraction, namely the preverbal subject phrase on the one hand and adjunct phrases on the other hand. Here, we are interested only in the difference between subjects and objects. In English, extraction out of a phrase in the preverbal subject position is strictly ungrammatical (16).

---

[36] 'Opaque domain' is the cover term for a domain that blocks extraction. Extraction out of an opaque domain is ungrammatical.

(16) a. * Who$_i$ did [a picture of e$_i$] impress you most?

    b. * Who$_i$ was [a picture of e$_i$] recognized by everyone?

    c. Who$_i$ did everyone recognize [a picture of e$_i$] ?

    d. * Which question$_i$ was [asking e$_i$] embarrassing?

    e. Which question$_i$ did everyone avoid [asking e$_i$]?

    f. * Which question$_i$ would [to have answered e$_i$ incorrectly] annoy you?

    g. (?)Which question$_i$ would it annoy you [to have answered e$_i$ incorrectly]?

    h. * Which spot will [on e$_i$] stand a huge tower?

    i. Which spot$_i$ will a huge tower stand [on e$_i$] ?

Extraction out of a subject-internal PP is ungrammatical, both for a primary subject (16a) as well as a derived one, as the passive subject (16b), although the picture noun phrase is in principle an extraction site (16c). Gerundive subjects (16d) are non-transparent, and so are clausal subjects (16f) and PP subjects[37] in the locative-inversion construction. The corresponding phrases are transparent for extraction if they are *not* in a subject position. For those who do not judge (16g) as fully acceptable, the reason is the dependency between the extraposed subject clause and its place holder in the subject position.

In German, the corresponding constructions are fully transparent. This fact was emphasized first in the 1980s (Haider 1983, 1989) and is by now widely accepted as an uncontroversial fact of German syntax, though with diverging strategies for modelling it.

(17a) is arguably a case of extraction out of an NP. (17b) is representative for extraction out of a subject clause. The clearest piece of evidence, however, is the extraction out of fronted object clauses (17c). The object clause precedes the subject. If the subject were in a spec position, the fronted object would have to be in an even higher position, and definitely VP-external, and hence non-transparent, too. But it is fully transparent. This follows if the subject is VP-internal, and if scrambling is VP-internal (see chapter 4.3 on scrambling, for details).

---

[37] PPs in locative-inversion constructions share an essential subject property with DP subjects, namely, the avoidance of *do*-support:

  (i)   On which spot stood a huge tower? Out of which cloud appeared a ghastly ghost?

  (ii)   On which spot *did there* stand a huge tower? Out of which cloud *did there* appear a ghastly ghost?

In the *there*-construction, the wh-PP triggers *do*-support (ii). In the absence of *there*, the PP behaves like a subject. If this is a correct assessment, (iii) must be regarded as a kind of quirky subject construction in English.

  (iii)   *On this spot* stood a huge tower. *Out of the corner* appeared a ghastly ghost.

(17)   a. Von welchem Künstler$_i$ haben [die frühen Werke e$_i$] die besten Preise erzielt?
        of which artist have [the early works] the best prices gained
        'The early works of which artist have gained the best prices?'

        b. Welche Frage$_i$ hätte [e$_i$ inkorrekt beantwortet zu haben] dich gestört?
        which question would-have [incorrectly answered to have] you annoyed
        'Which question would it have annoyed you to have answered incorrectly?'

        c. Welche Frage$_i$ hat [e$_i$ korrekt zu beantworten]$_j$ keiner e$_j$ vermocht?
        which question has [correctly to answer] nobody accomplished
        'Which question has no one been able to answer correctly?'

The explanation for the systematic contrast between English and German is this: German has an OV clause structure. In OV, the subject of the clause may remain in its VP-internal position. This is a position in the directionality domain of the head and hence its transparency qualities do not differ from those of its co-arguments. A VP-internal subject is as transparent as a VP-internal object. In English, a language with a VO clause structure, the VP-internal subject position is *not* within the directionality domain. The subject is raised to a functional spec position. This immediately accounts for the transparency differences.

Note that German respects the transparency restrictions in cases where they apply. Like English, German obeys the transparency restrictions for phrases in spec positions. This is easy to document with embedded V2 clauses. The phrase in the spec position of the embedded V2 clause is opaque for extraction, as expected (18b), but it is transparent in the clause-internal positions (18c). This confirms that the transparency contrast for subjects is structurally conditioned.

(18)   a. dass man glauben könnte, [[das Problem seriös zu lösen] [habe [keiner vermocht]]]
        that one believe might [[the problem seriously to solve][had [nobody accomplished]]]
        'that they might think that nobody has been able to solve the problem seriously'

        b. * Welches Problem$_i$, könnte man glauben, [[e$_i$ seriös zu lösen] habe keiner vermocht]?
        which problem might one believe [[seriously to solve] had nobody accomplished]
        'Which problem might they think that nobody has been able to solve seriously?'

    c. Welches Problem$_i$, könnte man glauben, [e$_i$ habe [e$_i$ seriös zu lösen] keiner vermocht]?
which problem might one believe [had [seriously to solve] nobody accomplished]
'Which problem might they think that nobody has been able to solve seriously?'

A second and independent class of data confirming the systematic structural difference between a VO clause structure (English) and an OV clause structure (German) is discussed in the chapter on wh-movement (chapter 3, especially in section 3.4 on wh-in-situ). The data and the structural interpretation were presented first in Haider (1986): an in-situ wh-subject is deviant in English (19b,d) but it is inconspicuous in German (20b,d):

(19)   a. And who has published this when?
           b. * And when did *who* publish this?
           c. It is fully unclear what has struck whom
           d. * It is fully unclear whom *what* has struck

(20)   a. Und wer hat das denn wann zuerst publiziert?
              and who has it PRT when first published

           b. Und wann hat das denn *wer* zuerst publiziert?
              and when has it PRT who first published

           c. Es ist nicht völlig unklar, was wem zuerst aufgefallen ist
              it is not entirely unclear what whom first struck has

           d. Es ist nicht völlig unklar, wem *was* zuerst aufgefallen ist
              it is not entirely unclear whom what first struck has

The interpretation discussed in chapter 3 on wh-movement will be this: in German, the in-situ wh-subject is VP-internal. In English, the subject is in a VP-external, functional spec position. This will immediately account for the difference since the syntactic properties of a wh-element in a spec position are predictably different from the properties of a wh-element in its VP-internal argument position.[38]

---

[38] If you search corpora, you easily find similar examples. Here are two specimens from newspapers:

    (i)   Wo wer im Schwimmbad hingehört, weiß offensichtlich jede
              'where who in-the swimming-bath belongs-to knows obviously everyone'
                                  (source: *Die Zeit*, 1988: 32, p. 41)
    (ii)   (Woran wir würgen oder:) *Wie* wird *wer* Akademiker?
              (on-what we choke or) how becomes who (an) academic?
                                (source: Presse 18 May 1996)

1.5   Summary

German clause structure is determined by the following parameters:

- The *finite* verb is obligatorily moved to the highest functional head position, if this position is accessible. The spec position is obligatorily lexicalized in the declarative clause structure. This is the pan-Germanic V2 property (exception: English).

- The phrasal projections of the major categories are *not uniform* with respect to the canonical position of the head. Verbal and adjectival projections are head final (as in OV languages). Nominal projections (NPs) and PPs are head initial (as in VO languages). All lexical functional heads (complementizers, articles) are head initial, and arguably, all covert functional head positions, too (see chapter 2 on clause structure).

- OV (head final) and VO (head initial) are alternative implementations of a *directionality* requirement. The head directionally identifies the merged elements in its domain. SVO and SOV differ with respect to the directionality domain of the head. In SVO, the subject argument is local to the head, but not within its directionality domain. In SOV, all arguments are within the directionality domain of the verbal head. This is the basic difference that triggers a cascade of contrasts between OV and VO structures. OV/VO is not a holistic property of a language, though, but clearly a property of the phrasal organization. The evidence for this is the fact that German head-initial projections share the properties of English head-initial projections:
  - compactness (in head-initial structures),
  - word order rigidity (in head-initial structures),
  - order and distribution of verbal particles (in OV vs VO),
  - verb clusters with verb order variation and clause union effects (in OV),
  - mandatory functional subject position; subject expletives; quirky subjects (in VO),
  - (missing) subject–object asymmetries (in OV).

- Head-final projections differ from head-initial ones at least in the following characteristics. The systematic correlation between OV and VO, and the set of syntactic properties that hold or do not hold, respectively, calls for a principled coverage in any grammar model that claims empirical adequacy.

- Here, these differences will be modelled as the effect of combining the directionality requirements with a universal constraint on merger, namely the universal exclusion of (internal) merger to the right. For a complex *head-initial* projection, this entails a shell structure, compact-ness, word order rigidity, multiple particle positions with strandable par-ticles, and a mandatory functional subject position.

Head-final projections are not compact, allow for word order variation, do not allow distant particle positions, cluster the verbs in subclausal or infinitival com-plement structures, do not have a mandatory functional subject position, and hence, do not show subject–object asymmetries conditioned by a functional sub-ject position.

2

The functional architecture of a German clause: facts and controversies

2.1   Introduction

Modern grammar theory produced the largely uncontroversial insight that the sentence structure is a verb projection embedded under at least one, but potentially more than one[1] (overtly realized) functional projection. For English and other Germanic SVO languages, it is obvious that the syntactic surface structure of a clause must provide at least three functional layers. It is obvious because of the positive evidence for at least four different verb positions. (1) depicts the familiar structural representation of an SVO clause with two functional layers above the VP. This is the familiar CP-IP-VP organization of a clause.

(1)

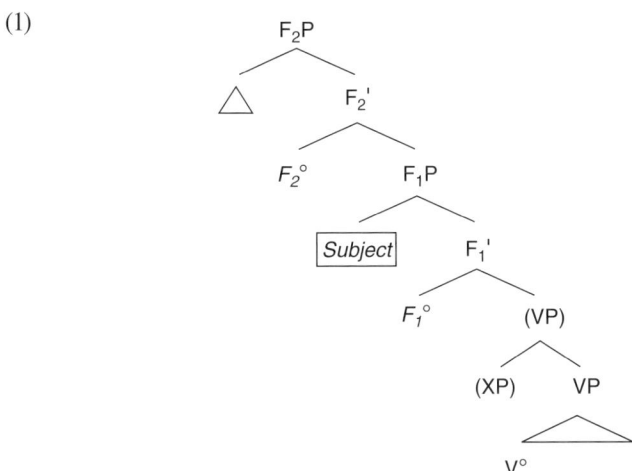

---

[1] For English, the structure of an unembedded main clause consists of at least a VP plus a functional projection, that accommodates the finite auxiliary and the subject. In the embedded clause structure, there is an additional functional layer that accommodates the complementizer that selects a functional verbal projection.

The $V°$ position is the position of the lexical head of the VP. XP is an example of an optional adjunct that precedes the VP, as in (2a).[2] F_1 is the position that is customarily referred to as the 'Infl' position. F_2 is the complementizer position, or alternatively the position of the fronted finite auxiliary. In (2a), the modal as the finite quasi-auxiliary verb occupies the F_1 position. Elements that occur in this position are fronted to the F_2 position in clauses with 'I'-to-C movement. Instances of this structure are the following clauses. (2b) is a clause with a clause-initial finite verb and an empty spec. In (2c), wh-fronting triggers the fronting of the finite auxiliary. In (2d), the trigger is the fronting of a negative quantifier.

(2)   a. that$_{F2}$ we should$_{F1}$ [much more carefully] evaluate$_{V°}$ the available evidence

        b. Should$_{F2-i}$ we [e$_{F1}$]$_i$ [much more carefully] evaluate$_{V°}$ the available evidence?

        c. What$_j$ should$_{F2-i}$ we [e$_{F1}$]$_i$ [much more carefully] evaluate e$_j$

        d. Under no circumstances should$_{F2-i}$ we [e$_{F1}$]$_i$ disregard$_{V°}$ the available evidence

        e. I think *(that$_{F2}$) [under no circumstances [should$_{F?-i}$ we [e$_{F1}$]$_i$ disregard$_{V°}$ positive evidence]]

The embedding of a clause like (2d) under a complementizer (2e) is evidence for the third functional layer. It is worth emphasizing that dropping the complementizer is ruled out in the case of an embedded V-to-'I' construction, although *think* is a verb that ordinarily allows dropping the complementizer. What (2d,e) teach us is this: the functional head position for the complementizer and the position for the fronted finite verb are not necessarily identical in English, nor are they – as illustrated in (3b) – in the Scandinavian languages or in Yiddish. In German, however, the distribution is strictly complementary. C-introduced clauses are verb final. Dropping the *dass* (that) complementizer triggers V2 fronting. Dutch, on the other hand, does not accept embedded V2 clauses, and it does not allow CP- internal V2 either.

In sum, the Germanic V2 clause structure is incompatible with a complementizer-introduced structure in Dutch and German, but not in the Scandinavian languages and in Yiddish. CP-internal V2 (3a,b) occurs in all Germanic VO languages (see Vikner 1995; Haider *et al.* 1995: 6), but not in the OV ones (3d), with the exception of Frisian (4).

(3)   a. Peter said *(that) [never before] *had* he read such a good article

        b. Peter sagde *(at) [aldrig før] *havde* han læst sådan en god artikel

Danish

---

[2] Note that adjunction is not limited to a single instance. In principle, adjunction is free.

Peter said (that) [never before] *had* he read such a good article

c. Peter sagte (*dass) [nie zuvor] *hätte* er so einen guten Artikel
gelesen   *German*
Peter said (that) [never before] *had* he such a good article read

d. Piet zegde *(*dat) hij *heeft* [nooit voordien] zo'n goed artiekel
gelezen   *Dutch*
Peter said (that) he *had* [never before] such-a good article read

Frisian allows both *CP-internal V2* (4b), and *V2-complements* (4c), as alternatives
to a complementizer-headed complement (4a).

(4)   a. Ik leau [*dat* hy him wol rêde *kin*]   *Frisian*
           I think [that he him well save can]

       b. Ik leau [*dat* hy *kin* him wol rêde]

       c. Ik leau [hy *kin* him wol rêde]

For CP-internal V2, de Haan and Weerman (1986: 84) note a constraint on the
class of selecting verb: 'The application of Move V in combination with a lexical
complementizer does not only depend on the nature of the matrix verb – a verb
such as "spite" (regret) does not have this possibility – but also on other properties
of the matrix clause: the matrix clause … cannot be negative, nor modalized.' The
restriction on the particular verb class is virtually identical with the restriction in the
continental Scandinavian languages noted by Vikner (1995: chapter 4): In Icelandic
and Yiddish (see Vikner 1995: 72), CP-internal V2 is a regular option (5a,b). In
Danish (6), and the continental Scandinavian languages, clause-internal V2 is possible only with those verbs that allow *that*-drop in English (7a,b). In Icelandic and
Yiddish (see Vikner 1995: 72), CP-internal V2 is a regular option (5a,b). In German,
these verbs allow a V2 complement in place of a *that*-complement (7b,c).

(5)   a. Jón efast um [að ámorgun *fari* María snemma á fætur]   *Icelandic*
           Jon doubts on [that tomorrow *will* Mary get up early]

       b. Jonas tsveyfelt [az morgen *vet* Miriam fri oyfshteyn]   *Yiddish*
           Jonas doubts [that tomorrow will Miriam early up-stand]

(6)   a. Vi *ved* (we know)   *Danish*

           (i) at Bo ikke [$_{VP}$*har* læst denne bog]
               that Bo not [$_{VP}$has read this book]

           (ii) at denne bog$_i$ *har*$_j$ [Bo ikke [$_{VP}$e$_j$ læst e$_i$]]
                that this book has [Bo not [$_{VP}$read]]

           (iii) at Bo *har*$_j$ ikke [$_{VP}$e$_j$ læst denne bog]
                 that Bo has not [$_{VP}$read this book]

b. Vi *beklager* (we regret)

    (i) at Bo ikke [$_{VP}$ *har* læst denne bog]
    that Bo not [$_{VP}$ has read this book]

    (ii) * at denne bog$_i$ *har*$_j$ [Bo ikke [$_{VP}$ e$_j$ læst e$_i$]]
    that this book has [Bo not [$_{VP}$ read]]

    (iii) *at Bo *har*$_j$ ikke [$_{VP}$ e$_j$ læst denne bog]
    that Bo has not [$_{VP}$ read this book]

(6a-i) and (6b-i) illustrate the 'standard' structure for the embedded clause, with the subject raised, and the finite verb in its VP-internal position. (6a-ii) and (6b-ii) are embedded V2 structures with a fronted object ('drop the complementizer, and you have a main clause structure'). This construction is ungrammatical for a verb like 'doubt' or a factive verb like 'regret' (6b-ii). (6a-ii) differs from (6a-iii) only in the (free) choice of the element moved to the spec of the functional head that is associated with the finite verb in the V2 position. In (6a-iii) it is the subject, in (6a-ii), it is the object. Keep in mind: (6a-iii) must not be mistaken for a case of V-to-'I'. It is a case of CP-internal topicalization construction. This is reflected in the selection restriction. Internal topicalization is licit only in the complement clause of a restricted class of verbs. V-to-'I' would not be restricted. There is no language in which V-to-'I' would be dependent on the type of selecting verb.

In English, the complementizer-drop variant (7a) is identical in word order with the main clause order. Complementizer-drop is not a free option for complement clauses, however. It depends on the type of matrix verb that selects the clause. Factive verbs do not accept the complementizerless variant (7b).

In German, the complementizerless variant is a V2 clause. The finite verb moves from its clause-final position to the position that is otherwise occupied by the complementizer. In (7c,d) this is string vacuous. But, if the clause is slightly augmented, the different order becomes transparent (7e,f). In (7f), the participle is fronted. But, just as well, the subject could have been fronted, instead.

(7)   a. He will think (that) it has rained

    b. He will regret *(that) it has rained

    c. Er glaubt (dass) es regnet
       he believes (that) it rains

    d. Er bedauert *(dass) es regnet
       he regrets (that) it rains

    e. Er glaubt, dass es nicht geregnet *habe*
       he thinks that it not rained has

    f. Er glaubt, geregnet$_i$ *habe*$_j$ es nicht e$_i$ e$_j$

Let us return to the problem posed by (2e), that is, by English clauses with CP-internal fronting of the finite auxiliary across the subject. What kind of functional head position is the position of the finite auxiliary verb in (2e)? Since it follows a topicalized phrase, it is expected to be in the same position as in the main clause counterpart (8a). If this is correct, what is the position of the complementizer in (2d), and is the position of the complementizer in (2d) identical with the position of the very same complementizer in (8b)? Obviously, these two assumptions are incompatible. If $C°$ is in F_2 in (8b), F_2 may alternatively be the position of the finite auxiliary in (8a), but not in (2e), since there is both a fronted auxiliary as in (8a) and a complementizer as in (8b).

(8)   a. Under no circumstances should$_{F2-i}$ we [e$_{F1}$]$_i$ disregard$_{v°}$ positive evidence

       b. that we should$_{F1}$ disregard positive evidence under no circumstances

There are alternative strategies for modelling the problem raised by data such as those in (2) and (8). One strategy is the strategy of *absolute cartography* (AC), see Rizzi (2004); Cinque (2004). The other strategy is that of *convergent structuring* (CS), see Haider (2005b).

AC assigns each individual functional element to a unique functional head position in the clausal architecture. In a UG perspective, the cross-linguistic evidence for functional heads is superimposed: if language X has an overt functional head H, any language must have this functional layer, and if it is not overt in language Y, it is covert. From an AC point of view, the position for the complementizer *that* in (2e) is structurally identical with the position of the complementizer in (8b). Consequently, (8b) is mapped on the same structural scaffolding as (2d). Hence, (9b) must involve an empty functional projection, namely F_2P.

(9)   a. that$_{F3}$ under no circumstances should$_{F2-i}$ we [e$_{F1}$]$_i$ disregard$_{v°}$ positive evidence

       b. that$_{F3}$ [$_{F2P}$ [$_{F2'}$ [e$_{F2}$ [we should$_{F1}$ disregard positive evidence under no circumstances]]]]

In an AC approach to sentence structure, UG directly determines the universal sentence structure. The language-specific differences are differences in terms of which positions of this universal structure are associated with lexical material.

The CS approach on the other hand characterizes the sentence structure as the minimal convergent projection for the terminals of the given clause. In other words, the grammar determines for a given array of terminals its grammatical status. If a given array is grammatical, its structure is the minimal syntactic structure that meets all grammatical requirements for this array. UG determines what is a possible grammar; the grammar of the individual language determines the possible structures for given arrays of terminals in this language.

From a CS vantage point, (9a) requires three functional layers, but (9b) requires only two, since there are only two elements that require a functional head position, namely the complementizer and the finite modal. The difference between (9a) and (9b) is one in terms of the system's potential of English grammar. The grammar of English allows a functional projection to intervene between the projection of the complementizer and the projection whose head accommodates the finite auxiliary. This projection is present only if it is instantiated by lexical material.

The question 'Is the position of the complementizer in (9a) identical with the position of the complementizer in (9b)' is an ill posed one in the CS perspective. The notion of 'identical position' is relative to the given structure. In both clauses, the complementizer is the head of the top-most functional projection, and in both clauses (9a) and (9b), the complement of the C°-projection is a projection with the finite auxiliary associated with a functional head. In a CS analysis, (9b) requires two functional projections, one for the complementizer, and one for the finite auxiliary. (9a), however, requires three functional projections since this clause involves a pre-subject XP in a spec position plus a concomitant functional head. In each case, the structure is the minimal convergent structure for the given clause.

In the CS analysis, the crucial property of the English clause structure in the case of (9a) vs (9b) is the availability of internal topicalization of the quantifier. It is this option of grammar that triggers the adequate structuring. A clause without an application of this option (8b, 9b) does not instantiate the structure required for internal topicalization.

With this in mind, let us return to the initial issue, namely the clausal architecture under a cross-linguistic perspective. What insights do the Scandinavian languages offer with respect to the functional architecture of a clause? All Scandinavian languages are V2 languages, but only Icelandic is an obligatory V-to-'I' language. In other words, the finite verb remains in-situ in non-V2 contexts in the other languages.

(10)   a. at han *ikke* [$_{VP}$ købte bogen]   *Danish*
            that he not [bought book-the]
            'that he did not buy the book'

        b. að hann keypti$_i$ *ekki* [$_{VP}$ e$_i$ bókina]   *Icelandic*
            that he bought not [book-the]
            'that he did not buy the book'   (Platzack 1986: 209)

In (10a), the Danish example, the finite verb follows the negation, which precedes the VP. In Icelandic, however, the finite verb precedes the negation. What applies to the negation in (10) would hold also for pre-VP adverbials. (11) illustrates V2-versions of (10), with the finite verb fronted to a clause-initial functional head position:

(11) a. Bogen$_j$ købte$_i$ han *ikke* [$_{VP}$ e$_i$ e$_j$]   *Danish*
          book-the bought he not

      b. Bókina$_j$ keypti$_i$ hann *ekki* [$_{VP}$ e$_i$ e$_j$]   *Icelandic*
          book-the bought he not

In the clause structure of the continental Scandinavian standard languages (dialectal variations will be considered below), the head of the functional projection that accommodates the subject remains empty. This resembles the English situation in clauses with a finite main verb. But unlike English, any finite verb is moveable (see 11), and on the other hand, any finite verb (main verb or auxiliary) stays in-situ in a context like (10a). Why should this be so?

A simple but controversial answer has been formulated as the RICH AGREEMENT HYPOTHESIS. In its *weak* form[3] it says: If a language has rich inflection then it has verb movement to Infl (Bobaljik 2002: 132). Verbal inflection in a given language is 'rich' iff finite verbs bear multiple distinct inflectional morphemes (Bobaljik 2002: 134), or in other words, if there is a morphologically differentiated inflection paradigm for person and number. Danish, Norwegian and Swedish finite verbs are uninflected for agreement. Morphology only marks tense. Faroese, Icelandic, Yiddish and the West Germanic languages inflect for tense and agreement. English is an exception, as usual.[4]

The RICH AGREEMENT HYPOTHESIS is not fully adequate because there is counterevidence in both directions: there are Germanic VO languages that do not move the finite verb despite rich inflection (Faroese; Hallingdalen dialect of Norwegian; see 12), and on the other hand there are languages that move the finite verb in spite of the lack of inflection (Kronoby dialect of Swedish; see 13).

(12) a. at Jón ofta *etur* tomatir   *Faroese* (Vikner 1997: 189)
          that Jón often eat tomatoes

      b. * at Jón *etur* ofta tomatir
      c. * at me kjøpæ *ikkje* bokje   *Hallingdalen, Norwegian*
          that we buy not book-the
      d. at me *ikkje* kjøpæ bokje
          that we not buy book-the   (Trosterud 1989: 91)

---

[3] Strong form: If and only if a language has rich inflection then it has verb movement to the Infl. position, that is, to the I^0 position (nowadays: T^0 or Agr^0).

[4] It marks *agreement* in general only for third singular present (unless the finite verb is a modal); for the auxiliary *be*, all persons are distinguished in the present (*am–are–is*).

Faroese has nearly as rich a verbal inflection paradigm as Icelandic,[5] but the finite verb stays in-situ.[6] The Norwegian Hallingdalen dialect morphologically marks tense and number (present sg. *kjøpa*; present pl. *kjøpæ*), but the verb does not raise. A number distinction in the past tense of strong verbs is also attested in the Hallingdalen variety of Norwegian and in the Skelleftemålet and Pitemålet varieties of Swedish, according to Bobaljik (2002: 146). None of these dialects shows evidence for movement of the finite verb to a pre-VP functional head position that is different from the V2 position.

Verb raising to a functional head position in spite of *poor inflection* (no subject–verb agreement) is attested in the Kronoby dialect of Swedish (Alexiadou and Fanselow 2002).

(13)   he va bra et an tsöfft *int* bootsen   *Kronoby Swedish*
        it was good that he bought *not* book-the

The variety of Swedish spoken in Kronoby, Finland, displays the verb-negation order indicative of verb raising even though the inflectional paradigm resembles the standard Swedish one in that it 'has no subject-verb agreement at all' (Vikner 1995: 135). A parallel case is the Tromsø dialect of Norwegian as described in Iversen (1918).

In sum, there is no manifest grammatical causality based on the morphological make-up of the finite verb that could serve as the unequivocal trigger for the raising of the finite verb in VO Germanic (see Hallingdalen Norwegian vs Kronoby Swedish or Tromsø Norwegian). Nevertheless, the pre-VP position of the subject that is obligatorily lexicalized is a manifest indicator of a functional projection below the CP and above the VP in the Germanic VO languages.

Table 2.1 summarizes the properties examined above and anticipates a property to be discussed in the following section, namely the lack of V-to-'I' in the Germanic OV languages (row (d)). This (i.e. no V-to-'I' in OV) is still a controversial issue, but the relevant facts are uncontroversial and robust counterevidence for the theory-driven V-to-'I' analyses in handbooks.

---

[5] Unlike Icelandic, the plural forms do not distinctly code for person. Rohrbacher (1999) took this (i.e. the fact that a paradigm contains at least one ambiguous form) as sufficient for the blocking of V-to-'I'. Vikner (1997) points out that in both the present indicative as well as in the past tense paradigm, Faroese marks only number but not person distinctions in the plural. He takes this to be crucial: V-to-'I' in VO, iff person morphology is found in all tenses (Vikner 1997: 207).

[6] According to Barnes (1987), there are speakers for whom raising is optional. This seems to be a dialectal variant that conserves the raising option that has become obsolete in the majority variant of Faroese.

Table 2.1 *CP-internal V2 in Germanic languages*

	V2	CP-internal V2	overt V-to-'I'
a. Icelandic, Yiddish	yes	yes	yes
b. Continental Scandinavian languages	yes	yes	no
c. Frisian	yes	yes	no
d. German, Dutch	yes	no	no
e. Romance (Italian, French, …)	no	no	yes

Faroese and the continental Scandinavian languages lack overt V-to-'I', irrespective of the differences in the morphological make-up of the finite verb. English is exceptional since V-to-'I' is restricted to a subclass of finite verbs, namely auxiliaries and quasi-auxiliaries (modals). French is an example of a language with a general V-to-'I' requirement in the absence of a V2 property.

(14)   a.   de ne PAS *manger* de chocolat   *French*
              to NEG$_{cl}$ NEG eat of chocolate

        b.   Il ne *mange*$_i$ PAS e$_i$ de chocolat
              he NEG$_{cl}$ eats NEG of chocolate

        c.   * de ne *manger*$_i$ PAS e$_i$ de chocolat

        d.   * Il ne PAS *mange* de chocolat

In French, the negation consists of two elements. One is the clitic *ne*, and the other one is the particle *pas*. This is the counterpart of English *not*. In an infinitival construction (14a), the particle precedes the verb. In a finite clause, however, the finite verb is moved across the particle to the pre-VP functional head position. Both conditions are obligatory (14c,d).

What you should keep in mind for the following section is this:

- Cross-linguistically, V-to-'I' is independent of the morphological shape of the finite verb.
- Some VO Germanic languages obligatorily apply V-to-'I', some do not allow it.
- English is exceptional. It requires V-to-'I' for (quasi-)auxiliaries but disallows it for main verbs. Typically, languages either require V-to-'I' for any finite verb (e.g. Icelandic, French) or disallow it for any verb (continental Scandinavian).

2.2   The position of the clause-final finite verb in German and Dutch: no overt V-to-'I'

This subsection briefly reviews the widely held but arguably incorrect assumption on the existence of *clause-final* functional heads as targets of V-movement and then presents in detail the data that patently militate against the alleged V-movement to a clause-final functional head position.

According to this view, the German clause structure is identical with the English one, except for the *position* of particular functional heads. In English, the functional head whose specifier is the functional subject position, precedes the VP. In German, this head is assumed to follow the VP, but the specifier is to precede the VP. In other words, this functional projection is head final, with both the complement (i.e. the VP) and the specifier preceding. The would-be finite verb is deemed to move to this right-hand finiteness head position. This analysis, however, is empirically inadequate.

With respect to V-to-'I' raising, German seems to behave like Faroese (see Vikner 1995: 148). The finite verb does not raise in spite of its morphologically well-coded finiteness features. The verb stays in its VP-internal head position and the finiteness features get checked in-situ (or, in Chomskyan terms, in a derivation *after* spell-out).

There is direct positive evidence for this claim, and it comes from verbs with multiple separable prefixes (Haider 1993: 62; Vikner 2001). A second, independent, domain of evidence is based on the ungrammaticality of exactly that type of structural constellation that has been the primary source of evidence for assuming V-to-'I'. Crucial evidence for assuming V-to-'I' in English, French or Icelandic, to name a few uncontroversial specimens, is the distribution of adverbials and negation relative to the finite verb: adverbials and negation follow if the verb is finite, but precede the infinite form. In other words, adverbials and negation intervene. German does not allow any intervener.

German is representative for all Germanic OV languages. There is no Germanic OV language with uncontroversial evidence for V-to-'I' raising of the finite verb to a clause-final functional head position, and this is not accidental. There is reason to assume that this is a general property of OV languages and that a grammar with this property would not be UG compatible.

Let us recapitulate the 'hand-book knowledge' on V-to-T-to-AgrS that is in need of revision. It is a theory-driven extrapolation of what turned out to be adequate for VO languages, modulo head final. This is important to keep in the front of your mind: the structural analysis in terms of head-final functional heads is not primarily a data-driven analysis but a theory-driven one. (1) illustrates widely assumed structural representations.

The guiding idea behind (1a) has been a minimal and conservative modification of the sentence structure that has proven useful for VO languages. In the simplest of all syntactic worlds, the OV structure would be isomorphic with the VO structure, modulo serialization. Consequently, the lexical and the functional heads are assumed to follow their complements in OV while they precede in VO structures. This hypothesis is legitimate as a hypothesis, of course, but it needs to be tested against the relevant empirical evidence.

(1)   German *V2 clause* structure with head-final functional heads
       (*to be dismissed!*)

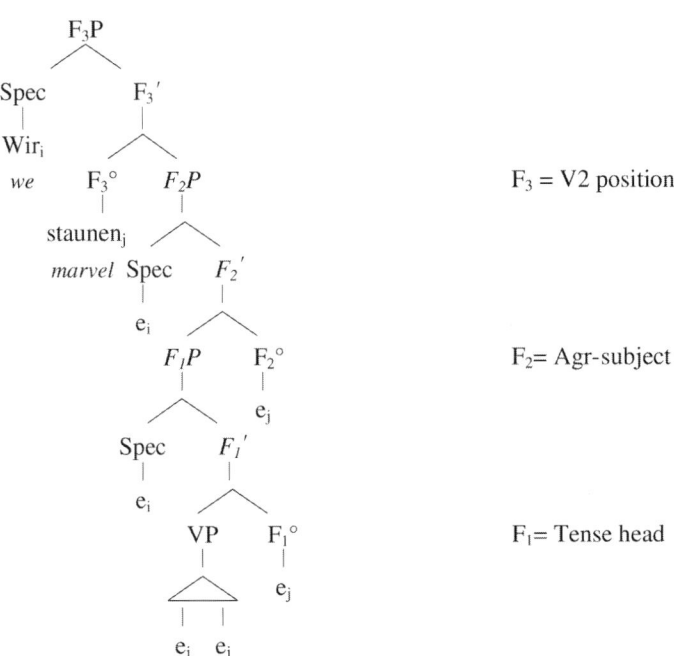

(2)   German *V-final* clause structure with head-final functional heads
        (*to be dismissed!*)

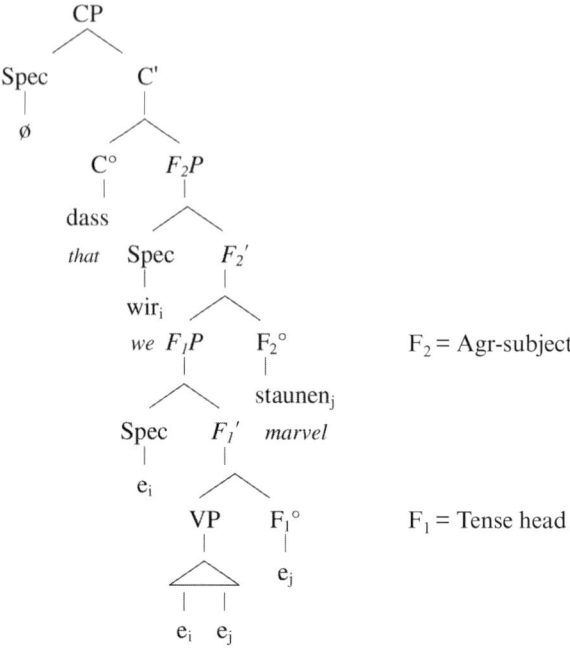

It is not enough to show that the typical word order patterns are compatible with the assumed structure. What has to be shown is that the structure captures all the relevant patterns and excludes the unacceptable ones. It will be shown that the structure both under- and overgenerates. It excludes acceptable patterns and it admits unacceptable ones. The evidence strongly points to the conclusion that the clause-final finite verbs in OV are not in a derived position but remain in their base position.

In recent years, the two original functional domains (IP, CP) have been each subdivided into several functional projections. Pollock (1989) started to decompose the I-domain (into AgrP and TP), and Rizzi (1997) argued for a cascade of functional projections within the C-domain. In addition to CP, he proposed functional projections for illocutionary functions (*force, finiteness, topic, focus*), some of which may be iterated or instantiated more than once (i.e. *topic*). The latter assumption is contested in Benincà and Poletto (2004), who proposed a finer grained notion of topics instead.[7]

---

[7] Grewendorf (2002) is a handy source for an overview of German in a minimalist perspective.

Table 2.2   *The lexical domain of V° and its functional extensions*

V-PROJECTION	verb (shells) with the arguments of the verb
I-domain	projection of tense (T), person (AGR), aspect (Asp), …; with the subject in a functional spec position
C-domain	selected features like [± wh]; sentence mood (interrogative, declarative, imperative); information structure (topic, focus)

For OV languages, there is much less consensus as to whether the decomposition into cascades of functional projections is empirically useful and adequate. Note that German does not provide any direct evidence for overt functional heads in the midfield[8] (since there is no possibility of either moving a finite verb to one of these hypothetical positions; see the discussion of CP-internal V2 above) nor is there uncontroversial evidence for functional spec positions (no EPP effect that calls for an expletive, no opacity effects on extraction, as will be discussed at length below).

The crucial property embodied in (1) and (2) is this: the finite verb raises out of the VP. In (1), the V2 structure, it ends up in the top-most functional head position. If this position is blocked by a complementizer, the finite verb's journey comes to a halt in the functional head position below. In the linearization of (2), the finite verb is clause final because the cascade of functional heads except for the C°-head is head final.

Note that this mixed headedness property of functional heads is a strange property from the point of view of grammar theory. What is it that determines the opposite headedness, namely the head-initial property of the top functional head in (1) and the head-final property of the functional heads below? All the functional heads in (1) are feature based. In other words, the headedness property is not a property of a specific lexical item and thereby coded and stored as a lexical property. This would be possible for the complementizer in (2),[9] since it is a lexical item, but not for the functional head that supplies the V2 position in (1).[10]

---

[8] 'Midfield' is the part of the clause in between the V2/C° position and the clause-final verb position.

[9] There are languages with two sets of complementizers, namely head-initial and head-final ones (see Bayer 1998 and 2001 on Bangla). In this case, it is reasonable to assume that the headedness property is a lexical property of the given subset, analogous to coexistent head-initial and head-final particle constructions ('prepositions' vs 'postpositions'), as in German.

[10] Note: if 'CP' is used for the highest functional head in a V2 clause in this book, e.g. for F3 in (1), then this is just for the sake of exposition. Of course, a functional head that is targeted by V-movement cannot be of the category C°, since V° and C° are clearly distinct categories with distinct features (see also Brandt *et al.* (1992)).

In addition to the theoretical concerns, there is immediate empirical evidence against moving the finite verb to the right. Here is the first of two empirical arguments. There are finite verbs that cannot move. This provides positive evidence for deciding on the position of a clause-final finite verb.

What we know from languages with V-movement is this: whenever a verb has moved to an *intermediate* functional head position, it cannot be prevented from moving to a higher functional position if movement to this position is required. A familiar instance of this is V-to-'I' followed by V-to-C in English: if a verb is moved by V-to-'I', it will move on, if 'I'-to-C applies. There are no cases of an exceptional subset of verbs that move only to I°, but do not move further. In other words, if a verb is moveable in the first step, it is moveable in further steps, too. On the other hand, verbs may resist movement (to intermediate functional heads) at all and stay in-situ, as for instance, English main verbs or finite verbs in mainland Scandinavian languages in non-V2 sentences. So we note: there is no exceptional subset of verbs that would allow V-to-'I' but resist further movement to C.[11]

With this in mind, let us analyse what the theory predicts for a specific verb class of German, namely verbs *with more than one* separable prefix (see Haider 1993: 62; Vikner 2001; Fortmann 2007). It is easy to find or to construct them because particle-verb formation is a productive word formation paradigm in German (see (6) for examples). Here are the ingredients. The prefix *vor* (before), as in (3a,b), and the prefix *an* (at, on), as in (3c,d), are two specimens out of the set of separable prefixes. They are obligatorily stranded if the verb moves.

(3)   a.   Er sagte$_i$ es *vor*-e$_i$
             he said it before
             'He told the answer'

       b.   * Er *vor*sagte$_i$ es e$_i$

       c.   Er sagte$_i$ es *an*-e$_i$
             he said it on
             'He announced it'

       d.   * Er *an*sagte es

Crucially, prefixation may be iterated, yielding a doubly prefixed particle verb. Let me illustrate this with *vor-an-kündigen* (literally: pre-ad-vertise) as a 'verb with two separable prefixes'. *Ankündigen* is derived from *kündigen* by prefixing *an*-, and this verb is the basis for deriving yet another verb by prefixing

---

[11] This does not exclude the converse, namely verbs that move to C°, but never stop and stay in 'I°'. One case is the case of mainland Scandinavian languages discussed in the preceding section, and another case could be the quotative inversion in English as in 'Blair exaggerated, *says* The Times' (see Collins 1997).

it with *vor-*. The result is *vorankündigen* with the word structure [vor$_P$° [an$_P$° [kündigen]$_{V°}$]] (preannounce).

Guess what is going to happen if a doubly prefixed verb has to move? You are by now able to predict the behaviour on the basis of the information given above, if you take into consideration what obligatory particle stranding (i.e. 'separable prefix') amounts to in terms of the grammatical properties of the particle. In a descriptive rendering of 'separable prefix' this reads as follows: a separable prefix is a prefix that must be stranded if V-movement applies to the complex verb. In other words, in V-movement contexts, the sister of the particle is the trace of the moved V. Analyse now the possible options of V-movement for a verb with double prefixing (see 4), and you will realize that there is no way to properly and simultaneously observe the stranding requirement for each of the particles involved.

(4)   a. * Er kündigte es *vor-an*-e$_i$
            he announced it pre-on
            'He preannounced it'

        b. * Er *an*-kündigte es *vor*-e$_i$

        c. * Er *vor-an*-kündigte es e$_i$

If in (4a), *kündigte* moves, as in (3a), and *an-* is correctly stranded, *vor-* would still be attached to a morpheme, namely *an-*, and not to a verbal trace, hence it would not count as stranded (4a). So it is ill formed, since *vor-* is a separable particle and thereby requires stranding. If, however, *vor* is stranded (4b), then *an-kündigte* must have moved. But then *an* is not stranded and is therefore ill formed, just like (4c), with no stranding at all.

Consequently, this amounts to a catch-22 situation. There is no way to meet the demands of both particles simultaneously. Therefore, the V-to-'I' theory is bound to predict that a derivation in which a finite verb with more than one separable particle has to move will crash.

Let us now compare the two competing analyses for a clause-final finite verb in German. Hypothesis *I* – the V-to-'I' hypothesis – assumes that a clause-final finite verb is always a verb that has string-vacuously moved to a clause-final functional head position. Hypothesis *II* – the checking in-situ hypothesis – assumes that clause-final finite verbs in German are checked in their VP-internal lexical head position and stay in-situ in the VP head position.

What are the respective predictions? Hypothesis *I* predicts that verbs with two particles cannot appear in finite form at all because they would trigger a *stranding conflict* (see 4) for the particles when the bare verb has to move to a function head position. Only forms that do not involve stranding (as a consequence of movement of the bare verb to a functional head position) would be admitted. According to this hypothesis, doubly prefixed verbs are always non finite.

Hypothesis *II* predicts a different outcome. Since hypothesis *II* presupposes that clause-final verbs stay in-situ, the stranding conflict does not arise in the clause-final position as this is the base position of the verb. It only arises once the verb moves to the clause-initial functional head position in a 'verb second' or 'verb first' clause. So the prediction is this: verbs with two separable particles may be used as finite verbs, but only in clauses that do not involve fronting the finite verb, that is, only in verb-final clauses.

What do the data tell us? There are doubly prefixed *finite* verbs, they occur in head-final positions and they must not be moved to the V2/V1 position. Hence, hypothesis *II* is supported, whereas hypothesis *I* lacks empirical support (see 5) and is discredited.

(5)   a.   wenn du uns voranmeldest
              if you us preregister   (lit. *pre-on-register*)

        b. * Du meldest$_i$ uns *voran*-e$_i$
              you register us *pre-on*

        c. * Du *an*meldest$_i$ uns *vor*-e$_i$

        d. * Du *voran*meldest$_i$ uns e$_i$

As (5b–d) show, a verb with *two* separable prefixes may occur as a finite verb, but it is well-formed only in the clause-final position (5a), and there is no way to derive a well-formed version with fronting. Hypothesis *I* fails because it predicts that the stranding conflict would already have arisen in the final position when the verb is allegedly raised to the hypothetical postverbal functional head position in order to check finiteness features.

In (6), more of these verbs are listed, for the sake of illustration. The crucial point is that this verb format is productive and the fronting failure is easy to understand. So, there is no room for the kind of doubts raised against the original argument (Haider 1993: 62), based on verbs that arise through back-formation[12] (see 7), namely that there might be some ill understood property of backformation verbs that blocks fronting (see Koopman 1995 on corresponding verbs in Dutch).

(6)   a. ab-drucken   – *vor-ab*-drucken   (lit. *pre-off-print*)

        b. an-melden   – *vor-an*-melden   (lit. *pre-an-nounce*, preregister)

        c. ein-teilen   – *um-ein*-teilen   (lit. *re-in-deal*, reorganize)

---

[12] Höhle (1991) was the first to note that these are finite verbs that do not front. For a recent study, see Fortmann (2007).

d. ein-steigen – *mit-ein*-steigen (lit. *with-in-step*, get on together)

e. aus-drucken – *mit-aus*-drucken (lit. *with-out-print*, print out jointly)

(7) a. auf-führen (lit. *up-lead)* 'perform, put on stage'

b. Aufführung 'performance' – Ur-aufführung '*ur*-performance = premiere'

c. *ur*-auf-führen 'show for the first time'

A verb like *uraufführen* is a backformation[13] from the deverbal noun *Aufführung* (performance) prefixed with *ur*. This, again, produces a clash with the stranding requirements for the sandwiched particle *-auf-*. In this case, the grammatical causality is not as immediately evident as in the case of doubly prefixed verbs above (see Fortmann 2007).

Note that these data do not only decide the controversy on potential V-to-'I' raising for finite verbs but also for *infinitival constructions*. The German infinitival marker *zu* – a cognate of English *to* – unlike its English counterpart, is not a lexical functional head element but an inflection particle prefixed to the verb. As illustrated in (8), verbs with two separable prefixes are perfect also in the infinitival construction. They would be ungrammatical if the infinitival verb had to raise to a functional head position.

(8) a. ohne sich (vor)an*zu*melden
    without oneself (pre)-on-*to*-register
    'without to preregister oneself'

b. anstatt es (mit)aus*zu*drucken
    instead-of it (with)-out-*to*-print
    'instead of printing it out jointly'

What the examples in (8) confirm is that sentential infinitival complements in German do not require V-to-'I' raising of the infinitival verb to the functional head position of the infinitival marker, and they confirm that the infinitival marker *zu* is a morpheme attached to the verb, and not a separate functional head. If it were an infinitival functional head like English *to*, the verbs in (8) would have to raise and this would cause a stranding conflict for the particles. Consequently, the examples in (8) would be ungrammatical, contrary to the facts. So we have to conclude: neither the finite nor the infinitival verb moves out of the VP to a (clause-final) functional head position.

---

[13] $[Ur[aufführ]_V ung]_N]_N$ is reanalysed (rebracketed) as $[[uraufführ]_V\text{-}ung]_N$, which yields *uraufführen* as a verbal base of the deverbal noun.

Let us dwell on this point for a moment and watch out for potential alternative accounts. Advocates of the established V-to-'I' approach tend to organize a retreat on two defence lines, a data challenging line and an analytic patch-up one. The first move is to question the data by introducing additional, supportive data. The second line of defence is a patch-up strategy. The preferred move is to protect it by an (ad hoc) assumption so that it becomes compatible with the evidence.

A case of the first attempt is Sabel's (2000) claim that there are instances of interveners, that is, non-verbal material that intervenes between a sequence of non-finite verbs and the clause-final finite verb. (9a) is an example, and it has an infinitival counterpart (9b). Does this[14] prove the point that the finite auxiliary *hat* in (9a) has moved out of the VP and that the PP item *dafür* has been extraposed?

(9)   a. (?/*) dass er viel gelernt *dafür* hat
             that he much learned it-for has

        b. (?/*) ohne viel gelernt *dafür* zu haben
             without much learned it-for to have

Data as (9a) would yield a point in favour of the raising hypothesis if indeed the intervener appeared right between the finite verb and the preceding non-finite one(s). This is not the case, however. The position of the intervener is ambiguous between a position immediately to the left of the finite verb (9a) or the infinitival verb (9b), and a position immediately to the right of the main verb. The unambiguous cases are (10b) and (10d). Here, the PP *dafür* would be in a position following the VP and preceding the allegedly raised verb. In (10e,f), the intervener is a full PP.[15] The strong unacceptability of this order shows that there is no space for intervening material between the right boundary of the VP and a supposed functional head position to the right of the VP. There is no space because the verb does not raise. The verbs form a compact verbal cluster (see chapter 7 for an extensive discussion of the clustering property).

Finally (10g) shows that the prepositional object *dafür* can indeed be extraposed to the right edge of the VP, if there is a VP. In sum, the pattern illustrated by the examples in (10) does not support hypothesis *I*, but rather lends additional support to hypothesis *II*.

---

[14] In my opinion, the order with an intervening PP is deviant. This personal judgement conforms with several checks with informants.

[15] If (10a,c) are felt to be less deviant than (10b,d), respectively, this points to a difference in terms of an accessible repair strategy. The PP item in (10a,c) can be reanalysed as a word level element (i.e. a preposition amalgamated with a pronoun) and this can be construed as cliticized to the main verb.

(10) a. ?/* dass er viel gelernt *dafür* haben muss
          that he much learnt it-for have must

      b. * dass er viel gelernt haben *dafür* muss
          that he much learnt it-for have must

      c. ?/* ohne viel gelernt *dafür* haben zu müssen
          without much learnt it-for have to have-to

      d. * ohne viel gelernt haben *dafür* zu müssen
          without much learnt have it-for to have-to

      e. * dass er viel gelernt *für das Examen* hat
          that he much learnt for the exam has

      f. * ohne viel gelernt *für das Examen* zu haben
          without much learnt for the exam to have

      g. [$_{VP}$ Gelernt haben *dafür/für das Examen*] muss er viel
          [learnt have it-for/for the exam] must he much

The inversion of full PP complements (10e,f) is strongly unacceptable. It is the ungrammaticality of this very order that is the crucial evidence against V-to-'I'. Extraposable material is the kind of intervener material that hypothesis *I* predicts to appear between the non-finite verb (in the VP) and the finite verb in the alleged clause-final functional head position. This type of evidence – interveners between potential V positions – has become the cardinal evidence for assuming functional layers to the left of the VP in VO languages. Hence, it should be a source of evidence for V-to-'I' in OV as well.

The ungrammaticality of these patterns not only contradicts Sabel's claim. It also provides the second empirical argument against V-to-'I', announced above: V-to-'I' should produce stranded particles. (11) lists the minimal set of data for this argument. First, it must be shown that the VP is an extraposition site for a PP, as (10g) and (11a) illustrate. The PP *damit* (with-it) is postverbal in (11a). Second, if the finite verb, according to hypothesis *I*, must leave the VP and target a clause-final functional head position, extraposition to VP ought to produce the kind of intervener that proves the actual movement. The extraposed phrase would end up right between the stranded particle and the raised finite verb, as in (11b). However, this is ungrammatical. Third, hypothesis *II* predicts the order in (11c). The finite verb stays in-situ and the extraposed PP follows the finite verb. This is the correct order.

(11) a. [$_{VP}$ Angefangen *damit*]$_i$ hat bloß einer e$_i$
          on-caught with-it has just one
          'Only one has started with it'

b. * weil bloß einer *an*-e$_i$ damit *fing*$_i$

c.   weil bloß einer *anfing* damit

What kind of patch-up strategy could one enlist for protecting the V-to-'I' hypothesis against the particle stranding evidence? Sufficient (and entirely ad hoc) would be the assumption that the particle is stranded only when the verb moves to the left, but not when it moves to the right.

Is it true that movement to the right never strands a particle in a language in which V2 movement strands a particle? The answer is: no. Here is an example. In Dutch verb clusters, particles are optionally stranded, and the distant verb is to the right, not to the left. In Haider (2003), the stranding variant is argued to follow from a movement process. It is the verb that moves, and it moves to the right within the cluster. (12b) cannot be the result of particle movement. First, particles like *op* (up) do not move, and second, movement would be able to skip intervening adverbials, contrary to the facts (12b).

(12)   a. dat ze deze mensen *opgebeld* hebben
            that they these people up-phoned have

        b. dat ze deze mensen *op* (*vrijwillig) hebben *gebeld*
            that they these people up (voluntarily) have phoned

What the Dutch particle stranding data teach us is this: particle stranding is not constrained to left-bound V-movement. It occurs also with a right-bound movement.[16] This undermines the patch-up strategy.

In this situation it seems wise to introduce additional, independent evidence. Let me as a proponent of the '*no clause-final 'I', hence no clause-final V-to-'I'*' hypothesis therefore call up one more witness, namely data from scopal relations: V-movement of the V-to-'I' kind leaves the domain of the VP. VP-internal material does not c-command the target position of V-movement since it is outside of the VP. If the verb is scope sensitive and the scope-bearing element is VP-internal, V-movement will remove the scope-sensitive element out of the domain of the scope-bearing element and the scopal relation will be destroyed, unless reconstruction may be applied (i.e. unless scope may be calculated with respect to the trace of the moved scope-sensitive element).

(13)   a.   (He said that the value would triple, and) tripled the value has
                indeed within one week

        b. * (He said that the value would *more than triple*, and) tripled the
                value has indeed *more than* within one week

---

[16] To be clear: this movement in Dutch is not movement to a functional head position. It is a kind of head-to-head cliticization: $[V° + V°]_{V°}$.

Why is (13b) ungrammatical? Note that the verb in (13b) contains the target of comparison: 'the value more than tripled' means that the degree to which the value grew is more than *three*-fold. In a comparative construction, the target of comparison must be in the c-command domain of the comparative expression. Reconstruction does not apply as (13b) demonstrates. Topicalization removed the target 'triple' out of the domain of 'more' and it is not reconstructed. Otherwise (13b) would be flawless.

With this in mind, we are prepared to construct the V2 counterpart of (13), and the predictions are obvious (see Haider 1997b). Hypothesis *I* predicts the comparative version to be ungrammatical both in the clause-final and the clause-initial version since in each case the verb has left the VP. Hypothesis *II* predicts that the clause-*final* version will be grammatical since the finite verb stays in-situ, but the *fronted* version will be deviant, because the verb as the carrier of the target of comparison has left the domain of the comparative operator. (14a) illustrates the comparative construction and (14b) is the corresponding equative construction. In (14b), the scope-bearing element is *so* (as).

(14)   a. dass sich der Wert (*mehr als*) verdreifachte (in diesem Jahr)
            that itself the value (more than) tripled (in this year)

        b. dass sich der Wert (*so gut wie*) verdreifachte
            that itself the value (as good as) tripled
            'that the value as much as tripled'

The crucial data are data with a fronted verb, as in (15b,d). The verb is fronted by finite verb fronting or by topicalization. In each case the result is robust, and it is deviant.

(15)   a. Der Wert verdreifachte sich (**mehr als*) (in diesem Jahr)
            the value tripled itself (more than) (in this year)

        b. Verdreifacht hat sich der Wert (**mehr als*) (in diesem Jahr)
            tripled has itself the value (more than) (in this year)

        c. Der Wert verdreifachte sich (**so gut wie*) (in diesem Jahr)
            the value tripled itself (as much as) (in this year)

        d. Verdreifacht hat sich der Wert (**so gut wie*) (in diesem Jahr)
            tripled has itself the value (as much as) (in this year)

Computing scope by means of reconstruction is obviously inapplicable in these cases, both for head movement (V2), and for phrasal movement (topicalization). With this in mind, let us evaluate the competing hypotheses on the clause-final position of a finite verb:

(16)   a. Hypothesis *I*: [... [$_{VP...}$ Q ...e$_i$] V°$_{fin-i}$]
        b. Hypothesis *II*: [... [$_{VP}$ ... Q ... V°$_{fin}$] ...]

If hypothesis *I* (16a) was the correct analysis, a clause-final finite verb would have moved out of the domain of the quantifier and the scope relation would crash. Hypothesis *II* (16b), however, correctly predicts that the clause-final finite verb is in the scope of a VP-internal quantifier, and it predicts that moving the finite verb to the clause-initial functional head position will destroy the scope relation.

The conclusions of the above discussion for the German clause structure are as follows:

(i)   there is no overt V° movement to a clause-*final finite* functional head position nor to a clause-final *infinitival* functional head;

(ii)   the finite verb remains in-situ, hence particle stranding is not at issue. Movement applies only when the finite verb moves to the V-second position, that is, the top functional head position;

(iii)   there is no overt V-movement to either a clause-medial or clause-final functional head. A clause-final finite verb is clause final as the head of the VP.

Conclusion (iii) is an indirect one. Given (i) and (ii), we can infer that the clause-final position of the finite verb is indeed the VP-head position and not a functional head position low enough so that the finite verb ends up as a clause-final element (followed by an empty subtree) in surface structure. Here is the reasoning. If finite verbs had to move to an *intermediate* functional head position to the left, particles would be stranded and doubly prefixed verbs would become deviant. Needless to say there is no construction in German or Dutch in which a stranded particle would follow the finite verb unless the verb is in the V2/V1 position.

This state of affairs has an obvious implication for the identification of functional head positions in German in general. If the finite verb stays in-situ and does not move to an intermediate functional position, simple inspection of data does not show whether the empty functional position is to the right or to the left of the VP, or if it is absent at all, maybe.

The fact that the lexical functional heads (complementizers, articles) are head initial points to the conclusion that empty functional heads are head initial, too, in German. After all, their position must follow from theoretical principles since there is no way to associate idiosyncratic directionality information lexically with an empty element.

At any rate, it is circumstantial evidence that plays the crucial role in finding out whether there are empty functional head positions at all in the German clause structure[17] and whether they have to be located as clause-medial or clause-final heads.

---

[17] I do not endorse the universal clause structure hypothesis. As argued for instance in Haider (1993, 2005b), I take clause structure to be the minimal complete structure for the given array of terminals. UG dictates the functional architecture as a function of

A central area of circumstantial evidence for functional projections is the predictable syntactic properties of the spec positions obligatorily associated with each functional head. The next subsections will focus on this area, and particularly on two aspects. One aspect is the alleged need of functional spec positions for accommodating arguments or adjuncts, and especially for accommodating the subject. A side effect of this is the obligatory lexicalization of the allegedly universal structural subject position. In Generative terms, this is known as the EPP property (*every clause has a functional subject position*). The second aspect is the syntactic behaviour of phrases in spec positions as opposed to phrases in VP-internal argument positions, namely, the subject–object asymmetry with respect to extraction. The discriminating property is the opacity effect for phrases in spec: a phrase in a functional spec position is an island for extraction. Extraction out of a phrase in spec is ungrammatical.

2.2.1   *Appendix on predicted interveners*

The raising-to-'I' hypothesis, with the finite verb targeting a clause-final 'I', makes a fully clear and fully wrong prediction for German: extraposed material intervenes between a stranded particle and the raised finite verb. The prediction follows from the following facts:

a.   a particle is stranded in the VP base position when the finite verb moves to a functional head position (see the V2 movement)

b.   VP is a target of extraposition (see also chapter 5)

Therefore, if both the finite verb moves to a clause-final functional head position and a phrase XP is extraposed to the right edge of the VP, the predicted order will be (1a), illustrated by the ungrammatical (1b). The grammatical order is (1c). (1d) shows that the VP is a target for extraposition.

(1)   a.   … [[$_{VP}$ … e$_j$ … *particle*-e$_i$] XP_j]$_{VP}$ V$_{\text{fin-}i}$

b.   * dass sie den Hund nicht an-e$_i$ [der dort saß] fasste$_i$
        that she the dog not on [who there sat] grabbed
        'that she did not touch the dog that sat there'

c.   dass sie den Hund nicht anfasste [der dort saß]
        that she the dog not on-grabbed [who there sat]
        'that she did not touch the dog that sat there'

the given inventory. If, for instance, a language does not have any morphosyntactic agreement relations (e.g. Chinese), the core grammar does not have to project agreement nodes.

    d. [Den Hund angefasst, der dort saß]$_{VP}$ hat sie nicht
        [the dog on-grabbed, who there sat] has she not
        'Touched the dog who sat there has she not'

The 'V-in-situ' hypothesis, on the other hand, predicts that extraposed material has to follow the finite verb, since the verb does not leave the VP.

   Note that the V-to-'I' hypothesis cannot be salvaged by the ad hoc assumption that the particle moves out of the VP, together with the verb, and that stranding takes place in the postverbal functional position only. In this case it suffices to replace (1a) by (2a). Here, the hypothesis wrongly predicts that an extraposed relative clause may end up preceding the finite verb.

(2)   a. … [[$_{VP}$ … DP-e$_j$ DP e$_i$] RC_j]$_{VP}$ V$_{fin-i}$

        b. * dass sie dem Hund^j etwas e$_i$ [der^j dort saß] gab$_i$
            that she the dog something [who there sat] gave
            'that she gave the dog that sat there something'

        c. dass sie dem Hund etwas gab [der dort saß]
           that she the dog something gave [who there sat]
           'that she gave the dog that sat there something'

        d. [Den Hund^j etwas gegeben, der^j dort saß]$_{VP}$ hat sie nicht
           [the dog something given, who there sat] has she not
           'Given something to the dog who sat there has she not'

As illustrated by (2b) once more, a VP is a target of extraposition. In this case, it is a relative clause that belongs to the first of two objects. If the finite verb indeed left the VP, (2b) would be grammatical, since the relative clause would be adjoined to the VP while the verb is raised across the VP to the final functional head position. If, however, the finite verb remains in situ, the predicted order is that of (2d), and this is indeed the grammatical order.

2.3   The position(s) of the subject

    Does German clause structure provide a unique structural position exclusively reserved for the subject? The answer is less evident than it is for VO languages like English or the Scandinavian languages. For VO languages, the subject position is very easy to identify. It is the only argument position that *precedes* the verb. In OV languages, all arguments precede the verb, and in many languages, the order among these arguments is variable, due to scrambling. So, a naive inspection of data is not sufficient. What we need to answer the question are structural criteria that allow us to clearly identify a structural subject position.

What is special about the subject in SVO languages? Although a subject argument is merged in a VP-internal position, this position is not in the canonical directionality domain of the verbal head since the VP-internal subject position is the highest argument position in the VP, and in SVO languages, the highest argument position precedes the lexical head $V°$ (1a).

(1)   a. SVO V-projection: $[_{VP}$ DP$_{Subject}$ $[_{V'}$ V° $\rightarrow$ ..... $]]$
        b. SOV V-projection: $[_{VP}$ DP $[_{V'}$ ..... $\leftarrow$V° $]]$

In an SOV language, all VP-internal arguments are within the canonical directionality domain of the head. There is no structurally unique VP-internal position in the sense that it differs from other VP-internal positions in its licensing property. In an SVO setting (1a), however, the VP-internal subject position is structurally unique since it is not on the canonical side of the head.

Next, let us take for granted that an argument must be licensed by a head in its canonical directionality domain. If this is so, we understand why a VP in an SVO language must be embedded under a functional projection. The functional head provides a structural licensing context for the subject:

(2) $[_{FP}$ DP$_i$ $[$F° $\rightarrow$ $[_{VP}$ e$_i$ $[_{V'}$ V° $\rightarrow$ ..... $]]]]$

Generative grammar started as a theory based mainly on data of a single SVO language, namely English. The Principles & Parameter model (Chomsky 1981) opened the typological horizon but the majority of studies are still based on VO languages, namely Romance and Scandinavian languages. OV languages like Dutch and German for some time did not attract the critical mass of researchers that is necessary for arriving at a big enough scientific community to systematically filter the diverse proposals for grammatical analyses. From the late 1980s onwards, this has changed.

When the discussion of the adequate analysis of German sentence structure gained momentum, a core issue was the question raised above, namely the quest for arguments for or against a unique and obligatory structural position for the subject in the midfield. The discussion has not yet reached a definitive answer. It is still impeded by the bias towards structural analyses that are nearly identical with the analyses for VO structures.

The controversy on the necessity, predictability and existence of a structural subject position is closely connected with the general issue of the functional architecture of the midfield of an OV clause. Before the split-Infl hypothesis turned out to be a useful concept for modelling the VO clause structure (Pollock 1989), the IP was considered the only functional shell between CP and VP.

Soon, additional functional projections were considered. On the basis of differences between wh-extraction and topicalization out of embedded sentences,

Müller and Sternefeld (1993) suggested a topic phrase (TopP) immediately below CP. Vikner (1995) realized that CP-internal V2 in Scandinavian languages calls for CP-recursion or a separate functional projection between CP and IP.

In the meantime, the space between the VP and the CP has become densely populated with numerous functional projections, especially since Rizzi (1997) proposed splitting the CP, as in (3). TopP, in contrast to other functional projections, is in Rizzi's model a freely serialized phrase that can be instantiated more than once, as in (3). Benincà and Poletto (2004) question the multiple instantiation of TopP and suggest a more fine-grained differentiation[18] among topics, with a functional projection for each topic category in terms of the information structure categorizations.

(3)   'split CP': [_{ForceP} [_{TopP} [_{FocP} [_{TopP} [_{FinP} .....]]]]]   (Rizzi 1997)

The following sentence (4) instantiates all phrases listed in the structure sketched in (3):

(4)   Credo [_{ForceP} che [_{TopP} a Gianni [_{FocP} QUESTO [_{TopP} domani [_{FinP} gli dovremmo dire]]]]]

         (I) believe [that to Gianni this tomorrow him we-shall-have-to tell

It is very easy to construct a sentence parallel to (4) in German (see 5), but it is very tough if not impossible to produce compelling arguments for the syntactic reality of the assumed functional projections. It is surely not enough to point out that functional heads are a neat way to structurally code notions that play a role in an information structure perspective, as for instance topic or focus. The fact that there are languages in which topic or focus is morphologically coded does not necessarily entail that this is so in every language, and, in particular, this does not necessarily entail that languages like English or German must have *functional projections* that structurally encode focus and topic.

(5)   Ich glaube [_{CP=ForceP} dass [_{TopP} Hans [_{FocP} DAS [morgen [_{FinP} jemand sagen müssen wird]]]]]

         I believe [that [(to) Hans-DAT [this [tomorrow [someone tell have-to will]]]]]

How can we find out whether the functional projections indicated in (5) really exist in the German clause structure? The verb does not move to, and stay in, any of the alleged functional head positions below C°, so the surface verb position

---

[18] Benincà and Poletto (2004, ex. 58) suggest the following cascade: [hanging topic [scene setting adv. [left dislocation [list interpretation [contrastive focus 1 [contrastive focus 2 [informational focus [_{FinP ...}]]]]]]]]

does not betray a functional head position. Hence, the potential functional projection will show only its spec position. Let us therefore rephrase the question in terms of properties of the spec position:

How can we find out whether a given position is a spec position of a functional projection? Here are some empirically valid diagnostic properties:

- obligatory expletives for unlexicalized spec positions (EPP effect),
- opacity for extraction of phrases in spec positions that precede the lexical main verb,
- primary lexicalizations of functional head positions by functional lexemes (e.g. complementizers, determiners, infinitive particles, etc.),
- secondary lexicalization of functional head positions by the finite verb in V-raising languages.

The alternative to a cascade of functional projections as in (5) is a structure with phrases adjoined to VP or to a functional projection. An instance of this is the adjunction analysis of scrambling (see chapter 4.4). Note that the difference between an adjunction solution and an analysis in terms of multiple specs seems to be a purely notational one as long as we look at the positions of the elements in the spec positions. Multiple specs are specs adjoined to a functional projection. But the difference ceases to be a notational one once we consider the syntactic properties of the projection. First, the functional projection must have a functional head, but the adjunction structures do not require a functional head. It is an extension-by-adjunction of a projection with its own head, lexical or functional. Second, a phrase in the spec of any functional head preceding the verb is opaque for extraction. Phrases adjoined to a VP on the canonical side (i.e. left-adjoined in OV) are not opaque.

If the diagnostic properties listed in the preceding paragraph are checked in German, positive evidence for intermediate functional projections turns out to be difficult to assess. There is no unquestionable and easy-to-pinpoint case of a functional projection between CP and VP in German.

The evidence from expletives to be discussed below ranges from negative to not conclusive. The systematic lack of opacity effects for extractions from a phrase in a given position indicates that the position of the given phrase is not a functional spec position. This will be the topic of the following subsection. Movement of the finite verb is a handy indicator for functional heads if the movement targets these heads. German moves the finite verb, but it is never found in any of the alleged intermediate positions where it should be found. Finally, the only lexical category for a functional head position in clause structure is the small set of complementizers (*dass* – that, *ob* – whether, *wenn* – if, etc.). There is no primary lexical element for any of the intermediate candidates; in particular, the infinitive marker *zu* (to) is not a functional head in German. In sum, direct evidence for intermediate functional projections is missing. So, circumstantial evidence needs to be checked carefully and judged sensibly in order to avoid premature and misguided conclusions.

2.4   Expletives for functional spec positions

In English and the Scandinavian languages, the spec position that accommodates the subject is structurally mandatory and it must be lexicalized. This is the EPP property of a VO sentence structure. German, however, shows disrespect for EPP and this is so because it is OV. Let us start with the passive of intransitive verbs.

(1)   a. Wurde (*es) applaudiert?
           was (it / there) applauded?

       b. Wäre (*es) zu applaudieren gewesen?
           would (it / there) to applaud been?
           'Would it have been necessary / possible to applaud?'

If there is a functional spec position for subjects, this spec position would have to be lexicalized for the satisfaction of the EPP. In the absence of a suitable subject argument, an expletive serves as substitute. But clause-internal expletives are ungrammatical in German subjectless constructions, and, arguably this cannot be explained away as a kind of pro-drop phenomenon.

Note first that German uses an expletive for the obligatory functional spec position in V2 clauses. Here, the spec position is lexicalized with an expletive, namely *es* (it), if no phrase is fronted. The V2 versions of the examples in (1) are given in (2):

(2)   a. Es wurde applaudiert
           it / there was applauded

       b. Es wäre zu applaudieren gewesen
           it would to applaud been
           'It would have been necessary / possible to applaud'

Why is *es* not used as a clause-medial expletive? Two reasons might be responsible. It could be so that *es* is covert (pro-drop conjecture), or that *es* cannot be placed because there is no room to accommodate it since there is no functional subject position in the German clause structure.

Is German a semi-pro-drop language? Semi-pro-drop means that expletive subjects drop, but referential subjects do not. Icelandic is semi-pro-drop. It drops the expletive in counterparts of the examples in (1), but not in embedded clauses[19] and, crucially, it drops quasi arguments (see Sigurðsson 1989; Haider 2001b). German does not drop quasi arguments, neither with weather verbs (3a) nor in the middle construction (3b). On the other hand, German forbids a clause-internal expletive in the counterpart of the English *there*-construction (3c,d) and in the subjectless passive construction (1).

(3)   a. Hat *(es) gestern geregnet?
        has (it) yesterday rained

      b. Hier würde *(es) sich gut leben   *intransitive middle construction*
        here would (it) REFL fine live
        'Here one would live well'

      c. Es ist hier noch nie jemand gestorben
        there is here never ever someone died
        'Nobody ever died here'

      d. Hier ist (*es) noch nie jemand gestorben
        here is (there) never ever someone died

Dutch is different and the difference is instructive. Dutch apparently allows an expletive in subjectless passives (4), and it forbids dropping it as in (4b), if the word order in the verbal cluster is head initial rather than head final (see Richards and Biberauer 2005: 142, who credit Hans Bennis for this observation).

(4)   a. Ik denk dat (er) gedanst werd
        I think that (there) danced was

      b. Ik denk dat *(er) werd gedanst

The contrast in (4) is a structural one since it depends on the verb order. The 'English-like' order obeys an 'English-like' constraint against an empty midfield, the 'German-like' verb order is happy with an empty midfield. This is not a pro-drop mystery; it is a facet of an 'EPP mystery'.

What we have not yet ascertained is this: is the *er* in (4b) an expletive for the *functional* subject position? There are good reasons for assuming that it is not. Here is one clear-cut piece of evidence. Dutch (see Koeneman 2000: 192) does not show any opacity effects for subject extraction in the presence of an allegedly subject expletive *er*.

In Dutch, the presence of *er* has no effect on the extractability of the subject argument, neither in interrogatives (5a) nor in declaratives (5b) when the

---

[19] For example (i) I gratefully acknowledge Höskuldur Thráinsson (p.c.).

(i)   að */?(Það) hefur verið dansað   *Icelandic*
        that (expl) has been danced

fronted subject has to cross an expletive *er* (Koeneman 2000: 192). Note that the *er* in (5) is strongly preferred rather than avoided.

(5)   a. Wie denk je dat [??](er) is aangekomen?
            who think you that (there) is arrived

        b. Syntactici denk ik niet dat [??](er) zijn aangekomen
            syntacticians think I not that (there) are arrived

In VO languages, however, an expletive in the functional subject position gives rise to a blocking effect on subject extraction across the expletive. This is so in English, but also in Scandinavian languages.

(6)   a. * Who$_i$ do you think that *there* arrived e$_i$?

        b. * Hwem$_i$ tror du at *det* kom e$_i$ igaar?   *Norwegian*
            who think you that there came yesterday

        c. * Hvaða málfræðingar heldur Þu að Það hafi lesið Barriers?
            what linguists think you that there have read Barriers?   *Icelandic*

What (5) plainly suggests is that the structural position of *er* is not the spec position of a functional projection. If this were the case, we would expect (5) to be as deviant as (6), but (5) is not deviant at all, and, moreover, it becomes nearly unacceptable only if the *er* is dropped. This is exactly the opposite of the VO pattern (6).

   Let us briefly recapitulate: neither German nor Dutch expletives provide unquestionable evidence for an obligatory functional subject position. The obligatory absence of a subject expletive in intransitive passives and in presentative constructions in German calls for a structural explanation. Invoking a language-specific pro-drop option is an ad hoc patch-up strategy that does not adequately capture the empirical situation. Accounts in terms of pro-drop as an independent parametric difference disregard important facts: first, an expletive for a functional spec position is available in German, namely for spec C, but this expletive does not drop (7). Second, an expletive in a functional subject position would block subject extraction, contrary to the facts of Dutch (5). Third, pro-drop would make the wrong prediction for extraposition (8).

(7)   a. Ich glaube, *(es) wurde zu wenig nachgedacht
            I think (it) was too little thought

        b. Ich glaube, *(es) wird mir niemand zuhören
            I think (it) will me-DAT nobody listen-to

In the German extraposition construction, a pronoun *es* correlating with an extraposed clause may be missing in some cases (8a). But it would not be wise to analyse this as a case of pro-drop. Pro-drop is the variation between a lexical and a silent pronoun with otherwise identical syntactic properties.

First, the pronominal correlate *es* (it) of an extraposed clause does not drop freely. The exact conditions of its distribution have successfully evaded a final conclusion until now, but the facts are clear. With a predicate as in (8a), there is free variation, but there are other predicates like that in (8b) that do not allow dropping. Second, since German does not allow referential pro-drop, the pronominal subject does not drop even if its reference is determined by the immediate context (8c).

(8)   a. Seit heute steht (es) fest, dass das nicht so ist
            since today stays (it) certain, that this not so is
            'Since today it is certain that this is not so'

        b. Seit heute ist *(es) peinlich, dass das nicht so ist
            since today is (it) embarrassing that this not so is

        c. (Wann findet die Sitzung statt?) Seit heute steht *(es) fest
            (when takes the meeting place?) since today stays (it) fixed

Third, the presence of *es* in combination with an extraposed clause makes the clause opaque for extraction. Opacity should be independent of the overt or covert status of the antecedent pronoun. The facts tell a different story, however. Extraction across an overt antecedent *es* is ungrammatical.

(9)   a. Wen$_i$ wurde (*es) erwartet, [e$_i$ dort anzutreffen]?
            who was (it) expected there to-come-across

        b. Was$_i$ wurde (*es) vermutet, [dort e$_i$ vorzufinden]
            what was (it) assumed there to-find

        c. dass (es) erwartet / vermutet wurde, [ihn dort vorzufinden]
            that (it) expected / assumed was him there to-find

This pattern becomes understandable if the *es* in (9) is the pronominal argument, and not an expletive, and the extraposed clause is dependent on it (see Bennis 1986 for Dutch). In this case, the extraposed clause is not selected and therefore opaque. If there is no *es*, the clause is argumental and hence transparent for extraction. If you assume a silent *es*, however, you are bound to assume, contrary to the facts, that it blocks extraction just like an overt one does.

The issue of a missing pronominal correlate of an extraposed phrase is broader than a matter of dropping a subject pronoun. First, the 'dropped' pronoun need not be a subject, as in (10), and second, the dropped element need not be a pronoun (11).

(10)   Man hat (es) erwartet / vermutet / zugelassen, dass das Dach einstürzte
'one has (it-ACC) expected / presumed / allowed that the roof collapsed'

The missing correlate can be a pronoun, as in (9c) or (10), but, for other verbs, it can be a PP, as in (11), with the amalgamated pronoun (*da*) precliticized to the preposition:

(11)   a. Ich habe sie (davor) gewarnt, dass sie das anfasst
            I have her (it-against) warned [$_{CP\text{-fin}}$ that she it touches]

         b. Ich habe sie (davon) abgehalten, das anzufassen
            I have her (it-from) off-held [$_{CP\text{-non-fin}}$ this to touch]
            'I prevented her from touching it'

The technical concept of pro-drop that has been successfully employed for the modelling of the syntactic behaviour of covert subject clitics in Romance or Slavic would not allow subsuming the case of dropping a PP as in (11) under regular pro-drop. We shall not engage in the investigation of these aspects any further, because for the present purpose of our discussion it is sufficient to realize that pro-drop is not the key for understanding why there is no overt expletive in German subjectless clauses.

We keep the two options in mind. The standard option – every clause in any language obligatorily provides a functional spec position for the subject (EPP) – is puzzling since it leaves us without an answer for the absence of EPP effects in German (and in OV languages in general).

The empirically adequate option seems to be this: only VO languages are EPP languages because of the particular syntactic property of the VP-internal subject position as the single position in the VP that is not within the canonical directionality domain of the verbal head since it precedes the head. In OV language, all arguments are within the directionality domain of the verbal head; so UG does not require/provide a functional projection for the subject. Since there is no obligatory functional projection for the subject, there is no EPP effect for a subject position, and there is no need or place for an expletive as secondary lexicalization of an otherwise empty functional subject position. So, the typological corollary of this option is (12):

(12)   EPP theorem
         VO languages require a subject expletive in clauses without an argumental subject for structural reasons, OV languages do not.

This follows from a parametric difference in canonical directionality. Only in VO is the VP-internal subject position not in the directional licensing domain of the verbal head, whence the need for a functional licenser.

Let us finish the discussion of the subject position(s) in a German clause with a comment on a particular claim. It has been argued (see Travis 1991; Zwart 1993) that a *clause-initial subject* in a German verb-second clause is not in spec C but rather in spec 'I'. According to this analysis, a subject-initial sentence is structurally different from a clause with a non-subject preceding the finite verb in a V2 clause. The subject-initial clause lacks the higher functional shell, namely the CP (13b).

(13)   a. [$_{CP}$ e [$_{C'}$ dass [$_{IP}$ ich$_i$ [$_{I'}$ e [$_{VP}$ e$_i$ das nicht glaube]]]]][20]
              that   I   this not believe

        b. [$_{IP}$ Ich$_i$ [$_{I'}$ glaube$_j$ [$_{VP}$ e$_i$ das nicht e$_j$]]]   (analysis to be dismissed!)
            I   believe   this not

        c. [$_{CP}$ Das$_i$ [$_{C'}$ glaube$_j$ [$_{IP}$ ich$_k$ [$_{I'}$ e$_j$ [$_{VP}$ e$_k$ e$_i$ nicht e$_j$]]]]]
            this   believe   I   not

If the analysis (13b) were correct, and the position of a clause-initial subject in a V2 clause was identical with the clause-internal position, the existence of an overt functional spec position for the subject could not be denied. Travis (1991: 359) takes as a crucial piece of evidence an apparent distributional restriction for the weak pronoun *es* in German: it may appear in the clause-initial position as subject, but as an object it is said to be deviant, as illustrated by (14b). There are data, however, that call for a more fine-grained account, namely the data in (14c–d).

(14)   a.   *Es* hat den Hund erschreckt
              It-NOM has the-ACC dog frightened
              'It has frightened the dog'

        b.   * *Es* hat der Hund erschreckt
              It-ACC has the-NOM dog frightened
              'The dog has frightened it'

        c.   (Ihr Geld ist nicht verloren.)   *Es* hat jetzt nur jemand anderer [21]
              (Your money is not lost.)   It-ACC has now only someone-NOM
                                                 else
              'Your money did not get lost. It is only in the hands of someone else'

        d.   (Das Schild können Sie genauso gut weglassen.) *Es* hat ohnehin
              keiner beachtet
              (The sign could you just-as-well omit.)   It-ACC has anyway
                                                           nobody observed

---

[20] The CP-IP structure is used here only for expository reasons.
[21] For this example, I gratefully acknowledge Werner Frey. Originally, it was cold comfort for investors who had lost their money in an investment fraud. The corresponding case in Dutch is not acceptable, as native informants tell me.

In brief, Travis's account of (14a) is this: the difference can be attributed to the failure of *es* to undergo A'-movement. If the initial *es* is the subject, it is fronted by A-movement to spec-I. If it is an object, it is fronted to spec CP by A'-movement. The first type of fronting is licit for *es*, the second type is not.

But this is not the only way of capturing the difference, nor is it the most straightforward one. The primary property of *es* is its stress avoidance as a weak pronoun. By definition, a weak pronoun is unstressed. Stressing of *es* is deviant in any position, and if fronting an object induces stress, *es* cannot be fronted. Why is the subject not stressed when fronted? The appropriate descriptive generalization is one in terms of the information structure (topic comment organization) of the clause: an element moved to spec C is not stressed if it is the highest element in the complement of C°. Moving a lower element changes the information structure, unless the fronted element re-instantiates the topic of the preceding utterance. This is illustrated by (14c,d). In these sequences, the fronting of a weak object pronoun is possible. It remains unstressed because it is contextually backgrounded.

Note that the sentences with object *es* in initial position in (14c,d) would be rated deviant if presented in isolation. What accounts for the contrast or the parallel between clause-initial subject *es* and object *es* respectively, is stressing and de-stressing rather than a structural difference. In (14c,d), de-stressing is a consequence of the information structure. In sum, there is no principled ban against having an object *es* in the sentence-initial position. This has been emphasized in Haider (2005a) and is discussed also by Meinunger (2007).

Let us recapitulate: the evidence discussed so far is evidence for two major properties of German clause structure (for a more detailed presentation see Haider 1997b). First, there is no evidence for *functional head* positions to the *right* of the VP, and second, there is no evidence for movement of the finite verb or the subject to intermediate functional head or functional spec positions, respectively.

From a comparative perspective, the lack of verb movement has a parallel in Faroese, but the lack of EPP effects is unparalleled, given that German, unlike Icelandic, does not provide a null expletive. This set of circumstances becomes understandable, however, if the stronger assumption holds. The subject resists moving to a spec position not because it must not move, but because it cannot. There is no functional subject position to accommodate it, and there is no functional head to trigger movement of the finite verb to this intermediate position. This result may become less 'appalling' once the reason for the need of a functional subject position in VO clauses has been appreciated (see 1.4.1 and 1.4.2 on quirky subjects).

2.5   Extraction out of subjects: no subject–object asymmetry

One important area of circumstantial evidence for the functional architecture of the clause is the evidence from extraction domains gained in the past three decades of intensive research in this field – in spite of the fact that these constraints are presently not a focal research area. The robust generalization that got established was and still is that a phrase in the functional spec position of the subject (formerly *spec I*) or in any higher spec position (and thereby *preverbal* in VO languages) is an *absolute island* for any type of *extraction*.

As a test criterion for the status of a functional spec position in clause structure, this descriptive generalization is easy to apply: if a given position is a functional spec position of the relevant kind, a phrase in this position must be opaque. If the phrase is not opaque, the position cannot be a functional spec position of the subject type or a structurally higher one. English subjects and phrases in higher spec positions are opaque. German subjects (1) and phrases preceding them (2) are not opaque, however. This is widely uncontroversial and clear cut, and (negligently or intentionally) ignored in current theorizing.

If the subject clause in (1) is VP-internal, as assumed here, extraction is expected to be possible. If, however, the subject clause were, as assumed by the competing analysis, in a spec position, extraction would be predicted to crash.[22]

(1)   a.   Mit wem$_i$ hätte (*es) denn [e$_i$ speisen zu dürfen] dich besonders
               gefreut?
               with whom had (it) PRT [dine to be-allowed] you-ACC especially
               pleased

         b. * Who(m)$_i$ would [to have dinner with e$_i$] please you ?

         c.   Who(m)$_i$ would it please you [to have dinner with e$_i$]?

The contrast between (1a) and the ungrammatical English construction (1b) is sharp and damaging for analyses that situate the infinitival subject clause in German in a functional spec position. A clause in a functional spec position corresponding to the English subject position, or in a higher one, is always opaque for extraction. The straightforward alternative is a subject-in-situ analysis for (1a). The clause remains in its VP-internal position and extraction is unproblematic. The contrast between (1c) and (1b) is one between a clausal subject in a functional spec position and in a VP-internal one, respectively.

---

[22] Note that this cannot be checked in Dutch: sentential infinitival complements are ungrammatical in VP-internal positions. Either clause union applies or the clause is extraposed or topicalized.

The argument against a clause-medial functional subject position in German is strengthened by the following data. Object clauses remain transparent for extraction when scrambled (2a) across the subject, but not if they are moved to a functional spec position like the clause-initial spec position in V2 (2b). (2b) is an embedded V2 clause, with the infinitival object clause in the initial spec position. If the subject in (2a) were in a spec position, the scrambled infinitival clause would have to be either in a higher spec position or adjoined to a functional projection. In any case, opacity for extraction is guaranteed in either environment and therefore the examples are expected to be strongly deviant. The data, however, contradict this expectation. Extraction out of an infinitival object clause preceding the subject does not make a clause deviant at all (2a). Extraction out of a clause in the initial spec position is ungrammatical.

(2)   a.   Was$_i$ hat (*es) [ihr e$_i$ zu erklären] keiner riskiert?
             what has (it) [her to explain] nobody risked

       b.   * Was$_i$ hat sie behauptet [$_{CP}$ [ihr e$_i$ zu erklären]$_j$ [$_{C'}$ habe [keiner e$_j$ riskiert]]]
             what has she claimed [her to reveal] [had [nobody risked]]]

So we are entitled to dismiss the premise that the overt subject position in German is an obligatory functional spec position. The simplest account for the lack of opacity of scrambled phrases is obvious: scrambling is a VP-internal phenomenon. Scrambling across the subject in German is scrambling across the VP-internal subject (see Haider and Rosengren 1998, 2003). The scrambled phrase remains in the VP, that is in the directionality domain of the V° head, and therefore remains transparent.

How could an advocate of the standard, structural subject approach defend his or her position? The first strategy is usually to find out whether the difference could be reduced to an intervening factor. The intervening factor has been suspected of being the head position of the VP: in German, both the VP-internal subject position and the VP-external, structural subject position precede the main verb, and so do the object positions. In English, the objects follow the verb, the subject precedes.

This is so, but why should this matter, one may ask oneself. The crucial point is that in both languages, the structural subject position would be the same kind of functional spec position. It is a spec position of a functional projection, whose complement is or contains the VP. This position is the identified source of opacity. The internal structure of the VP has no effect on the behaviour of the functional spec position in the standard approach.

The standard analysis of German clause structure with overt V-to-'I', which has been discredited in the preceding section, appears to provide a possible loophole. The fact that German, in contrast to English, does not make a difference between finite auxiliaries and main verbs with respect to V-to-'I', is an invitation to forge a tool for capturing the opacity effect on the hypothesis that an I-head that attracts full verbs could make its complement transparent for extraction. That this idea is doomed to fail becomes evident, once you take a side look at French or Icelandic. If V-to-'I' has the effect of lifting the restriction against extraction out of the functional subject position, the opacity effect would have to be absent in French (cf. Kayne 1981) or Icelandic, contrary to the facts.

Therefore, we are entitled to continue taking English as a representative case for opacity. A phrase in the spec position that is the functional subject position or in any higher spec position is opaque. Note that it does not matter whether it is a transitive subject (3a,c) or an object raised to the functional subject position, as in the case of passive (3b,d):

(3)   a. * Who$_i$ would [a picture of e$_i$] help the police?
      b. * Who$_i$ was [a picture of e$_i$]$_j$ shown to the police e$_j$?
      c. * What would [to release e$_i$ to the media] increase the popularity of the candidate?
      d. * What was [to release e$_i$ to the media]$_j$ suggested e$_j$ by the PR team?

The VP-internal position of the subject is irrelevant. This indicates that it is the surface structure position that matters for transparency.

A potential derivational escape route is blocked by the principle of the cycle. The blocked escape route is this: extract first, and move the containing phrase afterwards. Extraction prior to movement of the containing phrase is ruled out by the principle of the cycle since the containing phrase would target a lower position than the extracted phrase. The principle of cyclic application requires that the target of movement must not be lower than the target of any previous movement step.

From a representational point of view, the equivalent of the principle of the cyclic derivation is the ban against reconstruction. The phrases in the structural subject position in (3b,d) would not be opaque in their extraction site position e$_j$. However, opacity restrictions are operative in the surface position and therefore they are not reconstructible, that is, the phrases that contain the trace of the extracted wh-element cannot be checked for opacity at the trace position e$_j$ but only in the actual surface position.

An example of extraction out of a position higher than the subject position is extraction out of an internally topicalized phrase. The topicalized phrase in (4c,f) precedes the subject position. Hence, it is either adjoined to a functional projection, or it is a phrase in a spec position with a phonetically empty head. In any case, grammar predicts opacity, and the result of extraction is indeed a strongly deviant expression, as the examples in (4b,e) demonstrate:

(4)   a.   Who$_i$ did she chat [with e$_i$] in the hall?
         b.   * Who$_i$ did [with e$_i$] she chat in the hall?
         c.   I am sure [that [with him], she would not chat in the hall]
         d.   Who$_i$ would she surely appreciate [a picture of e$_i$]?
         e.   * Who$_i$ would [a picture of e$_i$] she surely appreciate?
         f.   I am sure [that [a picture of him] she would surely appreciate]

Let us recapitulate: there is uncontroversial and well investigated evidence for opaque domains in English and other VO languages as a result of at least two decades of research on this subject matter. The position of the subject in the spec of a functional head proved to be one of these uncontroversial opaque domains. In theory-neutral terms, this restriction is known as the 'subject condition'.

In German (and Dutch), the corresponding opacity effects are missing, and so is the uncontroversial evidence for the justification of assigning the subject to a functional spec position in these languages. In this respect, German is representative for OV languages. On the other hand, German and Dutch are by no means exceptions or quirky specimens of languages that show a defect in their opacity management system. In the uncontroversial instances of phrases in functional spec positions (see examples 5b and 2b), the predicted opacity effect is operative. So, we may safely conclude that in an OV language, the subject stays in its VP-internal position. In VO languages, however, the subject requires a special licensing environment.

(5)   a.   Von wem$_i$ haben [frühe Bilder e$_i$] denn bessere Preise erzielt als
              späte?
              by whom have [early pictures] PRT better prices made than late
              (ones)

         b.   * Von wem$_i$ wurde dir gesagt [$_{CP}$[frühe Bilder e$_i$] hätten bessere
              Preise erzielt als späte]?
              by whom were you told [[early pictures] would-have better prices
              made than late (ones)]

If the initial PP in (5b) is construed as the PP extracted out of the subject in its surface position in (5b), namely out of the spec position of an embedded V2 clause, the sentence is strongly deviant as a result of violating the opacity restriction. (5a) however is innocuous.[23]

---

[23] Note that the subject DP which the PP is part of precedes a particle, namely *denn*. This particle has been suspected of marking the left edge of the VP (Diesing 1992, and others). If this were true, the subject would have to be opaque since it would be outside the domain of its lexical head.

What are the implications of this result? The implications are far-reaching since they allow narrowing the range of admissible sentence structure models. The maze of functional projections extrapolated from the cumulative syntactic literature on German sentence structure gets pruned down significantly, once we take opacity as the syntactic touchstone.

What type of analyses are problematic if we take the opacity data for what they are? Here is an illustrative but not exhaustive selection for German.

It is empirically *not* adequate, even if it is 'politically correct' in terms of the presently accepted theoretical framework to hold that

- phrases scrambled to positions preceding the subject are positioned in the spec of functional projections (whose heads code for *information structure functions*).

The opacity facts have additional implications since they apply in any context in which a phrase that contains the extraction site precedes, or occupies, the spec of a functional projection. Hence it is not adequate to hold that

- an adverbial that precedes the VP is positioned in the spec of a functional head with *adverbial features* (Cinque 1999), because in this case any preceding phrase would have to be opaque, contrary to the facts, nor that
- (definite)DPs are positioned in the spec of functional projections whose heads are to *check case features* (Agr-S and Agr-O projections). For details on case see chapter 6.

In each case, the crucial test is this: take an (infinitival) clause, put it in the position immediately preceding the phrase P in the questionable position and check for opacity. The clause will not be opaque in German. This signifies that the phrase P cannot be in the spec of a functional projection. If it is in a spec position, any phrase preceding it must be in a spec position of a higher functional head, or it is in a position adjoined to the functional projection that accommodates P. In terms of the Minimalist Program, this would be a multiple-spec projection. In each case, the theory predicts opacity.

Why should you take an infinitival clause? First, it is a clearly identifiable embedded domain. Second, the set of verbs with infinitival complements is big enough. Third, infinitival clauses have a wide range of distributions; in particular they are well formed in clause-medial, clause-final and clause-initial positions in German. Finite clauses are preferred in extraposed positions. Fourth, there is no better domain for testing extraction out of embedded phrases because clear cases of extraction out of DPs are tough to defend against alternative analyses.

Before leaving this chapter we should address an essential issue: we have not understood an account fully as long as we have not understood why others have not suggested/accepted the alternative account earlier.

Why does German appear to be exceptional? It appears to be exceptional as long as you try to model it according to the limits of a VO system. But it is not exceptional; it is just a (partially) OV language. German becomes exceptional only if you disregard the principled differences between OV and VO clause structures that follow from the single basic parametric difference of directionality.

The lack of opacity appears to be exceptional at first, but only if you assume (correctly) that the opacity domains are universal and (incorrectly) that the clause structure is uniform across languages, and does not leave room for the kind of parametric differentiation described above. Opacity is a structurally conditioned and thus a genuine syntactic phenomenon. Predictable structural differences between an OV and a VO organization of clause structure entail predictable differences with respect to the transparency or opacity of clause-internal phrasal positions in OV and VO, respectively. This is positive evidence for a parametric difference rather than a weird exception of German.

2.6   Summary

Given the empirical facts reviewed in this chapter, the minimally necessary structural commitment for a German clause is this (Haider 1997b): there is at least one functional projection above the VP and it accommodates either the complementizer (1a) or the finite verb moved to the functional head position (1b).[24] The spec position of this functional head is the target of XP fronting (1c). The functional projection in (1) accounts for the family-specific property of the Germanic languages (except English), namely the V2 property (1c).

(1)   a. $[_{CP}\, C°\quad (\ldots)\ [_{VP} \ldots\ldots\ldots V_{fin}]]$
        b. $[_{FP}\, V_{fin-j}\quad (\ldots)\ [_{VP} \ldots\ldots\ldots\ e_j]]$
        c. $[_{FP}\, XP_i\, [_F°\, V_{fin-j}\quad (\ldots)\ [_{VP} \ldots e_i \ldots\ e_j]]]$

Contrary to handbook wisdom, there are no clause-*final* functional head positions and there is no head movement targeting such a position in German.

---

[24] In a bare phrase structure approach, it is not necessary to claim categorical identity for the functional head position in (1). It is not plausible to assume V2 to target a position of the category C°. Neither the verb as V° nor its finiteness features are categorically identical with C°. The verb targets, and thereby identifies the category of, an otherwise underspecified functional head. See Brandt *et al.* (1992) for empirical details.

As for clause-*medial* functional projections above the VP within the domain indicated by '(...)' in (1), the situation is controversial. First, there is no direct evidence of head movement to intermediate functional head positions. Second, opacity of extraction used as a test criterion for intermediate spec positions provides no positive result for the assumption of spec positions. Finally, the syntactic properties of the subject are characterized best as properties of a VP-internal argument that agrees with the finite verb. It is not restricted to a functional spec position. The absence of EPP effects follows from the absence of a structural configuration that would trigger the EPP effects.

3

Targeting the clause-initial position: German wh-constructions

3.1 'Wh-movement': movement to the clause-initial spec position

Chomsky's 'On wh-movement' (1977) has paved the way and since then it is common knowledge that wh-interrogative clauses are representative of a family of constructions that share syntactic properties of a particular movement type (*A-bar movement* = phrasal movement to a non-argumental spec position). This transformation places a phrase into the clause-initial functional spec position that is commonly referred to as the spec $C°$ position:

(1) $[_{CP} XP_i [C° [\ldots e_i \ldots]]]$

A prototypical representative of this construction is the interrogative clause construction in languages that (obligatorily) front wh-phrases, as in English or German and their Germanic kin. In these languages, a *single* wh-phrase is fronted.[1] This type of interrogative clause is just an instance of a bigger family of constructions. Other members (see section 3.2) are relative clauses (3.2.3), comparative and equative clauses (3.2.4) and, in V2 languages, the V2 declarative clauses (3.2.5). In each of these clause structures, a phrase is placed into the highest spec position.

(2)   a. [*Was*$_i$ [will [er uns e$_i$ erklären?]]]   interrogative main clause
           what wants he (to) us-DAT explain

         b. (Man fragt sich,) [*was*$_i$ [er uns e$_i$ erklären will]]   embedded
           (one asks oneself) what he (to) us explain wants   interrogative clause

         c. Alles, [*was*$_i$ [er uns e$_i$ erklären will]]   relative clause
           everything what he (to) us explain wants

---

[1] The only Germanic language with multiple wh-fronting as in Slavic languages is Yiddish (cf. Diesing 2001). This is most likely a contact phenomenon imported from the Slavic adstrate languages.

    d. [*Das*$_i$ [will [er uns e$_i$ erklären]]]   declarative main clause
       this wants he (to) us explain

    e. Er erklärte uns so^j viel, [*wie*$_i^j$ [wir e$_i$ verstehen konnten]]   equative
       he explained (to) us as much, as we understand could   clauses

    f. Er erklärte uns mehr^j, als [*O*$_i^j$ [ich e$_i$ verstehen   comparative
       konnte]]   clause
       he explained us more, than I understand could

In (2a-c), the moved phrase is the interrogative pronoun *was* (what), in (2d), it is the demonstrative pronoun *das* (this), in (e) it is the wh-form *wie* (how),[2] but in (2f), a moved phrase is apparently missing. However, as will be shown in section 3.2, there is good evidence for a covert syntactic item in spec C. Incidentally, Southern German dialects employ an overt wh-item, and it is in the expected target position, as illustrated in (3). This variant with its overt wh-element supports the analysis of the standard variety that posits a null wh-element.

(3)   Er hat uns mehr erklärt [als [*was*$_i$[3] [ich e$_i$ verstehen konnte]]]
                                    dialectal comparative clause
      he has us more explained [than [what [I understand could]]]
      'He has explained to us more than I could understand'

Let us now briefly check the characteristics of wh-movement constructions and their instantiation in the respective family of constructions in German.

    First, as already announced, wh-movement targets the *clause-initial spec* position. This position provides room for only a *single* phrase. Consequently, if there is more than one wh-element (cf. 4), only one can be moved and the other one(s) remain in-situ. In section 3.4, you will be engaged in a discussion on the 'traffic rules' that control which one of several items gets priority for being fronted.

(4)   a. *What* did you buy *when* for *whom*?

        b. *Was* hast du *wann* für *wen* gekauft?
          what have you when for whom bought

Second, wh-movement potentially produces *long-distance* dependencies, that is, wh-movement is not constrained by the boundaries of a single clause (5).

---

[2] Actually, *wie* (how) as a wh-pronoun is a manner wh-adverbial. The *wie* in equative constructions is the element corresponding to *so*. In the example (2e) it is construed as *wie viel* (as much), corresponding to *so viel* (so much).

[3] *Was* is pronounced [wo:s].

Note that wh-movement out of a C°-introduced clause is avoided in Northern varieties of German but it is common in the Southern German standard as well as in the southern German dialects. Paul (1919: 321f.) devoted a subsection of his German Grammar to long-distance wh-dependencies and referred to them justly as 'Satzverschlingung' (sentence intertwining):

(5)   a. [Wer$_i$ wohl meint er [dass e$_i$ ihm seine Arbeit hier bezahlen werde]]?
            who perhaps assumes he [that him his work here pay shall][4]
            'Who did he perhaps assume would pay him for his work here?'

        b. Alles [was$_i$ ich dachte [dass e$_i$ mich aufheitern würde]]
            everything [what I thought [that me cheer-up would]]
            'Everything that I thought would cheer me up'

Note further that in the examples in (5) chosen from Paul (1919: 321), the moved item is the subject of the embedded clause (see also the discussion of the examples (11) below). In English, the corresponding subject movement would crash since it is subject to the *that-t-constraint*: extraction of a subject wh-item adjacent to the C° position is deviant (cf. 6a). This constraint does not apply in German (6b), for a principled reason.

(6)   a. * What$_i$ do you think [that e$_i$ is responsible for the deviance]?

        b. Was$_i$ glaubst Du denn [dass e$_i$ verantwortlich ist für die
            Abweichung]?   *German*
            what think you PRT [that responsible is for the deviance]

The absence of the *that-t*-effect in German is just one out of a set of systematic differences between German and English (as a representative of a VO-clause structure) that can be shown to correlate ultimately with a basic difference between an OV-clause structure as in German and a VO-clause structure. In VO, the subject argument is not in the directionality domain of V° in the VP and is raised to a functional spec position. Subject extraction in VO leaves a trace in a spec position, namely in the functional subject position. In OV, however, the trace of subject extraction is VP internal. This is the basic difference between (6a) and (6b).

Third, since wh-movement targets spec C, an 'already' occupied spec C position blocks wh-movement. This is the source of the 'wh-island effects', first noted, described and named by John Ross (1967). The examples in (7a,b) provide a kind

---

[4] Note: *wohl* is a particle. Structurally, it is an apposition to *wer*. So, *wer wohl* is a single phrase and (5a) does not violate the V2 pattern, with a single phrase in the initial position.

of minimal pair. In each case, the embedded clause is a V2 clause.[5] In (7a), the spec C position of the embedded clause contains the trace of the wh-item that has moved to the matrix clause. In (7b), the position is occupied by a fronted element, so a well-formed chain of wh-movement could not originate in the embedded clause. This is the disambiguating feature for (7a,b). (7c) is ambiguous because the wh-item could be construed as a matrix item or as an item of the embedded clause.

(7)   a. Wie oft$_k$ hat sie gesagt [e$_k$ habe man sie e$_k$ angerufen]?
            how often has she said [has one her phoned]   unambiguous

        b. Wie oft$_i$ hat sie e$_i$ gesagt [man$_k$ habe e$_k$ sie angerufen]?
            how often has she said [one has her phoned]   unambiguous

        c. Wie oft$_{i/k}$ hat sie (e$_i$) gesagt [(e$_k$) dass [man sie (e$_k$) angerufen habe]]?
            how often has she said [that one her phoned has]   ambiguous

The wh-island effect is a special case of a blocked spec C position. In English, normally only wh-items move to spec C (8a). In German, spec C accommodates also non-wh-items, as in the case of the clause-initial phrase in a declarative clause. So, an embedded declarative clause with an occupied spec C (8c) blocks wh-movement just like an embedded clause whose spec C is occupied by a wh-item (8b). (8d) is the grammatical variant of (8c) with a trace in spec C.

(8)   a. * Who(m)$_i$ did she say [*where* [Bill met e$_i$]]?

        b. * Wen$_i$ hat sie gesagt [*wo* [Bill e$_i$ getroffen habe]]?
            whom has she said [where [Bill met has]]
            'Whom has she said Bill has met, and where?'

        c. * Wen$_i$ hat sie gesagt [dort [habe [Bill e$_i$ getroffen]]]
            whom has she said [there [has [Bill met]]]

        d. Wen$_i$ hat sie gesagt [e$_i$ [habe [Bill dort e$_i$ getroffen]]]
            whom has she said [has [Bill there met]]

---

[5] Note that this sentence is ambiguous between a long-distance extraction analysis and a parenthetical structure (see Reis 2000), though with different syntactic behaviour (Haider 2005a). In the parenthesis analysis, the matrix clause of (7a) corresponds to the parenthesis. A variant of (7a) as a parenthetical structure is (i). If the matrix verb in (i) were replaced by *behaupten* (claim), the parenthetical analysis would be deviant, since 'claim' does not refer to the speech act type of the clause, namely interrogative.

(i)   Wie oft habe man sie – hat er gesagt – angerufen?
            how often has one her – has he said – up-phoned

If the parenthesis is inserted right after the initial wh-phrase, the word order is identical to the word order in (7a).

Note that German, unlike English, does not allow wh-infinitives (9). So German fortunately cannot embarrass the grammarians with violations of the wh-island constraint in the case of wh-infinitives (10).

(9)   a.   She always has to tell him what to do and where to go

         b.   * Sie muss ihm stets erklären was zu tun und wohin zu gehen
             She must him always tell what to do and where to go

(10)   This is a man [who_i I do not know [$_{CP}$ *when* to ask [$_{CP}$ *where* to meet e_i]]]

Fourth, wh-movement dependencies must not lead into/out of adjunct domains. Adverbials are opaque domains for wh-extraction. Wh-elements must not be extracted out of an adverbial domain. In this respect, German does not differ from English, nor does any other language. In fact, the opacity of adverbials is just a subinstance of the general ban against extraction out of phrases that are not selected as argument by a head. This covers adverbials but also clauses that depend on an antecedent element, as for instance extraposed clauses with a pronominal antecedent (11c). The *es* (it) in (11c) is the argument of the matrix verb, with the extraposed clause depending on, and specifying, it (cf. Bennis 1986).

(11)   a.   * Who_i did she laugh [before Bill mentioned e_i]?

         b.   * Wen_i hat sie [ehe Fritz erwähnte e_i] gelacht?
             who has she [before Fritz mentioned] laughed
             'Who was the person such that she laughed before Fritz mentioned this person'

         c.   Wen hat sie (*es) prophezeit, dass er heiraten würde[6]
             whom has she (it) prophesied that he marry will
             'Whom has she prophesied that he will marry'

Fifth, there is a systematic difference between German and English (which is representative for VO in this respect) with respect to extraction out of subject phrases. In English, extraction out of a phrase in the functional subject position is strictly ungrammatical. In German, the subject is not generally opaque. This is once more a VO/OV-dependent effect. In German, the subject remains within

---

[6] In the declarative version of this clause, the *es* (it) is optional. This means that the extraposed clause is either construed as the object (in the case without *es*), or it is construed as predicating over the object pronoun *es*. In the latter case, the clause is opaque for extraction.

    (i)   Sie hat (es^i) prophezeit, [dass er sie heiraten würde]^i
            she has (it) prophesied [that he her marry would]

the directionality domain of the verb, that is, in its VP-internal position. In a VO language like English, the subject is the single argument that is not in the directionality domain of the verbal head. So it needs a licensing domain of its own, namely a spec position. As a phrase in a spec position, it is opaque for extraction. This is true for German, too, but only in cases in which a phrase is indeed in a spec position, as e.g. in spec C in an embedded V2 clause (12c).[7] In (12c), the infinitival clause is in the spec position of the embedded V2 clause. This is an option since the matrix verb allows either a C-introduced finite clause or a V2 clause as its complement.

(12)   a.   Mit wem$_i$ hätte [e$_i$ dort e$_i$ dinieren zu dürfen] dir Spaß gemacht?
            with whom had-SUBJUNCTIVE [there to dine to be-allowed-to] you
            pleasure make
            'With whom would it have pleased you to be allowed to have dinner
            with there?'

       b.   * With whom would [e$_i$ to be able to have dinner with e$_i$ there] have
            pleased you

       c.   * Mit wem$_i$ hat sie gesagt [$_{CP}$ [e$_i$ dort e$_i$ dinieren zu dürfen] [hätte [ihr
            Spaß gemacht]]]
            with whom has she said [[there dine to be-allowed-to] had-SUB-
            JUNCTIVE [her pleasure made]]]

If you want to double check on wh-extraction out of subjects in German, you should bear in mind that wh-extraction is universally constrained by yet another condition, namely the ill-understood *bridge-verb* property: only a subset of verbs with sentential complements allows wh-extraction out of the complement. These are typically verbs of saying and believing. Typical blocking verbs are verbs that presuppose their complement (see the contrast for sentential objects in 13a).

(13)   a.   Wen$_i$ hat sie prophezeit /gehofft /*übersehen /*eingesehen [dass er e$_i$
            heiraten würde]?
            whom has she prophesied / hoped / overlooked / realized [that he
            marry would]

---

[7] Wolfgang Sternefeld (1985) noted a curious and ill-understood intervening factor: acceptability is reduced when there is no 'verbal bracket' in the matrix, that is, when there is only the finite main verb, which gets fronted to the V2 position, rather than a fronted auxiliary, with the main verb as infinitive or participle remaining in the clause-final position. Arguably, directional licensing by an overt verb rather than merely by its trace is preferred.

   b. Wen$_i$ hat ihr geträumt /*gereicht [dass er e$_i$ heiraten würde]?
       whom has her dreamed / sufficed [that he marry would]

Verbs with the proper semantic relation (i.e. the kind of semantic relation between the verb and its argument that constitutes the 'bridge' quality for extraction out of the phrase that represents this argument) are much rarer with respect to subject arguments than with respect to object arguments. Hence the chance of finding a verb that does *not* allow the extraction out of its sentential argument is much greater for subjects than for objects. Nevertheless there are a few candidates. One is illustrated in (13b). So, if you find a case of a deviant extraction out of a subject clause, first check the matrix verb for its bridge quality with respect to the argument you experiment with.

Sixth, if a wh-item is not moveable but its containing phrase is, this phrase is moved, if this phrase is 'recognizable'[8] as a wh-phrase. This is the so-called *pied-piping effect*. In German, just as in English, DP specifiers or attributes cannot be extracted, hence the whole DP is wh-moved.[9]

(14)   a.   [Welches / Wessen Buch] hast du nicht gelesen?
            [which / whose book] have you not read

       b. * [Welches$_i$ / Wessen$_i$] hast du [e$_i$ Buch] nicht gelesen?
            [which / whose] have you [book] not read

       c.   Wieviele Bücher hast Du gelesen?
            how-many books have you read

       d. * Wieviele hast Du [e$_i$ Bücher] gelesen?
            how-many have you [books] read

Unlike English, German does not allow stranded prepositions, hence PPs are pied piped (15c). This contrast is not a simple OV/VO effect since there are also VO languages that do not allow preposition stranding (e.g. French).

(15)   a.   [Which train]$_i$ are you waiting for e$_i$?

       b. * [Welchen Zug]$_i$ wartest du auf e$_i$?
            [which train] wait you at

       c.   [Auf welchen Zug]$_i$ wartest du e$_i$?
            [at which train] wait you
            'For which train are you waiting?'

---

[8] The wh-item within the phrase must be in a position that makes the wh-property accessible from outside the phrase. This is the case if the wh-item is the determiner of the phrase or its specifier.

[9] This is a parameterized constraint. Slavic languages, for instance, are not subject to this restriction. They allow multiple wh-fronting.

Northern German vernacular varieties allow preposition stranding in a special case, namely in cases of an otherwise *amalgamated* weak pronoun and its interrogative counterpart. The weak pronoun is *es*. Instead of [$_{PP}$ P° es], the amalgamated version [$_{PP}$ *da* P°] is used,[10] with the interrogative version [$_{PP}$ *wo* P°], as for instance in *damit* (this with) or *womit* (where with) instead of *mit es* (with it) and *mit was* (with what), respectively.

(16)   a. Da$_i$ habe ich nichts [$_{PP}$ e$_i$ von] gehört
           there have I nothing of heard

    b. Da$_i$ habe ich keinen Sinn [$_{PP}$ e$_i$ für]
           there have I no sense for

    c. Wo$_i$ / Da$_i$ hat der nicht [$_{PP}$ e$_i$ für] gestimmt
           where / there has this-one not for voted
           'What has he not voted for / for this, he has not voted'

    d. Wo$_i$ / Da$_i$ hat der nicht gestimmt [$_{PP}$ e$_i$ für]
           where / there has this-one not voted for

    e. Daar$_i$ heb ik niets [$_{PP}$ e$_i$ van] gehoord   *Dutch*
           there have I nothing of heard

Note further that this type of stranding (16c,d) is, unlike in Dutch, not sensitive for extraposition. In Dutch, stranding is allowed only in the non-extraposed version, that is, in (16e) as the counterpart of (16a). The Dutch version of (16d) with the trace in the extraposed PP would be ungrammatical, although Dutch allows PP extraposition to the same extent as, or an even higher extent than, German.[11]

---

[10] The amalgamated version is mandatory, except for cases of disambiguation:

    (i)   Geld hat die Eigenschaft, dass man alles [in es] verwandeln kann
               money has the property that one everything [in(to) it] turn may
               'Money has the property that you can convert anything into it'
    The cliticized version *darin* would be the equivalent of [P Pronoun-DAT] and would receive a locative interpretation in the sense that money is the medium in which you can turn everything (into something else). Interestingly, the cliticized version is not ambiguous between the dative (= locative) and the accusative (= directional) version of the PP.

[11] It has been argued that PP stranding is absent in Germanic OV languages because stranding requires a *congruent* licensing directionality for the verb and the preposition. Hence stranding would be possible in VO but not in OV since the preposition and the verb license in opposite directions in OV. This cannot be the whole truth, however, since stranding in German is not allowed for *post*-positions either:

    (i)   [des Geldes *wegen*], [dem Freund *zuliebe*], [dem Freund *gegenüber*], …
               the money-GEN because-of, the friend-DAT for-sake, the friend-dat in-the-face-of, … 'because of the money', 'for the friend's sake', 'face to face with the friend', …

3.2   Wh-movement-type phenomena in German

This section illustrates the common properties of the wh-movement-type constructions for the following five instantiations in German, namely unembedded and embedded interrogatives, relative clauses, comparative and equative clauses, and for V2 declaratives. For each construction you will see examples for the local and the long-distance variant and for the typical opacity constraints (wh-island and adjunct opacity).

3.2.1   Direct questions

Main clause interrogatives are instances of the general V2 structure, with a wh-phrase in the clause-initial position. Bear in mind that extraction out of *that*-clauses as in (1c) is a feature of Southern German vernaculars, but rarely found in Northern German varieties.

(1)   a.   *Auf wen*$_i$ hat sie e$_i$ gewartet?
             for whom has she waited

       b.   *Auf wen*$_i$ glaubte man [e$_i$ habe [sie e$_i$ gewartet]]?
             for whom believed one [has [she waited]]
             'For whom did they believe she waited?'

       c.   *Auf wen*$_i$ glaubte man [e$_i$ dass [sie e$_i$ gewartet habe]]?
             for whom believed one [that [she waited has]]

       d.   * *Auf wen*$_i$ sagte er [*wo* [sie e$_i$ gewartet habe]]?   *blocked spec in*
             for whom said he [where [she waited has]]   *the complement*

       e.   * *Auf wen*$_i$ sagte er [*sie* habe [e$_i$ gewartet]]?   *blocked spec in the*
             for whom said he [she has [waited]]   *complement*

       f.   * *Mit welchem Mann*$_i$ war sie so kurzsichtig,
             [e$_i$ [dass [sie e$_i$ kollidierte]]]?   *adjunct island*
             with which man was she so myopic [[that [she collided]]]
             'Which man was it that she was so myopic that she collided with him?'

There are two special cases of unembedded interrogatives. First, there are interrogative clauses in the format of an *embedded* clause (see section 2.2), that is, the format with the finite verb in clause-final position. Examples are musing

(ii)   * Des Geldes$_i$ hat er sie [e$_i$ wegen] nicht geheiratet
         the money-GEN has he her [because-of] not married

(iii)   * Dem Freund$_i$ hat er es [e$_i$ zuliebe / gegenüber] nicht erwähnt
         the friend has he it [for the sake of / in the face of] not mentioned

questions, as in (2a), or exclamative clauses (2b). Second, there are interrogatives without wh-movement (2c,d).

(2)   a. Warum er das getan *hat*? – Ich habe keine Ahnung
         why he it done has   – I have no idea
         'Why has he done it? I have no idea'

      b. Wie hoch der springen *kann*!
         how high this-one jump can
         'How high he can jump!'

      c. A: Das hat sie nicht zu ◇◇◇ gesagt. B: Das hat sie nicht zu WEM gesagt?
         A: this has she not to ◇◇◇ told. B: this has she not to WHOM told?

      d. Und das hat dann *welchen* Effekt?
         And this has then *which* effect?

(2c) is an *echo question*. An echo question is a question following an utterance that asks to repeat an item of the previous utterance that the hearer has not properly perceived (namely the word or phrase that is masked by '◇◇◇' in 2c). Hence, echo questions are not *constructionally* interrogative. This also shows in the violation of syntactic constraints for wh-questions.[12]

Finally, (2d) is typical for 'unfaithful' questions, as for instance exam questions. The examiner is supposed to know or presuppose the answer. Hence it is not a speech act of asking for information unknown to the speaker, but rather a hint to produce a specific statement in order to be checked for accuracy.

3.2.2   *Embedded interrogative clauses*

The prototypical cases are complement clauses of verbs that select/ admit an interrogative clause. This is the case of so-called indirect questions (1). Furthermore, the interrogative clause format is employed for embedded exclamative constructions (2).

---

[12] Here is an example of a violation. (i) questions an item in an extraposed position. This is deviant for wh-questions such as (ii). The in-situ wh-item of a multiple-wh question must not be extraposed.

    (i)   Er hat nicht gesprochen mit wem?   (echo question)
    (ii)   *Wer hat nicht gesprochen mit *wem*?   (wh-question, with an *extraposed* in-situ wh-item)
    (iii)   Wer hat nicht mit *wem* gesprochen?   (wh-question, with an in-situ wh-item)

(1)   a.   Ich weiß nicht [*auf wen*$_i$ [sie e$_i$ gewartet hat]]
            I know not [for whom [she waited has]]
            'I don't know for whom she was waiting'

      b. * Ich weiß nicht [*auf wen*$_i$ man glaubte [e$_i$ [habe sie e$_i$ gewartet]]]
            I know not [for whom one believed [[has she waited]]]
            'I don't know for whom they believed she was waiting'

      c.   Ich weiß nicht [*auf wen*$_i$ man glaubte [e$_i$ [dass sie e$_i$ gewartet habe]]]
            I know not for whom one believed that she waited has

      d. * Ich weiß nicht [*auf wen*$_i$ er sagte [*wo* [sie e$_i$ gewartet habe]]]
            I know not for whom he said where she waited has   *blocked spec in the complement*

      e. * Ich weiß nicht [*auf wen*$_i$ er sagte [*sie* habe [e$_i$ gewartet]]]
            I know not for whom said he she has waited   *blocked spec in the complement*

      f. * Ich weiß nicht, *mit wem*$_i$ sie so kurzsichtig war, [e$_i$ [dass [sie e$_i$ kollidierte]]]
            I know not with whom she so myopic was that she collided   *adjunct island*
            'I do not know who it was that she was so myopic that she collided with him'

Note the contrast between (1b) in section 3.2.1 and (1b) above. Extraction out of an embedded V2 clause is subject to an intriguing constraint: each of the landing sites of the extraction must be a V2 clause, too.[13] In (1b), the fronted wh-element is in the spec of a V-final clause, whence its deviance.

Embedded wh-exclamative complements are not selected as wh-clauses. A verb like *glauben* (believe) does not admit a wh-clause as a complement (2b), except for a wh-complement with an exclamative interpretation (2a).

(2)   a.   Du glaubst nicht, *wie groß* er geworden ist!
            you believe not how big he become has
            'You won't believe how big he has become'

---

[13] An intervening V-final clause is not acceptable either. In (i), the final target is in a V2 clause, but the intermediate landing site is in a V-final clause.

   (i)   * Wen hat sie gemeint, [e$_i$ dass man gehofft *habe* [e$_i$ werde er e$_i$ heiraten]]?
            who has she thought [that one hoped has [would he marry]
            'Who did she think that everyone hoped that he would marry'
   (ii)   Wen hat sie gemeint, [e$_i$ *habe* man gehofft [e$_i$ werde er e$_i$ heiraten]]?

b. * Du glaubst nicht, *ob* er groß geworden ist!
you believe not whether he big become has
'You do not believe whether he has become big'

There is a clear difference between the embedded and the main clause interrogative construction. It is the positioning of the finite verb. As in English (subject–auxiliary inversion), embedded wh-clauses neither trigger nor allow the fronting of the finite verb. Why does the finite verb not move to the functional head position that accommodates the wh-element in embedded clauses?

This peculiarity – no finite verb fronting in embedded wh-clauses – includes the fact that there are no embedded V1 interrogatives as an alternative to an embedded interrogative clause with a complementizer. *Ob* (whether) does not alternate with V1 if the clause is a *selected* interrogative clause (3b). However, there is an alternation for non-selected clauses; (3c) vs (3d) illustrates this alternation for a non-selected clause.[14]

(3)   a. Es ist unklar, *ob* er sie gekannt hat
            it is unclear whether he her known has
            'It is unclear whether he has known her'

        b. * Es ist unklar, *hat* er sie gekannt
            it is unclear has he her known

        c. Er tut so, als [ob er sie gekannt habe]
            he acts so as [if he her known has-SUBJUNCTIVE]

        d. Er tut so, als [habe er sie gekannt]
            he acts so as [had-SUBJUNCTIVE he her known]

The key for understanding the distribution of the finite verb is the selection relation and the checking relation. If an embedded wh-clause is a selected clause, the matrix verb that selects this clause requires a clause with a wh-feature. This feature is checked at the head position of the selected phrase. In the case of a selected clause, the head is the functional head of the top-most functional projection of the clause. This functional head is either lexicalized as an interrogative complementizer (*ob* – whether) or it inherits the feature by spec head-agreement from the wh-phrase in spec.

(4)   [... V° [$_{CP}$ XP$_{[+wh]}$] [C°$_{[+wh]}$] [....]]]]

---

[14] Since there is also the construction *als wenn* (as if), and *wenn* (if) alternates with V1, just as in English, (3b) could be the V1 alternation for *wenn*, rather than for *ob*, but this is not easy to verify.

A wh-feature on C° is a non-verbal feature. So, this functional head position is not a target for fronting the finite verb in this case. Given this state of affairs, you are justified in asking immediately what to expect in the case of an *unem-bedded* interrogative clause. The situation is as follows. In the main clause, the wh-element is *directly* interpretable in terms of its illocutionary force. In other words, a wh-element in a main clause is interpreted as a question marker. It is not in a grammatical dependency relation to a selecting element. So the difference between the embedded and the non-embedded occurrence is one between a *semantically* interpretable feature and a *syntactical* one. Compare (5a) and (5b):

(5) a. *Wen* hat sie geküsst?
whom has she kissed

   b. Es ist nicht interessant, *wen* sie geküsst hat
it is not interesting whom she kissed has

   c. Es ist nicht interessant, *ob* sie ihn geküsst hat
it is not interesting whether she him kissed has

   d. * Es ist nicht interessant, *hat* sie ihn geküsst
it is not interesting has she him kissed

   e. *Hat* sie ihn geküsst?
has she him kissed

The wh-feature of the wh-element in (5a) is directly interpreted. Its interpretation is that of an *illocutionary* feature, namely the feature of an *erotetic*[15] utterance. In the case of (5b), the wh-feature of *wen* cannot be directly interpreted since the clause is not a question. Therefore, the feature must be checked in a spec-head configuration. This applies also to the embedded exclamative in (2a). The diffe-rence between (2a) and an indirect question as in (1a) and (5b,c) is the selection relation. An indirect question is a complement clause selected for a [+wh] feature. The exclamative clause (2a) is a wh-clause not selected for a wh-feature. So, the wh-item cannot be, and is not, interpreted as a question operator but as a different kind of operator (degree operator).

A fronted finite verb as in the embedded V1 clause (5d) is apparently incom-patible with a selected wh-feature. V1 clauses are ungrammatical in the position of selected wh-clauses. However, V1 is the standard structure of a yes/no question (5e). This is of course not a peculiarity of German. It is true for English as well, and in fact for all Germanic languages: embedded indirect questions are incom-patible with fronting the finite verb. What is the grammatical nature of this diffe-rence between main and embedded clauses?

---

[15] erotetic = having the function of the speech act of questioning.

The difference is obvious. Main clauses are not selected, but embedded ones are. Hence the latter, but not the former, must meet selection requirements, and the selectable feature is checked on the head of the embedded phrase. For an embedded clause, this is the head of its highest functional projection. A finite verb in this position is just a finite verb. There is no wh-variant of a finite verb. Hence it does not qualify as a selectable head with a [+wh] feature.

For matrix clauses, the situation is different. They have no selection requirement and they are interpretable as independent utterances. For a V1 structure, interpreted as a yes/no question, this is the direct interpretation of the constructional 'meaning' (*Satzmodus*) of this structure.

3.2.3   *Relative clauses*

In German, there are two distinct *relative* constructions. One is the postnominal wh-movement type (1a–c), the other one (1d) is a type of construction familiar from OV languages, namely a prenominal participial construction:

(1)   a. ein Mensch^i, [der^i dieses Beispiel analysiert]
            a human-being [who this example analyses]
            'a human being who analyses this example'

         b. Alles^i, [was^i man analysiert]
            everything [what one analyses]
            'everything that they analyse'

         c. wer dieses Beispiel analysiert   *headless relative*
            who this example analyses
            'who(ever) analyses this example'

         d. ein [PRO^i dieses Beispiel analysierender] Mensch^i
            a [this example analysing-NOM-SG-MASC] human-being
            'a human being analysing this example'

The format of the relative clause in (1a) is the format of a dependent finite clause with a relative phrase (consisting of the relative pronoun *der*) moved to the top spec position. The functional head of this spec position remains empty. The finite verb must not move to this position. This is the pattern familiar from embedded wh-clauses.

The moved relative phrase is a relative pronoun or a pied-piped phrase that contains the relative pronoun. In German, the relative pronouns are recruited from the set of *demonstrative* pronouns. Only in a subgroup is the relative pronoun a *wh-pronoun*, namely for relative clauses that relate to quantifiers like *nichts* (nothing) or *alles* (everything), as in (1b), and for 'free' relative clauses, that is, relative clauses without a nominal head, as in (1c).

The attribute construction (1d) does not involve wh-movement. Its empty subject is construed with the noun the participle agrees with. This construction is a subinstance of OV-type relative constructions: the relative clause contains a null element that relates to the antecedent of the relative clause and the verb of the relative clause is morphologically marked and agrees with the head noun of the NP. The lexical head of the attribute in (1b) is a participle that agrees with the noun in gender, number and case, just as attributes in German do. The null element in the construction (1d) is the subject argument.[16]

The wh-movement properties of wh-movement relative clauses are illustrated in (2).

(2)   a.   der Tag [*auf den*$_i$ [sie e$_i$ gewartet hat]]
            the day [for which [she waited has]]

       b.   * der Tag, *auf den*$_i$ man glaubte [e$_i$ [habe sie e$_i$ gewartet]]
            the day for which one believed [[has she waited]]
            'the day for which they believed she had been waiting'

       c.   der Tag, *auf den*$_i$ man glaubte [e$_i$ [dass [sie e$_i$ gewartet habe]]]
            the day for which one believed [[that [she waited has]]]

       d.   * der Tag *auf den*$_i$ er sagte [*seit wann*   *blocked spec in*
            [sie e$_i$ gewartet habe]]   *the complement*
            the day for which he said [since when [she waited has]]
            complement
            '*the day for which he said since when she has been waiting for'

       e.   * der Tag *auf den*$_i$ er sagte   *blocked spec in*
            [*sie* habe [e$_i$ gewartet]]   *the complement*
            the day for which he said [she has [waited]]

---

[16] It is a PRO-subject. This can be verified with predicates, like *einer nach dem anderen* (one after the other):

(i)   DEN [PRO^i *einer nach dem andern* ins Wasser springenden] Männern^i
       the-DAT [one-NOM after the other into-the water jumping] men-DAT
       '(to) the men (that are) jumping into the water one after the other'

The case of the predicate in (i) is nominative. The source of the nominative is agreement with the subject. This is familiar from control constructions, as in (ii):

(ii)   Sie hat den Männern geraten [PRO^i *einer nach dem andern* ins Wasser zu springen]
       she has advised the men [one-nom after the other into-the water to jump]
       'she has the men advised to jump into the water one after the other'

f. * der Mann, *mit dem*$_i$ sie so kurzsichtig war,
[e$_i$ [dass [sie e$_i$ kollidierte]]]   *adjunct island*
the man with whom she so myopic was [[that [she collided]]]
'the man such that she was so myopic that she collided with him'

As in the case of embedded interrogative clauses (see 1b in section 3.2.2), extraction out of a V2 complement (2b) is deviant, since the target position is in a V-final clause.

Headless relative clauses (1c) are finite wh-clauses that represent a DP, but there is no overt nominal head of this DP. The structure in (3) is an analysis that parallels the standard relative clause construction, with an empty DP-head though. This construction is subject to a peculiar restriction, namely a *matching* requirement: the case that is assigned to the DP must be identical with the case assigned to the relative phrase. As a consequence thereof, the construction gets deviant once the case of the relative phrase within the relative clause (the XP in 3) and the case of the DP that the headless relative clause represents do not match. In other words, the case assigned to the relative phrase within the relative clause must be the same case as the case assigned from outside to the DP that the headless relative clause represents.

(3) $[_{DP} e^i [_{Rel.cl} XP^i_{Rel.} \dots\dots]]$

In the deviant cases in (4b,c), the case of the relative pronoun and the case of the DP are different; in the well-formed examples (4a,d), both candidates have received the same case, from different case assigners, of course.

(4)   a.   Er widerspricht [$_{DP-DAT}$ wem-DAT sie widerspricht]
                 he contradicts [whom-DAT she contradicts]

           b. * Er widerspricht [$_{DP-DAT}$ wen-AKK sie kritisiert]
                 he contradicts [whom-AKK she criticizes]

           c. * Er widerspricht [$_{DP-DAT}$ wer-NOM sie kritisiert]
                 he contradicts [who-NOM criticizes her]

           d.   Getadelt wird [$_{DP-NOM}$ wer-NOM sie kritisiert]
                 reproached is [who-NOM criticizes her]

           e. * Getadelt wird [$_{DP-NOM}$ wem-DAT sie widerspricht]
                 reproached is [whom-DAT she criticizes]

The exact (mis)matching conditions are more complicated than a simple case identity condition would have it.[17] The grammar-theoretic source of the matching

---

[17] See Bausewein (1991) and Pittner (1995) for a characterization in terms of ranked conditions, and van Riemsdijk (2006) for a detailed survey.

requirement is not entirely clear: if the free relative is analysed as a DP with an empty N° or D° head plus a relative clause (see 3), the case checking of the empty N° head should be independent of the case checking of the relative phrase. On the other hand, if the relative phrase is taken to be head of the whole DP, this would require a raising analysis (as proposed by Vergnaud (1985) for relative clauses). A third guess is that the matching conditions are part and parcel of the identification requirements for the empty head of the DP.

3.2.4   Comparative and equative clauses

In standard German, just as in English, comparative clauses display the properties of wh-movement constructions, but there is no *overt* wh-item involved. Fortunately, dialects of German provide immediate evidence for the involvement of wh-elements. Example (1a) is a dialectal one (written with standard German lexemes); example (1b) is the standard German version.

(1)   a. Er hat mehr Geld^i ausgegeben als [*wos*^i_j ich je e$_j$ verdienen werde]
             he has more money spent than [*what* I ever earn shall]   *dialectal*
             'He has spent more money than I shall ever earn'

         b. Er hat mehr Geld^i ausgegeben als [*O*^i_j ich je e$_j$ verdienen werde]
                                                                        standard

         he has more money spent than [I ever earn shall]

Obviously, the comparative clause contains a gap. In (1b), the object is missing, in (1a) the object is the fronted wh-item. The missing/moved element is the target of comparison. Second, the island (2b) and adjunct (2c) effects of wh-movement are properties of this construction:

(2)   a.   Er hat mehr Geld ausgegeben, als (*wos*)[18] man vermutete,
              dass er verdient hat
              he has more money spent than (what) one supposed
              that he earned has

         b. * Er hat mehr Geld ausgegeben, als (*wos*) man sagt,
              womit er verdient hat
              he has more money spent than (what) one said
              what-with he earned has

         c. * Er hat mehr Geld ausgegeben, als sie so talentiert war,
              dass sie verdiente
              he has more money spent than she so talented was that she earned

---

[18] The variant with *wos* is dialectal. The standard variant has a phonetically empty wh-operator.

Note that – as expected – extraction out of a subject clause is not deviant (3a). This is parallel to the extraction out of subjects in the case of wh-questions (section 3.1, ex. 12a). In English, extraction out of a subject is strictly ungrammatical (3b).

(3)   a.   Sie hat mehr Leute^i eingeladen [als O^i_j [PRO e$_j$ zu bewirten]] mir Spaß gemacht hat
        she has more people invited [than [to entertain]] me fun made has

    b.   * She has invited more people^i [than O^i_j [PRO to entertain e$_j$]] was fun for me

The 'siblings' of comparative clauses are equative ones. German *equative* clauses display a wh-element, namely *wie* (how), hence their wh-nature is easy to identify:

(4)   a.   Er hat soviel^i Geld ausgegeben [*wie*^i_j er e$_j$ verdient hat]
        he has as much money spent [how he earned has]
        'He spent as much money as he earned'

    b.   Er hat soviel^i Geld ausgegeben [*wie*^i_j man dachte [dass er e$_j$ verdient habe]][19]
        he has as much money spent [how one thought [that he earned has]]

    c.   * Er hat soviel^i Geld ausgegeben, [wie^i_j sie so talentiert war, dass sie e$_j$ verdiente]
        he has so-much money spent [as she so talented was that she earned]

In German dialects, the two constructions – comparative and equative – are strictly parallel, with *als was* for comparative clauses and *als wie* for equative clauses. As in the corresponding German standard construction, *als* is a preposition whose complement is a clause, whose spec is the target of wh-movement.

Finally, there is a kind of equative construction for proportional relations, as in (5).[20]

(5)   *Je* mehr Geld du ausgibst, *desto* größer wird dein Minus am Konto
    the more money you spend, *the* bigger shall-become your deficit on-the account

---

[19] Note that the wh-item is not the full wh-form of the target of equation. It is an operator. In its 'full version', the clause would read roughly like this:

(i)   *so* viel Geld … [*wie*~~viel Geld~~$_i$ man dachte, dass er e$_i$ verdient habe]
                                               German
    so much money …[how ~~much money~~ one thought that he earned has]

[20] Dutch employs a wh-item in each of the two spec positions, namely *hoe* (how):

(i)   *Hoe* meer geld je uitgeeft, *hoe* groter zal je minus worden   *Dutch*
    how more money you spend, how bigger shall your deficit become

In each of the two clauses in (5), an operator phrase is placed in the highest spec position. Note that the first sentence (*je* ...) has the form of an embedded sentence, with a clause-*final* finite verb. It is related to the main clause by means of the second operator (*desto*). Structurally, (5) has the form of a left-dislocation construction: the dependent clause is adjoined to the matrix clause and associated with a cross-referencing element in the spec of the matrix clause. A structurally parallel case to (6a) is (6b), with a left-dislocated conditional clause.

(6)   a.   [Je^i mehr Geld du ausgibst], [desto^i größer [wird dein Minus am Konto]]
              [the more money you spend] [the bigger [becomes your minus on-the account]]

        b.   [Wenn^i du zuviel Geld ausgibst], [dann^i wird [das Minus auf deinem Konto größer]]
              [if you too-much money spend] [then becomes [the deficit on your account bigger]]

3.2.5   *Declarative V2 clauses*

The clause-initial phrase in a V2 declarative clause is a phrase moved to the top-most spec position, hence a V2 clause is an instance of the family of wh-movement constructions, and the properties of this construction are expected to hold for V2 clauses as well. It is easy to see this if you merely replace the wh-item in a main clause interrogative by the element that could serve as an answer. The examples in (1) are the declarative counterparts of the questions in (1) in section 3.2.1.

(1)   a.   *Auf ihn*$_i$ hat sie e$_i$ gewartet
              for him has she waited

        b.   *Auf ihn*$_i$ glaubte man [e$_i$ habe [sie e$_i$ gewartet]]
              for him believed one [has [she waited]]
              'For him they believed she waited'

        c.   *Auf ihn*$_i$ glaubte man [e$_i$ dass [sie e$_i$ gewartet habe]]
              for him believed one [that [she waited has]]

        d.   * *Auf ihn*$_i$ sagte er [*wo* [sie e$_i$ gewartet habe]]   *blocked spec in the*
              for him said he [where [she waited has]]   *complement*

        e.   * *Auf ihn*$_i$ sagte er [*sie* habe [e$_i$ gewartet]]   *blocked spec in the*
              for him said he [she has [waited]]   *complement*

f. * *Mit dem Mann*_i war sie so kurzsichtig, [e_i [dass [sie e_i kollidierte]]]
adjunct island
with the man was she so myopic [[that [she collided]]]
'As for this man, she was so myopic that she collided with him'

What determines whether a V2 clause is typed as an interrogative clause or a declarative clause? It is the element in the spec position, evidently. If it is an interrogative element, the clause is typed[21] 'interrogative', if it is non-interrogative, the clause is typed 'declarative'.[22] For a theoretician, this account might seem too superficial. S/he might prefer a feature-based account: an interrogative clause has a head with an interrogative feature [+wh] that needs to be 'checked' by a phrase with a matching interrogative feature in the spec position. Analogously, the declarative clause has a [-wh] feature. Which of these accounts – the feature-based one or the contextual one – is more adequate?

If you think the two accounts are merely notational variants, you might be surprised to learn that actually these accounts differ empirically once we take into consideration a specific fact of German, namely the interpretation of wh-pronouns in-situ in comparison to the interpretation in a spec position:

(2)   a. Gestern hat das *wer* erzählt
yesterday has this who told
'Yesterday someone told this'

b. *Wer* hat das gestern erzählt *(?)   *interrogative only*
who has this yesterday told?

c. Gestern hat sie *wen* besucht
yesterday has she whom visited
'Yesterday, she has visited someone'

d. *Wen* hat sie gestern besucht *(?)   *interrogative only*
whom has she yesterday visited?

e. *Wer* hat wen besucht?
who has someone/whom visited

The sentences (2a) and (2c) are declarative clauses with the wh-item interpreted as an indefinite pronoun (i.e. *someone*). (2b,d), however, are *interrogative*

---

[21] The Clausal Typing Hypothesis (Cheng 1997) proposes that languages must syntactically mark (or 'type') a wh-question and that they do so with either wh-movement or a question particle.
[22] This does not exclude that the declarative pattern with an interrogative intonation contour may be used for questioning. In this case, the *interrogative intonation* contour is the interrogative force indicator.

only.[23] (2e) is ambiguous, but only for the construal of the second wh-element. It can be interpreted as an interrogative pronoun in-situ or as an indefinite pronoun. In each case, the wh-element in the sentence-initial position must not be interpreted as an indefinite pronoun. Here is a sketch of an answer: it follows from the contextual approach, but not from the feature approach.

If the surface position of a wh-item is a spec position, the wh-item is obligatorily interpreted as a wh-operator since by virtue of being in a spec position, it is in an A'-position and binds a variable (namely at least its trace). If, on the other hand, the wh-item is in its base position, it is ambiguous. Either it is interpreted as an indefinite or, if bound by a higher wh-item, it is interpreted as a wh-element.

The feature-based approach would allow both interpretations (wh or indefinite) also for the spec position and therefore would be inadequate, for the following reason. A wh-item is specified as either [+wh] or [-wh], corresponding to the interrogative and the indefinite construal, respectively. If the value is [+wh], the wh-element in spec is interpreted as Q-operator. If the feature is [-wh], the wh-element in spec would be interpreted as a [-wh] element, viz. an indefinite. Hence (2d) should be ambiguous, contrary to the facts. It is interrogative only. So, the contextual approach seems to be superior:[24] a wh-element in the spec position is

---

[23] The inaccessibility of a declarative reading for the fronted wh-element, interpreted as an indefinite pronoun, cannot be attributed to the avoidance of stress. First, a topicalized subject is not stressed. So, (2b) should be open for a declarative reading, contrary to the facts. Second, destressing, for instance by focusing on another element, does not save the declarative reading:

    (i)   Wen hat SIE$_{focus}$ gestern besucht (interrogative/*declarative)
                someone-acc / whom has she yesterday visited

Note, however, that there may be an additional factor that interacts in ruling out an indefinite reading in the clause-initial spec position: the generic reading of *einer* (one) is not available in this position either:

    (ii)   In Salzburg wird einem im Sommer viel Mozart serviert
               in Salzburg is one in summer much Mozart served
               'In Salzburg, in summer, they serve you much Mozart'

    (iii)   Einem$_{*generic}$ wird in Salzburg im Sommer viel Mozart serviert
               (to) one is in Salzburg in summer much Mozart served
               'one is served much Mozart in Salzburg in summer'

[24] If you object and hypothesize that there might be a [+wh] feature involved that must not be cancelled, you should take into consideration that [+wh] features may be cancelled in German, as the following example demonstrates:

    (i)   (Er gab auf.) Hatte er *doch* keine wirkliche Chance mehr
               (he gave up) had he PRT no real chance any-more
               '(He gave up.) In fact, he had no real chance any more'

The example is representative for declarative V1 sentences. The assertive particle *doch* is incompatible with an interrogative reading. So it *cancels* the constructional

a wh-operator. A wh-element in-situ is construed as wh-in-situ, if bound by a wh-operator, and as an indefinite pronoun otherwise.

3.3   Partial wh-movement

The examples in (1a,b) illustrate a construction frequently heard in spoken vernacular German. Let us refer to (1a) as the *was*-construction (WC) and to (1b) as the *copy* construction (CC). A detailed cross-linguistic survey of this construction and a survey of the research literature is presented in Fanselow (2006). The bridge-verb conditions of partial wh-movement and full wh-movement constructions are not completely identical (see Reis 2000).

(1)   a. *Was* glaubt sie, *wen* sie gesehen hat?
          what believes she whom she seen has
          'Whom does she believe that she saw?'

       b. *Wen* glaubt sie, *wen* sie gesehen hat?
          whom believes she whom she seen has
          'Whom does she believe that she saw?'

In both constructions, a wh-element is moved at least into the nearest comp (i.e. the spec- C position) All higher comps are either filled with the item *was* (what) or a copy of the moved wh-item (see 2).

(2)   a. *Was* meinst du, *was* sie glaubt, wen sie gesehen hat?   WC
          what think you what she believes whom she seen has
          'Whom do you think that she believes she has seen?'

       b. *Wen* meinst du, *wen* sie glaubt, wen sie gesehen hat?   CC
          whom think you whom she believes whom she seen has

       c. *Was* meinst du, *wen* sie glaubt, wen /*was sie gesehen hat? WC+CC
          what think you whom she believes whom /*what she seen has

       d. *Was* meinst du, *wen* sie glaubt, dass sie gesehen hat?   WC+CC
          what think you whom she believes that she seen has

These examples illustrate the following properties of this construction: *was* never appears in positions that *follow* the surface position of the moved wh-item. Hence, in (2c), the lowest *was* is ungrammatical since obviously the wh-item *wen* has moved to the intermediate comp. So, the lowest clause is just the complement clause of 'believe', with the expected complementizer *dass* and the trace in comp

interrogative reading (i.e. the reading as a yes/no question) that is normally associated with V1 clauses, namely the reading as a yes/no question.

(i.e. Spec-C in today's diction). The other licit possibility is the *copy* construction, in combination with the *was*-construction. In (2c), the intermediate comp contains a copy while the highest comp contains *was*. In other words, the intermediate clause instantiates the CC and the matrix clause uses the WC. In (2d) the wh-item *wen* is moved to the intermediate comp but not any further, with *was* in the highest comp. This is a combination of WC and standard wh-movement.

These constructions (WC, CC) share the constraints of the wh-movement constructions (e.g. wh-islands) and there are additional constraints that apply to them but not to the standard wh-movement construction. (3) illustrates the wh-island constraint.

(3)   a. * Wen^i behauptete sie, *wann* er sagte, wen^i er gesehen habe?
            whom claims she when he said whom he seen has
            '*Whom did she claim when he said that he has seen'

        b. * Was^i behauptete sie, *wann* er sagte, wen^i er gesehen habe?
            what claims she when he said whom he seen has
            '*What did she claim when he said whom he has seen?'

Without going into too much detail – for a detailed survey see Fanselow (2006) – three factors that distinguish the WC and the CC from the standard wh-movement construction need to be taken into consideration. *First*, the class of verbs that admits the construction is more narrow than the class of bridge verbs (i.e. the verbs that allow long-distance wh-extraction). *Second*, the CC is restricted to monolexical wh-expression; in other words, complex wh-phrases are excluded. (4) contrasts wh-extraction with WC and CC. *Third*, the lowest wh-item must not remain in-situ.

As for the class of matrix verbs, volitional verbs like *mögen* (want), *wünschen* (wish) or *hoffen* (hope) are not compatible with the WC or CC although they are bridge verbs[25] for wh-extraction.

(4)   a. Wen möchtest / wünschst du [dass ich befrage]?
            who want / wish you [that I question]

        b. * Was /*Wen möchtest / wünschst du [wen ich befrage]?
            what / whom want / wish you [whom I question]

---

[25] Volitional verbs are remarkable in yet another aspect: they are bridge verbs but they do not allow a V2 clause instead of a *that*-clause. Most bridge verbs allow for this variation.

   (i)   Er möchte, {dass ich sie anrufe, *ich rufe sie an}
          he wants {that I her up-phone, *I phone her up}

   (ii)   Wen$_i$ möchtest du, dass ich e$_i$ anrufe
          who want you that I up-phone

     c.   Wen hat sie gehofft [dass man dort antreffe]?
        whom has she hoped [that one there meets]

     d. * Was /*Wen hat sie gehofft [wen man dort antreffe]?
        what / whom has she hoped [whom one there meets]

In fact, it seems to be easier to list the verbs that do allow the WC or CC than to enumerate the verbs that do not permit it. Acceptability is guaranteed for verbs of the class (believe, think, say, ...), that is, verbs of wanting, saying and believing. What is still missing, though, is a representative field study on this construction in order to ascertain the range of verbs and the variation in acceptability.

    The second restriction applies to the CC only. It is a restriction on copy candidates. The higher copy must not contain pied-piped material. This excludes phrasal wh-expressions (5a). The amalgamated PPs that result from the combination of a preposition and a neuter wh-pronoun are marginally acceptable, though (5b).

(5)   a. Was /*[*Mit wem*] glaubst Du [mit wem sie rechnet]?
        what / with whom think you [with whom she reckons] [26]

     b. Was /(?)*Womit* glaubst du [womit sie rechnet]?
        what / what-with think you [what-with she reckons]
        'With what do you think she reckons?'

     c. Was / *wann* glaubst du [wann sie damit rechnen wird]?
        what / when think you [when she it-with reckon will]
        'When do you think that she will reckon with it?'

The third difference is a ban against leaving the wh-item in-situ (6a). It must be moved at least to the local spec C. Although the WC and the CC are a kind of multi-wh construction, WC and CC clearly differ from the wh-in-situ constructions (6b) to be discussed in the following subsection:

(6)   a.   Wen / Was glaubst Du [wen sie (*wen) gesehen hat]?
          whom / what think you [whom she whom seen has]
          'Whom do you think that she has seen'

     b.   Wo / Weshalb glaubst du [dass sie *wen* gesehen hat]?
          where / why think you [that she whom seen has]
          'where / why do you think that she has seen whom'

     c. * Wo /*Weshalb glaubst du [wen$_i$ sie e$_i$ gesehen hat]?
          where / why think you whom she seen has

---

[26] 'Reckon with' is chosen here because it allows both a literal interpretation (calculate with the use of an instrument) and an idiomatic interpretation (take someone into consideration). This opens the possibility of using animate and inanimate forms in the example.

Both the CC and the WC require at least one step of overt wh-movement. The wh-phrase must be moved at least into the local spec position. It must not remain in-situ (6a), unlike in a multiple wh-construction (6b). The second wh-item in a double question must not be moved, as (6c) demonstrates, irrespective of the source domain of the wh-item in the clause-initial position. So, for local wh-movement, the WC and the CC do not come into play. For long-distance movement, the WC is a way to avoid non-local movement. Instead, the unmarked wh-item *was* (third person neuter) marks all higher comps as a means of marking the scope domain and the path to the lower wh-expression it is in construction with. Analogously, the CC traces the path from the top position as the scope position to the lowest comp position.

From the point of view of structure processing, scope-marking by placing an overt copy of the moved wh-item tracing is obviously parser-friendly. It reduces the working memory load for keeping the initial wh-item in the buffer until its source position has been reached, and it puts clear signs in the intermediate comps that direct the parser towards the source position.

(7)   a. Wann dachte sie, dass er gedacht habe, dass er sein Ziel erreicht habe
        when thought she that he thought had that he his goal reached has

       b. Was / Wann dachte sie, was / wann er gedacht habe, wann er sein Ziel erreicht habe
        what / when thought she what / when he thought had when he his goal reached has

The version (7a) is three-way ambiguous. *Wann* could be construed with the matrix clause, the intermediate clause, or the most deeply embedded clause. (7b) is unambiguous. So, with the CC and the WC construction, the grammar provides disambiguation options with parser-friendly side effects.

Finally, what could be the source of the restriction against full copies? Fanselow (2006) refers to Hiemstra (1986) for a theoretic modelling of this aspect. Her approach is roughly this: wh-movement is in general movement of a wh-feature and languages only differ to the extent of what needs to be pied-piped when the wh-feature moves. In the unmarked case, long-distance wh-movement moves the (minimal) moveable wh-expression. Alternatively, grammars may restrict movement to the wh-feature only. In this case the wh-feature to be spelled out at the landing site needs a carrier. This gets realized phonetically as the most unmarked wh-expression of the language: *was* in German. In addition, there is supposed to exist an intermediate case of feature pied-piping in which person–number features of the wh-phrase are also moved. So, for instance (wh, 3rd. sg., ACC) will then be spelled out as the corresponding wh-word *wen* in German. This, according to

Hiemstra (1986), is the source of the CC. Since the spell-out of a feature set is always an atomic wh-item, the CC is restricted to atomic wh-items.

While this account is empirically adequate for the WC, the details of the German CC are not captured precisely. First, the examples of the type (5b), i.e. amalgamated PPs, are not covered. A PP, unlike a pronoun, cannot be regarded as a mere *pronominal* person–number feature bundle, but nevertheless the construction is acceptable.

The particular example in (8) combines the WC and the CC. The wh-item in the intermediate clause is a copy of the item in the lowest clause, namely a wh-pronoun amalgamated with the preposition, forming a PP. The matrix wh-element is the scope marking *was*. The contrast between the amalgamated, monolexical variant (8a) and the phrasal variant (8b) needs to be accounted for.

(8)   a. *Was* glaubst Du, *wofür* sie meint [*wofür* das gut sei]
           what believe you what-for she thinks [what-for it useful may-be]
           'What do you believe she thinks it may be useful for?'

       b. *Was* glaubst Du, was /*[*für wen*] sie meint [[*für wen*] das gut sei]
           what believe you what / [for whom] she thinks [[for whom] it useful
           may-be]
           'Who(m) do you believe she thinks it may be useful for?'

What is the structural difference between a monolexical wh-expression (*wofür*) and a phrasal one (*für wen*)? In the case of a phrasal wh-expression, the maximal c-command domain of the wh-item is the phrase it is contained in. If we posit that a scope-marking wh-item must c-command its dependent(s), phrasal wh-expressions are immediately ruled out. The wh-item within the PP in the intermediate comp does not c-command the wh-item in the lower PP, whence the ungrammaticality.

In sum, the WC appears to be the underspecified variant of the CC. In the WC, we see the unmarked wh-item *was* in its scope-marking function; in the CC, the scope-marking wh-item is a 'copy' of the dependent, and therefore 'overspecified', in comparison to *was*. This overspecified scope marker is licit as long as the basic requirement, namely the c-command relation between copy and dependent, is not infringed.

3.4   Wh-in-situ in multiple-wh interrogative clauses

From a German vantage point, English posits 'strange' restrictions on the potential candidates for wh-items that have to be left in-situ (Haider 1986). Most of these restrictions turn out as VO effects that are absent in a clause with a basic OV organization (Haider 2004b), for principled reasons. Hence, the set of facts characteristic of English wh-in-situ must not be mistaken as reflections of universally valid constraints; they may be valid for VO languages though. Let us briefly review the relevant contrasts.

English in particular, and VO languages in general, restrict the contexts for *in-situ wh*-elements more narrowly than OV structures do. These restrictions, for principled reasons, do not hold for OV languages (like Japanese or German). In English, special restrictions hold for wh-elements in the *functional subject* position, and for wh-elements that function as '*higher type*' *adverbial* wh-elements (viz. *how, why*).

3.4.1   Background

The adequate characterization and theoretic reconstruction of restrictions on English multiple-wh constructions with respect to the in-situ wh-elements have played an important role in the study of conditions on transformations. The key data are asymmetries in multiple-wh constructions as to which wh-item has to move and which one must stay.

Chomsky's (1973) *superiority* condition[27] is the first formulation of a general traffic rule for wh-movement. The structurally higher candidate receives priority over the lower candidate as the candidate for movement to the spec position. The *Minimal Link Condition*[28] (MLC; Chomsky 1995: 264) is a more recent rendering of Chomsky's (1973) original concept of '*Superiority*'.

(1)   a.   (It is unclear) what$_i$ e$_i$ shocked *whom*[29]

       b.   * (It is unclear) whom$_i$ *what* shocked e$_i$

       c.   (Es ist unklar) was *wen* schockierte
             (it is unclear) what whom shocked

       d.   (Es ist unklar) wen$_i$ *was* e$_i$ schockierte
             (it is unclear) whom what shocked

---

[27] Chomsky (1973: 246): 'No rule can involve X,Y in the structure [...X...[...Z... WYV...]...], where the rule applies ambiguously to Z and Y and Z is superior to Y.' 'Superior' is defined as follows: 'Category A is superior to category B in the phrase marker if every major category dominating A dominates B as well but not conversely.'

[28] Note that the MLC is not a condition on transformations; it is a condition on the choice of a candidate out of a set of alternative derivational continuations of a given input structure (hence, a transderivational constraint): if a given structure allows alternative derivational continuations, the MLC determines the choice of the appropriate candidate, namely the derivation with the *shorter* movement step.

[29] Kayne (1983:235 fn.13) emphasizes the following contrast between (i) and (ii):

(i)   ?I know who(m) I should give what to
(ii)   *I know who(m) what should be given to

According to the superiority constraint, *whom* in (1b) is not a licit candidate for movement to spec C because there is a superior one, namely *what*. Analogously, the chain link in (1a) is minimal in comparison to the chain link in (1b). So, the 'minimal link' requirement selects (1a) and disqualifies (1b).

Given these facts and these accounts, why is there no corresponding effect for the German examples? (1c,d) are fully representative of the construction. They are optional variants with no difference in meaning.[30] The subject–object asymmetry for wh-in-situ is absent in German. And so are two other asymmetries characteristic of the in-situ constructions. One is the ban against in-situ wh-subjects (2), and the second is the ban against unmoved higher adverbial wh-operators (*why, how*). Both restrictions are absent in German, and in fact in OV languages in general. The discussion of superiority effects has been too narrowly focusing on English and therefore these two restrictions have been mistakenly subsumed under the domain of Superiority.

As for the first contrast between English and German – and this is directly related to the source of the deviance of (1b) – in-situ wh-subjects are deviant in English (2), but this is independent of the superiority constraint. The following examples (2) are taken from Chomsky (1981: 236). Neither Superiority nor a minimal link condition could be applied in these cases since there is no competition between two wh-elements for the same spec C target.

(2)   a. I know perfectly well *who* thinks (that) she/*who* is in love with him

       b. I don't know *who* would be happy that she/*who* won the prize

       c. I don't remember *who* believes that she/*who* read the book

Whatever condition rules out an in-situ wh-subject in a finite clause[31] as in (2), will rule out an in-situ wh-subject in (1b). This condition will rule out an in-situ wh-element in the subject position in general, independent of crossing or non-crossing movements. Hence, there is in fact no justification for invoking the superiority constraint or the MLC for explaining the deviance of (1b).

In German, this condition does not apply, as the corresponding examples in (3) illustrate. Why does it not apply? It does not apply because the context of application is not given. The wh-in-situ data are valuable counterevidence for the assumption that in surface structure, German subjects are VP-external and

---

[30] The only difference is one of information structure: the first wh-element is the sorting key for value assignment. Elements of the set the first wh-element ranges over are the items which are paired with elements from the set the lower wh-element ranges over. The difference between (1c,d) is only one in terms of the choice of the sorting key.

[31] Bresnan (1977) accepts an in-situ wh-subject in the subjunctive construction. Note that in this construction, subject–verb agreement is waived in English: *Who recommended that [who be fired]*.

situated in a functional spec position. If a subject is *not* in a spec position, a condition that applies to wh-subjects in spec positions trivially does not apply.

(3)   a. Ich weiß ganz genau *wer* glaubt, dass sie / *wer* in ihn verliebt ist
         I know very exactly who believes that she / who with him in-love is

       b. Ich weiß nicht, *wer* Freude haben würde, wenn sie / *wer* den Preis gewönne
         I know not, who pleasure have would if she / who the prize win-would

       c. Ich erinnere mich nicht, *wer* glaubt, dass sie / *wer* das Buch gelesen habe
         I remember myself not, who believes that she / who the book read has

Note that the contrast between English and German in this respect is not due to an idiosyncrasy of either English or German; it is a VO- vs OV-related effect. VO languages share the asymmetry with English while OV languages share the free variation with German. So, for instance in Japanese, there is no deviance effect for a wh-subject preceded by a wh-object.

(4)   a. *Dare-ga nani-o* katta no?   *Japanese*
         who-NOM what-ACC bought Q-PRT?

       b. *Nani-o dare-ga* katta no?
         what-ACC who-NOM bought Q-PRT ?

       c. *Wer*-NOM hat *was*-ACC gekauft?   *German*
         who has what bought

       d. *Was*-ACC hat *wer*-NOM gekauft?
         what has who bought

What is the specific OV/VO dependent trait that is responsible for the contrast? More than one differentiating trait is potentially relevant. It might be a difference in the position of the subject, or it might be a side effect of another OV property. The latter position has been argued more than once in the literature. For instance, OV languages scramble (see, among others, Fanselow 1997; Wiltschko 1998). So, if the object is scrambled across the subject, the starting position of the scrambled object is higher than the subject position, hence no superiority violation occurs, and as a result of scrambling the object will end up nearer to the spec C position than the subject, hence no MLC violation can arise. (5) illustrates a scrambling derivation of (1d). Is this a satisfactory account?[32] Certainly, it is questionable, both on theoretical as well as on empirical grounds.

---

[32] Wiltschko's (1998: 123f.) basic claim is this: German permits scrambling. Scrambling 'imbues' the scrambled phrase with the d-linking quality, which cancels superiority.

(5)   (Es ist unklar) [$_{CP}$ wen$_i$ [e$_i$ was e$_i$ schockierte]]
       (it is unclear) [whom [what shocked]]

From a theoretical point of view, a scrambling account for (1d) as in (5) appears to be a ploy for tricking out a restriction otherwise imposed by the grammar. Scrambling as in (5) would be applied only for the purpose of bypassing the restrictions of MLC or Superiority, but not for the purpose of genuinely scrambling a specific item. Scrambling in (5) is completely neutralized since the scrambled item never stays in its scrambled position. Granted, you may think, but could it not be the case that wh-items are items that are scrambled anyway, just as pronouns are fronted in German? Here comes the empirical indication mentioned above: wh-items resist scrambling.

Unlike personal pronouns (6a,b), wh-pronouns are *not* fronted to a clause-internal position in German. This is expected since a wh-pronoun is indefinite, if it is not interrogative, and indefinites are preferably clause final in German. In fact, fronting them yields a result with judgements from marginal to deviant (6c). It does not matter how you interpret the pronoun *wer* – either as an in-situ interrogative or as an indefinite pronoun ('someone') – the judgements are the same.

(6)   a.   Es ist unklar, ob ihn$_i$ wer e$_i$ schockiert hat
             it is unclear whether him who shocked has
             'It is unclear whether someone shocked him'

       b.   *Wem* ist unklar, ob ihn$_i$ *wer* e$_i$ schockiert hat
             whom-DAT is unclear whether him who shocked has
             'For whom is it unclear who has shocked him'

       c. ??/* Wann hat *was*$_i$ wer e$_i$ beobachtet
             when has what who observed

       d.   Was$_i$ hat *wer* e$_i$ beobachtet
             what has who observed

       e.   [Was$_i$ *wer* e$_i$ beobachtet hat] ist unklar
             [what who observed has] is unclear

Hence, according to her assumption, wh-subjects that remain in-situ stay in a scrambled position, with scrambling being triggered by the d-linking feature. But, here is immediate counterevidence:

(i)   * A priest must never reveal what *who* has confessed to him
(ii)   Ein Pfarrer darf niemals preisgeben, was ihm *wer* gebeichtet hat
         a priest may never reveal what him-dat *who* confessed has

You may utter this sentence without any discourse-linking of *who* or *what* since it discusses a general property of priests. The common ground of the utterance may be empty with respect to sins, sinners and priests.

If the source for the missing MLC effect in (6d,e) is scrambling as in (6c), why is (6c) deviant but (6d,e) are not? If wh-items refuse to be scrambled (6c), why wouldn't they refuse scrambling in the derivation of (6d,e)? Of course you might try to find yet another excuse; for instance they might refuse scrambling only if their trip is doomed to end up in the scrambled position and if the wh-item would not step over to the wh-trail. But this is tinkering a way out rather than sculpting a satisfactory account since crucially, scrambling would not be caus-ally involved but would only provide an accidental sideline opening a technical back-door exit.

Scrambling is not a likely source for an adequate and successful solution for a simple reason. It necessarily remains completely silent on the contrasts with the examples in (2). This pattern is absent in OV, and this is evidence for the subject position as the crucial piece of the solution. In VO languages, the subject is obliga-torily placed into a functional spec position above the VP. In OV, the subject, just like any other argument of the verb, may remain within the domain of the head. So, if (2) reflects a ban against wh-in-situ in a spec position, this ban does not apply to VP-internal argument positions irrespective of their grammatical function.

In sum, the missing asymmetry in OV between object and subject in-situ is arguably not a by-product of scrambling. It is a reflex of the different structural status of the surface position of a subject in VO vs OV. The in-situ wh-subject in OV is a wh-item in a VP-internal position. In VO, the subject is in a func-tional spec position. The observation that a language with wh-subjects in-situ is also a language with scrambling is factually correct but explanatorily spurious. Scrambling is just another by-product of the head-final organization.

3.4.2   Wh-in-situ from the perspective of an OV clause structure

Imagine Chomsky's mother tongue had been German (or any other wh-movement OV language) when he was analysing the wh-in-situ patterns that led to his publication on the conditions on wh-movement (Chomsky 1973, 1977). He would have found no compelling reason to appeal to Superiority unless he had been aware of the English patterns. In this case, he would have been driven to real-ize that the English patterns are most likely just a parametric variant, namely a VO effect, rather than a universal setting of grammars. What would a minimally repre-sentative set of data have looked like for him? Table 3.1 summarizes the data.

The data for the pattern in row a. of table 3.1 have been introduced in the subsection above, with reference to Superiority and the MLC. When there is a subject–object asymmetry, this is a VO property and it follows from the obliga-tory requirement of placing the subject into a functional spec in VO, with subject and object ending up in different syntactic domains.

Table 3.1 *Synopsis of German–English wh-in-situ contrasts*

	English	German[33]	VO source	OV source
a. Wh-subject in-situ	*	√	subject in spec	subject in VP
b. Wh[$_{-why/-how}$] …why/ how…	*	√	scope domain	scope domain
c. why < how / how < why	*	*	semantic universal	semantic universal
d. X_{wh-i} … Y_{wh-j} e_j … e_i if X and Y are non-distinct	*	*	parsing	parsing

What is special about a wh-element in a functional spec position compared to an argument position within the VP? A wh-element in a functional spec position becomes an operator for this reason: as a potential operator element, the wh-item is turned into an active operator by virtue of occupying an operator position. In English, an in-situ wh-subject is a wh-element in a spec position because a subject is obligatorily assigned to the functional subject position. Hence, a wh-subject is automatically construed as an operator element since the position is the position for an operator.

Here are two pieces of evidence for the claim that a spec position is an operator position for a wh-element. One piece is the fact that a wh-item in an unequivocal spec position in German, namely the clause-initial spec position, is obligatorily interpreted as an operator (see the discussion of (2) in section 3.2.5). The interpretation as an indefinite pronoun is unavailable in this position, as discussed in detail by Pasch (1992). The second piece is a kind of 'amnesty' phenomenon that has been observed for English wh-subjects in-situ. This property is characteristic of operators.

(1)   a.   * I'd like to know where *who* hid it

       b.   (?) I'd like to know where *who* hid it *when*   (Chomsky 1981: 238;
                                                                  Kayne 1983: 235)

       c.   (?) What$_k$ did who$^{i/*j}$ reveal e_k about his^i mother   (Hornstein 1995:
                                                                  144; ex. 84d)

---

[33] The situation in Dutch is analogous to German (Haider 2008), modulo the recruitment of *er* (there):

(i)   (?) Ik weet niet, welke wijn *er wie* bestelde (checked with native informants in Antwerp)
          I know not which wine there who ordered

It is known that a lower, *properly licensed* wh-element mitigates the deviance of an in-situ *wh-subject* (1b) c-commanding it. Less well appreciated is the phenomenon illustrated by (1c). (1c) is unequivocal evidence that the property at stake for the wh-subject is its *operator status*. What do (1b) and (1c) have in common and what makes them different from (1a)?

(1a) is the standard case of deviance for a wh-subject in-situ. Why should the occurrence of a lower wh-item matter? It matters if the lower item, namely *when* in (1b), is dependent on the higher wh-element. If this dependency is construed as an operator-variable dependency, the wh-subject in (1b) performs an operator function which it does not in (1a). An uncontroversial instance of an operator function is the binding of a pronominal variable in (1c). Note that (1c) is deviant if *his* is not interpreted as a bound variable but as a deictic pronoun. In this case, the operator quality of the wh-subject is not satisfied.

The rows (b) and (c) in table 3.1 deal with the peculiarity of two adverbial wh-items, namely *why* and *how*. Unlike other adverbial wh-items (e.g. *when, where*), they must not be left in-situ in English. This is not the case in German or in other OV languages like Japanese,[34] Dutch, Yiddish:

(2) a. Who left *when /*why /*how*?

  b. Dare-ga *naze* soko-ni itta no?   *Japanese*
      who-NOM *why* there-to went Q-PRT   (Saito 1994: 195)

  c. Wie heeft het *waarom / hoe* gedaan?   *Dutch*
      who has it why / how done
      'Who did it why / how?'

  d. Ver hot *farvos / vi azoy* gezungen?   *Yiddish*
      who has why / how sung   (Diesing 2001, ex. 8,9)

  e. Wer hat *warum / wie* gesungen?   *German*
      who has why / how sung

There is a robust contrast in English in particular, and in VO languages in general, between in-situ manner and reason wh-expressions on the one hand and in-situ place and time wh-adverbials on the other. This contrast is absent in OV.

---

[34] In Japanese, as expected, a wh-subject may be dependent on an object fronted (by scrambling), as in (i). A wh-subject combined with *why* is perfect, as in German. Thanks to Naoki Suzumura for re-checking the data.

  (i)   Nani-o *dare*-ga katta no?
         what-acc who-nom bought Q-PRT
         'What did who buy?'

  (ii)   Dare-ga *naze* kita no?
         who-nom *why* came Q-PRT
         'Who came why?'

(3)   a.   Who leaves *when*? Who lives *where*?
        b.   * Who leaves *why*? *Who lived *how*?

What is special about *why* and *how*? Szabolcsi and Zwarts (1993) noted that the difference is best characterized as one in terms of the *semantic type* of the wh-operator. *Why* and *how* are *not* ranging over *individuals* but over *higher-order entities*.[35] *Where* and *when*, on the other hand, are 'ordinary' individual type operators, ranging over individual locations and individual points of time, respectively. So, what is special about higher order operators that could account for the observed OV vs VO patterns? It is the surface position of the in-situ adverbial. What – in descriptive terms – is the difference between the pattern in (2b–e) and the patterns in (2a) and (2b)?

In the former patterns, the wh-operator *precedes* the (head of the) VP. In the latter patterns, the wh-adverbial follows. And what does this mean in structural terms? The crucial difference is the difference in the c-command domain of the wh-operator. Semantically, the c-command domains are mapped on the scope domains. In (2b–e), the wh-operator c-commands the head of the VP, in (2a) and in (3b) it does not.[36] If we assume that higher order operators need to c-command the (head of the) phrase that denotes their semantic target in order to acquire the required scope over its target domain, then, in VO and OV, a higher order wh-element must precede. For VO, the only option to achieve precedence is to move to the spec of C because there is no room for a wh-adverbial in the region between C° and the left VP-boundary, for independent reasons. In OV, there is room. This difference is a difference between head-initial and head-final projections. Head-initial ones are compact. So, the contrast is ultimately a consequence of a property of head-initial structures. Owing to their compactness, they do not provide the required room for placing the adverbials in a preverbal position.

What will happen if there is more than a single higher-order wh-operator? The prediction for VO is clear. There is no way to satisfy the c-command requirements of each of the candidates simultaneously since there is only a single empty place

---

[35] 'Higher-order entities are entities of a *higher type*': this refers to the kind of denotation ('type') a category is semantically assigned to. 'Higher types' are types that are more complex than the type of an *individual entity*. Example of a basic type: FUGU denotes a set of individual entities, namely the set of fugus in a given context. 'Poisonous' refers to a property, that is, a *set of sets*, namely all (sub)sets of entities that have the property of being poisonous (fugus, vipers, toadstools, …). This is a higher-order type, i.e. more complex than a set of individual entities: {i, j, k, ….} vs {{i, j, k, …}, {l, m, n,…}, … }.

[36] Be aware that this statement presupposes that postverbal adverbials are embedded in the VP, rather than adjoined, as in: '(They told me that he would talk gently to Mary) and [$_{VP}$ talked *gently* to Mary] he has.'

in spec and no room elsewhere, in positions preceding the VP. So, the clause will
be deviant (4a,b). But why is the corresponding clause deviant in OV as well, and
– bold prediction! – in fact in any language of the world?

(4)   a. * *Why* did he fix it *how*?

       b. * *How* did he fix it *why*?

       c. * *Weshalb* hat er es *wie* repariert?
          why has he it how fixed

       d. * *Wie* hat er es *weshalb* repariert?
          how has he it why fixed

The descriptive generalization is this: a higher order quantifier cannot be
construed as dependent on a higher order quantifier. This construal would
entail a distribution function over sets of sets rather than sets of individuals.
In other words, the brain seems to have no problem when mapping individuals onto sets, but it is not prepared to generate this mapping with sets, both
as values and as range elements. This accounts for the difference between (5a)
and (5b):

(5)   a. *Wer* hat es *warum / weshalb* (nicht) repariert?
          who has it why / why[37] (not) fixed

       b. * *Wie* hat er es *warum / weshalb* (nicht) repariert?
          how has he it why / why (not) fixed

If you double check on this empirical generalization, you should be aware that
for some people *how* is easily type-shiftable into *what way* or *in which way*, and
the latter versions denote individual-type operators, ranging over a set of different ways. Reinhart (1998: 31) notes the following non-shifted, that is, standard
judgement that illustrates this difference between *how* and *what way*.

(6)   Who fainted, when you attacked him/whom *what way/*how*?

Finally, the incompatibility of *why* and *how* teaches us an important lesson on
the licensing relation between the in-situ wh-elements and the moved item. What,
in your opinion, licenses a third or fourth or any other wh-item in-situ, as for
instance in (7)?

(7)   Who fixed *what when* for *whom*?

---

[37] *Weshalb* (lit. who-for) and *warum* are synonymous. Both mean 'why'.

You might be tempted to say that what holds for the first in-situ element will hold for any other in-situ element, namely, that it is licensed by the element that has moved.[38] Is there another way of looking at this situation, too? Your first generalization might be formulated like this:

> **G1** = An in-situ wh-element is licensed if it is linked to a c-commanding wh-item in spec C.

Another way of looking at (13) would be this:

> **G2** = An in-situ wh-element is licensed if it is linked to a c-commanding licensed wh-element.

According to the first generalization (G1), all wh-elements in-situ in (7) would depend on *who*. Under the second generalization, the third wh-element in (7) would depend on the preceding one, namely *what* and the fourth one would be dependent on the third one, and so on. At first glance, these generalizations seem to be equivalent, but this impression is misleading. What is the difference and how can we decide which one is the correct one? There is a crucial difference that comes into play once we combine *why* and *how*:

(8)   a. Wh$_x$ ... why ... how   ['wh$_x$' = any individual level type wh-element]

        b. Why ... wh$_x$ ... how

According to G1, (8a) is grammatical and (8b) is ungrammatical. In (8a), both *why* and *how* are licensed by the 'wh$_x$' in spec C. In (8b), however, *why* in spec C would have to license both the 'wh$_x$' and *how*. The latter instance of licensing is illegal since the licenser and one of the licensees (namely *how*) are higher-type wh-elements.

G2 produces exactly the inverse grammaticality assignments: (8a) is predicted to be ungrammatical because the last wh-item, namely *how* would have to be licensed by the preceding, c-commanding *why*. This is illegal since both are higher order type wh-elements. (8b), on the other hand, is well formed since 'wh$_x$' is licensed by *why* in spec C, and *how* is licensed by the preceding, c-commanding and licensed wh$_x$.

The different predictions cannot be checked in VO languages since the structures we have to test involve a *why* or *how* in situ, and this structure is deviant in

---

[38] For an adequate semantic treatment of multiple wh-constructions see Reinhart (1998). She argues for interpreting the dependency relations between the wh-elements in terms of choice functions.

VO independently.[39] But, fortunately, there is German (and other OV languages), and it provides the evidence needed:

(9)   a. Warum hat man was /*das wie organisiert?
           why has one what / this how organized

       b. Wie hat man was /*das warum organisiert?
           how has one what / this why organized

       c. Wie hat man wann /*warum was organisiert?
           how has one when / why what organized

       d. Waarom heeft men wat /*dat hoe geregeld?   *Dutch*
           why has one what / this how organized

The data in (9) clearly support G2. *Why* and *how* may indeed coexist in a single clause, but only if they do not depend on a higher order wh-item. Let us examine (9a). The first in-situ wh-element *was* (what) is licensed by the fronted wh-item *warum* (why). The third wh-element *wie* (how) is licensed by the preceding (and c-commanding) licensed wh-element *was*. Hence there is no immediate dependency between two higher order wh-items.

   This set of affairs is expected if G2 holds, but crucially not if G1 is applied. G1 would rule out all four sentences in (9). (9d), the Dutch counterpart of (9a), shows that G2 is, as expected, not specific for German but likely to be representative of OV structures in general.

3.5   Is the *'d-linking'* effect a *discourse-linking* effect?

There is a by now well known difference between bare wh-elements and phrasal wh-items, that is, phrases that contain more than merely the wh-element. 'D-linked' is the technical term for what Pesetsky (1987) takes to be 'discourse-linked'. But, in fact, d-linking is a technical concept that just discriminates between bare wh-items (1a,c) and phrasal wh-expressions (1b,d):

---

[39] The deviance is likely to be somewhat mitigated by a variant of the amnesty effect referred to above:

(i)   (??)Why did you fix what how?

There is a single chain of licensing relations. *Why* licenses *what* and *what* licenses *how*, and they are combined into a single, complex interpretation function. So, if you judge (i) less deviant than a corresponding clause with *the car* in place of *what*, this may be the result of a repair attempt that transfers the c-command requirement from *how*, to the licensing chain of *how*.

(1)   a. * What did *who* eat?

        b.   What did *which gaijin* eat?

        c. * Mary asked what$_i$ *who* read e$_i$ (Pesetsky 1987:104)

        d.   Mary asked what$_i$ [*which men*] read e$_i$?   (Pesetsky 1987:104)

Which gaijin or *which men* refers to a contextually established set of individuals that have the property of being 'Gaijin' or 'man' in the given context. In other words, (1b) presupposes that there are foreigners in Japan and (1d) presupposes that the common ground of the present discourse contains men. *Who*, on the other hand, is contextually unrestricted. It only bears a sortal restriction, namely that it ranges over animate entities. However, d-linking is not the key to a perfect solution of the problem posed by (1), as will become transparent immediately.

In Pesetsky's (1987) account, (2b,d) are ruled out by stipulating *how many* as inherently unable to be d-linked. Note that this complicates and potentially voids the notion of d-linking. *Which customers* asks for a property of the set of customers in the given context, and so does *how many customers*. For (2a), the answer may be: 'The Japanese-speaking customers bought the book with Fugu recipes.' A possible answer for (2b) is 'The book with Fugu recipes was purchased by three customers.' *How many* asks for the cardinality of a set. A possible answer is a number. *Which N* can be answered by naming an individual or a set of individuals. This seems to be the relevant distinction for (2), namely a distinction in terms of the semantic type category.

(2)   a.   What /which book did *which customers* buy?

        b. * What /which book did *how many customers* buy?

        c.   I need to know *how many people* voted for whom

        d. * I need to know whom$_i$ [*how many people*] voted for e$_i$
                                                              (Pesetsky 1987:107)

        e.   Ich muss wissen, wen$_i$ wieviele Leute e$_i$ gewählt haben
             I must know whom how-many people voted-for have

If the type category is the key for understanding the difference between (2a) and (2b), we have to expect that *which N*, but not *how many N*, may be licensed in-situ by a higher-order wh-item:

(3)   a.   Why did you talk to which people?

        b. * Why did you talk to how many people?

        c.   Warum hast Du mit welchen /*wie vielen Leuten gesprochen?
             why have you with which / how many people talked

First, the contrast in (3a,b) confirms that *how many* is a higher-order wh-type since it must not depend on a higher-order wh-operator. As expected, this holds for German (3c) as well. An appropriate answer to (3a) could be this: 'I talked to my immediate neighbours, because ..., and to my parents because ..., and to ...' An answer to (3b) would be of a different type. It would have to sound like 'I talked to a group of 5 people, because ..., and to a group of 9, because ..., but not to a group of 13, because I suffer from triskaidekaphobia.'

Which N is processed as an individual type operator. You may answer the wh-phrase *which book?* with *this one* or *the one on the table*. Semantically, *which* is an operator that binds an NP-*internal* variable. *How many*, however, is a higher-order operator. Its range is a set of sets. Your answer to *how many books?* is the cardinality of the respective set, that is, a number. Therefore, just like *how* itself, *how many* or any other combination with *how* (*how much, how often, how high,* ...), these higher-order wh-items cannot depend on a wh-item which is higher type itself (3b).

The contrasts in (1a–d) are contrasts between a bare wh-item and a phrase that contains a wh-item. The bare wh-item is a wh-item in a functional spec position. This accounts for its special syntactic behaviour. The wh-item in the subject wh-phrase in (2b,d) crucially is not the subject of the clause. The subject is the whole phrase. Therefore we do not expect that a bare wh-item and a phrase-internal one behave alike. Note that this involves a structural difference and that recourse to a pragmatic/semantic notion is therefore not necessary.

D-linking does not provide the appropriate partitioning. Both in the case of *which* N and in the case of *how many* N, the DP consists of a wh-item and a restrictor (i.e. the NP). The restrictor triggers the presupposition of a reference set in each case. This is d-linking. However, the difference between *how many* and *which* is not one of d-linking but one of the semantic type of the wh-items involved.

As for the contrast between (2d) and (2e), this is parallel to what we already have seen for *how* and *why* and reflects an OV/VO-triggered difference. The precise details of the domain requirements that are ultimately responsible will not be worked out in detail here (see Haider 2004b).

Finally, the difference between a phrase-internal wh-item and a bare wh-item shows in yet another construction. In German, a *was für N* phrase (lit.: 'what for N', meaning: 'what kind of N') may be split by wh-movement. *Was* is moved and the rest of the phrase is stranded (4b). Splitting is an alternative to pied-piping the whole phrase (4a).

(4)   a. [*Was für Autos*] hast du wie / warum repariert?
        [what for cars] have you how / why fixed

b. *Was* hast du [*für Autos*] wann /*wie /*warum repariert?
   what have you [for cars] when / how / why fixed

Was in (4b) is a bare wh-operator ranging over kinds, that is, properties of sets, and therefore it is a higher order operator (see Pafel 1996). So, as expected,[40] it is incompatible with higher order in-situ wh-elements directly dependent on it. This explains the deviance in (4b).

In (4a), the expression *was für Autos* (what for cars; 'what kind of cars') is a phrasal wh-expression, and the phrase itself provides the range set for *was*, namely *Autos* (cars). So, the expression as a whole is interpretable analogously to 'which cars' and this is a wh-expression that can be construed as ranging over a set of individuals, namely a set of cars. Hence it is a licit licensing element for an in-situ higher order wh-element.

3.6   A residue of *Superiority*?

If superiority (or, alternatively, a minimal link condition, or a shortest move requirement) is a constraint of core syntax, one of its clearest contexts of application is one in which the wh-elements involved are contained in separate clausal domains. Data like those in (1) are usually cited as cardinal evidence for this kind of superiority phenomenon.

(1)   a.   Who persuaded who(m) [to visit you]?
        b. * Who$_i$ did you persuade who(m) [to visit e$_i$]?
        c.   Who$_i$ did you persuade her [to visit e$_i$] ?
        d.   Who$_i$ did you persuade e$_i$ [to visit who(m)] ?

From a derivational perspective, the offending property of (1b) is this: a wh-element from a lower clause is moved across a wh-element of the higher clause. In other words: the more distant wh-item is moved, and the wh-element closer to the target position is left in-situ. In a representational view, the trace of the moved wh-phrase is c-commanded by a closer potential antecedent (i.e. the in-situ wh-element). So, in any case, a minimal link requirement seems to provide the empirically correct distinctions.

But there are facts that are less easy to handle. Some of them are known at least since Fiengo's (1980) detailed study, and Pesetsky (1987) accounted for them in terms of his d-linking proposal:

---

[40] I gratefully acknowledge that Gereon Müller (pers. comm.) made me aware of the consequence of the approach developed above for the *was-für* construction.

(2)   a.   Who$_i$ did you introduce [*which* people] to e$_i$?
        b. * Who$_i$ did you introduce *who* to e$_i$?
        c.   What$_i$ did you tell [*which* people] about e$_i$?
        d. * What$_i$ did you tell *who* about e$_i$?   (Fiengo 1980:126)

The contrast between (2a,c) and (2b,d), respectively, is less easy to reconcile with
a minimal link condition on movement or on the antecedent-trace relation. (2b,d)
obviously violate superiority, because there is an alternative derivation that obeys
the minimal link condition. The very same consideration should rule out (2a,c),
however. The crucial differentiating factor for the sentences in (2) seems to be
the structural difference between the wh-phrases involved. Fiengo (1980: 125)
not only contrasts bare wh-pronouns with DP-internal ones (as in 2) but also with
PP-internal ones in contrast with P-stranding (as in (3)).

(3)   a.   What$_i$ did you give e$_i$ to whom ?
        b.   [To whom]$_i$ did you give what e$_i$?
        c. (*) Who(m)$_i$ did you give what [to e$_i$]?

The pattern in (3b) matches the patterns in (2a,c) in a relevant aspect: when the
wh-elements are categorically distinct, there is no superiority effect attested. This
is unexpected in a minimal link scenario. Category distinctions should not matter because the crucial property, namely minimal link, is category independent.
What matters for a minimal link algorithm is just the property of being a wh-
phrase, that is, a phrase with a wh-feature that needs to be checked or licensed.
The type (3c) is hard to file since the judgements in the literature differ.[41] If the
difference between *who* and *what* is perceived as a formal difference, it should
be acceptable.

    German is particularly instructive in this respect because the distinctions are
more fine grained since bare wh-elements can be distinguished in terms of case.[42]
Crucially, apparent superiority effects arise only with wh-elements that are *non-
distinct* in form, as in (4a,e), but not if the form is different (4b,c,d).

(4)   a. * Wen$_i$ hat er denn *wen* gebeten [davon e$_i$ abzuhalten] ?
                who-ACC has he PRT whom-ACC asked [from-it to-keep-away]

        b.   Was$_i$ hat er denn *wen* gebeten, [für ihn e$_i$ zu erledigen] ?
                what-ACC has he PRT whom-ACC asked [for him to-carry-out]

---

[41] In Fiengo's judgement (1980: 123) it is starred. This judgement is not shared uniformly,
though. Culicover (1997: 220, ex. 2b) does not judge (3c) as deviant.

[42] For a more detailed discussion see Fanselow (1991: 330), Müller (1995: 323f.) and
Haider (2004b).

    c.   *Wohin$_i$* hat er denn *wem* versprochen [die Schlüssel e$_i$ zu legen]?
       where$_{PP}$ has he PRT whom-DAT promised [the keys to put]

    d.   *Wem$_i$* hat er denn *wen* gebeten [die Nachricht e$_i$ zu übermitteln]?
       whom-DAT has he PRT whom-ACC asked [the message to transmit-to]

    e.   *Wer$_i$* glaubt er/*wer* wohl [dass e$_i$ ihm seine Arbeit hier bezahlen werde]?
       who-NOM thinks he/who PRT [that e$_i$ him his work here pay will]

The wh-elements in the unacceptable examples (4a) and (4e) are identical in form. In (4b), only the form (and consequently the denotation: animate vs inanimate) differs, but the case is the same, as in (4a). This is sufficient, as the acceptability contrast shows.[43] As expected, category differences (4c) or case-driven form differences (4d) suffice, too. Note, however, that a case difference is not enough, if the forms do not differ (5b). For the neuter pronoun, there is no case distinction between nominative and accusative in German, and a covert case difference is not enough to save acceptability (5b). Note that this is independent of the wh-status of the *was* in the matrix. (5b) is unacceptable even with *was* construed as an indefinite pronoun.

(5)   a.   *Wen$_i$ /was$_i$* hat dieser Umstand ihn bewogen [für diese Aufgabe e$_i$ auszuwählen]?
         whom-ACC / what-ACC has this circumstance him prompted [for this task to-choose]

---

[43] Fanselow (1997) judges the following example as deviant. It involves extraction out of a finite complement clause:

   (i)   ?* *Wen* glaubte *wer*, [dass der Peter ihr e$_i$ vorstellte]?
        whom-ACC believed who-NOM, that the Peter-NOM her-DAT e$_i$ introduced
        'Whom did who believe that Peter introduced to her?'

The acceptability of this example can easily be improved, though. If the matrix clause has an overt right boundary verb, and if the forms of the fronted wh-item and the matrix wh-element are clearly distinct, and if, eventually, a discourse particle typical for questions (*denn*) is inserted into the matrix clause, then the pattern becomes inconspicuous in the variants of German that tolerate extraction out of a finite complement clause:

   (ii)   *Womit$_i$* hat denn *wer* gedacht, [dass sie es e$_i$ geöffnet habe]?
        what-with has PRT who thought [that she it opened has]
        'What has who thought that she has opened it with?'

   (iii)   *Woraus* hat man denn *wem* erzählt, [dass sie es e$_i$ geformt habe]?
        what-out-of has one PRT whom told [that she it formed has]
        'What have they told whom that she has made it from?'

b. *Wen$_i$ /*was$_i$* hat *was* ihn bewogen [für diese e$_i$ Aufgabe auszuwählen]?

whom-ACC / what-ACC has what-NOM him prompted [for this task to-choose]

'Whom / what did what / something prompt you to choose for this task?'

What these (un)acceptability patterns point to is not so much a grammar-based constraint but a processing restriction. Identity of form (despite differences in grammatical functions) is not a plausible parameter of a principle of syntax but a factor that is obviously relevant for processing. Hence, under these circumstances, the apparent superiority effects can be reconstructed as an impediment of a processing routine: the parser does not accept two identical forms in the buffer that compete for an extraction site. The antecedent-gap computation algorithm halts at the very moment in which a wh-element is encountered that is identical in form with the wh-element whose antecedent-gap relation is still under computation.

The sheer identity of form in a potential trace position of the fronted wh-element seems to be an insurmountable obstacle for the parser in its successful scouting for the wh-movement path. The parsing algorithm probes for the trace of the first wh-element. The second, non-distinct wh-element is identical in form, but it must be kept distinct. This seems to interfere with the search for the trace of the moved wh-item. The in-situ item needs to be blocked from being taken as a closer potential antecedent of the trace, but since it is identical in form with the real antecedent, this makes the parse crash.

The antecedent-trace relation on the one hand, and the binding relation between a moved wh-element and the in-situ one, on the other hand, is formally not distinct, whence the breakdown of the processing algorithm. In other words, the processing conflict is this: when the processor has an uncompleted chain in its buffer, it cannot assign a *second, identical* item it encounters to a different chain, but it is bound to automatically analyse the second item as a trace copy belonging to the current chain, with the result that in the examples discussed above, the chain structure becomes deviant.

3.7   Summary

German is a wh-movement OV language that fronts (or pied-pipes) a single wh-phrase. The following contrasts between German and English are arguably collateral effects of the OV vs VO contrasts:

- no subject–object asymmetry for long-distance wh-movement (no *that-t*-effect)
- no subject–object asymmetry for in-situ wh-elements (superiority)
- no general restriction against higher type wh-elements in-situ (i.e. *why, how*)

The absence of the subject–object asymmetry known from VO languages is both immediate and corroborative evidence for the different structural status of subjects in the German clause structure in comparison to the English one. The following constructions involve wh-movement to the clause-initial spec position in German:

- declarative V2 clauses,
- wh-interrogative clauses, as main clauses or as dependent clauses,
- relative clauses and free relative clauses,
- comparative and equative clauses.

Partial wh-movement (WC, CC) is in free variation with the matrix wh-movement construction. It is limited to a small class of matrix verbs, however. The CC is restricted to word-level wh-expressions. This is arguably a by-product of the c-command requirement that holds between the higher and the lower copy.

4

Targeting left: clause-internal word order and word order variation

4.1   Introduction

First, the word order variation usually referred to as *scrambling* in German is typical for OV languages. In fact, it is not a holistic property of a language but a property of head-*final* phrases. German with its mixed headedness is a good test case. Head-initial phrases (e.g. NPs) are ordered strictly, while head-final phrases (AP, VP) are the territory of scrambling. Scrambling is a property of all Germanic OV languages, but its domain of application differs according to the grammar-specific features of the individual languages. Dutch, for instance, does not allow change to the relative order of DP arguments, but a PP object may be scrambled across another object.

Second, all Germanic languages front pronouns. The target for pronoun fronting is the leftmost position of their respective domain. Pronoun fronting is not a subinstance of scrambling, although the order variation it produces may be analogous to scrambling. Pronoun fronting, for example, must not change the relative order of the pronouns. In principle, scrambling produces all possible permutations of arguments. In the Scandinavian languages, *object shift* is a device of the grammar that apparently allows the movement of an object pronoun out of the VP, but object shift in general must not change the relative order of the objects (Thráinsson 2001). This is a clear difference between object shift and scrambling.

Scrambling is still a controversial issue in grammar theory. As for the modelling of this phenomenon of OV grammars, by now all theoretically available options within generative theorizing have found their (at least part-time) advocates. Scrambling has been taken to be the result of movement (majority opinion), but also the result of base generating the word order variation (minority opinion). Movement approaches have been formulated as adjunction operations or as movement to functional spec positions. The latter implementation has led to various recalcitrant questions (e.g. What kind of functional projections? What kind of functional heads?) and especially to the fruitless search for a *grammatical* trigger of scrambling.

This chapter will present the empirical background of scrambling and pronoun distribution in German, evaluate the major approaches to the grammar-theoretical modelling of scrambling, and present an analysis of scrambling that characterizes it as part of the system's potential of an OV grammar that is exploited, but not triggered, by information structuring. Unsurprisingly, this is an analysis that has been put forth by the author (Haider and Rosengren 2003).

4.2   Word order of pronominals

Unstressed pronouns in German – as in many other languages – have distributional properties of their own that differ from non-pronominal DPs:

- earliness: preference for the left edge of their locality domain
- rigid serialization template: in German, *nominative* before *accusative* before *dative*[1]
- serialization restrictions with respect to particles sensitive to information structure and higher adverbials (propositional attitude and frame adverbials).

4.2.1   Earliness

Unstressed pronouns (especially personal and reflexive pronouns) tend to be fronted. In German, a pronoun is fronted to a position following the topmost functional head, that is, to a position following the complementizer (1a) or the finite verb (1b), or it stays put (1c). The target position is in the area between the functional head position and the highest argument position. In Germanic linguistics, the theory-neutral term for the area immediately following the 'second' position (i.e. the V2 position or, alternatively, the C° position) is the *Wackernagel*[2] *position*.

(1)   a. dass [*es* jeder heimlich zurückstellte]   *German*
          that [it-ACC everyone secretly back-put]
          'that everyone put it back secretly'

      b. Zurück stellte *es* jeder heimlich
          back put it everyone secretly

---

[1] Dutch has the same order restriction: nominative before direct object before indirect object.

[2] The term honours the grammarian Wilhelm Wackernagel (1806–1869), who was the first to point out the importance of the 'second' position (in today's terminology: the functional head position of the fronted finite verb in Germanic languages) for the description of word order in historical stages of Germanic languages.

    c.   dass jeder *es* heimlich zurückstellte

    d. * dat het$_i$ iedereen [e$_i$ voorzichtig terugzette]   *Dutch*
        that it everyone [carefully back-put]

    e.   that everyone carefully [put it$_i$ back e$_i$]

    f.   that everyone carefully [put back the book/*it]

The German example (1a) is representative of the distribution of unstressed pronouns, like personal and reflexive pronouns in any grammatical function. They are all preferably fronted to the Wacknernagel position.

In Dutch, the domain of fronting is more narrow than in German: object pronoun fronting may in general not cross an unergative subject (1d).[3] In English, pronoun fronting is obligatory in the VP, relative to the particle of a particle verb (1e vs 1f). In the continental Scandinavian languages (2), there is a fronting process that is contingent on verb movement ('object shift'). If the verbal head of the VP is fronted, this apparently enlarges the domain of fronting for pronouns. Since, in this case, the position of pronouns following the (fronted) verb precedes clause-internal adverbials and negation, the pronouns end up preceding these elements. This is the so-called obligatory *object-shift* configuration (cf. Holmberg 1999; Vikner 1994). The common trait of all these fronting processes is this: pronouns are fronted to the left edge of their maximal domain of reordering. This domain is not identical across languages, however.

In spite of the cross-linguistically apparently diverse patterns, the serialization of unstressed pronouns in the Germanic languages is determined uniformly. The seemingly diverse patterns are the parametric diversification of a single condition: if a pronoun can/must be fronted, it is fronted to the left edge of the minimal domain of its licensing V° head, without crossing the overt head position. Once it is acknowledged that German and Dutch may differ minimally in the structure of the VP with respect to the position of the transitive subject argument (due to the absence of morphological case in Dutch), it is possible to provide a uniform descriptive generalization for the range of fronting in a Germanic OV language: pronoun fronting targets the highest accessible position *in the domain*

---

[3] Note, however, that the pronoun *zich* (him/herself), as the reflexive object of an *inherently reflexive* verb, may be fronted across a transitive subject according to the standard Dutch grammar *ANS*:

  (i)   Op deze plaats schijnt *zich* gisteren een meisje opgehangen te hebben
                                           (*ANS* 1997: 1314)
        on this spot seems herself yesterday a girl hanged to have
  (ii)   Hier heeft *zich* een drama afgespeeld   (*ANS* 1997: 1315)
        here has itself a drama played (note: 'play itself' = take place)

of V°. The languages mentioned above differ with respect to the architecture of the V° domain for principled reasons.

In German, the left edge of this V° domain is arguably the left edge of the VP that is selected by the functional head that accommodates the finite verb in V2 or by the complementizer.[4] In Dutch, the left edge of the corresponding domain apparently follows the position of the transitive subject since Dutch arguably has a more complex VP structure as a trade-off effect of its lack of a morphological case system. So, the target position of pronoun fronting is lower. There are however data in Dutch descriptive grammars that show that non-referential pronouns (e.g. inherent reflexives) may be fronted across an unergative subject (see footnote 3).

In VO languages, pronouns targeting the left edge of the VP end up in positions immediately following the V° head. Pronoun fronting does not cross the licensing head. In the Scandinavian languages, there is an additional possibility, namely *object shift*. The pronouns may be fronted to the left edge of the projection headed by V, provided that the *overt* head of the VP is not crossed. Processes that front the lexical verb (V-second, topicalization) enlarge the domain of pronoun fronting (Holmberg 1999) in Scandinavian languages, as illustrated in (2a).

(2)   a. Studenterne læste$_j$ *den$_i$/*artiklen$_i$* alligevel ikke [$_{VP}$ e$_j$ e$_i$]   *Danish*
            students read it/article-the after-all not

        b. Studenterne læste$_j$ alligevel ikke [$_{VP}$ e$_j$ *artiklen/*den*]
            students read after-all not [article-the/it]

A pronoun is *obligatorily* fronted across pre-VP adverbials and negation, if the VP does not contain any lexical material to the left of the base position of the pronoun.[5] Note that pronominal object shift in Scandinavian and pronoun fronting in German produce a word order variation that is taken advantage of by identical semantic interface conditions (see the following section). A common trait of all pronoun fronting processes – in English (1e) as well as in Scandinavian languages, and in fact in all Germanic languages – is the conservation of the canonical relative order. Pronoun fronting must not change the relative order of argumental pronouns in Scandinavian languages.

---

[4] Note that this interpretation is the author's view and not generally assumed. The majority prefers an interpretation in which the 'midfield' (i.e. the part of the clause between C°/V2 and the clause-final verbs) consists of the VP embedded under a cascade of functional projections. In this interpretation, pronoun fronting must be either movement to a higher spec position or a kind of clitic movement process that adjoins the fronted pronoun to a higher functional head position.

[5] This is the case if the verbal head is fronted to V2 and no other elements in the VP (stranded particle, preceding argument, etc.) intervene between V° and the pronoun.

4.2.2   *Fronted pronouns: a case for the syntax–semantics interface*

In German, the distributional restrictions for fronted pronouns differ from those for scrambled non-pronominal DPs. Information structuring particles like *ja* or *doch* (1), or 'light negation',[6] may precede scrambled DPs, but they must not precede fronted pronominals (see Haider 2006). In other words, fronted pronouns must precede these particles, full DPs may precede or follow. Is this a specifically structure-based or just a construal-based difference, or maybe both?

(1)   a.   dass unter diesen Umständen *sie* ja/doch keiner erreichen könnte
          that under these circumstances her PRT/PRT nobody reach could
          'that under these circumstances, nobody could reach her'

      b.   * dass unter diesen Umständen ja/doch *sie* keiner erreichen könnte

      c.   dass unter diesen Umständen ja/doch *die Frau* keiner erreichen könnte
          that under these circumstances PRT/PRT the woman nobody reach could
          'that under these circumstances, nobody could reach the woman'

      d.   dass unter diesen Umständen *die Frau* ja/doch keiner erreichen könnte

      e.   Ob *sie* nicht jemand rechtzeitig erreicht hat?
          whether her not someone on-time reached has
          'Could it be that someone has not reached her on time?'

      f.   Ob nicht *die Frau/*sie* jemand rechtzeitig erreicht hat?[7]
          whether not the woman/her someone on-time reached has?
          'Could it be that someone has not reached the woman/her on time?'

Both the pronoun or the full DP may be placed before the particle, either directly after the complementizer or after an adverbial (1a,d), but only the full DP may alternatively follow the particle (1c vs 1b). If a particle of the kind mentioned above precedes, the result is ungrammatical for a pronominal but the very same order is unproblematic for a non-pronominal DP. In (1), in each case, the object precedes the subject. Hence the object has been fronted in each case.

---

[6] 'Light negation' is rhetoric negation and different from sentence negation ('Wouldn't you agree that … ?'). It is licit only in non-asserted clauses (i.e. conditionals, indirect questions). Semantically, it does not negate the clause. (1e) does not assert that 'she was not reached'. It means: 'Could it not be the case that …'.

[7] The variant with the pronoun is of course grammatical with a different structure and reading, namely, with *nicht* adjoined to *sie* as phrasal negation, i.e. 'not her, but someone else'.

Here is evidence for the interface nature of the constraint. The following examples show that the restriction against pronouns in the position that c-commands the particles, including light negation, is independent of fronting. It holds in the base position, too. An unstressed pronominal object is unacceptable in a base position (2a). Stressed ones behave like lexical DPs.

(2)   a. dass ja doch irgendwer *die Frau/*sie* gesehen hat
             that PRT PRT someone the woman/her seen has
             'that someone has seen her/the woman after all'

     b. dass *sie/die Frau* ja doch irgendwer gesehen hat
             that her/the woman PRT PRT someone seen has

The contrast between (2a) and (2b) is parallel to the contrast in (1), hence it is independent of scrambling. What is the source of the constraint against pronouns in the domain of these particles? It is a pragmatic one, namely the *information structure* (IS) effect of these particles. They separate the topic domain (left) from the comment domain (right).[8] The crucial property of pronouns is this: pronouns are *inherently topical* by virtue of their antecedent-dependent bound interpretation. Full DPs may be topical or not. Reinhart (1995) suggests a criterion for differentiating, namely this one: cataphoric pronouns refer to *topics* only. In the following example (3), the cataphoric *er* (he) relates to *Max*. So *Max* must be topical, and if topicality is at issue for the serialization of pronouns relative to IS-particles, we predict also for full DPs that the co-referent DP must precede the particle, simply because it is topical.

(3)   a. Da er[i] Japanisch spricht, wird jetzt Max[i] seine Gäste *doch* auf Japanisch begrüßen
             since he Japanese speaks will now Max his guests PRT in Japanese welcome
             'Since he speaks Japanese, Max will now welcome his guests in Japanese after all'

     b. ? Da er[i] Japanisch spricht, wird jetzt *doch* Max[i] seine Gäste auf Japanisch begrüßen
             'Since he speaks Japanese, after all Max will now welcome his guests in Japanese'

---

[8] The 'comment domain' properly includes the domain of assertion, but is not identical with it. Clear evidence is the fact that sentence adverbials follow the particles, but they are not asserted.

   (i)   Da hat ihn *ja leider* niemand gekannt
          there has him PRT unfortunately nobody known
   (ii)   * Da hat ihn *leider ja* niemand gekannt

    c.   Da er[i] Japanisch spricht, frage ich mich, ob das Max[i] nicht lesen sollte (*light negation*)

        since he Japanese speaks ask I myself whether this Max not read should

        'Since he speaks Japanese, I wonder whether Max shouldn't read it'

    d. ? Da er[i] Japanisch spricht, frage ich mich, ob das nicht Max[i] lesen sollte (*light negation*)

        since he Japanese speaks ask I myself whether this not Max read should

The examples in (3) illustrate that a topical DP just like a pronoun precedes these particles (including light negation). (3b,d) are pragmatically odd,[9] but otherwise well formed. Would the correlation with topicality justify the assumptions of a *categorical* position for a topic, as Frey (2004) suggested? He argues for a functional topic position right below the clause-initial functional projection. Fanselow (2003, section 4) reviews Frey's data basis in detail and arrives at the opposite conclusion, namely, that '*there is no evidence in favour of the structurally distinct topic position*' and that the adduced evidence '*can be explained semantically*':[10] a topic interpretation is unavailable for DPs in the domain of elements that separate topics (preceding) from non-topics (following). Such elements are the aforementioned particles but also sentence adverbials (4). Since unstressed personal pronouns are inherently topical, they have no other option than to precede, otherwise the syntactically well formed clause becomes pragmatically odd. Syntax provides several options, pragmatics singles out one of them.

    This modular interface effect becomes especially clear in the case of object shift discussed at the end of the preceding section. Object shift is a strictly

---

[9] Note that the very same order is acceptable for a non-topical 'Max':

    (i)   Ich frage mich, ob das nicht Max/jemand der Polizei erzählen sollte

                                                     (*light negation!*)

            I ask myself whether this not Max/somebody the police tell should

            'I ask myself whether Max/somebody shouldn't tell this to the police'

[10] Frey's evidence is word order differences that correlate with topicality. These differences could be captured semantically. The syntax just has to provide information about the relative domain inclusions in terms of relative order and the corresponding c-command domains. Genuine syntactic evidence would be specific evidence for a functional spec position (e.g. an expletive in this position in the absence of a fronted topic) or a functional head position lexicalized by a fronted finite verb. The absence of this predictable evidence is a problem for the assumption of a functional projection. The semantic solution is unaffected by these structure-specific problems.

structure-controlled operation. It is dependent on the V° head having been fronted. If the syntactic context does not allow this, object shift cannot apply. This crucially does not make the clause pragmatically deviant. So, pragmatics does not trigger object shift in a grammatically causal sense. Pragmatics just takes a free ride on the system's potential of grammar and is parasitic on structural syntactic possibilities.

Note that topicality is not the only property that makes a phrase escape the domain of particles or sentence adverbials. The generic *man* (indefinite 'one') is not a topic but nevertheless it precedes.

(4)   a. * dass (ja) leider *man es hier* übersieht
                that (PRT) unfortunately one this here overlooks
                'that unfortunately one overlooks this here'

        b. dass *man es hier* (ja) leider übersieht
                that one this here (PRT) unfortunately overlooks

In sum, at the interface that correlates structure and interpretation, the pragmatics module takes advantage of the word order freedom provided by the grammar, assigning different interpretations according to the c-command domain of the given phrase.

4.2.3   Order restriction for pronouns: NOM < ACC < DAT

There is a uniform relative order for pronouns that holds irrespective of the verb class-specific base order pattern for DPs determined by the given verbal head (e.g. DAT–ACC for a verb like *vorstellen* 'introduce' vs ACC–DAT base order for a verb like *aussetzen* 'expose'). Unlike full DPs, pronominal arguments are *canonically* ordered according to the *case-based* template in the headline. Only if a pronoun is focused may it deviate from this order: in (1b), the subject pronoun is focused and it remains in the position where a lexical noun would occur, with the object pronouns preceding. In other words, it is not subject to the ordering template for unstressed pronouns.

(1)   a. dass niemand / er *mich ihr* vorstellte
                that nobody / he-NOM me-ACC (to) her-DAT introduced

        b. dass *mich ihr* niemand / (sogar) ER vorstellte
                that me-ACC her-DAT nobody / (even) he-NOM introduced
                'that nobody / even he introduced me to her'

        c. dass er *sie ihr* ja ausgesetzt hat
                that he-NOM them-ACC her-DAT PRT exposed has
                'that he has exposed them to her'

      d. ?? dass er *ihr sie* ja ausgesetzt hat
         that he-NOM her-DAT them-ACC PRT exposed has

The analogous ordering pattern (NOM-ACC-DAT) holds for Dutch (NOM-DO-IO).[11] This is remarkable because it contrasts with the rigid IO < DO order for non-pronominal DP objects in Dutch and the prohibition against scrambling a direct object across the indirect object. So this is additional evidence for the claim that the order of pronominal arguments could neither be a result of scrambling, nor could it be regarded as an indicator of the canonical base order of arguments in general, as Müller (1995) would like to have it for German, for instance.

For both issues, Dutch provides the relevant (counter)evidence. In Dutch, DP objects cannot be reordered by scrambling, so the pronoun order cannot be the result of scrambling. On the other hand, if the pronoun order were an indicator of the canonical order of arguments in general, the Dutch order for non-pronominal arguments, namely IO before DO, would contradict this. It would have to be analysed as an instance of scrambling of the IO across the DO. But, objects do not scramble across each other in Dutch.[12]

The examples under (2) show that personal pronouns serialize in the order DO before IO, whereas a demonstrative like *dat* (this) or a strong form of a personal pronoun, like *haar* (her) instead of *ze* (her) are ordered like non-pronominal DPs.

(2)   a. Had Jan/*hij het zich* niet ingebeeld?
        had Jan/he it himself not imagined

      b. Had Jan/*hij zich dat* niet ingebeeld?
        had Jan/he himself this not imagined

      c. Eigenlijk had Jan/*hij zich haar* heel anders voorgesteld
        actually had Jan/he himself her completely different imagined

      d. Eigenlijk had Jan/*hij ze zich* heel anders voorgesteld
        actually had Jan/he her himself completely different imagined

---

[11] Note that, like English, Dutch has no morphological DAT–ACC distinction, except for a single instance namely third person plural:

    (i)   Ik heb hun-DAT het boek gegeven.
          I have them-DAT the book given
    (ii)   Ik heb ze-ACC aan mijn broer gegeven
          I have them-ACC to my brother given

[12] Of course there are, as always, conceivable technical implementations. The indirect object could be generated below the direct object and raised into an object spec position in a VP-shell structure. But this would affect a pronoun and a non-pronominal DP equally. The problem remains that the surface order for non-pronominal DPs is IO–DO, but for pronouns it is DO–IO.

It is worth emphasizing that the order pattern NOM-ACC-DAT is not a restriction on *fronted* pronouns only. It is a general restriction on the *relative order* of pronouns (3b) and it holds both in the Wackernagel position as well as in their midfield position. Of course, non-pronominal DPs (4) or strong pronouns (demonstratives, focused personal pronouns) are not subject to this restriction.

(3)   a.   dass endlich wer *sie uns* vorstellen/zeigen sollte
              that after-all someone them-ACC us-DAT introduce/show should

        b.   ?? dass endlich wer *uns sie* vorstellen/zeigen sollte
              that after-all someone us-DAT them-ACC introduce/show should

(4)   a.   dass endlich einer *den seltsamen Gast der Gastgeberin* vorstellen
              sollte
              that after-all someone the strange guest-ACC (to) the host-DAT intro-
              duce should

        b.   dass endlich einer der Gastgeberin den seltsamen Gast vorstellen
              sollte
              that after-all someone (to) the host-DAT the strange guest-ACC intro-
              duce should

Both orders in (4) are equally grammatical. (4b) is the base order for non-pronominal DPs with this class of verbs (experiencer-theme verb). For pronominals, however, the order in (3b) is deviant. The examples are intentionally constructed with an indefinite non-specific, non-generic wh-indefinite subject, just in order to demonstrate that the subject itself is most likely in its base position and not scrambled.

As for the theoretical reconstruction of the syntactic causality of the ordering template for pronouns, an insightful and generally accepted theoretical model is presently lacking.

4.2.4   *The special case of* es *as a defective pronoun*

Not only in German and Dutch is the third person neuter pronoun (Germ. *es*; Dutch *het*) special. It is in Cardinaletti and Starke's (1999) terminology a *defective* pronoun. Not only is it, like other weak pronouns, stress-avoiding, but it is categorically unstressable. Ungrammaticality is the result if this pronoun is stressed or placed into a stress-attracting position. Focus, for instance, results in stress. Hence, unstressable pronouns cannot be focused (1b,d).

(1)   a.   Ich habe nur *ihn* gesehen
              I have only him seen

b. Ich habe (*nur) *es* gesehen
    I have (only) it seen

c. *Ihn* habe ich gesehen
    him have I seen

d. * *Es* habe ich gesehen
    it have I seen

However, if the pronoun in the sentence-initial position can be de-stressed, the contrast between *es* and stressable pronouns disappears. Here is an example. In (2), the sentence-initial object pronoun is a topic, and crucially, it is not focused since it merely re-addresses a discourse participant introduced in the immediately preceding utterance without focusing it.

(2)   a. Ihr Geld ist nicht verloren. *Es* hat jetzt nur jemand anderer[13]
           your money is not lost. It has now only someone else
           'Your money is not lost. Just someone else has/owns it now'

       b. Dieses Schild können sie genauso gut weglassen. *Es* hat ohnehin
           keiner beachtet
           this sign could you just-as well remove. It has anyway nobody
           observed

Note that the sentences with object *es* in initial position in (2) would be rated deviant if presented in isolation, that is, as utterances that are not a continuation of an immediately preceding utterance. In this case, the fronted object pronoun would be interpreted as foregrounded, that is, focused and thus stress-attracting. If (2b) is presented in isolation, without *ohnehin* (anyway), it is felt to be deviant. *Ohnehin* mitigates the effect, since it suggests a topic continuation.

Avoidance of a stress position is the key for understanding another peculiarity of German *es*. It avoids prepositional phrases. Prepositional objects are the lowest ranking objects. So they usually precede the clause-final verb position. This is the nuclear stress position. Stress (i.e. pitch accent) is placed on the lowest argument position, and within this phrase, on the head element of the lowest phrase. This would be the pronoun in the PP in (3b). Here is what you find instead:

(3)   a. Ich habe auf *ihn* gewartet
           I have for him waited

       b. ?? Ich habe auf *es* gewartet
           I have for it waited

---

[13] For this example I gratefully acknowledge Werner Frey (pers. comm.). It was originally cold comfort for investors who had lost their money in an investment fraud. For Dutch, an informant tells me that the corresponding case remains deviant.

c. Ich habe *da*rauf gewartet
   I have there-for waited

d. *Wo*rauf hast Du gewartet?
   where-for have you waited
   'What did you wait for?'

e. Auf *was* hast Du gewartet?
   for what have you waited

Instead of the pronoun *es* as complement of the preposition (3b), German employs an amalgamated form that looks like a preposition with a pre-cliticized *da* (3c). The interrogative form is *wo*+ preposition, as illustrated in (3d). Although the version (3e) in place of (3d) is dispreferred in the German standard variety, it is widely used in the Southern German colloquial variants.[14]

4.3   Word order variation with non-pronominal arguments: scrambling

In comparison with other Germanic OV languages, as for instance Dutch, the potential of word order variation in German is greater. For example, all of the six possible permutations of the three DPs in (1a) yield fully grammatical orders. One of the five alternative serializations for (1a) is given in (1b). In Dutch, only PP arguments may be reordered, whereas DP arguments must not be permuted (see the discussion of property (vii), below).

(1)   a. dass das Objekt dem Subjekt den ersten Platz streitig macht
          that the object-NOM the subject-DAT the initial place-ACC contested
          makes
          'that the object contends with the subject for the initial place'

       b. dass den ersten Platz dem Subjekt das Objekt streitig macht
          that the initial place-ACC the subject-DAT the object-NOM contested
          makes

---

[14] In some cases, the amalgamated form is not available, for semantic reasons. In this case, the pronoun *es* is used nevertheless, as a kind of no-way-out option. Here is an example that I overheard in a broadcasting report. The amalgamated form *darin* cannot be used, since in the absence of a case distinction, its meaning would be locative (in it), and not, as required, directional (into it):

(i)   Geld hat die Eigenschaft, dass man jegliche Waren [*in es*] verwandeln kann
        money has the property that one any commodity [in(to) it] transform can
        'money has the property that any commodity can be transformed into it'

Ross (1967) not only furnished the name for this phenomenon (*Scrambling*), but also placed it outside grammar proper and treated it as a stylistic rule. In the Minimalist Program (Chomsky 1995: 324), a similar approach is considered. However, the fact that scrambling interacts with structurally determined phenomena (e.g. anaphor binding and quantifier-variable binding) plus the fact that the very existence of scrambling in a given language is grammatically conditioned[15] militates against attempts to disqualify scrambling as a genuine phenomenon of syntax. The following grammatical properties that are characteristic of scrambling in German (Stechow and Sternefeld 1988; Grewendorf and Sternefeld 1990; Müller 1995a: 95–102; Haider and Rosengren 1998, 2003) – some of which are inappropriately characterized in the literature – will be discussed in the given order:

(i)   Scrambling proper is *clause bound* (in German).

(ii)   There is *no* instance of syntactically *obligatory* scrambling.

(iii)   Scrambling applies to arguments of *diverse categories* (e.g. DP, PP, CP), but not to complements in general (e.g. not to VP).

(iv)   Scrambling of potential binders *extends* their respective *binding domains*, and conversely it *disrupts* binding when a bindee is scrambled across its binder.

(v)   Scrambling *extends the scope domain* and produces *scope ambiguities*, since scope may be computed either on the derived order, or on the order before movement, which is accessible via the trace of the scrambled item.

(vi)   Scrambling is *not a singular process*, that is, more than one constituent in the given domain of scrambling may be scrambled.

(vii)   Scrambling *re-serializes* arguments (Scandinavian *object shift* does not – see discussion of property (vii), below).

(viii) Scrambling operates in head-final phrases only, not in head-initial ones.

Scrambling is usually discussed as a clausal phenomenon. But, in fact it should be seen as a more general phenomenon in the context of head-final projections (Corver and van Riemsdijk 1997; Haider 1997e, 2000a). In German, scrambling is found within VPs (see 2) and within APs (see 3), but not within NPs and PPs, as they are head *initial* (see discussion of property (viii) below).

---

[15] A necessary condition for scrambling within a projection P is this: (i) P must be a head-final projection, and (ii) the arguments of the head of P must be licensed relationally, that is, the identification of the given argument phrases does not depend on unique structural positions for each argument (see Haider 1992/2000; Corver and van Riemsdijk 1997; Haider 1997b; Haider and Rosengren 1998).

(2)   a. [$_{VP}$ Dem Subjekt den ersten Platz streitig gemacht] (das) hat das Objekt

(to) the subject-DAT the first place-ACC contested made (this) has the object-NOM

b. [$_{VP}$ Den ersten Platz$_i$ dem Subjekt e$_i$ streitig gemacht] (das) hat das Objekt

the first place (to) the subject contested made (this) has the object

The examples in (2) illustrate scrambling in a clause-initial VP. The VP is either *topicalized* – this is the variant without *das* (this) – or *left-dislocated*. The latter is the variant with the resumptive *das* (this) in the clause-initial position, and with the left-dislocated VP adjoined to the clause. Topicalization is an instance of wh-movement while a left-dislocated phrase is generated as a clause-adjoined phrase and associated by means of the pronominal correlate.

(3)   a. der [$_{AP}$ *dem Briefträger* in vielen Merkmalen ähnliche] Sohn der Nachbarin

the [the postman-DAT in many features similar] son (of)-the neighbour

'the son of the neighbour resembling the postman in many features'

b. der [$_{AP}$ in vielen Merkmalen *dem Briefträger* ähnliche] Sohn der Nachbarin

the [in many features the postman-DAT similar] son (of)-the neighbour

Since there are no transitive adjectives, the demonstration of scrambling within an AP is limited to dative and to prepositional objects (3).

Property (i): Scrambling proper is clause bound.

The claim that scrambling is clause bound is uncontroversial for cases in which scrambling would amount to extraction out of finite clauses, as illustrated in (4), but it holds also for extraction out of infinitival clauses. Apparent counterevidence is merely a misinterpretation (see chapter 7, on clause union). Some misinterpret a clause union construction as a construction with an embedded clausal infinitive and are surprised that this apparently violates the clause mate constraint for scrambling. But, if there is no embedded infinitival complement clause in these clause union cases, scrambling cannot violate locality (see 4e).

Long-distance scrambling as in (4a) and (4c) is unacceptable in German. The examples (4b) and (4d) are cases of *focus fronting* (FF; see Neeleman 1994: 395f. for Dutch; for German: Reis 1987, and Haider and Rosengren 1998). It is a construction that is almost exclusively used in spoken language, presumably because of the necessity of a manifest intonation contour, that is, a rise–fall contour, indicated here by / and \ , respectively. Keep in mind that scrambling and FF are two clearly distinct phenomena. For instance, FF may be applied to elements that do not scramble, even to selected manner adverbials (4e) or VPs (4f).

(4)   a.   Scrambling
                * dass [die Lösung]$_i$ niemand geglaubt hat, [dass er e$_i$ gefunden hätte]
                that the solution no-one believed has [that he found had]

        b.   Focus fronting
                dass [/so eine Lösung]$_i$ NIE\mand geglaubt hat, [dass einer e$_i$ finden würde][16]
                that such a solution no-one believed has [that someone find would]
                'that no one believed that anyone had found such a solution'

        c.   Scrambling
                * dass niemand [sie zu besuchen]$_i$ glaubt, [dass er sich e$_i$ leisten kann]
                that no-one [her to visit]$_i$ believes, [that he REFL afford can]

        d.   Focus fronting
                dass [sie zu be/suchen]$_i$ NIE\mand glaubt, dass er sich e$_i$ leisten kann
                that [her to visit] no-one believes that he REFL afford can
                'that no one believes that he can afford to visit her'

        e.   Focus fronting of a selected manner adverbial
                dass ja [/so frugal]$_i$ KEI\ner von uns glaubte, dass man e$_i$ leben könnte
                'that PRT [so frugal] nobody of us thought that one live could'

        f.   Focus fronting of a VP
                dass ja [mit Anstand ver/LIEren]$_{VP-i}$ unser Team leider NICHT\ e$_i$ kann
                that PRT [with grace lose] our team unfortunately not can
                'that our team is unable to lose with grace'

        g.   Clause union infinitival construction (*third construction*)
                Da habe ich *mich*$_i$ angefangen, [e$_i$ damit zu beschäftigen][17]
                there have I *myself*$_i$ begun [therewith to engage]
                'So I began to engage myself for it'

In (4a) and (4c), the scrambled constituent is in the midfield of the matrix clause, that is, the clause that embeds the clause with the trace of the scrambled constituent. This type of long-distance displacement is ungrammatical in German,

---

[16] Capitals in these examples indicate the locus of the rise–fall pitch accent.

[17] This is a sentence uttered by the author Stefan Heym in a broadcast interview that I overheard.

with the exception of focus fronting: (4b) and (4d) are acceptable, but only with a specific focus intonation contour. This construction is the result of long-distance movement.

(4g) is an example of a construction that is discussed in more detail in chapter 7.1, the so-called *third* (*infinitival*) *construction* (den Besten and Rutten 1989; Grewendorf and Sabel 1999; Haider 2003: 244–7). It still awaits a generally accepted analysis. In the literature you may find claims that it involves a non-local type of scrambling, that is, scrambling across the boundary of an extraposed infinitival clause. In chapter 7, it will be argued that this construction, if analysed properly, does not provide evidence for long-distance scrambling in German, that is, scrambling across a clause boundary. It is a variant of a clause union construction.

Property (ii): Syntactically, scrambling is optional. There is no *core syntax* trigger.

Scrambling is optional in the sense that there is no genuinely syntactic context that requires scrambling. This is generally acknowledged (see for instance Müller 1995a: 95–100; Fanselow 2003). On the other hand, scrambling has semantic (e.g. scope, construal of indefinite DPs) or pragmatic (information structure) effects. But these effects that accompany scrambling cannot be taken to be *grammatical* triggering factors of scrambling since the specific interpretation effects that might be claimed to trigger scrambling are found with the canonical order as well. Moreover, in many cases, scrambling seems to *reduce* rather than to *enhance* or *change* the interpretation potential. Here is an example.

(5a) has the definite DP after an indefinite pronoun subject (morphologically identical with the interrogative form and specifically chosen here because it does not scramble). So the definite DP is likely to be in-situ. Analogous considerations apply to (5b,c). Generic interpretation (5a), indefinite specific (5b) and definite specific (5c) interpretations are available for DPs in-situ as well as for scrambled DPs. What may *get lost* by the scrambling of indefinites is the *existentially bound* interpretation. Note, however, that the strong interpretation (generic (5a) or specific (5b)) is available in the base position as well. The grammar theoretic reason will be analysed below.

(5)   a. (existential *or* generic)
            dass ja WER (*die*) *Pockenviren* ausrotten sollte
            that PRT who (the) pockvirus-PL exterminate should
            'that surely someone should exterminate the pockvirus'

        b. (indefinite specific)
            wenn WER *eine rothaarige Frau* sucht, dann ist das Lisa
            if who a red-haired woman seeks, then is this Lisa
            'if someone is looking for a red-haired person, then this is Lisa'

c. (definite specific)

dass er WEM *ihr Kleid* gezeigt hat, hat Lisa nicht gefallen

that he who-DAT her dress shown has, has Lisa-NOM not liked

'that he has shown her dress to someone Lisa did not like'

The only case for allegedly obligatory scrambling (cf. 6a) – indefinites must not occur in the domain of negation in German – rests on a controversial premise, namely the premise that the negation universally c-commands the whole VP. This premise is unfounded, at least for German or Dutch,[18] see section 4.4.2, issue (i). There are elements, for instance indefinite wh-pronouns, that do not scramble (cf. 6b), but must not be in the domain of the negation (6a,c).

(6)   a. *   dass jemand nicht *wen* verjagte

that someone not *someone* chased

b. */?? dass mitunter wen$_i$ jemand e$_i$ beleidigt, kommt vor

that sometimes someone-ACC someone-NOM offends happens PRT

'that it happens that someone sometimes offends somebody'

c.   dass mitunter wer wen nicht beleidigt, kommt vor

that sometimes someone-NOM someone-ACC not offends happens PRT

'that it sometimes happens that someone does not offend somebody'

The fact that scrambled indefinites may lose their indefinite or unspecific interpretation is but an epiphenomenon, and not the *trigger*, of scrambling. (6b) is ungrammatical because an obligatorily indefinite pronoun that has been scrambled out of the *minimal domain of argument-projection* (MAC = minimal argument complex)[19] cannot receive an existential reading: it has left the domain of existential closure.

---

[18] Universally, the position of the negation particle for sentence negation is a position that in most cases minimally c-commands the finite verb or its trace. This is one reason why a negation particle in the role of sentence negation cannot appear in a VP-internal position in a VO language since the verb is VP initial.

(i)   * He has [$_{VP}$ talked *not* to Mary]

(ii)   Er hat [$_{VP}$ mit Maria nicht gesprochen]

he has with Mary not talked

In an OV language, the negation particle, just like adverbs of all semantic types, is VP internal since any immediately VP-internal position necessarily c-commands the finite verb in its base position.

[19] The MAC is the minimal projection of the head that contains all argument positions of the head. This is a modification of Diesing's (1992) claim that the VP is the domain of existential closure. The VP in an OV language may be larger than the MAC. This is the case if scrambling is analysed as adjunction to VP. In head-initial projections, however, the left boundary of the MAC is identical with the left boundary of the VP.

The generic or indefinite-specific interpretation that indefinites receive outside the MAC is incompatible with the lexical semantics of indefinite pronouns.

The examples in (7) illustrate that the very interpretation that is applicable to scrambled indefinites is available in the base position as well. In other words, scrambling *eliminates* interpretation options (by altering the c-command domains), but it does not *add* or *generate* them. In a triggering account, the 'generated' interpretation would be an element of the triggering mechanism, however.

(7)   a. dass ja Fisch/einen Fisch keiner bestellte
          that PRT fish/a fish nobody ordered
          'that nobody ordered fish/a fish'

       b. dass ja keiner Fisch/einen Fisch bestellte
          that PRT nobody fish/a fish ordered

The bare indefinite '*Fisch*' (fish) in (7) is interpreted generically in (7a), and in (7b) it can be so interpreted as well. But a preferred reading for (7b) is that of an existentially bound indefinite. This is not a natural reading for (7a). The loss of the existential reading in (7a) is a by-product of scrambling. The scrambled DP has left the minimal argument complex (MAC), which means that it has left the domain of existential closure.

Property (iii): Scrambling applies to all *argumental* categories (i.e. DP, PP, CP).

Scrambling is not restricted to nominal arguments. Any argumental category, that is, DP, PP (8a), *finite* clause (8b), or *infinitival* clause (8c), may be scrambled.[20]

(8)   a.   dass dort jetzt [auf Peter]$_i$ jemand e$_i$ wartet
             that there now [for Peter] someone waits
             'that someone is waiting for Peter there now'

       b.   (?) weil ja heutzutage [dass die Erde rund ist]$_i$ niemand e$_i$ ernsthaft
             bezweifelt
             since PRT today [that the earth round is] nobody seriously doubts

       c.   dass doch [diese Tür aufzubrechen]$_i$ keiner je e$_i$ versucht hat
             that PRT [this door open to force] nobody ever tried has
             'that nobody ever tried to force this door open '

Note that in these examples, the scrambled constituent is to the left of the subject but to the right of information structure-sensitive particles (*ja, doch*) and

---

[20] There are some restrictions with respect to genitival objects, however (cf. Rosengren 1993, 1994). Since this is of no relevance in this connection, we shall not discuss it further.

temporal adverbials. This, in addition to the fact that they are well-formed in the absence of focus intonation, indicates that focus movement is not at stake. However, as the question mark in (8b) indicates, non-extraposed finite clauses are marginal; but they are equally marginal in the position of the trace (i.e. the canonical argument position) as well. Their preferred position is clause final because extraposition is strongly preferred for ease of processing reasons (avoidance of centre embedding).

A remark on the *scrambling properties of adjuncts* seems to be appropriate here: an analysis in terms of scrambling presupposes a unique base position for the given adjunct. But, on the other hand, if we assume that an adjunct may be generated in alternative positions, this would account for alternating orders without having to invoke scrambling. For Dutch, this is suggested by Neeleman (1994), and Neeleman and Weerman (1999), for German by Haider (2000a). Arguments for alternative base domains of adverbials in German have been worked out in great detail by Frey and Pittner (1998).

Property (iv): Scrambling of possible binders extends their respective binding domains.

In the literature on scrambling, binding properties are the key properties for distinguishing scrambling from A'-movement fronting processes, since A'-movement is undone for binding, but scrambling is not. Binding operates on the output of scrambling.

Scrambling of a potential binder enlarges its *binding domain* because scrambling enlarges the *c-command domain* on the binder. This holds for principle-A effects (9a), for principle-C effects (9b) and for Q-binding of pronouns (9c).[21]

In the examples below, binding does not apply in the respective base positions[22] because of the lack of c-command: the unscrambled version of (9a) would be deviant because the reciprocal pronoun needs to be properly bound by a c-commanding antecedent. (9b) would be grammatical in the unscrambled position because no occurrence of *Peter* c-commands the other, and in (9c), the pronoun would not be qualified for a quantifier-bound reading, because the pronoun would not be c-commanded and therefore not in the scope of the quantifier.

(9)   a. dass wer die Kandidaten^j_i einander^j e$_i$ präsentierte
          that one the candidates-ACC (to) each-other-DAT presented
          'that someone presented the candidates to each other'

---

[21] Note that the discussion of Q-binding in scrambling constructions in the literature may be complicated by controversial data judgements (see Frey 1993; Moltmann 1990; Müller and Sternefeld 1994).

[22] In the following example, the subscript is the trace index; the superscript is the binding index.

b. *dass man Peter$_j^i$ [Peters^i Vater] e$_j$ nicht übergeben hat
   that one Peter [(to) Peter's father-DAT] not surrendered has
   'that one has not handed over Peter to Peter's father'

c. dass man [fast jeden^i]$_i$ seinem^i Vorgesetzten e$_i$ ankündigte
   that one [almost everyone] (to) his boss-DAT announced
   'that almost everyone was announced to his boss'

The counterpart of an *extended* binding domain due to the *scrambling* of a potential *binder* is the *diminishing* or *destroying* of the binding domain of an element by *scrambling* the *bindee* across a binder. Note that this is not a property of A'-movement. A'-moved bindees are reconstructed for binding. For instance, topicalizing a bindee would not affect its binding properties because they are computed in the position from where topicalization starts (see (11), below), and not in the target position. For scrambling, the target position is the relevant position for computing binding properties.

Scrambling a bindee across a binder destroys binding relations that hold in the base position for principle-A effects (cf. (10a) in comparison with (9a)), for principle-C effects (10b), and for Q-binding (10c).

Binding of a fronted reflexive by a nominative (10e) appears to be exceptional. The fronted reflexive is bound by the subject although the subject does not c-command. This is not a peculiarity of a subject, as the comparison with an ECM subject in (10d) shows. It is a peculiarity of a subject that agrees with the finite verb (Haider 1989).

In Haider (1993: 167), the crucial factor is seen in the bipartite relation of the finite subject. 'Nominative' is a bipartite relation because the nominative DP obligatorily agrees with the finite verb. Hence it is in a relation with a functional head that c-commands the nominative and the finite verb. It is this functional head that c-commands the reflexive. The binding domain of the subject is the c-command domain of the functional head since this head shares the nominal features of the subject (by agreement). For a detailed discussion and implementation see Frey (1993). Note that this is a property of the nominative subject. ECM subjects do not agree. Hence there is no functionally extended binding domain for them (10d).

(10) a. * dass man nebeneinander$_i$ die Kandidaten^i e$_i$ setzte
        that one next-to-each-other the candidates seated

   b. dass man [den Hut des Polizisten^i]$_j$ dem Polizisten^i/ihm^i e$_j$ nicht übergeben hat
      that one [the hat-ACC of the policeman] the policeman/him-DAT not handed-over has

'that the hat of the policeman was not handed-over to the policeman/
him'

c.   dass man [seinen^i Vorgesetzten]$_j$ jedem*$^{/??i}$ e$_j$ ankündigte
     that one [his boss-ACC] everyone-DAT announced

d. * dass man sich$_i$ keinen^i e$_i$ vorstellen ließ
     that one himself nobody introduce let
     'that one lets nobody introduce him/herself'

e.   dass sich$_i$ bei diesem Fall viele^i e$_i$ geirrt haben
     that REFL with this case many erred have
     'that in this case many erred'

These examples demonstrate that binding applies at the target position of scrambling and not at the respective base positions (see Frey 1993). Hence, reconstruction is not at issue. Note that this distinguishes structures resulting from
scrambling from those resulting from topicalization (11a,b):

(11)   a.   Aneinander$_i$ hat man die Bilder^i e$_i$ angeglichen
            to-each-other has one the pictures assimilated
            'The pictures were assimilated to one another.'

       b. * [Aus Peters^i Wagen]$_j$ hat man ihn^i e$_j$ gezerrt
            [out of Peter's car] has one him dragged
            'Peter was dragged out of his car.'

In A'-chains, binding is checked in the lower, that is, in an A-position. So, (11a)
meets condition (A) because A binding for the A'-moved anaphor is checked in the
position of the trace. (11b) violates condition (C) since the A'-moved PP contains
a referential expression, namely *Peter*, and checking the PP in the position of the
trace detects a principle C violation. The relevant contrasts are (10a) versus (11a),
and (10b) versus (11b).

Property (v): Scrambling produces scope ambiguities.

Scrambling of a quantifier across another quantifier produces scope ambiguities
between these quantifiers. Scope computation, unlike binding, has access to any
chain link. Binding operates only on the highest element of a movement chain.
Scoping, on the other hand, operates on chain links (cf. Frey 1993): a quantifier Q
can get a wide scope reading with respect to a phrase E, if Q c-commands at least
one member of the chain of E (see also Aoun and Li's 1993 *scope principle*).[23]
Since scrambling – under most of the current analyses – is the result of movement

---

[23] 'An operator A may have scope over an operator B iff A c-commands B or an A'-element
that is coindexed with B.'

and therefore produces chain links, it is predicted to produce chain-based scope ambiguities.[24]

(12)   a. dass man [*mindestens ein* Bild]$_i$ *fast jedem* Experten e$_i$ zeigte

(ambiguous scope)

that one [at-least one picture-ACC] (to) almost every expert-DAT showed

'that there is at least one picture that was shown to almost every expert'

'that for almost every expert it is true that at least one picture was shown to him'

b. dass man *mindestens einem* Experten *fast jedes* Bild zeigte

(unambiguous scope)

that one (to) at least one expert-DAT almost every picture-ACC showed

'that for almost every expert it is true that at least one picture was shown to him'

The ambiguity of (12a) is a scrambling effect. The wide scope reading of the existentially quantified expression follows from its surface position. It c-commands the universal quantifier. The universally quantified expression, on the other hand c-commands a trace of the scrambled existential quantifier expression. Hence this phrase can be reconstructed into the scope of the lower quantifier. The order of the objects in (12b) – DAT before ACC object – is the base order for the head verb *zeigen* (= show). The c-command domains of the quantifiers are unambiguous, and so are their scope domains in (12b).

Property (vi): Scrambling may apply more than once in its domain.

A scrambling domain may contain more than one scrambled phrase. Note that this is different from typical A'-movement, like wh-movement in German. A'-movement targets a specific spec position and this position provides room for a single item only. In each instance of wh-movement (see chapter 3), only a single phrase is moved to the target position.

Given that (13a) reflects the base order, (13b) is the result of scrambling the two objects across the subject. Note that the resulting order of the scrambled objects is free: changing the order of the dative and the accusative object in (13b) does not affect grammaticality.

---

[24] In German, there is a possibility of forcing reconstruction. This is the use of a rise–fall double focus contour with focus on the element to be reconstructed and on the element preceding the trace at the reconstruction site. See Jacobs (1988, 1997); Büring (1997); Haider (2001c), and section 3.2 of Haider and Rosengren (2003).

(13)   a. dass das Objekt dem Subjekt den ersten Platz streitig macht
        that the object-NOM the subject-DAT the initial place-ACC contentious
        makes
        'that the object contends with the subject for the initial place'

        b. dass dem Subjekt den ersten Platz das Objekt streitig macht
        that the subject-DAT the initial place-ACC the object-NOM contentious
        makes

Property (vii): Scrambling *reorders* arguments (*object shift* does not).

In a genuine scrambling language like German (or Japanese, Turkish, etc.), scrambling produces the complete set of permutations of argument order variants for a given clause (see the discussion of example (1) at the beginning of this section 4.3). In particular, an argument may be scrambled across a transitive subject.

In the Germanic OV languages, scrambling as characterized above applies in German and Yiddish, but not in Dutch (14b) or Afrikaans. This correlates with the fact that in the course of language change, Dutch and Afrikaans reduced and lost their morphological encoding of case. DPs are morphologically indistinct for case. This leaves only PP arguments as *morphologically distinct* arguments, and in fact, a PP object may be scrambled across another object in Dutch (14d) and Afrikaans. So, at least to a limited extent, all Germanic OV languages allow for scrambling for the purpose of changing the order of arguments.

(14)   a.   Toen hebben de autoriteiten de moeder *het kind* teruggegeven
                                                                              Dutch
              then have the authorities the mother the child back-given

        b. * Toen hebben de autoriteiten [*het* kind]$_i$ de moeder e$_i$ teruggegeven

        c.   Toen hebben de autoriteiten het kind *aan de moeder* teruggegeven
              then have the authorities the child to the mother back-given

        d.   Toen hebben de autoriteiten *aan de moeder*$_i$ het kind e$_i$
              teruggegeven

                                                            (Geerts *et al.* 1984: 989f.)

The change of the base order is a crucial difference between *scrambling* on the one hand and *object shift* in Scandinavian VO languages on the other hand. Object shift never changes the canonical order of the arguments. It just changes the order of an argument relative to a preceding adverbial or a preceding negation particle. So, attempting to subsume these two phenomena under the same heading would merely confound the terminology. The Dutch type of so-called scrambling must be distinguished from object shift, too, since object shift does not apply to PPs and presupposes V-fronting (see the discussion of object shift, below in section 4.4.1, issue (v)).

Property (viii): Scrambling applies in head-final phrases but not in head-initial ones.

In German, two of the four major lexical projections are head final (namely VP and AP), and two are head initial (DP, PP). The functional architecture in the clause is head initial. Scrambling is licit in the head-final phrases, but not in head-initial ones.

This is easy to demonstrate by comparing on the one hand the word order variation within the VP and on the other hand the rigid order within the NP. The comparison is as close as one could wish, since a German infinitival verb can either be the head of a VP, or by category conversion, the head of an NP ('nominalized infinitive').

(15)   a.   [$_{VP}$ Mails an die Behörde schicken$_{V}$°]
              mails-ACC to the authority send

        b.   [$_{VP}$ an die Behörde$_i$ Mails e$_i$ schicken$_{V}$°]
              to the authority mails send

        c.   das [$_{NP}$ Schicken$_{N}$° der Mails / von Mails an die Behörde]
              the [send(ing) the mails-GEN / of mails to the authority]

        d. * das [$_{NP}$ Schicken$_{N}$° [an die Behörde]$_i$ der Mails/von Mails e$_i$]
              the [send(ing) [to the authority] the mails-GEN / of mails]

Note that the German NP structure is identical with the English one. This is so because the NP (and its functional extension as DP, too) is head initial in both languages. This accounts for the rigid order as a collateral property of the compactness property of complex head-initial phrases. In the NP, the direct object of the verb corresponds to the genitive object or, alternatively, to the prepositional object, with *von* (of). English has only the latter option, in the absence of an oblique case.

The other head-final domain in German is the AP. Consequently, it is a domain of scrambling. This is true for APs with a basic A° category (16a,b) as well as for deverbal participial constructions (16c,d).

(16)   a.   ein [$_{AP}$ jedem-DAT an Dummheit ebenbürtiger] Kandidat
              a [(to) everyone-DAT in stupidity equal-AGR] candidate
              'a candidate who is a match to everyone in stupidity'

        b.   ein [$_{AP}$ an Dummheit$_i$ jedem-DAT e$_i$ ebenbürtiger] Kandidat
              an [in stupidity (to) everyone-DAT equal-AGR] candidate

        c.   ein [$_{Participial-P}$ die Zuhörer mit seinen Argumenten überzeugender] Kandidat
              a [the audience with his arguments convincing-AGR] candidate
              'a candidate convincing the audience with his arguments'

d. ein [_Participial-P_ mit seinen Argumenten die Zuhörer überzeugender]
Kandidat
a [with his arguments the audience convincing-AGR] candidate

The theoretic modelling of scrambling in the literature almost exclusively focuses
on scrambling as a *clausal* phenomenon. But, in fact, scrambling is a phenomenon
of head-final phrases in general, and hence scrambling phenomena occur not only
in head-final VPs. Note that some theories of scrambling in clausal domains may
turn out to be inappropriate since they do not cover scrambling in an adnominal
AP or participial attribute because the structural prerequisites assumed in the
particular model are clause specific.

4.4   Scrambling in a grammar-theoretical perspective

The preceding section has presented syntactic properties of scrambling
constructions. In this section, implications of these properties for the theoretic
modelling of scrambling will be addressed. What follows is a list of issues that
will be discussed in detail in this section. After recapitulating the properties of
the scrambling phenomenon, partitioned in less or more controversial aspects,
the major theoretical approaches will be briefly compared.

Uncontroversial empirical issues (section 4.4.1)

(i)   German scrambling is clause bound.
(ii)   Scrambling affects binding properties (extending/reducing binding
         domains).
(iii)   Scrambled phrases remain transparent for extraction.

Controversial empirical issues (section 4.4.1 continued)

(i)   Scrambling is variation in the serialization of arguments (≠ 'object
         shift').
(ii)   Object shift is not scrambling, scrambling is not object shift.
(iii)   Scrambling is tied to head-final projections.
(iv)   There is no evidence for scrambling from parasitic gaps in German.

Controversial theoretical issues (section 4.4.2)

(i)   Is scrambling syntactically optional?
(ii)   What could be a potential syntactic trigger of scrambling?
(iii)   Does scrambling involve chain formation?
(iv)   What kind of syntactic process produces scrambling?

4.4.1 *Uncontroversial and controversial empirical properties of scrambling*

The empirical issues (i) and **(ii)**, that is, the fact that scrambling in German is clause bound and that binding properties change when a binder or a bindee is scrambled, are uncontroversial. In a theoretical perspective, these properties do not match A'-movement properties, that is, properties of movement to functional spec positions at the periphery of a clause. A'-movement is reconstructed for the computing of binding. Moreover, A'-movement is not clause bound, but scrambling is. In terms of the Principles & Parameters terminology (Chomsky 1981), scrambling seems to be more adequately captured by an A-movement approach rather than an analysis in terms of A'-movement.

Issue (iii): the transparency of scrambled phrases for extraction

A robust and characteristic property of a phrase moved to a spec position is the opacity effect for extraction ('freezing' effect). A phrase in a preverbal functional spec position becomes opaque for extraction. This is the unequivocal harvest of the intensive research on extraction domains in the 1980s. Consequently, extraction out of this phrase is ungrammatical. As for scrambling, extraction out of scrambled phrases is fully acceptable in the clear cases of extraction (1). Hence, an approach that assigns the scrambled phrase to a functional spec position is unlikely to be empirically adequate.

Uncontroversial, clear cases of extraction out of a scrambled phrase are extractions out of a scrambled infinitival clause, as in (1). The infinitival clause in (1) is scrambled without doubt. It precedes the transitive subject. The particle preceding the scrambled clause is an information-structuring one. It is used here in order to make clear that the scrambled clause does not need to be adjacent to the V2 position.

(1)   a. Was$_i$ hat denn [e$_i$ damit zu beweisen]$_j$ einer schon öfters e$_j$ versucht?
         what has PRT [it-with to prove] someone already often tried
         'What has someone already often tried to prove with this?'

      b. Wen$_i$ hat denn [e$_i$ damit zu beeindrucken]$_j$ keiner e$_j$ wirklich beabsichtigt?
         who has PRT [it-with to impress] no-one truly intended
         'Who has nobody truly intended to impress with this?'

Extraction out of DPs is a less clear-cut phenomenon cross-linguistically. It is dependent on the semantics of the governing verb to a great extent. But, also for this type of extraction, if it is extraction at all,[25] scrambling is no impediment.

---

[25] It is not entirely clear whether the separation of a PP from NP involves movement at all (in German), as de Kuthy (2000) argues.

Extraction in the scrambled version (2a) is as acceptable as in version (2b), with extraction out of the object in its base position.

(2)   a. Von Mozart$_i$ hat ja [die ersten Symphonien e$_i$]$_j$ kaum einer e$_j$ auf CD aufgenommen

    of Mozart has PRT [the first symphonies] hardly anyone on CD recorded

    'Hardly anyone has recorded the first symphonies of Mozart on CD'

    b. Von Mozart$_i$ hat ja kaum einer [die ersten Symphonien e$_i$] auf CD aufgenommen

    of Mozart has PRT hardly anyone [the first symphonies] on CD recorded

The only case of a 'freezing' effect caused by scrambling that has been raised in the literature is evidence from the ill understood[26] phenomenon of '*was-für*' (what-for) split in German. Diesing (1992: 32f.) has claimed that the contrast between examples like (3a) and (3b) is due to a freezing effect caused by scrambling. But note, first, that (3c) is deviant too, without scrambling, and second, that in this example, the nominative is the subject of an unaccusative verb, that is, it is a nominative on an object argument in its object position. So the split should be unproblematic.

(3)   a.   Was$_i$ erzählte denn jeder von euch [e$_i$ für Witze]?

    what told PRT everyone of you [for jokes]?

    'What kind of jokes did every one of you tell?'

    b. */? Was$_i$ erzählte [e$_i$ für Witze]$_j$ denn jeder von euch e$_j$?

    what told [for jokes] PRT everyone of you?

    c.   ? Was$_i$ missglückten [e$_i$ für Witze] (jedem von euch)?

    what failed [of jokes]$_{-NOM}$ ((for) each one of you)?

    'What kind of jokes failed?'

Even though the acceptability of (3b,c) is degraded – personally, I do not regard them as completely unacceptable[27] – this cannot be the result of scrambling. The effect is independent of scrambling, as (3c) illustrates: the split in (3c) is marginal despite the fact that the subject is the subject of an unaccusative verb that may stay

---

[26] It is ill understood because it is not entirely clear whether it is a case of extraction at all. If it is an extraction, it seems to violate the left branch constraint ('do not extract an item that is the top left branch of a phrase'). Note that there is always an alternative construction with pied-piping the whole phrase. See Pafel (1996) for details.

[27] Note that acceptability improves if the clause has both a fronted verb and a verb in clause-final position, as in (4a) in comparison with (3b).

in its base position. We conclude that (3b) is deviant for some other reason than scrambling. Here is more evidence that renders Diesing's premise[28] problematic.

(4)   a. Was$_i$ hat denn jeder von euch den jeweils anderen [e$_i$ für Witze erzählt]?
         what has PRT each of you the respective others [of jokes told]
         'What kind of jokes did each of you tell the others, respectively?'

       b. Was$_i$ hat denn jeder von euch [e$_i$ für Witze]$_j$ den jeweils andern e$_j$ erzählt?
         what has PRT each of you [of jokes] the respective others told

       c. Was$_i$ hat denn [e$_i$ für Witze]$_j$ jeder von euch gestern e$_j$ erzählt
         what has PRT [of jokes] each of you the respective others told

One of the two orders of the objects in (4a,b) must be the result of scrambling. Most would agree that it must be (4b). Extraction, however, is perfect in both orders. But note that extraction even out of a pre-subject position (4c) is acceptable. There can be no doubt that (4c) is an instance of scrambling. In sum, the data Diesing has adduced as evidence for the alleged islandhood of scrambled constituents are not directly relevant for the issue. They tell more about the preferred positioning of information structure particles like *denn* or *ja* relative to scrambled phrases than about the opacity of scrambled phrases. The clear cases, namely extraction out of scrambled infinitival clauses, are incompatible with an opacity claim.

Let us turn now to some of the controversial issues in the scrambling debate. The *first issue* to be raised critically is the equivocation of scrambling and variation in adverb placement, as in the discussion of Dutch (5b) or Scandinavian object shift (6), below.

Issue (iv): Scrambling re-serializes arguments.

In the literature on word order variation in Dutch, the term scrambling has been introduced for the variation in the placement of adverbs as in (5a) and (5b). In analogy to English, it has been assumed that V and its object have to be adjacent. Consequently, (5b) had to be the result of moving the object out of the VP into a position in front of the adverb. This analysis neglects two important facts. First, compactness of the VP is VO specific since it holds for *head-initial* phrases, like the English VP,[29] but not in head-final phrases. Second, since compactness does not

---

[28] Thanks to Marga Reis (pers. comm.) for making me aware of these examples.

[29] Note that there are VP-internal adverbials in English, too, namely in contexts where compactness is not at issue, as in the case of extraposable PPs:

(i)   (He said he would talk politely to Noam, and) [$_{VP}$ talked *politely* to Noam] he has indeed.

hold for a *head-final* VP, as in Dutch, the order variation in (5a,b) can be captured without invoking scrambling. It is simply a variation in adverb placement in a phrase that provides several slots for adverbs. For Dutch, this alternative analysis has been argued for by Neeleman (1994) or Neeleman and Weerman (1999).[30]

Keep in mind that Dutch does not allow the reordering (i.e. scrambling) of DP arguments, but PP objects may be scrambled (5e), even across a transitive subject (5f), if the subject is indefinite. This contrasts with the absence of PP scrambling in a VO language like English. English does not scramble objects, neither as PPs nor as DPs. So, be aware that the term 'scrambling' in the way it is applied to Dutch refers to a set of circumstances that is entirely different from 'scrambling' as variation in the sequencing of DP arguments, as in German or other fully scrambling OV languages.[31]

(5)　　a.　dat Sofie *vandaag* dat boek moet lezen　　　　　　　　　　　*Dutch*
　　　　　　　that Sofie today this book must read

　　　b.　dat Sofie *dat boek*$_{(i)}$ *vandaag* (e$_i$) moet lezen[32]

　　　c.　* dat *dat boek*$_i$ Sofie *vandaag* e$_i$ moet lezen

　　　d.　Toen heeft hij oplossingen *aan de studenten* verdeeld
　　　　　then has he solutions to the students distributed

　　　e.　Toen heeft hij *aan de studenten*$_i$ oplossingen e$_i$ verdeeld

　　　f.　Toen heeft (alvast) *aan de studenten*$_i$ (?)iemand/*Paul/*hij oplossingen e$_i$ verdeeld
　　　　　then has (meanwhile) to the students someone/Paul/he solutions distributed

　　　g.　* Then, he distributed to the students solutions

The order variation of a nominal object and a prepositional object as in (5d,e) is acknowledged in standard grammars (cf. Geerts *et al.* 1984: 989f.). The fronting of a PP object across a subject (5f) is restricted in Dutch, however. Even indefinite subjects are hard to cross. In English, which is representative of the situation in VO, an object must not be scrambled (5g), neither across an object nor across a subject.

[30] This presupposes an analysis of adverbials as adjuncts, that is, items adjoined to a verbal projection. This is incompatible with the hypothesis that adverbials are placed in the specs of adverbial functional heads (Cinque 1999).
[31] If scrambling is invoked for generating an object–adverb order, the very same process ought to generate a direct object before indirect object order, simply by moving the direct object across the preceding indirect object. However, the latter outcome is ungrammatical in Dutch.
[32] The brackets apply in a base-generation analysis, as in Neeleman (1994) or Neeleman and Weerman (1999).

Issue (v): Scrambling is not object shift.

Another instance of confounding terms is the equating of the order variation in Dutch with 'object shift', as in the Scandinavian languages. Superficially, it seems to be justified, given the fact that in both cases the order variation only concerns the order of objects relative to adverbials or negation, with the relative order of arguments remaining unaffected. But there are at least two crucial differences. Object shift proper affects only DP objects, and object shift proper applies only if there is no lexical material in between the shifting phrase and the left edge of the VP (Holmberg 1999).

Object shift is commonly described as the fronting of one or more DP objects out of the VP to a position preceding the negation or a pre-VP adverbial, as in the Icelandic example (6b). This operation has to observe a 'strange' constraint, though. The DP to be shifted must be the leftmost lexical item in the VP. If there is any preceding lexical material in the VP, object shift is blocked. This material may be the lexical head of the VP, as in (6c), or a stranded particle of the fronted finite verb, as in (6d). The example is taken from Swedish because Swedish, unlike Danish, never allows us to *strand* a particle behind an object. Hence its base position precedes the objects.

Interestingly, any 'clearance' operation in the VP may feed object shift. The typical way of clearing the way out of the VP for object shift is the fronting of the verbal head to the V2 position. If the head is not finite, as in (6c), V2-fronting would not help. But, as Holmberg (1999) points out, even topicalization of the verb feeds object shift, as in (6e).

(6)   a.   Í gær las$_i$ Jón *ekki* [$_{VP}$ e$_i$ *bækurnar*]   *Icelandic*
             yesterday read Jón not books-the

       b.   Í gær las$_i$ Jón *bækurnar$_j$ ekki* [$_{VP}$ e$_i$ e$_j$]   object shift
             yesterday read Jón books-the not

       c. * Jón hefur *bækurnar$_j$ ekki* [$_{VP}$ lesið e$_j$]
             Jon has books-the not read

       d. * Dom kastade$_j$ mej$_i$ inte [$_{VP}$ e$_j$ *ut* e$_i$]   *Swedish*
             they threw me not out

       e.   *Kysst$_i$* har jag *henne$_j$ inte* [$_{VP}$ e$_i$ e$_j$] (bara hållit henne i handen)
                                                                        Norwegian
             kissed have I her not (only held her by hand-the)

Let us briefly halt for an interim recapitulation of the differences between object shift and scrambling, and the differences between full scrambling in OV and the situation in Dutch:

Object shift versus scrambling: an adequate account of object shift must recognize at least three generalizations. First, in all Scandinavian languages, object shift is contingent on removing the verbal head out of the VP. Second, in all Scandinavian languages, object shift preserves the relative order of arguments. Third, object shift applies only to DPs, and not to PPs. Icelandic is the only Scandinavian language with object shift for pronominal as well as non-pronominal DPs.[33] None of these generalizations is characteristic of scrambling. But nevertheless, scrambling and object shift have one property in common, namely the extension of the VP domain for the distribution of arguments.

Scrambling in German vs Dutch: German displays the full potential of scrambling. Arguments of any category may be permuted. In Dutch, only PP objects may be scrambled across other arguments. The relative order of DP arguments must not be changed by scrambling in Dutch. The so-called 'scrambling' of DP objects in Dutch is an order variation between an *object* and an *adverb* (preceding vs following). This can be captured in terms of the alternative adverb placements that are typical for an OV language.

Issue (vi): Scrambling is contingent on head-final projections.

It is a reasonably uncontroversial assumption that a head-final clausal architecture is a sufficient condition for scrambling (cf. Corver and van Riemsdijk 1997: 77ff.). It is controversial, however, as to whether this is a necessary condition as well. In other words, is scrambling restricted to OV, or is it a general option of grammar, available both in OV as well as in VO languages?

In the pertinent literature, you will find the claim that there are languages described as VO that allow scrambling. Is this damaging for the assumption of a cross-linguistic correlation between scrambling and a head-final organization? It is not, since there is an alternative analysis for these scrambling languages that are apparently VO. These languages are neither strictly VO, nor strictly OV. They are of a third kind.

Here is a preliminary characterization of this 'third' kind. The crucial property is the directionality value of the head. In the third type, the directionality parameter is un(der)specified. This means, that each of the two fixed directionality options (VO, OV) is freely available, and the value may be switched within the merging operation of the very same structure. Consequently, you find head-final structures, head-initial ones, and crucially also apparently mixed ones, with the

---

[33] Holmberg and Platzack (1995: 172f.) report that, to a very limited extent, non-pronominal arguments may shift also in Norwegian, varieties of Swedish, and in Faroese: only in double object constructions. A non-pronominal object DP may be shifted, but only if it is the first of two DPs in a double object construction. Again, the relative order must be preserved. Single, non-pronominal objects do not shift.

very same verbal head. What appears to be the result of VO plus scrambling merely is the result of V-fronting in the VP. Let me demonstrate this with Yiddish. Yiddish is a well-known case of this third type, but Slavic languages should be listed in this group as well, among quite a few other languages.

The examples in (7), taken from Diesing (1997: 402), illustrate the crucial property of Yiddish. One of the four variants is a perfect English order (namely 7a), and two are perfect German orders (namely 7b,d). In German, (7d) would be a scrambling variant. The crucial order for the point to be made here is (7c). It is ungrammatical both in English and in German.

(7)   a. Maks hot [$_{VP}$ gegebn Rifken das bukh]   *Yiddish*
         Max has given Rebecca the book   ⇐ VO base order ?

      b. Maks hot [$_{VP}$ Rifken dos bukh gegebn]   ⇐ OV base order ?
         Max has Rebecca the book given

      c. Maks hot [Rifken gegebn dos bukh]   ⇐ ???
         Max has Rebecca given the book

      d. Maks hot [dos bukh Rifken gegebn]   ⇐ scrambled order ?
         Max has the book Rebecca given

The canonical order for the variants in (7) is not immediately evident. For Diesing, (7a) reflects the base order of the VP, with (7b–d) as scrambling variants. But, if this is true, Yiddish is a puzzling exception. It would be the sole *Germanic VO language* that allows scrambling. Moreover, filing Yiddish as a Germanic *VO language* would make it exceptional in many more respects (see below). But if Yiddish is OV, (7a) and (7c) are likewise unexpected and these patterns would require extraposition of DPs, which is not attested in Germanic OV languages otherwise.

Given this affair, is Yiddish either an (exceptional) VO or an (exceptional) OV language? It is neither. Yiddish combines properties of both OV and VO. It is basically OV, but with one additional property, namely the possibility of V-fronting within a VP-shell structure. The existence of this property has independently been ascertained for Hindi (Mahajan 1997). What superficially might look like scrambling to the right in an OV language, as in (8a), turns out to be the result of (VP-internal) V-movement to the left, that is, optional VP-shell formation (as in 8b).

(8)   a. * [[[XP [e$_j$ [e$_i$ V°]]] YP$_j$] ZP$_i$]
      b.   [XP [V$_i$° [YP [e$_i$ ZP]]]]

In grammar-theoretic terms, this state of affairs represents a genuine third type, besides strict OV and VO, namely a language with an *adjustable directionality value*. It combines the properties of an OV projection with those of a VO projection. In other words, the Yiddish verbal head may license to the left and project a head-final structure like German, but alternatively it may license to the right and project a VP shell, and moreover, both options may be combined in the merger of a VP. What this amounts to is this: merger may start as in VO and then continue as in OV, producing first a *VP shell* and then optionally switch to OV and continue producing a layered V-projection familiar from OV. Let me illustrate this in (9):

(9a) and (9b) are the result of uniformly licensing to the left or to the right, respectively. They represent the OV and the VO type, respectively. The 'third type' comprises both the patterns (9a,b) as well as the patterns in (9c).

(9)   a. [XP [YP [ZP V°]]]   OV
        b. [XP [V$_i$° [YP [e$_{V°-i}$ ZP]]]]   VO
        c. { [XP [YP [V° ZP]]], [XP [V$_i$° [YP [e$_{V°-i}$ ZP]]]] } adjustable

The OV and the VO options are the result of a standard merger with the directionality value implemented either as consistently *left* or as consistently *right*, just like in (9a) and (9b). The possibilities that are available in the 'third type' only are the combination of (9a), (9b) *and* (9c). The two patterns in (9c) result from fixing directionality in either order and from changing the directionality in the course of merging. The first variant in (9c) starts out with *directionality = right*, licensing a complement to the right, and then the value switches to *left*. The second variant in (9c) is string- and structure-identical with (9b), except for the possibility of directionally licensing the XP by the verb.

Why should there be a language with this property? In other words, how could UG allow for a language with licensing alternations? In brief, all we have to admit is this: UG allows the un(der)specification of the value for the licensing parameter in a given language. So, in the course of building a projection either of the unspecified values may be instantiated, and moreover, the instantiated value may be changed in the course of merger.

This is the right place, it seems, to point out a crucial implication for diachronic syntax, namely the historic split of the Germanic languages in an OV group and a VO group. If the historic variants of Germanic languages are regarded from this perspective, the development of the Germanic languages is much easier to understand. The basic change was one from an adjustable underspecified headedness value to a rigid one. Before the split, the Germanic languages were languages with an underspecified directionality. The historic change was from an underspecified to a specified directionality value, with rigid directionality as a result.

This change required the choice of either one of two values as the canonical value. The choice of the value was in principle free. So, it happened that one dialect fixed it in the OV way and became the mother dialect of the West Germanic OV branch. The other dialect fixed it in the VO way and became the mother dialect of the North Germanic branch. This choice was independent of the morphological inventory. So, for example, two very similar languages in terms of their morphosyntactic make-up, namely Icelandic and German, ended up in different directionality systems by accident. The accident is the choice of the directionality value when giving up the adjustability option. Similarly, each group contains languages with hardly any morphosyntactic inventory, namely Afrikaans in the OV group, and the continental Scandinavian Germanic language in the VO group.

The rest of this section is devoted to a sceptical reader's desire for solid empirical evidence for the claim that the Yiddish VP clearly shows OV properties (besides the obvious VO-like order variants in the VP), and that Yiddish is – contra Diesing (1997) – not simply a VO language with scrambling options. Vikner (2001) offers a detailed and carefully argued demonstration that Yiddish has typical OV properties that are not found in any Germanic VO language. Here, just two data areas will be highlighted, namely (i) the *verb particle order* and (ii) the *auxiliary order.*

Vikner (2001: 37) characterizes the relevant facts as follows: 'In Yiddish and the (other) Germanic OV-languages, particle verbs whose particles are postverbal under V2 (separate) nevertheless always have preverbal particles in non-V2 contexts, whereas in the Germanic VO-languages, particle verbs whose particles have to be stranded under V2 never have preverbal particles in non-V2 contexts.'

(i) Verb particle order

The verb particle order follows the canonical directionality of licensing. Only if Yiddish is an OV language like German and Dutch, and not a VO language like English or Danish, would it be expected to have particles in the preverbal position in non-V2 constructions as in German and Dutch. Note that preverbal particles of particle verbs are never preverbal in a VO language. So, the crucial cases are (10d) and (11d). Both in the infinitival as well as in the participial construction the unmarked order in Yiddish is identical with the Dutch and German order. This order is ungrammatical in a VO language like Danish or English.

(10) a. * Den Brief wird er schicken *ab*   *German*
            the letter will he send off
      b.   Den Brief wird er *ab*schicken
      c. ?? Den briv vet er shikn *avek*   *Yiddish*
      d.   Den briv vet er *avek*shikn
      e.   Brevet vil han sende *afsted*   *Danish*
      f. *   Brevet vil han *afsted* sende
      g.   He will send *off* the letter   *English*
      h. *   He will *off* send the letter

(11)   a.   * Den Brief hat er geschickt *ab*   *German*
             the letter has he sent off
        b.   Den Brief hat er *ab*geschickt
        c.   ?? Den briv hot er geshikt *avek*   *Yiddish*
        d.   Den Briv hot er *avek*geshikt
        e.   Brevet har han sendt *afsted*   *Danish*
        f.   * Brevet har han *afsted* sendt
        g.   He has sent *off* the letter   *English*
        h.   * He has *off* sent the letter

The marked order (10c) and (11c) that is marginally available in Yiddish is ungrammatical in Dutch or German. It is the reflex of the potential switch of the directionality.

(ii) Variation in auxiliary verb orders

Two aspects are of interest here. First, the order of auxiliaries and quasi-auxiliaries follows the canonical licensing directionality. Second, in VO languages there is *no order variation* among these verbs, but in the Germanic OV languages, the order among auxiliaries and quasi-auxiliaries typically is variant (Vikner 2001), with language-specific clustering of properties. So, both the inverse order pattern as well as the fact that there is variation is a reliable indicator of the OV quality. Yiddish shows this order variation, and, as expected, it allows the head-final order as one of its options, the head-initial order as another option and the variation typical of the head-final variant.

Yiddish fits into the picture of German OV languages, but it would be the single outstanding exceptional case within the VO group. It shares the verb word order of German plus the variation that derives the Dutch order from the German basic order (see Haider and Rosengren 2003). Let me emphasize once more that there is no Germanic VO language that shows anything similar. Hence, Yiddish again is a well-behaved Germanic OV language in this respect. (12b) illustrates the OV-type verb–auxiliary order in the passive. (14) presents the variants for causative constructions. Here the dependent verb is an infinitive, and not a participle, as in (12). For the infinitive, both orders are attested. For an exhaustive overview of the whole class of auxiliaries and quasi-auxiliaries, including modals, in tense formation, passive, and with causative and perception verbs, see Vikner (2001: 73).

(12)   a.   * Di shtub iz *gevorn opgebrent*   *Yiddish*
             the house is been up-burned
             'The house has been burnt down'

        b.   Di shtub iz *opgebrent gevorn*

        c.   Das Haus ist *abgebrannt worden*   *German*
             the house is up-burned been

    d.   The book will *be bought*   *English*

    e.   * The book will *bought be*

    f.   Bogen vil *blive købt*   *Danish*
        book-the will be bought

    g.   * Bogen vil *købt blive*

The patterns with the passive auxiliary that are illustrated in (12) are representative of other constructions with auxiliaries and of the causative construction with *let*. In VO languages the relative order is invariant, without any exception, for all combinations of auxiliaries and semi-auxiliaries: the dependent verb follows. Therefore, (13a) and (13c) are grammatical, and (13b,d) are ungrammatical in VO languages (represented by English and Danish).

(13)   a.   He has *let* us *wait*   *English*

         b.   * He has us *wait let*

         c.   Han har *ladet* os vente   *Danish*

         d.   * Han har os *vente ladet*
            he has us wait let

Yiddish (14a,b) shows the order patterns known from its closest kin. (14a) is the order of Dutch (14c). (14b) is the German order (14f).[34]

(14)   a.   Er hot undz *gelozt vartn*   *Yiddish*
            he has us let wait

         b.   Er hot undz *vartn gelozt*
            he has us wait let

         c.   Hij heeft ons *laten wachten*   *Dutch*
            he has us let wait

         d.   * Hij heeft ons *wachten laten*

         e.   * Er hat uns *lassen warten*   *German*
            he has us let wait

         f.   Er hat uns *warten lassen*
            he has us wait let

On the basis of the extensive, robust and diverse enough evidence, in combination with the scrambling property of Yiddish, Vikner (2001: 86) concludes that

---

[34] Unlike German and Dutch, Yiddish does not employ the switch from the participial form to the bare infinitive (IPP, or *Ersatzinfinitiv*). IPP constructions do not exist in Yiddish (Vikner 2001: 71).

it is obvious 'that an account of Yiddish as an OV language will have far fewer problems to deal with than an account of Yiddish as a VO language would.' Nevertheless, Yiddish is not like Dutch or German with respect to the relative order of the verb and its DP arguments. No Germanic OV language allows DPs to follow the base position of their verbal head (except for cases of heavy NP shift), but Yiddish does, just like any VO language does. This conflict disappears once we acknowledge the crucial difference. In Yiddish, the verb is 'mobile'. So, Yiddish is a language with both OV properties and VO properties, simply because the adjustable directionality property makes both types of merger available in a single clause structure.

With Yiddish as a representative case for a property common to historic stages of Germanic languages, we arrive at this result: OV and VO are but the opposite settings in a system of merger with *fixed* directionality values. But crucially, this pair of settings is not exhaustive. There is a third possibility, namely an *adjustable* directionality value. This property is responsible for the mixed appearance of linear order in languages like Yiddish, and it is the key for understanding the diachronic development of Germanic languages. The change started from a common stage with adjustable directionality values and ended up with a split into two groups when the values got fixed. Fixing meant the choice of one of two available implementations, namely 'right' or 'left', with VO and OV as the resulting appearance. Since the split is completely independent of the morphosyntactic set-up, it is no surprise any more that both groups contain languages with ample and with scarce morphology.

Issue (vii): There is no evidence for scrambling from *parasitic gaps (pg)* in German.

The phenomenon of parasitic gaps (15) has been considered a cardinal diagnostic for A'-dependencies, since A'-dependencies (15a) license parasitic gaps, but A-dependencies do not (15b). So, if scrambling licenses parasitic gaps, scrambling must be an instance of A'-movement.

(15)   a. ? Which books$_i$ did you file e$_i$ [without reading pg_i]
        b. * These books$_i$ have been filed e$_i$ [without reading pg_i]

An English example like (15a) is usually paired with a German example like (16a) or (16b), as in Webelhuth (1992: 410f.), Müller (1995a: 173), or Grewendorf and Sabel (1999).

(16)   a. Er hat jeden$_i$ Gast [ohne pg_i anzuschauen] seinem^i Nachbarn e$_i$
            vorgestellt
            he has every guest [without to-look-at] his neighbour introduced
            'He has introduced every guest to his neighbour without looking at
            (him)'

b. Er hat die Gäste$_i$ [ohne *pg*$_i$ anzuschauen] einander^i e$_i$ vorgestellt
   he has the guests [without to-look-at] each other introduced
   'He has the guests introduced to each other without looking at
   (them)'

However, as has been emphasized by Webelhuth (1992: 410f.), the impact of
these data from German is more confusing than revealing. If (16a,b) are parasitic gap constructions, their collateral properties are inconsistent with standard
assumptions for another area of grammar. On the one hand, a parasitic gap
supposedly needs an A'-chain in order to be licensed, but on the other hand,
A'-antecedents should not bind anaphors but would trigger weak crossover violations. In (16a), the scrambled quantified DP binds a pronoun without any weak
cross-over effect, and in (16b) the scrambled object binds an anaphor. These
properties are the signs of A-positions. Since, under standard assumptions,
a position cannot simultaneously be treated as A and A', there are either two
movement steps involved (cf. Mahajan 1994), or the dichotomy must be relaxed
(cf. Deprez 1994), or the data must be re-evaluated for their validity. We advocate the third option.

At least for German, the identification of constructions like (16) as parasitic gap
constructions is highly questionable. First of all, the gaps in adverbial infinitival
clauses do not have the properties of parasitic gaps in English (see Haider and
Rosengren 2003: 243; Postal 1993).[35]

Second, Fanselow (1993) has noted parallels between this construction and
conjunction reduction and he concludes that *ohne* (without) and *anstatt* (instead
of) function syntactically like coordinating heads. The alleged parasitic gaps are
the result of a kind of coordination ellipsis (cf. 17b) rather than the result of the
parasitic gap-type variable binding mechanism. Viewed from this perspective, it
is not surprising any more that the alleged parasitic gap construction may contain
multiple gaps (17a), which would be illicit for parasitic gaps, but characteristic of
ellipsis constructions (17b).

(17)   a. dass er eine Frau$_i$ einem Mann$_j$ e$_i$ [anstatt *pg*$_j$ *pg*$_i$ vorzuziehen] unter-
           ordnen wollte
           that he a woman-ACC (to) a man-DAT [instead-of to-prefer] (to) subor-
           dinate wanted
           'that he wanted to subordinate a woman to a man instead of prefer-
           ring her to him'

---

[35] For arguments against the alleged evidence for A'-dependencies adduced from parasitic
gaps in Dutch, see chapter 2.3 of Neeleman (1994).

b. dass er eine Frau$_i$ einem Mann e$_i$ zuerst unterordnete und dann
[–^{36} vorzog]
that he a woman-ACC (to) a man-DAT first subordinated and then
[– preferred]
'that he first subordinated a woman to a man and then preferred her
to him'

The currently approved technical implementation for the case of genuine parasitic gaps is an analysis in terms of an empty operator that binds the parasitic gap and receives its interpretation from the licensing wh-item. It is for this reason that parasitic gaps are singular, since in spec C there is room for a single operator only.

Once it is realized that elliptic infinitivals are not cases of parasitic gap constructions in German (and the very same considerations apply to Dutch), the dilemma that scrambling apparently displays A- as well as A'-properties disappears, and so does the prime indicator for an A'-movement nature of scrambling in German: scrambling does not feed parasitic gaps, so parasitic gaps do not support the claim that scrambling chains are A'-chains. Since the elliptic infinitival adverbial clauses do not involve genuine parasitic gaps, it should not come as a surprise any more that these alleged parasitic gap constructions have properties that differ significantly from English parasitic gap constructions (see Haider and Rosengren 1998, section 3.2.3).

Note, finally, that the alleged 'parasitic gap' construction of German would have to scramble elements that do not scramble (easily). Wh-elements in-situ (18) license the alleged parasitic gaps, both in the function of a wh-interrogative (18a) as well as in the function of a wh-indefinite (18b), that is, 'someone'. (18a) is grammatical in each of the two interpretations of *wen* (whom/someone). Wh-elements do not scramble, neither as wh-in-situ nor as indefinite pronouns.

(18)   a. Wer hat seinem Nachbarn wen$_i$ [ohne [–] anzuschauen] e$_i$
vorgestellt?
who has his neighbour whom [without to-look-at] introduced
'Who introduced whom/someone to his neighbour without looking
at (him)?'

b. Er hat seinem Nachbarn wen$_i$ [ohne [–] anzuschauen] e$_i$ vorgestellt
he has his neighbour whom [without to-look-at] introduced
'He introduced someone to his neighbour without looking at (him)'

---

^{36} '–' is used to signify the position of the missing element(s) in a neutral way, that is, without commitment to analysis as ellipsis or parasitic gap.

It should be borne in mind that the alleged parasitic gaps have to be interpreted as bound pronouns. This is easy to understand when the antecedent is a quantifier.[37] This strengthens the parallel to coordination constructions.[38]

4.4.2   Controversial theoretical issues

Issue (i): Is scrambling syntactically optional?[39]

This issue has continuously produced controversies in the literature. These controversies are nourished by the desire to axiomatically ban optional movement from the realm of Universal Grammar. Scrambling appears to be a cardinal case of a syntactically *optional* tool of grammar. Present-day Generative Grammar favours a deterministic approach. This excludes truly optional syntactic operations. Each operation has to be uniquely triggered. Scrambling is an embarrassment for this policy since, until now, it defied any attempt to successfully unveil an uncontroversial syntactical trigger. Scrambling seems to be just a system's potential of an OV language exploited and synergistically occupied by modules of grammar at the respective interfaces (e.g. scope domains in semantics, or information structure effects in pragmatics).

---

[37] This becomes particularly clear, as Ulli Lutz (pers. comm.) pointed out, with negated quantifiers as antecedents:

(i)   Sie hat keinen$_i$ [ohne *pg* anzulächeln] e$_i$ begrüßt
        she has no-one [without smiling-at] welcomed
        'She did not welcome anyone without smiling'

The negative indefinite has wide scope. It cannot be reconstructed into the adverbial phrase/clause.

[38] Here is an example:

(i)   Heute hat fast jeder einen Gast mitgebracht und ihn mir nicht vorgestellt
        today has almost everyone a guest-ACC along-brought and him-ACC (to) me-DAT not introduced
        'Today, everyone brought a guest along and he did not introduce him to me'

The reading of i) is this: For every x, there is a guest y, such that [[..y..] and [..y..]].

[39] Müller (1995a: 95–100) emphasizes the optionality of scrambling in German. For optionality of scrambling in Japanese, see Fukui (1993), Saito and Fukui (1998: 440) and Miyagawa (1997). Bošković and Takahashi (1998), contrary to Saito and Fukui, assume that scrambling involves covert movement: the scrambled element is base-generated in its overt non-theta position and is moved back in LF to the position where it receives its theta role. This hypothesis is motivated primarily by the desire to find a consistent way of integrating optional scrambling into the Minimalist Program, even at the price of assuming lowering rules. We interpret this as a demonstration of the obvious difficulties of dealing with an optional system's potential rather than a convincing solution.

So, let us check whether scrambling is indeed optional in German and whether there is a trigger for scrambling. Two cases have been suspected as cases of obligatory scrambling, namely the serialization of objects relative to the negation particle, and the counterparts of the Dutch object-adverbial order variation.

In order to demonstrate the obligatoriness of scrambling, one would have to demonstrate a case with the scrambled order as the *only* grammatical order. Such a case could be constructed on the ban against wh-indefinites in the domain of particle negation, cf. (1a–d) (see Jacobs 1982; Haider 1996), and the position of the negation particle in relation to objects in general. The grammatical versions of (1c,d) require a negative indefinite, that is, *nichts* (nothing) instead of *nicht was* (not something) and *kein Gesindel* (*no* rabble), instead of *nicht Gesindel* (*not* rabble), respectively.

(1)   a.   dass hier wer was *nicht* begreift
                that here who what not grasps
                'that someone does not grasp something here'

        b.   dass er hier Gesindel *nicht* duldet
                that he here rabble not tolerates
                'that he does not tolerate rabble here'

        c.   * dass hier wer *nicht* was begreift
                that here somebody not something grasps

        d.   * dass er hier *nicht* Gesindel duldet
                that he here not rabble tolerates

If scrambling is invoked for (1a,b), we end up in a dilemma because indefinite wh-pronouns do not scramble, as (2a,b) illustrates, nor does an indefinite collective noun like *Gesindel* (rabble). In (2a), the order of the indefinite pronouns is the base order for a verb like *erklären* (explain). Scrambling is possible for indefinite DPs (2c), but not for indefinite pronouns. But this is exactly what is required for removing an indefinite out of the scope domain of negation.

(2)   a.   Hier will ich jetzt wem was erklären
                here want I now whom-DAT what-ACC explain
                'Here, I now want to explain something to someone'

        b.   */?? Hier will ich jetzt was$_i$ wem e$_i$ erklären
                here want I now what-ACC whom-DAT explain
                'Here, I now want to explain something to someone'

        c.   Hier will ich jetzt ein Problem$_i$ einem Leser e$_i$ erklären
                here want I now a problem-ACC a reader-DAT explain
                'Here, I now want to explain a problem to a reader'

At this point we have to rethink a tacit assumption, namely the assumption that the position of the negation particle *universally* is a pre-VP position. If you think you need obligatory scrambling for removing indefinites out of the scope of negation, you presuppose that the objects are generated/merged in a domain that is (potentially) in the scope of negation. This domain is the VP and the negation particle is assumed to be generated above the VP. But, and this is crucial, negation need not precede the *entire* VP. The alleged evidence for postulating a universal pre-VP position of negation comes from *head-initial* languages only. Only in VO and VSO languages does the negation particle precede the VP (3a). In OV languages, the negation particle is positioned close to the verb and thus follows the arguments (3b). This has been typologically attested by Dryer (1988).

(3)   a. ... [*Neg* [$_{VP}$ V$_{(fin)}$ –]]   head-initial VP
        b. ... [$_{VP}$ – *Neg* (...) V$_{fin}$]   head-final VP

If so, what is the universal, cross-linguistically valid structural requirement of sentence negation? The finite verb is the exponent of the tense features and tense situates the proposition. This is the domain negation operates on. The negation particle in the function of sentence negation must *c-command the finite verb* or its *trace*, if the verb is moved for finiteness reasons (e.g. the trace in the position out of which it is raised to an F-head in V2 languages).

The very same c-command requirement implemented in VO and OV produces different outcomes, respectively. Only in an OV language can the c-command requirement be fulfilled by a VP-internal negation, with the finite verb in the VP-*internal* position (3b). In VO (and VSO), however, the lowest c-commanding position for negation is the position preceding the entire VP, simply because the verb is VP-*initial*. In an OV language, however, the finite verb remains in its VP-internal base position. Any VP-internal particle c-commands the finite verb. So the negation particle can be placed in the lowest position preceding the finite verb. As a consequence, and in the absence of compactness in OV, argument positions, and in particular the positions of indefinite wh-pronoun arguments, easily precede the VP-internal position of the negation particle. Thus, the scrambling dilemma for indefinite wh-pronouns disappears. Indefinite pronouns do not scramble, they are generated/merged/projected in a position that precedes the negation particle, and there is no candidate for obligatory scrambling left.

The Dutch type of 'scrambling' is of the very same nature. The object is not scrambled, but merged above the adverbial. Since a head-final VP is not compact, it provides room for VP-internal adverbials. They may be merged immediately above their minimal domain of semantic integration. So, the position of the object relative to an adverb does not tell anything about scrambling.

The semantic difference between (4a) and (4b) follows immediately from the respective scope domain of the frequency adverbial. In (4a), the indefinite *was* (something) is in the scope of the frequency adverbial, in (4b) it is not and has wide scope. An analogous difference holds for the versions with a topicalized VP (4c,d).

(4)   a. Er hat *mehr als einmal* was angefasst
          he has more than once something touched

       b. Er hat was *mehr als einmal* angefasst
          he has something more than once touched

       c. [Was *mehr als einmal* angefasst]$_{VP}$ (das) hat nur einer
          [something more than once touched] (this) has just one

       d. [*Mehr als einmal* was angefasst]$_{VP}$ (das) hat nur einer
          [more than once touched something] (this) has just one

Note that a scrambling analysis of (4b) would incorrectly predict ambiguous scope, since scrambling would leave a trace within the scope of the adverbial. Genuine scrambling is indeed scope ambiguous, adverb placement is not:

(5)   a. Er hat ja fast allen *mindestens zwei* Fragen gestellt
                                                        unambiguous scope
          he has PRT almost all at-least two questions put
          'He has put almost all (of them) at least two questions'

       b. Er hat ja *mindestens zwei* Fragen$_i$ fast allen e$_i$ gestellt
                                                        ambiguous scope
          he has PRT *at least two* questions almost all put
          'He has put at least two questions (to) almost all (of them)'

       c. Er hat ja fast immer allen *mindestens zwei Fragen* gestellt
                                                        unambiguous scope
          he has PRT almost always (to) all at-least two questions put

       d. Er hat ja *mindestens zwei* Kandidaten fast immer dieselbe Frage
          gestellt   *unambiguous scope*
          he has PRT (to) at-least two candidates almost always the same question put
          'At least two candidates, he has almost always asked the same question'

For (5b), the scope inverse to the linear order is available because of the trace of the scrambled item. For (5d), inverse scope is not a natural option.[40] This follows if

---

[40] A decided scope judgement is a notoriously subtle phenomenon for elicitation. If you want to double check on these data, you should systematically vary the quantifiers in

(5b), but not (5d), is a case of genuine scrambling. In (5b), the trace is in the scope of the lower quantifier. This accounts for the possibility of a wide scope reading for *allen* (to all). In (5d), however, *fast immer* (almost always) does not have a wide scope reading. If the object had been scrambled across *fast immer*, this secondary, wide scope reading should be available, just as in (5b). Scrambling would leave a trace in the scope domain of the quantifier.

Issue (ii): What could be a potential syntactic trigger of scrambling?

Approaches within present-day Generative Grammar expect grammatical operations to be triggered. In the recent rendering of this working hypothesis this means that a grammatical feature is involved that needs to be taken care of by a particular structural position. So, the element with the particular feature has to move to the particular position, otherwise grammaticality becomes faulty.[41] For instance, the agreement feature(s) of the English subject are taken to be checked in a functional agreement position. So the subject DP must move to this position. This accounts among other things also for the movement in the passive that obligatorily displaces the object to the subject position in English. Successful trigger hypotheses would have to produce a trigger for scrambling that is as effective as the trigger for subject-with-spec-Agr agreement in English. This is the trigger that is responsible for the obligatory raising of the subject to the spec position.

The basic problem with triggering accounts is this: either they are begging the question and/or they are too strong, or too weak. It is evidently begging the question, if a '[+ scrambling]' feature is postulated just in order to trigger scrambling for the item this feature is assigned to (cf. Sauerland 1999).

An example of too weak an account is one that categorically restricts the features to DP-type case features (e.g. van den Wyngaerd 1989; Mahajan 1994; Miyagawa 1997, for IP-adjunction). Various empirical facts, e.g. the existence of VP-internal scrambling and the lack of opacity of scrambled phrases, notably of scrambled infinitival clauses, speak against scrambling being triggered by a property of only DS, namely their need to be case-licensed in specific case positions (i.e. functional spec positions). More generally, DP-feature-triggered scrambling does not cover non-DP scrambling. In scrambling languages, scrambling is not categorically restricted to DPs. PPs and CPs scramble, too.

---

the stimulus sentence. You are likely to harvest a clear informant feeling with stimulus sentences with negated frequency quantifiers.

(i)   Er hat ja zumindest eine Frage fast nie gestellt   (unambiguous scope)
        he has PRT at-least one question almost never asked

[41] The Generative literature on scrambling is full of attempts to identify a triggering feature for scrambling. See for instance Ko (2007), Sabel (2001), or Sauerland (1999), who considers even a [+*scr*] feature.

In German, CPs – both finite as well as infinitival ones – and PPs may scramble. So, accounts in terms of case-driven movement (= movement into F-specs of case-checking heads) are *undergenerating*. At the same time, these accounts are too strong, if they entail that scrambling is obligatory (i.e. because features must be obligatorily and overtly checked). This is evidently counterfactual.

The optionality problem could in principle be solved if the scrambling order and the canonical order were disjoint relative to some grammatical or semantic function. That is, the scrambling order would meet a property that the canonical order is not compatible with. However, the facts clearly tell that this is not the case. There is no property that could not be met in the canonical order as well. Here are some candidates: *case, givenness, focusing/focus avoidance, semantics* (*'strong' reading of indefinites*).

It is not case. Assume that in German (or any odd scrambling languages) case is checked by a functional head probing into the base position of the case carrier either by attracting it to the spec position or by attracting just the abstract case feature, and assume that scrambling is just the overt movement of the cased phrase to the case position. Why is this not a particularly adequate account? First, simply because scrambling is not restricted to cased elements. PPs and clauses scramble as well, and they are not case marked. Second, this account just shifts the optionality problem from 'optional movement' to the option of either attracting the bare feature or the feature plus its carrier DP. And third, the order of scrambled phrases would be determined by the functional cascade. But, crucially, if more than one DP is scrambled, the relative order among the scrambled DPs is free.

It is not givenness (or another pragmatic feature of a similar kind). Both the analytic inspection of data (6) as well as experimental studies (see for instance Skopeteas and Fanselow 2007)[42] show that givenness is not a trigger but rather a beneficiary of scrambling. Scrambling allows us to neatly partition the clause into 'given' (preceding) and 'asserted' (following) in terms of word order, but this partitioning of the clause is not mandatory.

The introductory question in (6) displays three discourse participants (*he, set of apples, the bag*) as given, and asks for the identification of a new, fourth one, namely the recipient. Lenerz (1977) already demonstrated that in question–answer pairs, scrambling may be applied for achieving a given-before-new order, with the new item ending up to the right of the given ones. In addition, he showed that the order (6b) would be infelicitous if uttered as an answer for a different question, namely one that asks for the direct object, namely *Äpfel* (apples).

---

[42] This study reports that the test subjects scrambled a 'given' object across an agentive 'new' subject only in one out of 64 cases. In seven out of 64 cases, the 'given' object was topicalized. In sum, 'givenness' as a 'trigger' would account for only one out of eight, but it would fail for 7/8 of the stimuli.

In this case, 'the apples' would constitute the new piece of information that is scrambled into the area of the given information. So, there is a restriction on scrambling, but not a trigger.

(6)   Wem hätte *er* denn *die Äpfel in die Tasche* tun sollen?
        Whom-DAT had he PRT the apples into bag put been-obliged-to
        'For whom should he have put the apples into the bag?'

   a. Meiner Meinung nach hätte er den KINdern *die Äpfel*$_{given}$ in die Tasche
      tun sollen
      my opinion according-to had he the kids the apples into the bag put
      ought-to
      'In my opinion, he should have put the kids the apples into their bags'

   b. Meiner Meinung nach hätte er *die Äpfel*$_i$ den KINdern e$_i$ in die Tasche
      tun sollen
      my opinion according-to had he the apples the kids into the bag put
      ought-to
      'In my opinion, he should have put the kids the apples into their bags'

It is not focus. This pair of examples (6a,b) not only illustrates *givenness*, but also *focusing*. In the answer to the question, the element that answers the question word is put into focus, indicated by capitals in (6). The focus is the answer for 'wem' (whom-DAT), that is, the indirect object of the verb. The answer clause may either stick to the canonical order (6a) or it may be reordered such that the answer item ends up in the position preceding the verb (and its co-predicate)[43] as in (6b). Here, scrambling appears to have an *altruistic* effect. It produces an order in which the focused element appears as the argument closest to the verb, by removing the interveners. The preverbal position is a preferred position in a clause for a focused argument.[44] Altruistic movement is hard to reconcile with triggering, however. The trigger would be a 'kick out' feature that chases away all elements out of the domain of the item. This would not be the kind of feature conceived of as triggering features, namely features that travel to their checkpoint because they are attracted by a particular functional head.

It is not meaning. The claim that scrambling is syntactically optional does not deny that scrambling has semantic and/or pragmatic effects. But, first of all, these effects are not exclusively dependent on scrambling, otherwise languages without

---

[43] The example involves a complex predicate (Neeleman 1995; Haider 1997d), that is, the verb plus the preceding directional (= resultative) PP. This type of PP cannot be scrambled. PPs that scramble are argumental PPs, that is, PP objects.

[44] Note that the nuclear stress position is normally the *deepest* argument position in a phrase structure. So, in a head-final clause, this is the preverbal position. All other argument positions to the left are higher in structure.

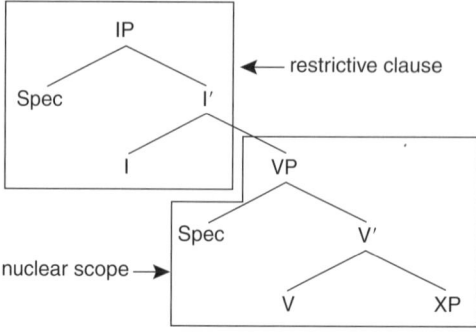

Figure 4.1 *Tree splitting (cf. Diesing 1992)*

scrambling would be seriously underprivileged. Second, the fact that scrambling is enlisted for pragmatic functions must not be equated with scrambling being syntactically *triggered* by these functions.

So, once more, semantic interpretation (see e.g. Adger 1994) does not provide a *syntactic* trigger, since the reading that is associated with a scrambled constituent is available in the canonical order, too. Scrambling may *cancel* a reading available in the canonical order, namely the reading with existential closure, but it does not *provide* a new one that is not already available in the canonical order. The cancelling effect is the effect of fronting across domain-sensitive elements. Let us examine an exemplary case of a meaning-based, in particular an information structure-based, account of scrambling by de Hoop (1992), drawing on Diesing's (1992) tree-splitting hypothesis (see figure 4.1).

A crucial area of evidence for the tree-splitting hypothesis is the interpretation of indefinite DPs, notably bare plurals. If a bare plural DP precedes a frequency universal as in (8b) and in (9b), the existential reading is unavailable. Instead, the preferred reading is generic. 'Generic' vs 'existential' interpretation roughly refers to the distinction illustrated by (7):

(7)   She published *papers on English grammar*
       (i) existential: X_{she} published a set of Ys, and each Y is a paper on English grammar
       (ii) generic: If Y is a paper (of her) on English grammar, X_{she} typically published Y

The existential reading of (7i) refers to individual entities that are papers on English grammar. The generic reading refers to properties of a kind ('genus', something common to a whole group or class). So, in the generic reading (7ii), we talk about a kind, namely the class of 'papers on English grammar' and a typical property.

Diesing (1992) proposes a specific syntax–semantics correspondence:

• The VP is mapped on the *nuclear scope* domain of the semantic representation of a clause. This is the domain of existential binding.
• The domain above the VP is mapped on the *restrictor* domain.

The existential reading is not appropriate for the order in (8b) and (9b). This is derived from tree splitting on the assumption that both in Dutch (8) and in German (9) the position of the frequency adverbial precedes the VP:[45] if the VP is the domain of existential closure and the adverbial precedes, a preceding bare plural DP is outside the domain of existential closure.

(8) a. dat de politie *altijd krakers* oppakt   *existential or generic*
        that the police always squatters arrests

     b. dat de politie *krakers altijd* oppakt   *generic*
        that the police squatters always arrests   (de Hoop 1992)

(9) a. dass Otto *immer [Bücher über Wombats]* liest

                                                           existential or generic
        that Otto always [books about wombats] reads

     b. dass Otto *[Bücher über Wombats immer]* liest   *generic*
        that Otto [books about wombats] always reads   (Diesing 1992)

German scrambling provides another instance of the alleged tree-splitting effect, or alternatively, of a domain effect. In (10a) and (10c), the object is scrambled across the subject (quantifier) and the existential reading becomes unavailable. Crucially, the same effect appears if an object is scrambled over an object and does not cross the subject (10e).

(10) a. dass *[Bücher über Wombats]*$_i$ keiner e$_i$ liest   *generic*
        that [books about wombats] nobody reads

     b. dass keiner *[Bücher über Wombats]* liest   *existential or generic*
        that nobody [books about wombats] reads

     c. dass Hausbesetzer$_i$ die Polizei e$_i$ verhaftet   *generic*
        that squatters-OBJ the police-SUBJ arrests

     d. dass die Polizei Hausbesetzer verhaftet   *existential or generic*
        that the police-SUBJ squatters-OBJ arrests

---

[45] Note that this could be made to follow from a different assumption. Instead of identifying the domain of existential closure with a specific subtree, a relative characterization would suffice. Existential closure is possible only in a narrow scope domain. In (8b) and (9b), the crucial item precedes a universal frequency quantifier and therefore its domain properly contains a domain of quantification.

e. wenn wer [*Bücher über Wombats*]$_i$ niemandem e$_i$ zeigen will

generic

    if someone [books about wombats] nobody-DAT show wants
    'If books about wombats, someone wants to show to nobody'

f. wenn wer niemandem [*Bücher über Wombats*] zeigen will

existential or generic

    if someone (to) nobody-DAT [books about wombats] show wants

For Diesing (1992), the scrambled object in (9) has left the VP as the nuclear scope domain and entered the domain of the restrictor. Hoop (1992), who characterizes scrambling as optional A-chaining, maintains that 'strong' case positions are associated with 'strong' readings (e.g. generic, specific, partitive), and therefore, only 'strong' DPs may scramble. Scrambled DPs are assumed to target higher functional spec positions, whose heads are 'strong' case heads. The 'strong' case position is incompatible with existential closure.

Note first of all that these approaches share a disadvantage of all accounts that invoke functional specs as targets for scrambling: if there is a cascade of Case heads above the VP, the relative order of the cascade of functional heads would predict a fixed order for the scrambled DPs, contrary to facts.

Second, the tree-splitting or 'strong' case approach misses an essential generalization: scrambling *cancels* one of several interpretation options (namely existential closure), but it crucially does not produce one. A so-called 'strong' interpretation (e.g. the generic one) is not a function of scrambling. It is available also in the unscrambled order. Scrambling does not make available interpretation options; it cancels one. Hence, a trigger relation is not the most promising way of modelling this set of facts.

Third, (10e) shows that tree splitting at the VP boundary misses an essential point. Whenever an indefinite is scrambled across a quantified item, it loses its existential reading. But, in (10e), unlike the usually adduced examples with scrambling across a subject, the target position of scrambling follows the subject. In (10e,f), the subject *wer* (who) is a wh-pronoun used as an indefinite pronoun (with the reading *someone*). These pronouns are inert for scrambling. So, it is unlikely that both the subject *wer* and the scrambled object *Bücher über Wombats* are outside the VP. A straightforward account is that scrambling in (10e) just skips the object. This is confirmed by the fact that scrambling is licit also within topicalized VPs,[46] with the very same effect on the interpretation of the scrambled indefinite.

---

[46] Here is an example:

(i)   [[Bücher über Wombats]$_i$ niemandem e$_i$ zeigen]$_{VP}$ würde nur einer
          [[books about wombats] nobody-DAT show] would only one
          'There is only one who would show books about wombats to nobody'

Fourth, for an account based on tree splitting (with or without 'strong' functional case) it is unexpected that the existential reading does not get lost in scrambled positions in certain contexts, namely in the scope of higher quantifiers, as Ruys (2001) noted, who credits Kerstens (1975) for this observation.

(11)   a. dass der Premierminister *oft* (einen) Journalisten weggeschickt hat
                                                                        existential
            that the prime-minister often (a) journalist(s) away-sent has

        b. dass der Premierminister (einen) Journalisten *oft* weggeschickt hat
                                                                        *existential
            that the prime-minister (a) journalist(s) often away-sent has

        c. dass *jeder* Premierminister (einen) Journalisten *oft* weggeschickt hat
                                                                        existential
            that every prime-minister (a) journalist(s) often away-sent has

Note that the relative order between the indefinite/bare-plural DP and the frequency adverbial in (11b,c) remains constant. Nevertheless, the interpretation options differ. (11b), as predicted by Diesing and Hoop, does not invite an existential reading, but the existential reading is available in (11c). What is crucial is that in (11c), the indefinite DP is in the scope of a higher quantifier, namely the quantified subject. Hence, it is not just the position of the DP that strictly determines the interpretation. In Ruys' (2001: 65) words this reads as: 'There is no evidence that scrambled weak NPs must become strong or presuppositional; indeed, this is often very clearly not the case.[47] And those interpretive effects that do arise with scrambling affect not only weak NPs but strong ones as well and seem related to scope and focus much more than to strength.' Schenner (2004) demonstrates with a wide range of data that an empirically adequate account of the partitioning problem is a cross-modular effect, fed in part by information structure dependent conditions (focus, clausal topic, discourse topic, presupposition) and in part by structural conditions (different c-command domains).

In sum, it seems safe to conclude that the syntax–semantics interplay in the interpretation of indefinites constitutes compelling evidence neither for scrambling as (triggered) movement to higher functional spec positions nor for semantic features as triggers of scrambling.

---

[47] Here is an example with a scrambled bare plural that may receive an existential reading:

(i)   Damals hat ja doch [einer *Geheimdokumente*ᵢ Journalisten eᵢ übergeben]
                                                                (Haider 2000a: 36)
            then has PRT [someone secret-files (to) journalists over-handed]
            'In those days, someone has handed over secret files to journalists'

Note that there is a typological implication: if scrambling was movement triggered by higher functional heads, it ought to be operative also in some Germanic VO languages as well, for instance, in Icelandic, with its rich morphological system of case marking (Kress 1982). This is not the case, however (cf. Collins and Thráinsson 1996: 410). Although a pre-VP position is accessible for object shift, this movement conserves the base order, both for subject–object order (12a,b) as well as for double object constructions. In German, both orders are available (12c,d).

(12)   a.   Í gær las Jón bækurnar$_i$ ekki e$_i$ *Icelandic*
              Yesterday read John books-the not
              'Yesterday John did not read the books'

        b.   *Í gær las bækurnar$_i$ Jón ekki e$_i$
              Yesterday read books-the John not

        c.   Gestern las Hans die Bücher nicht (= 12a)   *German*
              Yesterday read Hans the books not

        d.   Gestern las die Bücher Hans nicht (= 12b)
              Yesterday read books-the Hans not

If there was a syntactic trigger for scrambling in German, the difference between the availability of scrambling in German and the lack of scrambling in Icelandic would have to be reduced to an accidental property: it so happens that the relevant feature is strong in German but weak in Icelandic. The difference is *not* accidental, however. It is a difference that relates directly to the difference between OV and VO. So, arbitrary assignment of strong/weak values is but a technical option, but the relevant generalization would not be captured. The discussion does not honour the typological moment, namely the correlation with the directionality parameter. The absence of the compactness property in head-final phrases provides headroom not only for adverbial positions but also for scrambling positions. This seems to be the principal source of a word order variability unknown for strict VO languages.

It is not driven by a scrambling feature. No insight is gained by (optionally) assigning a feature [+*scr*] to a phrase that is to be scrambled (see Sauerland 1999). Of course, there is no way to prove that such a feature does not exist in the grammatical reality because the non-existence of a feature is impossible to prove since it is a system-internal construct with no ontological qualities outside of the formal system. It is sufficient, though, to keep in mind that this implementation of feature triggering is an ad hoc technical device. It is the kind of feature that a grammar theory must not admit, namely an isolated, system-internal feature whose only function is that of launching a movement operation.

Issue (iii): Does scrambling involve chain formation?

What would be the alternative to movement and chain formation? The alternative is that the order variation called scrambling is merely the result of base-generating alternative orders. This is presently a minority position, advocated for instance by Fanselow (1993, 2001, 2003). The majority position is one that favours scrambling by movement.

Fanselow (2003) suggests that the merging operation that combines a head with its arguments is free, that is, merger may apply in any order. Languages with rigid word order would be languages that overtly move the arguments to functional spec positions for licensing whereas languages with free word order move the arguments covertly. So the free surface word order is the free basic word order in these languages.

Why is it that difficult to present conclusive evidence for the simple question: does scrambling involve traces? First, scrambling is strictly local, and second, scrambled arguments display the properties of A-moved elements. So, there is no obvious difference between a DP in a scrambled position or in a base position with respect to locality or A-related properties, like binding. Third, it is clear that the target of scrambling cannot be a functional spec position since this would produce a freezing effect for extraction. But there is no freezing effect. So, scrambling must be re-merging[48] in the domain of merger, that is the VP. The result only minimally differs from base generation. The only difference is a trace.

(13)   a. $[X\ Y\ V^\circ]_{VP}$ assumed base order
       b. $[Y_i\ X\ e_i\ V^\circ]_{VP}$ scrambling by movement
       c. $[Y\ X\ V^\circ]_{VP}$ scrambling by alternative merger

So, what we would need is positive evidence for a trace. Conclusive evidence is hard to present, however. Here is first an inconclusive piece, for the sake of illustration. It is evidence from crossing violations, that is, from the result of moving the containing phrase of the trace across the antecedent of the trace.

It is well known that in English the pied-piping of an infinitival complement that contains the trace of a raised subject does in general not affect grammaticality (14a). Only with a *there* subject does a crossing violation result (14b).

(14)   a.   [How likely [t_i to win the match]] are some of our favourites$_i$? (cf. Postal 2004: 126)

        b. * [How likely [t_i to be a riot] is there$_i$

        c.   [Seinen Gästen e_i serviert] hätte er Champagner$_i$ sicherlich nicht
             [his guests served] has he champagne surely not

---

[48] *Re-merger* in the VP amounts to *adjunction* to (a sub-projection of) the VP in terms of the P&P model.

    d. */??[Sich e$_i$ vorgestellt]$_j$ hat ihr$_i$ Max nicht e$_j$
          [himself introduced] has (to) her Max not

    e.   [Ihr vorgestellt]$_i$ hat sich Max nicht e$_i$
          [(to) her introduced] has himself Max not

The acceptability of (14c) surely does not signal a crossing violation. This indicates that crossing is not at issue for scrambling. The fact that (14d) is deviant seems to be a side effect of the rigid order template for pronouns (see section 4.2.3).[49] The accusative precedes the dative in the pronoun order. Since the fronted phrase contains the accusative, the dative that would have to occur in between the accusative and the verb must not be crossed.[50] (14e), however, is analogous to (14c). So, for scrambling in general, crossing is not the source for conclusive evidence for a trace.

Let us turn now to more productive sources of evidence. One area of evidence has been introduced already above, namely scoping (section 4.3, property (v)). This evidence is construal based. It is not a matter of grammaticality or ungrammaticality, but one of the availability of one or the other reading. So, in the literature you will find incongruent data judgements. This makes it difficult to use as a source for the positive proof of a debated structure.

Much more robust are the judgements on nuclear stress contours and the decision whether stress in a given order entails narrow focus or not (Höhle 1982). Stress on the nuclear stress position is unmarked stress and so the focus is not constrained to the minimal phrase that contains the stressed item. Here are examples. Capital letters identify the stressed item.

(15)   a. Soeben hat jemand einem Verletzten einen ARZT besorgt
                                             (*maximal focus*)

        b. Soeben hat jemand einen Arzt$_i$ einem VerLETZTEN e$_i$ besorgt
                                             (minimal focus)

        c. Soeben hat jemand einen ARZT$_i$ einem Verletzten e$_i$ besorgt
                                             (minimal focus)

---

[49] The problem is not the reflexive fronted across its binder since (i) is perfectly acceptable:

(i)   [Stolz auf sich^i] war nicht einmal Max^i
       [proud of himself] was not even Max

[50] This clause is as deviant as the following clause (i). The required (relative) order is ACC–DAT, as in (ii). Of course, *ihr* (her) may be fronted across the subject.

(i)   */?? dass ihr Max sich nicht vorgestellt hat
           that her-DAT Max himself-ACC not introduced has

(ii)   dass sich-ACC Max ihr-DAT nicht vorgestellt hat
         'that himself Max (to) her not introduced has'

   d. Soeben hat jemand einem VerLETZTEN einen Arzt besorgt

                                                  (minimal focus)

   e. Soeben wurde einem Verletzten ein ARZT besorgt

                                                  (*maximal focus*)

   f. Soeben wurde ein ARZT$_i$ einem Verletzten e$_i$ besorgt

                                                  (minimal focus)

   g. Soeben wurde ein Arzt$_i$ einem VerLETZTEN e$_i$ besorgt

                                                  (minimal focus)

Note that each sentence in (15) in which the stressed phrase is immediately preceding the verb but does not allow maximal focus, is a sentence that involves
scrambling. Only in the base order does stress on the preverbal argument produce
a neutral nuclear stress pattern[51] (that is compatible with maximal focus). Why
should this be so?

   The position preceding the verb in the VP is the lowest position in the VP. If an
entire (complex) phrase is in focus, the phonetic focus is on the stressed syllable
of the head of the most deeply embedded phrase. So, if a whole clause is in focus,
the stressed syllable must be the head of the lowest phrase in the VP. If this phrase
is scrambled, however, the lowest phrase position is the position of the trace and
phonetically empty. Hence, the required stress contour is unavailable and therefore, scrambling of the lowest argument, as in (15b,c,f,g), is bound to yield narrow
focus. However, this follows only if scrambling leaves a trace, since it is this trace
that occupies the lowest position.

   In the passive variants, (15e,f,g), maximal focus is available, as expected, only if
the passive subject stays in its original object position. If it is scrambled, the focus
potential is reduced and there is no stress pattern that would yield maximal focus.

   The base generation approach is not compatible with this structure-based account
of focus since for this approach, at least (15b,c) would not contain a trace. The indirect object would be closest to the verb and it would be the lowest argument and
therefore it would have to be compatible with maximal focus when it is stressed.

   Unfortunately, Fanselow (2003) remains silent on the directionality issue, that
is, the question as to why, for instance, in German, the verbal arguments should
be licensed by covert movements while the arguments of the noun should have
to be licensed by overt movement and thereby would end up in a rigid order. The
answer could be one just in terms of setting the value 'overt'/'covert', completely

---

[51] A 'neutral nuclear stress pattern' is one in which focus is not constrained. The whole
     clause may be in focus. In other words, the clause is a felicitous answer to a question
     that does not presuppose anything, as for instance: 'What happened?' Minimal focus
     is focus on the minimal phrase. In this case, the clause is partitioned into focus and
     background. In the 'neutral' case, the utterance does not contain or mark backgrounded
     material.

disregarding the directionality difference between DPs and VPs, of course. But this would be a highly superficial level of accounting.

If scrambling is just a parametric difference between covert and overt movement of arguments to their respective functional licensing position, nothing seems to prevent this parameter from cutting across the OV/VO distinction. What could prevent a VO language such as Icelandic or Faroese with morphologically distinctly coded cases from applying covert licensing and thereby enjoying free word order for postverbal arguments in the VP? The answer would have to be that it simply happens that these two languages end up with the parameter setting for the value 'overt'.

So, for the time being, the preferred answer to the question 'Does scrambling involve traces?' is largely a theory-internal one. Whether the theory should provide multiple base orders for the arguments of a given head or whether it should determine a single base order is a theory-internal issue. This issue goes beyond the German scrambling data.

Issue (iv): What kind of syntactic process produces scrambling?

Up to now, all available theoretical approaches within the range of generative theories have found their (at least part-time) advocates in the literature: see Haider (1997e), and Corver and van Riemsdijk (1997) for a survey of the first generation of scrambling theories:[52] scrambling has been analysed in terms of either A or A'-movement to functional spec positions, in terms of adjunction as A-movement within the VP, or by A'-movement to positions outside the VP, or freely base-generated serializations. Second generation scrambling theories follow the premises of the Minimalist Program and try to implement it in terms of movement triggered by the need for feature checking. Accounts differ mainly in terms of the proposed triggering features (e.g. Richards 2004).

Given this state of affairs, it is worthwhile asking what might have prevented a general consensus on one of the solutions filtered out in this long-lasting discussion until now. One reason is that scrambling is used to refer to a wide range of word order variation phenomena (typical OV scrambling with the full range of permutation of arguments; argument–adverb order as in Dutch; string vacuous movement for evacuating the VP;[53] object shift; and so on). Any attempt at uniformly

---

[52] Implementations of scrambling within the framework of Optimality Theory have been proposed by Büring (2001), Choi (1999) and Müller (1999, 2000).

[53] Topicalization of what appears to be a subprojection of a VP (see (i) and (ii)) is often analysed as the result of evacuation plus topicalization of a VP ('remnant topicalization'; see den Besten and Webelhuth 1990). Equating this postulated evacuation operation with scrambling merely confounds the terminology. The evacuation movements are motivated only by the desire to have only entire phrases, that move, and not subprojections.

(i)   [e_j e_i Geschmückt] hat man den Sieger$_j$ mit einem Lorbeerkranz$_i$
       [decorated] has one the winner with a laurel-wreath

reconstructing these phenomena in a theory of grammar is bound to fail, if they do not constitute a consistent domain. Another reason is the dominant idea within generative theory that (overt and covert) movement is triggered movement and hence there cannot exist such a phenomenon as syntactically optional scrambling. So, much effort is devoted to uncover hidden triggers. Third, the empirical basis is still very narrow. Sufficiently peer-reviewed, detailed, in-depth analyses are available for only a few languages (mainly Germanic on the one hand, and Far Eastern OV languages on the other hand).

4.5   Outcomes and implications

Let us recapitulate the three principal alternative strategies of handling scrambling within grammar theory:

- Base generation approach: the scrambled orders are alternatively generated orders
- Derivation by movement in a functional-checking approach: the scrambled orders are derived orders. The scrambled elements are accommodated by functional spec positions
- Re-merger-by-adjunction approach: the scrambled orders are derived orders. The scrambled elements are locally (left)-adjoined to the phrase that contains the base position and thus remain within the directionality domain of the head.

For a comparative evaluation of these approaches you should check how straightforwardly each approach is able to account for at least the following properties: scrambling (a) is strictly clause bound, (b) may (not) target functional spec positions, (c) is non-string-vacuous, (d) may target any alternative positions within the (extended) VP, (e) is syntactically optional, (f) can apply to more than one phrase, (g) extends the binding domain of scrambled elements and gives rise to scope ambiguities, and finally, (h) presupposes a head-final domain of scrambling. The empirical evidence surveyed above is the basis of the following summary of generalizations on scrambling in German.

- *First*, scrambling arguably involves chain-formation. The evidence is the restriction on the focus domain once the lowest argument is scrambled. The trace in this position makes the nuclear stress assignment inapplicable.

(ii)   [e$_j$ Mit einem Lorbeerkranz geschmückt] hat man den Sieger$_j$
(iii)   (?) [Den Sieger mit einem Lorbeerkranz geschmückt] hat man

Table 4.1 *Checklist for the theoretical coverage of the characteristics of scrambling*

Scrambling theory properties	Checking-driven movement to spec	Alternative, base-generated orders	Re-merger = adjunction (to VP)
a. Moves {DP, PP, CP, (…)}	no[54]/ yes	–	yes
b. Freezing effect (opacity)	yes	no	no
c. Head-final domains only	no	???	yes
c'. OV languages only	no	???	yes
d. Feature-driven	yes	no	no
e. Optional	no	yes	yes
f. Creates a trace	yes	no	yes
g. Iterative	no (unless[55])	–	yes
h. Full range of permutation	yes (but[56])	yes	yes
i. Potentially string vacuous	yes	no	no
j. Creates A-type properties	yes/ no	yes	yes
k. Necessarily strictly local	no	yes	yes
l. Applies only in clausal XPs	yes (unless[57])	no	no

[54] 'No' applies to theories that take scrambling to be driven by DP features (e.g. case).

[55] Scrambling of more than a single phrase presupposes more than a single target position. This entails that there is either the possibility of targeting the same spec more than once (multiple spec) or that there is more than one functional phrase for checking the feature that triggers scrambling. Both options are equally unattractive. Multiple spec accommodation would make the sequence of scrambled phrases a syntactic unit that could not be interrupted by intervening material. But scrambling sequences with interveners are not ungrammatical in German. Multiplication of the functional projections for a single feature, on the other hand, is an unfounded assumption.

[56] The same problems as noted in the footnote above re-addressed: alternation in the order of multiple scrambled items is either variation in the order of multiply targeting a single spec (with the clear counterevidence from interveners) or variation in the targeting of multiple functional projections for the very same feature.

[57] In the current proposals, scrambling is framed in the functional architecture of a clause. If it is to apply in non-clausal domains, these domains would need the same kind of functional architecture as a clause.

- *Second,* the target position of scrambling is not a functional spec position. The evidence is clear and robust. It comes from the absence of a 'freezing' effect for extraction out of scrambled phrases.
- *Third,* scrambling correlates with headedness. It is a phenomenon of head-final projections. In German, scrambling is operative in the VP and the AP, which are the head-final projections in German. In head-initial structures (e.g. a complex NP, or in the head-initial projections of VO languages), scrambling is not found. The reason is this: left-adjunction to a VO structure creates a position that is not in the identification domain of the head of the projection. It would *precede* the head, whose canonical directionality domain comprises elements that *follow.*
- *Fourth,* only elements with a unique base position, i.e. selected elements, can be said to scramble. Alternative serializations of adjuncts relative to arguments and relative to each other are adequately described as generated in alternative positions (see Haider 2000b, 2004a).
- *Fifth,* scrambling chains come into being only when the surface order differs from the base order, i.e. scrambling is not string vacuous. This excludes two cases, namely the case in which scrambling of B across A is followed by A across B, with the scrambled order (AB) identical with the base order (AB). The second case would be pseudo-scrambling. The scrambled item would string-vacuously move into a higher position.
- *Sixth,* scrambling is optional, clause bound, category neutral and it may be applied to more than one phrase per domain of scrambling.
- *Seventh,* scrambled elements are possible binders and take scope.
- *Eighth,* scrambling is a free system potential of head-final phrases that is exploited in a cross-modular fashion for the semantic and information structure interface with syntax.

Let us finally briefly compare the principal approaches to scrambling with respect to these generalizations: there is a clear-cut opposition in at least six properties listed in table 4.1 between the movement-to-spec account and the re-merger account. So, empirical evidence and theory-internal coherence considerations should be enough for determining which approach is likely to provide the more successful modelling of the phenomenon.

Note that the 're-merger' approach characterized in the right-most column is intended to be in a direct and continuous relation to the empirical facts. Hence, whenever there is a difference between this column and the first or second one, the respective facts are challenges for the other theories, that is, the checking theories and the base-generation theory.

5

Targeting the right edge: extraposition

5.1   What is (at) the right edge?

The right edge[1] of a clause in German accommodates the phrases that, in the terminology of Generative Grammar, are said to be 'extraposed'. In general, the prime candidates for the right edge of a sentence are *embedded clauses* of any type, and *PPs*. Argumental noun phrases are excluded from the right edge, except for 'heavy' DPs ('heavy NP' shift). APs and VPs are banned from the right edge, too. Here are some representative examples. The examples in (1d–f) feature an optional pronominal correlate. (1e) is representative for PPs, with the pronoun (*da* = *there* instead of *es = it*) amalgamated with the preposition.

(1)   a. Man hat geglaubt, [die Sonne drehe sich um die Erde]

   finite V2 complement

   One has believed [the sun rotates itself around the earth]

   b. Man hat geglaubt, [dass sich die Sonne um die Erde drehe]

   finite CP complement

   One has believed [that itself the sun around the earth rotates]

   c. Man hat geglaubt, [diese Ansichten verbieten zu müssen]

   infinitival CP complement

   One has believed [these opinions forbid to have-to]

   d. Ihr hat (es) nicht gefallen, [wie man über ihn redete]

   wh-clause complement

   Her has (it) not pleased [how one about him talked]

   e. Man hat ihn (*dazu*) gezwungen, [das Land zu verlassen]

   infinitival CP complement

   One has him (*it*-into) forced [the country to leave]

---

[1] In the Germanic linguistics tradition this has become known as the 'Nachfeld' (postfield) of a clause. It starts right after the clause-final V-position.

    f. Er hat (es) nicht ausgeschlossen, [dass es so gewesen sein könnte]
                                             finite CP complement
        He has (it) not excluded [that it so been have could]

The extraposed *V2 sentence* in (1a) is the only type of embedded sentence that cannot occur in the preverbal domain as an alternative to the right edge. For finite clauses in general, the preverbal position is felt as clumsy rather than as ungrammatical, because of centre-embedding, but with adequate phrasing, informants will give you their consent. This is true for declaratives (1b) as well as for interrogatives (1d). Infinitival clauses are as acceptable in the midfield as in the right edge, and in the initial position as well, but only in the variant without a pronominal correlate, of course.[2]

If a sentence contains more than one embedded clause, multiple occupancy of the right edge is the consequence, with particular order effects. In (2a), the right edge contains two *dass*-introduced CPs, one of which is the object clause and one is a result clause depending on *so viele* (so many). The object clause precedes, the adjunct clause follows. In (2b), the object clause is an infinitival clause, and the following adjunct clause is a comparative clause. In (2c), however, the argument clause follows the relative clause. This is a cross-linguistically valid ordering pattern.[3] Cross-linguistically valid, too, is the ban against having two argument clauses in the right edge (2d–f).

(2)   a.   Mir haben soviele Leute versichert, [dass es so sei], [dass ich es selbst auch schon glaube]
                me have so-many people assured [that it so would-be] [that I it myself also already believe]
                'So many people have assured me that it would be so, that I myself believed it too'

---

[2] Keep in mind that in Dutch, infinitival clauses are obligatorily extraposed or topicalized, that is, fronted to the clause-initial position of a V2 clause. If not, they are ungrammatical. The only licit construction for non-moved infinitivals is the clause union construction with verb cluster formation (see chapter 7).

[3] Here is a small selection (see Haider 1997a). Note that the inverted order with the argument clause preceding the relative clause is unacceptable.

English: It struck an Austrian grammarian last century [*who analysed it*] [that this clause is grammatical]

Italian: Ho detto a qualcuno ieri [che mi aveva chiesto la strada] [*che non lo sapevo*]
           (I) have said to someone yesterday [who me asked the street] [that (I) not it know-1.P.Sg]

Swedish: Någon berättade [*som just hade lyssnat på nyheterm*] [att Ruczkoy hade fänglats]
           someone said [who just had listened to the-news] [that Ruczkoy had been-arrested]

  b.   Sie haben ihm öfter[i] vorgeschlagen, [eine andere zu heiraten], [als[i] er ertragen konnte]

    they have him more-often suggested [a different-one to marry] [than he bear was-able-to]

    'They have suggested to him to marry someone else more often than he could bear'

  c.   Mir hat ein Mann versichert, [den ich nicht kannte], [dass das Ende nah sei]

    me has a man assured [who I not knew] [that the end near would-be]

    'A man assured me who I did not know that the end would be near'

  d.   * Würde (es) beweisen, [dass sie ihn geküsst hat], [dass er ihr Liebhaber ist]?

    would (it) prove [that she him kissed] [that he her lover is]?

    '*Would it prove that she kissed him that he is her lover?'

  e.   * Würde (es) bedeuten, [ihn anzurufen], [ihn einladen zu müssen]?

    would (it) imply [him to-phone-up] [him invite to have-to]

    '*Would it mean to phone him up to have to invite him'

  f.   * Würde (es) bedeuten, [ihn anzurufen], [dass man ihn einladen müsste]?

    would (it) imply [him to-phone-up] [that one him invite would-have-to]

    '*Would it mean to phone him up that one would have to invite him'

Let us push the right edge capacity closer to its processable limit by constructing a sentence with at least three clauses in the right edge. The recipe is simple. Take a verb with an object clause and make sure you have an antecedent for a relative clause and for an adjunct clause. Again, the relative clause precedes the argument clause[4] that is sandwiched between the relative clause and the adjunct clause.

---

[4] Here are two examples sampled from a novel by Thomas Mann (*Doktor Faustus*, Frankfurt 1990) for readers who might think that a crowded right edge is just a generativist's whimsical invention.

  (p. 54): So brauchte etwa nur irgendwo im Reiche ein Bach-Fest bevorzustehen, [Rel.cl. zu dessen stilgerechten Aufführungen man einer Oboe d'amore bedurfte], [Adjunct cl. damit das alte Haus an der Parochialstraße den Kundenbesuch eines hergereisten Musikers empfing].

(3) Er hat so^i vielen Leuten^j gesagt, [denen^j er im Foyer begegnet war], [dass der Vortrag entfiele], [dass^i kein Mensch im Hörsaal erschien]
he has so many people told [who he in-the lounge met had] [that the lecture cancelled-was] [that no man in-the lecture room showed-up]
'he has told so many people who he had met in the lounge, that the lecture has been cancelled, that nobody showed up in the lecture room'

Since the right edge leaves room for adverbial clauses, too, the capacity of the right edge is not exhausted by the three clauses in (3), but we shall not push it any further here. Instead, we turn to PPs. It is a fact acknowledged by standard descriptive grammars of German that PPs may appear at the right edge. Here are examples; (4a,b) are from Schulz and Griesbach (1970, section E61, p. 395), (4c–e) are from the Duden grammar (1966, § 7055), which samples quotes from belletristic authors.

(4) a. Ich habe gestern noch im Büro gearbeitet *bis spät in die Nacht*
I have yesterday still in-the office worked till late in the night

b. Gestern sind viele Leute in München gewesen *trotz des schlechten Wetters*
yesterday have many people in Munich been despite the bad weather

c. Er wird sich rächen *für seinen Verrat*   (Max Frisch)
he will himself revenge for his betrayal

d. Morgen soll ich den Dienst antreten *in diesem Haus*
                                                              (Thomas Mann)
tomorrow shall I the duty up-take in this house

e. Trotzdem sah das doch sehr unsorgfältig aus *bei uns*
                                                              (Annette Kolb)
nevertheless looked it surely very untidy PRT with us

f. Sie will nichts mehr wissen *davon*   (Max Frisch)
she want nothing more know it-of
'She does not want to have anything to do with it'

For PPs, the grammatical function is a restricting factor. PPs in the function of (secondary) predicates (e.g. resultative, directional) are rejected if put into the right edge.

(p. 67): Wendell Kretzschmar huldigte dem Grundsatz, [$_{Rel.cl.}$ den wir wiederholt aus seinem zuerst von der englischen Sprache geformten Mund vernahmen], [$_{Adjunct cl.}$ dass es nicht auf das Interesse der anderen ankomme].

(5)   a. * Er hat es geschnitten [in kleine Stücke]   resultative predicate
          he has it cut [into small pieces]

       b. * Er hat sie gestellt [in eine Ecke]   directional predicate[5]
          he has her put [into a corner]

       c. * Es ist gewesen [in einem schlechten Zustand]   predicative PP
          it is been [in a bad shape]

DPs at the right edge are well formed only if they are *adverbial* (6a), or if they are so 'heavy', viz. lengthy, that the working memory relief overrides the restrictions of grammar (6b). In some contexts of utterance, as for instance in the case of announcements on train platforms, heaviness and shifting the crucial information to the focus of attention at the end of the message produce the same result in combination (6c).

(6)   a. wenn sie nicht geheiratet hätte *letztes Jahr /*seinen Nachbarn*
          if she not married had last year /*his neighbour

       b. Da hat auch noch angerufen *ein Herr Schmitt aus Castrop-Rauxel, der von dir wissen wollte, ob es stimme, dass man im Deutschen beliebig viele Sätze ausklammern dürfe*
          'There has also phoned a person named Schmitt, from Castrop-Rauxel, who wanted to know from you, whether it is correct, that German allows to extrapose arbitrarily many sentences'

       c. Auf Gleis Eins fährt ein *der Regionalzug aus Salzburg mit Planankunft um 10:17*
          on platform one moves in the local-train from Salzburg with arrival-time at 10:17
          'The local train from Salzburg with arrival time 10:17 is arriving on track one'

APs (7a) and VPs (7b) do not occur in the right edge in general, nor do wh-phrases in-situ (irrespective of their heaviness) (7c,d). The first restriction is one in terms of the category, the second one is the result of restrictions on the handling of in-situ wh-items (see chapter 3 on wh-constructions).

(7)   a. * Sie hat ihn gefunden [$_{AP}$ für die Aufgabe ungeeignet]
          she has him found [for the job unqualified]

       b. * Sie hat gesehen / gelassen [$_{VP}$ ihn abreisen]
          she has seen / let [him depart]

---

[5] A directional predicate is a subcase of a result predicate: the PP names the location an item ends up as the result of the process named by the directional verb.

    c.   Wann soll er den Dienst antreten hier /*wo?
        when shall he the job take-up here /*where

    d.   Wo hat er gewartet auf sie /*auf wen, als du ihn observiertest?
        where has he waited for her / for whom when you him observed

The availability of a right edge is not a property limited to clausal constituents. The availability of a right edge is a structural property of phrases in general, as the examples in (8) and (9–11) illustrate. A topicalized VP (8) provides a right edge, of course, and so do PPs, APs and NPs (9). In fact, the right edge of a clause is the right edge of the VP of the clause.

(8)   a. [$_{VP}$ Gesagt, *wo sie wohnt*], hat sie keinem
          [told *where she lives*] has she none

     b. [$_{VP}$ Einen Satz konstruieren, *der kein Nachfeld hat*], kann jeder
          [a sentence construct *that no postfield has*] can everybody

     c. [$_{VP}$ Gewartet *auf mich*] hat sie nicht
          [waited *for me*] has she not

Nominal phrases provide a right edge, too, as shown in (9a,b,e,g), and so do APs, as in (9d) and (10), and PPs as in (11).

(9)   a.   mehr^i Phrasen, *als^i nur die VPs*
           more phrases *than only VPs*

     b.   ein klügerer^i Mann, *als^i der Autor einer ist*
           a more-smart man, *than the author one is*

     c. * ein klügerer [*als der Autor (es ist)*] Mann
           a more-clever [*than the author (it is)*] man

     d.   [$_{AP}$ Klüger *als er es ist*] war keiner
           [more-clever *than he it is*] was none

     e.   [$_{DP}$ So^i viele Sätze, *wie^i du generieren kannst*]
           so many sentences *as you generate can*

     f. * [$_{DP}$ So^i viele, *wie^i du generieren kannst* Sätze]
           so many *as you generate can* sentences

     g.   [$_{DP}$ Der Anruf [$_{DP}$ der Leute^i] bei der Polizei, *die^i Hilfe holen wollten*] kam zu spät
           [the phonecall [(of) the people] at the police *who help seek wanted*] arrived too late

The comparative clauses in (9a,b) and the equative clause in (9e) are dependent on a comparative or equative expression. But they must be extraposed because they must not intervene between the head of the modifier of the NP, viz. the AP, and the NP node itself. This is illustrated by (9c): an AP allows a right edge (9d), but only if the AP is *not* a *preceding* modifier phrase of a head-*initial* phrase.[6] In this case, the head of the AP must be adjacent to the NP ('edge effect'). So, the intervening clause is placed to the right of the NP. Of course, this applies to the non-extraposed variant of (9e), too, as in (9f). Sentence (9g), finally, illustrates a relative clause placed at the very end of a DP, whose distant antecedent is an embedded DP, namely the genitive DP.

APs are head *final*, but PPs and clauses may follow the adjectival head in the AP (10a,b). This is a right edge phenomenon, since only clauses or PPs may follow, but DPs must not follow the head (10e) and can only precede (10f). Note that (10a,b) have variants (10c,d) with the clause or the PP in the right edge of the matrix clause.

(10)   a.   [$_{AP}$ Sicher, *ob es funktioniere*] war er sich nicht
              [sure whether it works] was he himself not

        b.   [$_{AP}$ Zufrieden *damit*] war kaum einer
              [content with-it] was hardly anyone

        c.   [$_{AP}$ Sicher] war er sich nicht, *ob es funktioniere*
              sure was he himself not whether it works

        d.   [$_{AP}$ Zufrieden] war kaum einer *damit*
              content was hardly anyone with-it

        e.   * [$_{AP}$ Sympathisch *allen*] war er nicht wirklich
              likeable (to) all-DAT was he not really

        f.   [$_{AP}$ *Allen* sympathisch] war er nicht wirklich
              (to) all-DAT likeable was he not really

For PPs, the right edge may be mistaken for the complementation position, since both, the complement and the 'right-edge' candidate, follow the preposition. The rare cases of post-positions in German as in (11a) allow differentiating clearly between right edge and complement position, however. The PP in (11a) offers room for the detached relative clause. For prepositional PPs there is indirect evidence. In German, unlike in North Germanic languages, prepositions do not

---

[6] Note that in English, the very same restriction is responsible for the adjacency of the head of a preverbal adverbial phrase and the VP it modifies. This follows from the fact that the English VP is a head-*initial* phrase, just like the NP in German. Adjunction of a modifier to a head-*initial* phrase is subject to this adjacency restriction (Haider 2000b, 2004a).

    (i)   He has [more often] won *than I*
    (ii)   * He has [more often *than I*] won

select clauses as complements. Hence, the clause in (11b,d) is not a complement. It is dependent on the amalgamated pronominal *da* (there), which is the complement. So, the clause in the fronted PP in (11b,d) must be identified as a clause in the right edge of the PP.

(11)   a. [PP Des Freundes wegen_P* *den er dort vermutete*] war er gekommen
            [(for) the friend's sake *whom he there expected*] was he come
            'It was for the friend's sake whom he expected (to be) there that he came'

        b. [PP Dazu, *dass ich das glaube*] kann man mich nicht zwingen
            [into-it *that I this believe*] can one me not force
            'one cannot force me to believe this'

        c. [PP Dazu] kann man mich nicht zwingen, *dass ich das glaube*
            [into-it] can one me not force *that I this believe*
            'one cannot force me to believe this'

        d. [PP Damit, *dass es explodiert*] konnte niemand rechnen
            [with-it *that it explodes*] could nobody reckon

        e. [PP Damit] konnte niemand rechnen, *dass es explodiert*
            [with-it] could nobody reckon *that it explodes*

Let us recapitulate: clauses and PPs but not DPs, VPs or APs are optionally placed at the right edge of the phrase they are contained in. In most cases this is simultaneously the right edge of their matrix clause. In each case (except for V2 clauses in the right edge) this is an optional variant. The advantage of shifting material to the right edge becomes obvious once we regard the variants with and without extraposition from the point of view of parsing. Here is a stacked version of a sentence (12a), and its extraposition variant, with the embedded clauses shifted to the respective right edges (12b):

(12)   a. Diejenige, die diesen Satz, der eine einzige Phrase, die ein Nachfeld, das mindestens eine weitere Phrase enthält, aufspannt, fehlerfrei wiederholen kann, verdient einen Preis
            she who this sentence that a single phrase that a postfield, that at-least one additional phrase contains, provides, correctly repeat is-able-to, deserves a prize

        b. Diejenige verdient keinen Preis, die diesen Satz fehlerfrei wiederholen kann, der keine einzige Phrase enthält, die ein Nachfeld aufspannt, das mindestens eine weitere Phrase enthält
            this person deserves no prize who this sentence correctly repeat is-able-to, that contains not-a single phrase, that provides a postfield, that contains at-least-one additional phrase

Evidently, the availability of shifting embedded clauses to the right edge makes it much easier for the cognitive parsing system to follow the flow of speech in an on-line parse. The problem with (12a) is its centre-embedding structure which overloads the working memory buffer of the parser. Note, however, that the availability of a right edge cannot be *dictated* by the ease of parsing, simply because there are strictly head-final languages which do not provide a right edge (e.g. Japanese) and therefore do not allow extraposition.

5.2   What is the structure of the right edge? Problems and puzzles

There is a tradition to analyse the right edge as the target of a special type of *movement* to the right, namely 'extraposition'. Extraposed phrases have been assumed to be right-adjoined to their matrix phrase (e.g. the VP) or to the phrase that contains the matrix phrase (e.g. the IP that contains the VP). This turns out to be unfounded, however, once the relevant data are analysed in due detail.

Let us briefly look at the extraposition-by-adjunction hypothesis and a paradox for movement accounts: the following set of data has been taken to be indicative of different adjunction sites by Reinhart (1980, 1983) or Culicover and Rochemont (1990). The rule for disjoint reference, that is principle C of the binding system of Chomsky (1981), apparently differentiates between extraposed *argument* clauses on the one hand and extraposed *relative* clauses on the other. If this is a difference in terms of different binding domains, relative clauses must be adjoined higher than the object position but lower than the subject position.

(1)   a. I sent her^i many gifts *last year* [that Mary^i did not like]

(C&R 1990: 29)

b. I sent her^i many gifts [(that) Mary^{*i} did not like] *last year*

(C&R 1990: 29)

c. She^i was sent many gifts *last year* [that Mary^{*i} did not like]

(C&R 1990: 28)

d. It bothered her^i (*greatly*) [that Rosa^{*i} had failed]

(Reinhart 1983: 49)

If the examples in (1b,c,d) are assumed to reflect structurally conditioned binding effects, these effect are captured if the extraposed clause is in a position c-commanded by the pronoun of the matrix clause, since in each of these cases, disjoint reference applies.

The contrast between (1a) and (1b) seems to indicate that the extraposition site of a relative clause is not c-commanded by the pronoun in the (indirect) object position of the matrix. This is the case if the relative clause is adjoined at least as high as the VP. That position, however, is in the c-command domain of the matrix subject, that is, the 'spec-I' position. This accounts for the unacceptability of (1c) and thereby for the subject–object contrast. Furthermore, the extraposed subject clause (1d) must be in a position that is c-commanded by the indirect object. So it must be lower than the indirect object position.

Reinhart (1983) assumes an n-ary branching, flat VP in which the arguments c-command each other. Current theorizing favours binary branching. In a binary branching, head-initial VP, the extraposed clause is situated in a position that is more deeply embedded than the indirect object. This is the XP position in (2a).

(2)   a. $[_{VP} V_i [NP [e_i XP]]]$
       b. It has [bothered$_i$ [her e$_i$ [that Rosa had failed]]]

Culicover and Rochemont (1990: 29–35) claim that relative clauses extraposed from object NPs are attached to the VP that contains the NPs. They adduce evidence mainly from ellipsis and the serialization of the parenthetical phrases. What their data show, however, is not that these relative clauses are *adjoined* to the VP. They only show that the attachment site is *not higher* than the VP. On the basis of contrasts like the ones in (3), they feel obliged to admit that in addition to VP adjunction, adjunction to IP must be another available option. VP topicalization (3b) must not pied-pipe an extraposed relative clause. So, they assume that an extraposed relative clause that relates to the subject may adjoin to IP (Culicover and Rochemont 1990: 35).

(3)   a.   They said that a man would come in, and come in a man did *who lives in N.Y.*

       b. * They said that a man would come in who lives in N.Y., and [[come in] *who lives in N.Y.*] a man did

There is, however, an independent reason for the ungrammaticality of (3b). The crucial defect for (3b) is the fact that the topicalized VP does not contain the antecedent of the relative clause. So the relative clause is not c-commanded by its antecedent. This requirement is easy to verify in a language like German. The relative clause must not be attached to the topicalized VP unless it contains the antecedent (cf. 5a vs 5b). In (4), the antecedent precedes, and, arguably, it c-commands the following relative clause. In (5a) it is clear that the relative clause is not c-commanded by its antecedent in the given structure.

(4)   a. Sie hat *dem Mann* etwas zugeflüstert, *der dort steht*
         she has (to) *the man*-DAT something whispered, *who (over) there stands*
         'She whispered something to the man who stands over there'

         b. Sie hat dem Mann *etwas* zugeflüstert, *das er nicht verstand*
         she has (to) the man-DAT *something* whispered, *that he (did) not understand*
         'She whispered something to the man that he did not understand'

The topicalized VP in (5a,b) is identical, except for the relative clause. In (5b), but not in (5a), the topicalized constituent contains the antecedent for the relative clause, whence the ungrammaticality of (5a).

(5)   a. * [Etwas zugeflüstert, *der^i dort steht*], hat sie *dem^i Mann*   (cf. 4a)
            something whispered who there stands has she (to) the man-DAT

        b. [*Etwas* zugeflüstert, *das er nicht verstand*], hat sie dem Mann
                                                                                    (cf. 4b)
           something whispered that he not understood has she (to) the man-DAT

        c. Nobody has told her^i until now [that the police suspects Rosa*^{i}]

        d. Niemand hat ihr^i bis jetzt gesagt [dass die Polizei Rosa*^{i} verdächtige]
           nobody has her until now told [that the police Rosa suspected]

Let us briefly recapitulate the argumentation reported above: an extraposed *argument clause* must be in the c-command domain of an object since *disjoint reference* applies (5c,d). The intervening adverbial shows that the clause is not in the object position. Nevertheless disjoint reference applies. So the clause must be in the c-command domain of the pronominal object. On the other hand, disjoint reference between an object pronoun and a referential expression does not apply if the latter is contained in an extraposed *relative clause*, as in (1a). Hence, the relative clause must be adjoined higher, the extraposed argument clause must be adjoined lower. This cannot be true, however: there is robust evidence (noted first in Haider 1992/2000) that had been ignored in previous studies, despite its ease of accessibility and its relevance. It is the relative order of extraposed clauses. If the extraposed relative clause is attached higher than an extraposed argument clause, it necessarily *follows* the argument clause.

This is contrary to the empirical evidence, however. It is a cross-linguistically valid fact that an extraposed relative clause *precedes* an extraposed argument clause.[7] The following sample illustrates the ordering restriction.[8]

(6i)   *English*
   a.   It struck a grammarian last century [*who analysed it*] [that this clause is grammatical]
   b.   * It struck a grammarian last century [that this clause is grammatical] [*who analysed it*]

(6ii) *Italian*
   a.   Ho detto a qualcuno ieri [che mi aveva chiesto la strada] [*che non lo sapevo*]
        (I) have said to someone yesterday [that me has asked the street] [that (I) not it know]
   b.   * Ho detto a qualcuno ieri [*che non lo sapevo*] [che mi aveva chiesto la strada]

(6iii) *Swedish* [9]
   a.   Någon berättade [*som just hade lyssnat på nyheterm*] [att Ruczkoy hade fänglats]
        someone said [who just had listened to the-news] [that Ruczkoy had been-arrested]
   b.   ??Någon berättade [att Ruczkoy hade fänglats] [*som just hade lyssnat på nyheterm*]

(6iv) *German*
   a.   Es fiel im vergangenen Jahrhundert einem Grammatiker auf [*der das untersuchte*] [dass dieser Satz grammatisch ist] (= 6i-a)
        it struck in-the past century a grammarian PRT [*who this investigated*] [that this sentence grammatical is]

---

[7] If you check this with English, make sure that the two clauses are indeed extraposed. In the following example, the argument clause is not extraposed: 'Many people said they were sick who weren't sick.' This can be inferred from the fact that the complementizer is dropped. So, better put an adverb in between the verb and the two extraposed clauses.

[8] The order may change if focus is involved. If the NP is focused, the relative clause may follow the argument clause:
   (i)   She told someone yesterday who had asked her that my lecture has been cancelled
   (ii)   She told *only those* people that my lecture has been cancelled who had asked her

[9] Note that the Swedish example (6iii-b), according to E. Engdahl (pers.comm.), is judged less acceptable despite the fact that the object clause appears in a position that could be its base position. The insertion of an adverbial between the verb and the object clause in (6iii-b) yields ungrammaticality.

b. * Es fiel im vergangenen Jahrhundert einem Grammatiker auf [dass dieser Satz grammatisch ist] [*der das untersuchte*] (= 6i-b)
it struck in-the past century a grammarian PRT [that this sentence grammatical is] [*who this investigated*]

The very same ordering pattern applies at the right edge of a DP (7a). The order remains unaffected by extraposition to the clausal right edge in (7b) vs (7c), as Wiltschko (1994: 25) illustrates with the following example:

(7)   a.   Sie hat [das Argument, das er präsentiert hat, dass rauchen gesund sei], widerlegt
she has [the argument that he presented has that smoking healthy is] refuted

b.   Sie hat das Argument widerlegt, das er präsentiert hat, dass rauchen gesund sei
she has the argument refuted that he presented has that smoking healthy is

c.   ??Sie hat das Argument widerlegt, dass rauchen gesund sei, das er präsentiert hat[10]
she has the argument refuted that smoking healthy is that he presented has

The particular structural account of the ordering restriction documented above immediately creates an apparent *binding paradox*. Since the relative clause precedes the argument clause, it cannot be analysed as attached higher up than the argument clause. Nevertheless the relative clause differs from the argument clause with respect to disjoint reference:

---

[10] Do not confuse the NP-internal order with the order resulting from extraposition to the right edge of the NP versus the right edge of the matrix clause of the NP.

   (i)   Er hat [den Befehl, der ihm erteilt worden war, die
       Brücke zu sprengen], missachtet   extraposition within the NP
       he has [the order that him given was the bridge to blast] ignored
   (ii)   Er hat [den Befehl, die Brücke zu sprengen, der ihm
       erteilt worden war] missachtet   NP-*internal* base order
   (iii)   Er hat [den Befehl, die Brücke zu sprengen,] missachtet,
       der ihm erteilt worden war   relative cl. extraposition to CP
   (iv) * Er hat [den Befehl, der ihm erteilt worden war] missachtet,
       die Brücke zu sprengen   object cl. extraposition to CP

Note that a relative clause may be extraposed to the level of the matrix clause. An object clause is confined to NP.

(8)   a. Someone has told him^i [who John^i had not met before] [that John^{*i} is in danger]

        b. Es hat ihr^i jemand prophezeit, [dem Ida^i blind vertraut], [dass Ida^{*i} uralt werde]
           it has her someone prophesied [whom Ida blindly trusts] [that Ida very-old will-get]

Since the reverse order, namely argument clause before relative clause, is deviant, there must be a non-structural reason which immunizes the relative clause against disjoint reference enforcement violations. Crucially, binding-induced disjoint reference patterns as discussed above differ from other cases of binding such as, for instance, binding of a pronoun by a quantifier (9). The binding relations between quantifiers and pronouns contrast sharply with the disjoint reference patterns: an object quantifier may bind a pronoun in an extraposed relative clause:

(9)   I told nobody^i all the details at once [that he^i might be interested in]

The ordering restrictions as well as the binding puzzle suffice to cast doubt on the validity of the particular adjunction analysis for extraposition sketched above. The ordering restriction is a useful basis for a transitive reasoning: if a clause is attached low, the preceding clause must be equally low or lower. Therefore: a relative clause cannot be taken to be attached higher than an argument clause if the extraposed relative clause precedes the extraposed argument clause. This insight is unavoidable and it is in conflict with what had been assumed in the literature since Reinhart (1983), namely, that an argument clause is adjoined lower than a relative clause.

Brody (2004: 151) objects to this conclusion and writes that 'there are a number of analyses compatible with the observation in (10) [HH] and a c-command dependent principle C'. He suggests a 'right node raising' derivation for the complement clause and illustrates it with the following structure assignment.

(10)   Someone has told [her^x (that *Mary^x will ...)] [who Mary met] [that Mary will prevail]

What this amounts to is binding under reconstruction. In his words, 'since principle C is sensitive to elements in A'-trace positions ... disjointness ... can be determined in the trace position and the extraposed complement clause could be stacked higher than and on the right of V and its complements.' What this suggestion completely ignores is the anti-reconstruction property of a CP in an A'-position.

It is well-known (van Riemsdijk and Williams 1981, on anti-crossover) that in principle-C contexts, uncontroversially A'-moved *clauses* are *not* reconstructed.

(11a) is an A'-moved clause, and it contrasts with the extraposed clause (11b) with respect to disjoint reference. Therefore, it is not evident that the disjoint reference effect with extraposed clauses can be attributed to reconstruction. There is a clear difference between *A'-moved bindees* (they are reconstructed) and *pied-piped bindees* that (indirectly) end up in an A'-position by virtue of being contained in a clause that is A'-moved. A clause is not 'altruistically' reconstructed.

(11)   a. [Dass Michas^i Position unhaltbar sei]$_j$ hat ihm^i keiner e$_j$ gesagt
            [that Micha's position untenable is] has him nobody told

        b. Keiner hat ihm^i (e$_j$) gesagt, [dass Michas*^{i} Position unhaltbar sei]$_j$
            nobody has him told [that Micha's position untenable is]

It is essential to realize that c-command is just a *necessary*, but *not* a *sufficient* requirement for a disjoint reference effect. First, adverbial clauses are opaque for disjoint reference, independent of extraposition (see 12). Second, it is easy to see that this binding opacity is independent of extraposition. Therefore, the absence of a disjoint reference effect does not warrant the inference that this is caused by the lack of c-command, as Reinhart (1983) suggested.

(12)   a. Ich werde ihm^i, [wenn ich Karl^i sehe], sein Paket übergeben
            I shall him [if I Karl meet] his package hand-over

        b. Man hat ihm^i, [obwohl / als Karl^i protestierte], den Zutritt verweigert
            they have him [although / when Karl protested] the admittance denied
            'They denied him the admittance although / when Karl protested'

In (12), a pronoun preceding a conditional clause (12a) or an adversative clause (12b) does not trigger a disjoint reference effect. This property of course does not change when the clause is extraposed.

This – the principle-C opacity of non-selected clauses – is the reason for the apparent paradox that extraposed relative or adverbial clauses are opaque for disjoint reference whereas extraposed argument clauses are affected. This is once more illustrated by (13a,b).

(13)   a. Someone has prophesied her^i [who Sue^i had met at a party] [that Sue*^{i} will win]

        b. Ich werde ihm^i nicht sagen, wenn ich Karl^i sehe, dass du Karl*^{i} suchst
            'I shall not tell him if I meet Karl that you are looking for Karl'

Reconstruction would not help because, as Wiltschko (1994: 28) noted, the effect does not change even when the relative clause belongs to an embedded clause. In (14), the extraposed object clause contains an extraposed relative clause. Both are c-commanded by the pronominal subject of the main clause. Since extraposition is clause bound, the relative clause must be contained in the extraposed object clause, and hence it is necessarily within the c-command domain of whatever element c-commands the object clause. There is no reasonable way to avoid the conclusion that the matrix subject *sie* (she) c-commands the co-referent *Lisa* in the relative clause that is contained, as an extraposed clause, in the extraposed complement clause.

(14)   a. Sie^i hat gesagt, [dass Lisa*^{i/ k} jemand^j gesehen habe, [der^j Lisas*^{i/ k} Vater ähnelt]]
        she has said [that Lisa someone seen has [who-NOM Lisa's father-DAT resembles]]
        'She has said that Lisa saw someone who resembles her father'

        b. Lisa^i hat gesagt, [dass sie^i jemand^j gesehen habe, [der^j Lisas^i Vater ähnelt]]
        Lisa has said [that she someone seen has [who-NOM Lisa's father-DAT resembles]]
        'Lisa said that she saw someone who resembles her father'

In sum, stay sceptical when you read that binding effects (especially disjoint reference) for extraposed elements are easy to capture if one admits reconstruction. If you check the relevant data, you will find out that they are neither easy nor captured.

In the next section, the sources of evidence that bear on the principal structure hypotheses for extraposition will be surveyed. The main issue is this: is the extraposition site an adjunction site and therefore *higher up* than the argument positions in the VP, or is the extraposition site lower down in the VP, at the bottom of the VP shell? Or is the question ill posed since extraposition is outside core syntax and rather a PF related serialization phenomenon? (Truckenbrodt 1995).

5.3   Towards an adequate theoretical modelling of the right edge

An adequate account of the structure of the right edge of a clause is obliged to offer insightful answers to at least the following questions on the grammatical nature of extraposition:

- Is extraposition an operation of *core syntax*, or rather a *post-syntactic* PF-serialization option ('delayed spell-out of lengthy portions of speech'), if extraposition is an instance of a *movement* operation?
- If extraposition is an instance of A'-*movement,* why does this instance of a movement operation disregard the core constraints on movement, for instance, the conditions on extraction domains (see section 5.3.1)?

- If extraposition is an instance of a *movement* operation that *right-adjoins* phrases higher in structure, why do extraposed phrases not behave like higher-adjoined phrases (opacity, linearization, binding, reconstruction failures)?
- If the failure of the adjunction-to-the-right approach is acknowledged, what would be an adequate alternative account, capturing the fact that the extraposition area is structurally low and more like a base structure than a derived one? – Is a base-generation approach with different dependency relations feasible?
- Are 'extraposed' clauses really extraposed, or could it be that the 'extraposed' clauses are stranded in their base-positions, as the result of 'intraposing' the 'non-extraposed' material?

Our dilemma will be this: first, if extraposition is an instance of movement, we expect to see the properties and restrictions of movement operations. The expectations are definitely not fulfilled, however. Extraposition violates the core domain restrictions of movement. Second, if extraposed phrases are derivationally adjoined phrases, they should have the syntactic properties of adjoined phrases, but they do not. If, on the other hand, extraposition is base generated, the tool kit of grammar theory should provide the right kind of tools to handle it. But it does not.

Let us start with the problems for movement accounts. These accounts assume that embedded clauses or PPs are moved out of their base position and merged / adjoined to the right of their matrix phrase or a phrase that dominates this phrase.

(1)   a. Hier können sie [[[einen Satz^j e$_i$] lesen] [der^j das illustriert]$_i$]
            here can you a sentence read which this illustrates

        b. [[[Einen Satz^j e$_i$] lesen] [der^j das illustriert]$_i$]$_k$ können sie hier e$_k$
            a sentence read which this illustrates can you here
            'Read a sentence that illustrates this you can here'

The following subsections will highlight evidence that bears on the empirical adequacy of movement accounts of extraposition. Extraposition by movement to the right creates an A'-dependency. So, the properties of extraposed elements need to be compared with well-established cases of A'-movement, like topicalization, that is, the movement to the sentence-initial spec position. If the grammatical properties modulo directionality of movement are sufficiently congruent, the movement account is successful. But it will become evident that the congruency is less than satisfactory. This casts doubt on the empirical adequacy of a model of extraposition that assumes optional rightward movement to adjunction sites.

Equally unsatisfactory are stranding accounts of extraposition in terms of left-bound movement, with the 'extraposed' clauses stranded in their surface position. This will be discussed after having reviewed the following phenomena. We shall primarily compare topicalization as a typical case of A'-movement with extraposition and stress the absence of A'-properties.

- Topicalization respects adjunct islands, but extraposition does not (5.3.1)
- Phrases introduced by focus particles can be topicalized but not extraposed (5.3.2)
- Adjuncts, arguments, or predicates are topicalized freely, but not extraposed (5.3.3)
- Inconsistent reconstruction properties of A'-chains (5.3.4)
- Evidence against PF movement (5.3.5)
- Missing extraction site (5.3.6)
- Split antecedents in coordinated structures (5.3.7)
- Extraposition plus reconstruction over- and undergenerates (5.3.8)
- VP topicalization and stranded adjuncts (5.3.9)

The conclusions will be, first, that neither adjunction by movement nor base-generated adjunction captures the grammatical properties of 'extraposed' constituents. Second, extraposition by stranding (as in Kayne's (1994) antisymmetry approach) turns out to be empirically inadequate, as well. The option that seems to be promising but presently hard to accept for the mainstream is a base-generation account: extraposed arguments are postverbal complements. Extraposed dependent clauses are base generated postverbally as locally dependent elements, with an obligatory antecedent relation (e.g. relative clauses, comparative clauses, result clauses). OV languages with 'extraposition' are head-final languages that allow for a restricted set of 'VO'-like structures, namely structures with postverbal elements. If this characterization is correct, the following generalization emerges: there is no VO language that does not allow extraposition. This is so because in a VO language, any dependent element, except for the subject, is postverbal. Since 'extraposition' is a variety of postverbal complementation, there is no way for a VO system to block this variety. For OV, extraposition is a parametric option that is responsible for the existence of *strict* OV languages and OV language with extraposition.

5.3.1   *Lack of islandhood of extraposed constituents and of their mother phrases*

If extraposition is the result of movement, this result should reflect the standard constraints on movement. This issue has two aspects, namely restrictions on the extraction site and restrictions on extraction out of the landing site. Extraction out of an opaque domain (cf. CED[11] contexts) is ungrammatical; hence extraposition out of an opaque domain should be ungrammatical. But the data contradict this straightforward expectation. First, extraposition out of movement islands is not deviant; second, extraction out of extraposed phrases is not deviant, either. So it is unlikely that extraposition is an instance of A'-movement.

Let us start with the opacity properties. In English, extraction out of subjects and extraction out of adjuncts is strongly deviant. This is known as the 'subject condition' and the 'adjunct condition', respectively (CED). But, as pointed out by Culicover and Rochemont (1990), extraposition clearly violates these constraints. For the examples in (1), the extraction site for extraposition would be internal to a *subject* (1a–c) or internal to an *adjunct* (1d) in a position as high as, or higher than, the functional subject position.

(1)   a. *A man* came in [with a pink beard]   PP-extraposition

        b. *A girl* rushed out [that hates pink beards]   relative clause
                                                               extraposition

        c. *More* girls rushed out [than pink beards could deter]   comparative
                                                               clause extraposition

        d. *So* long was the pink beard   comparison
           [that he even could step on]   and result clauses

If extraposition involved movement, it would be completely mysterious why extraposition by movement is not blocked by a barrier created by a non-selected constituent, that is, by an adjunct or a phrase in a functional spec position. The following German examples re-emphasize the absence of opacity effects with extraposition out of adjuncts.

(2)   a. Er hat [die ganze Nacht e_i] geschlafen, [die er im Verlies zubrachte]$_i$
           he has [the whole night] slept [which he in-the dungeon spent]

        b. Er hat [häufiger e_i] protestiert [als ich (zugestimmt habe)]$_i$
           he has [more-frequently] protested [than I (have agreed)]

        c. Er hat [so e_i] gesungen [wie er gesprochen hat]$_i$
           he has [so] sung [as he spoken has]

In (2a), a relative clause would have to be extracted out of an adverbial DP, namely the temporal adverbial DP. In (2b), a comparative clause would have to

---

[11] CED = condition on extraction domains (Huang 1982): *unselected* domains are opaque. This applies to the functional subject position ('subject condition') as well as to adverbials ('adjunct condition').

be extracted out of an adverbial AP, namely the frequency adverbial phrase, and in (2c), the extraction site would be a pronominal manner adverbial. Note that we need not test the subject effect for German since it is absent for a principled reason. German subjects are not opaque because they are VP internal. Subject opacity is a side effect of the spec position for subjects in a VO language like English.

Let us turn now to the second aspect, namely the transparency of extraposed phrases. In an OV language like German, it is easy to recognize whether a clause is extraposed or not, by simple inspection. The extraposed clause follows the clause-final verb(s). It is equally easy to recognize that extraction out of extraposed clauses is grammatical if the general conditions for extraction are met.

(3)   a. Wen$_i$ hast du erwartet, [dort e$_i$ zu treffen]
           whom have you expected [there to meet]
           'Whom did you expect to meet there?'

        b. Wem$_i$ hat der Mann versucht, der dort steht, [e$_i$ die Brieftasche zu stehlen]?
           whom did the man try who over there stands [the wallet to steal]
           'Whom did the man who stands over there try to steal the wallet from?'

Extraction out of an extraposed object clause is grammatical, as illustrated in (3). (3b) is instructive because of multiple extraposition. The extraposed relative clause precedes the extraposed argument clause that contains the trace of the wh-extraction. VP topicalization (4) confirms that the 'target position' for extraposition is VP internal:

(4)   a. [Erwartet, ihn dort zu treffen]$_{VP}$ hat sie nicht
           [expected him there to meet] has she not

        b. [Versucht, mir die Brieftasche zu stehlen]$_{VP}$, hat er nicht
           [tried me the wallet to steal] has he not

Let us discuss now an alleged counterexample. Büring and Hartmann (1997), who try to defend a movement analysis, correctly note that there is a clear acceptability contrast between (5a) and (5b) with respect to extraction. Their immediate conclusion is this. It is a subject effect, but 'for the base analysis, all clauses – being sisters to V – should be transparent' (Büring and Hartmann 1997: 9). Hence, a base-generation analysis would be in trouble, wouldn't it?

(5)   a. Wen$_i$ glaubst du, dass Hans e$_i$ besucht hat?
           whom think you that Hans visited has
           'Who(m) do you think that Hans has visited?'

b. * Wen$_i$ überrascht dich, dass Hans e$_i$ besucht hat
   whom surprised you that Hans visited has
   'Who(m) did it surprise you that Hans has visited?'

On the level of observational adequacy, Büring and Hartmann are right, but not on the level of descriptive adequacy. Extraction out of the extraposed complement of *überraschen* is possible, but only with a pronominal correlate[12] of the extraposed subject clause (cf. 6a,b). Moreover, there is an additional effect that reduces the acceptability of (5b): the fronted verb is the main verb. Extractions of this type astonishingly[13] improve if the fronted finite verb is an auxiliary (cf. Haider 1993: 159), and this is independent of psych verbs, as in (5) and (6).

(6)   a. Wen$_i$ hat ?(es) dich denn gefreut/überrascht [dort e$_i$ anzutreffen]?
          whom has it you PRT pleased / surprised [there to meet]
          'Whom did it please / surprise you to meet there?'

       b. Wen$_i$ hat ?(es) dich denn gefreut / überrascht [dass sie dort e$_i$ angetrof-
          fen hat]?
          whom has it you PRT pleased / surprised [that she there met has]
          'Whom has it pleased / surprised you that she has met there?'

The restrictions on extraction out of subject clauses of psych verbs in English also support the base-generation hypothesis of extraposition. Extraction is possible in the extraposed but not in the non-extraposed position (Haider 1993: 158).

(7)   a. * Who(m)$_i$ would [to have dinner with e$_i$] please you?
       b.   Who(m)$_i$ would it please you [to have dinner with e$_i$]?

It is safe to conclude then that extraposed subject clauses are indeed selected by the verb in their surface position and therefore transparent for extraction. If, however, the verb is not a bridge verb[14] with respect to the subject-argument,

---

[12] The 'correlate' is the antecedent of the extraposed clause. Puzzling and surprising is the fact that for object clauses, the presence of the optional pronominal correlate makes the extraposed clause opaque for extraction:

(i)   * Wen$_i$ hat sie es prophezeit dass er e$_i$ anrufen werde
            whom$_i$ has she it prophesied that he e$_i$ phone-up will

[13] This effect has been noted by Günther Grewendorf (in connection with a dispute between Wolfgang Sternefeld and the author), but its grammatical source is still ill understood.

[14] The property of being a *bridge verb* is a property with respect to a specific argument of a verb and not a global property for all arguments of a verb. Typical bridge verbs are propositional attitude verbs and verbs of saying. The bridgehood quality holds for the clause that denotes the proposition to be qualified. There are only a few verbs with a subject clause in a comparable semantic relation. In German, *please* is a bridge verb, but *tire* is not:

extraposition will not improve transparency. In this case, the extraposed clause will be as non-transparent as it would be in any other position.

Note that the contrast in (7) is at the same time evidence against reconstruction. Since extraction is possible in (7b), the extraposed subject clause must qualify as selected by the verb as an argument in the 'extraposed' position. The pronoun in 'spec-I' must be an expletive pronominal correlate of the clause. If reconstruction could apply at LF, the expletive pronoun would be replaced by the 're-intraposed' subject clause. In this case, however, (7b) would be predicted to be as bad as (7a) since the chain of the extracted wh-item would start in an opaque domain.

In a sophisticated derivational approach to extraposition, Müller (1996: 195f., 1997) tried to figure out a loophole for extraction in order to circumvent the predicted opacity of the extraposed clause ('anti-freezing' property). It is a combination of an adjunction analysis plus a technical by-pass of the strict cycle. The derivational loophole he devised – first extraction, then extraposition (= adjunction of the clause to a phrase not lower[15] than the position of the extracted element) – does not stand empirical tests, however (see section 5.3.8 for details).

As for the PF approach to extraposition, transparency should be a neutral property. Extraposition should not have any effect on transparency. If the clause is transparent in its base position, it will remain transparent, and vice versa, since the operation of extraposition would be post syntactic and affect the spell-out properties only.

5.3.2 *The distribution of phrases with a focus particle*

Bayer (1990) noticed a robust difference in the distribution of phrases with an attached focus particle of the type *only* or *even* in German in particular, and in OV languages in general. These phrases may be fronted, but they must not be extraposed. If extraposition is movement, this asymmetry is unaccounted

(i)   Auf wen$_i$ würde dich denn [stundenlang e$_i$ warten zu müssen] nicht freuen?
        for whom would you-acc prt [for-hours wait to have-to] not please
        'For whom would it not please you to have to wait for?'

(ii)   * Auf wen$_i$ würde dich denn [stundenlang e$_i$ warten zu müssen] nicht ermüden?
        for whom would you-acc prt [for-hours wait to have-to] not tire
        'For whom would it not tire you to have to wait for hours?'

The fact that there are hardly any bridge verbs for subject clauses is but a reflex of the fact that there are hardly any verbs with a subject argument that is semantically parallel to the object argument of the major class of bridge verbs. This covers the great majority of extraposed subject clauses. These clauses are non-transparent in the extraposed and in the non-extraposed position, just like object clauses without the bridge quality are.

[15] Otherwise, the strict cycle condition would be violated.

for. If, on the other hand, the extraposition position is a base position, Bayer's account in terms of canonical government yields the empirically correct result: the focus particle must be within the canonical licensing domain of a lexical head. In German, the canonical licensing directionality is to the left. The extraposed phrase is to the right of the head of the extraposition domain.

(1)   a.   [*Nur* [wenn es nicht regnet]] werde ich kommen
               [only [if it not rains]] shall I come
               'Only if it does not rain shall I come'

        b. * Ich werde kommen [*nur* [wenn es nicht regnet]]
               I shall come [only [if it not rains]]

        c.   Ich werde *nur* kommen [wenn es nicht regnet]
               I shall only come [if it not rains]

The essential contrast is that between (1a) and (1b). Topicalization is an instance of A'-movement, and A'-movement obviously (cf. 1a) does not interfere with focusing, but extraposition does (1b). The pattern illustrated in (1) is representative for all categories of extraposed phrases. The ungrammaticality of extraposing a focused phrase (see 1b) is evidence against movement. In (1c), the focus particle is preverbal and associated with the extraposed clause (association with focus).

     According to Bayer (1990), operator phrases must be linked to a canonically licensed position. Since licensing is mediated by a trace in (1a), extraposed phrases should be licensed as well, if there was a trace. If there is no movement, however, there is no trace. If extraposed phrases are in a base position, the extraposition position in an OV language is not a canonical licensing position, because it is postverbal. So, the contrast follows. Note that a PF account would overgenerate, too. There is no obvious reason why a focus particle that travels with the topicalized phrase in (1a) should not be spelled out with the clause in the right edge.

5.3.3   Immobility of AP, VP and DP

     If extraposition is A'-movement, phrases that can be A'-moved should be extraposable. In German (cf. 1), APs, DPs, or VPs can be topicalized but not extraposed. Extraposition is more selective. The class of extraposable constituents is not the class of constituents that can be A'-moved. If constraints on extraposition are constraints on licensing rather than restrictions on movement this pattern can be accounted for. Licensing restrictions are at work in base-generated constructions.

(1)   a.   [$_{AP}$ Stolz auf sie, (wie kein anderer es je war)] ist er gewesen
               [proud of her (like no-one else it ever was)] has he been
               'He has been proud of her in a way no one else ever has been before'

b. * Er ist gewesen [$_{AP}$ stolz auf sie (wie kein anderer es je war)]
   he has been [proud of her (like no-one else it ever was)]

c. [Eine NP] wurde hier verschoben
   [an NP] was here moved

d. * Hier wurde verschoben [eine NP]
   here was moved [an NP]

e. [$_{VP}$ Nach Rom gefahren] ist er nicht
   [to Rome travelled] has he not

f. * dass er nicht ist [$_{VP}$ nach Rom gefahren]
   that he not is [to Rome travelled]

Every type of CP can be extraposed, depending on the context. PP extraposition is subject to constraints, depending on their grammatical function. VPs, APs and argumental DPs are not extraposed at all. There is no parallel constraint on topicalization. If extraposition indeed was A'-movement to the right, DPs should be able to adjoin to the right just like CPs. They would be linked to their base position, which they are assumed to c-command as the antecedent of the trace, just as in any case of A'-movement to the left. The movement plus reconstruction approach, as well as the PF approach, is obviously at odds with this set of facts. Moveable constituents must be extraposable, if the movement approach to extraposition is correct.

5.3.4   Inconsistent reconstruction properties of A'-chains

The movement plus reconstruction hypothesis suffers from a general deficit. It has to attribute different *reconstruction* properties to A'-chains: A'-chains of movement to the left do not reconstruct for variable binding extraposition chains appear to do so, however. If both forms of dependencies are A'-dependencies, the theory is at a loss. Note that 'reconstruction' in this case restores the c-command relations, as if the extraposed phrase was not adjoined higher. The approach that base-generates extraposed constituents in the lowest shell of the projection does not have this problem. The extraposition area is within the c-command domain of preverbal elements.

(1)   a.   Sie hat jeden^i aufgefordert, [*seinen^i* Namen zu nennen]
            she has everyone summoned [his name to say]

       b.   Sie hat jeden^i [*seinen^i* Namen zu nennen] aufgefordert
            she has everyone [his name to say] summoned

       c.   ? [*Seinen^i* Namen zu nennen] hat sie jeden^i aufgefordert
            [his name to say] has she everyone summoned

    d.   Sie hat jeden^i [zu seinem^i Alibi] befragt
        she has everyone [about his alibi] questioned

    e.   Sie hat jeden^i befragt [zu seinem^i Alibi]
        she has everyone questioned [about his alibi]

    f.   ? [Zu seinem^i Alibi] hat sie jeden^i befragt
        [about his alibi] has she everyone questioned

The quantifier binds the variable in the extraposed infinitival clause in (1a) as perfectly as in the base order (1b), and this is analogously true for the PP (1d,e). If a phrase is A'-moved to the front across the binder, quantifier-variable binding fails and a weak-crossover violation arises (1c,f). This shows that A'-moved phrases are *not* reconstructed for the purpose of *variable binding*. The extraposition-by-movement hypothesis would be supported if binding in (1a) and (1e) was on a par with (1c) and (1f), respectively, contrary to the facts. There is no plausible reason for constraining A'-reconstruction by directionality, that is, for allowing reconstruction for right-moved items but not for left-moved ones.

    Büring and Hartmann (1995), who favour a reconstruction approach, cite the following case as cardinal evidence against a base-generation option. They argue that the principle-C effect in (2b) cannot be captured unless the extraposed CP is reconstructed, the reason being that the extraction site is DP internal and hence the DP-internal possessive pronoun would not c-command the extraposition site. This is correct, but irrelevant.

(2)   a. Wir haben [seine^i Aussage, dass Max*^{i} zu Hause gewesen sei], überprüft
          we have [his deposition that Max at home been has] checked

     b. Wir haben [seine^i Aussage] überprüft, [dass Max*^{i} zu Hause gewesen sei]
          we have his deposition checked [that Max at home been has]

What this reasoning does not pay sufficient attention to is a third factor. The DP-internal clause in (2) is an *identificational* clause. Semantically, the relation between *his deposition* and *that Max was at home* is that of referring to an identical proposition, namely the fact that he was at home. In these cases, extraposition is an irrelevant factor, as the following examples demonstrate:

(3)   a. Seine^i Aussage lautet, dass Max*^{i} zu Hause gewesen sei
          his deposition runs that Max at home been has

     b. Seine^i fixe Idee ist, dass Max*^{i} ein Vampir sei
          his fixed idea is that Max a vampire is
          'His obsession is that Max is a vampire'

The embedded clause in (3) is clearly external to the DP that contains the possessive pronoun and the clause is not extraposed out of the DP and nevertheless the quasi principle-C effect obtains. This is the result of the particular semantics of the verb. It identifies the proposition which the DP and the clause jointly refer to. So, the disjoint reference effect in (2) follows from the same set of circumstances and does not, contrary to appearance, bear at all on reconstruction.

Büring and Hartmann (1995) and Sternefeld (2007), who accept this conclusion, raise another case against base-generated extraposition. They point to the following contrasts in variable binding and suppose that a base-generated extraposed phrase would have to be in the scope of a preceding quantifier. Their objection is this: if a relative clause in the right edge is in the scope of the quantifier in the midfield, why is variable binding deviant in (4c)? In their opinion this is again a point for reconstruction. They argue that reconstruction captures the parallel between (4b,c), but base generation would not.

(4)   a.   Sie hat jedem[i] [*das Bild, auf dem er[j] abgebildet war,*] gezeigt
             she has everyone [the picture on which he depicted was] shown

       b.   ? Sie hat [*das Bild, auf dem er[j] abgebildet war,*] jedem[i] gezeigt
             she has [the picture on which he depicted was] everyone shown

       c.   ? Sie hat *das Bild*, jedem[i] gezeigt, *auf dem er[j] abgebildet war*
             she has the picture everyone shown on which he depicted was

What they fail to take into consideration, however, is an explicit concept of the syntax–semantics interface. C-command is a necessary but not a sufficient condition for variable binding. In (4c), the c-command domain for the relative clause and the scope domain for the DP plus the relative clause differ. The *antecedent* DP of the relative clause is *not* in the c-command domain, hence the DP plus the relative clause are not both in the scope domain of the object quantifier. This is essential: if the pronoun in the relative clause is bound by a quantifier, the whole DP, and crucially not the relative clause alone, receives a distributive reading (i.e. set of pictures, on each of which a person of the set *he* ranges over is depicted). Hence, the entire DP must be in the scope of the quantifier, and not only an extraposed part of it.

What Büring and Hartmann as well as Sternefeld failed to check is a DP with an extraposed clause that does not denote an individual but an abstract condition that does not receive a countable, referential denotation. This is the case for instance for propositional attitudes. The bracketed DP in (5a) denotes a propositional attitude (i.e. impression). In this case the embedded clause does not restrict the denotation range of the DP in the way an intersective reading of a relative

clause would do, and variable binding becomes acceptable in (5c), in contrast to
(4c), as expected.

(5)   a.   Sie hat jedem[i]/keinem[i] [den Eindruck, dass er[i] ihr gefiele]
             vermittelt
             she has (to) everybody/nobody [the impression that he her pleased]
             conveyed
             'she has conveyed everyone/nobody the impression that he pleased
             her'

       b.   ? Sie hat [den Eindruck, dass er[i] ihr gefiele] jedem[i]/keinem[i]
             vermittelt
             she has [the impression that he her pleased] (to) everybody/nobody
             conveyed

       c.   Sie hat den Eindruck jedem[i]/keinem[i] vermittelt, [dass er[i] ihr
             gefiele]
             she has the impression (to) everybody/nobody conveyed [that he her
             pleased]

In sum, the alleged evidence for a movement plus reconstruction approach is not
compelling. Upon closer scrutiny, the objections raised against a base-generation
account turn out to be empirically or theoretically questionable.

5.3.5   *Evidence against PF movement: troubles with extraposition out of DPs*

Relative clauses are extraposed freely, irrespective of the depth of the
embedding (cf. 1a–d) in the DP. Argument clauses[16] cannot be extraposed out of
a DP (cf. 4c), relative clauses can (cf. 4a). Comparative clauses must be c-commanded by the comparative DP, that is, the DP that contains the comparative
morpheme (cf. 3). If extraposition was just a matter of movement and reconstruction, these differences between the clause types should not exist because reconstruction would always restore the base situation. And they should definitely not
exist, if extraposition was just a matter of PF management (postponed spell-out of
clausal constituents) because at the PF level a clause is just a potentially lengthy
constituent of the category 'clause' and subtle syntactic differences do not matter
at the post-syntactic level of spell-out.

---

[16] Examples with acceptable complement extraposition out of reduced DPs are light-verb
constructions (cf. Guéron 1980: 638).

(1)   a.   Er hat *das Bild*ⁱ untersucht, *das*ⁱ ich gekauft habe
            he has the picture examined that I bought have

       b.   Er hat [den Rahmen *des Bildes*ⁱ] untersucht, *das*ⁱ ich gekauft habe
            he has [the frame of the picture] examined that I bought have

       c.   Er hat [die Farbe des Rahmens *des Bildes*ⁱ] untersucht, *das*ⁱ ich
            gekauft habe
            he has [the colour (of) the frame (of) the picture] examined that I
            bought have

       d.   Er wird [die Zusammensetzung der Farbe des Rahmens *des
            Bildes*ⁱ] untersuchen, *das*ⁱ ich gekauft habe
            he will [the composition (of) the colour (of) the frame (of) the pic-
            ture] examine that I bought have

       e.   */??Er hat [den Auftrag [das *Bild*ⁱ zu kaufen]] erteilt, *das*ⁱ man ihm
            empfohlen hat[17]
            he has [the order [the picture to buy]] given that one him recom-
            mended has
            'he has given the order to buy the picture that has been recom-
            mended to him'

Relative clause extraposition is clause bound (1e), but the depth of embedding of
the antecedent within a DP does not have a degrading effect, as (1d) illustrates.
This is not true for attributive clauses (see 2). Apparently, the overt agreement
relation that holds between a relative clause and its antecedent is the crucial differentiating factor.

(2)   a.   Ihr hat *die Idee* gefallen, *dass* ...
            her has the idea pleased, that ...

       b.   * Ihr hat [der Kritiker *der Idee*] gefallen, *dass* ...
            her has [the critic of the idea] pleased that ...

The relation between a comparative clause and its antecedent is studied in detail
in Haider (1995) and (1997a). The detached comparative clause of the non-elliptic

---

[17]   Relative clause extraposition out of a clause that is embedded in a DP is marginal, but
       not as sharply deviant as one might expect. In my judgement, this applies also to rela-
       tive clauses extraposed out of relative clauses:

       ?(?) Sie hatte [Briefe, die mit *einer Tinte*ⁱ geschrieben waren] untersucht, *die*ⁱ sehr
            schnell verblasst
            she has [letters which with an ink written were] examined which very fast fades

type (cf. Haider 1997a: 117) reveals a clear dependency: the comparative clause must be c-commanded by a comparative phrase in surface structure. This is illustrated in (3) with VP topicalization. If the licensing comparative phrase is within the topicalized VP, the comparative clause must be within the VP, too. This is not true for relative clauses (3d). But note that the extraposed relative clause precedes an extraposed comparative (3e). Consequently, if the comparative clause is within the c-command domain of the object in (3e), that is, within the VP, the relative clause must be within this domain, too.

(3)   a.   dass nur einer das Endspiel *öfter* gewonnen ~~hat~~, *als* ~~er es~~ verspielt
            hat
            that only one the finals more-often won has than ~~he it~~ lost has

       b.   [Das Endspiel *öfter* gewonnen *als* verspielt] hat nur einer
            [the finals more-often won than lost] has only one

       c.   * [Das Endspiel *öfter* gewonnen] hat nur einer [*als* verspielt]
            [the finals more-often won] has only one [than lost]

       d.   [*Sätze*^{i} konstruieren] kann man leicht, [*die*^{i} das beweisen]
            [sentences construct] can one easily [which this proves]

       e.   Er hat *mehr* Sätze^i konstruiert, die^i seltsam klangen, *als* ich kommentieren möchte
            he has more sentences constructed, which strange sound, than I
            comment would-like-to

Eventually, there is a clear contrast between relative clauses and argument clauses (see Haider 1997a: 126). The latter cannot be extraposed from an NP-internal complement position (4c,d), but the former can (4a,b). This is not so much a peculiarity of argument clauses, but rather one of relative clauses, which may be extraposed from their internal positions. As illustrated in (2b), NP-internal attributive clauses cannot be extraposed, either. The same is true for NP-internal comparatives (see examples (5); Haider 1997a: 118).

(4)   a.   Man hat [die Frau *des Boten*^{i}] beschimpft, *der*^{i} den Befehl
            überbrachte
            one has [the wife of the deliverer] scolded who the order delivered

       b.   Er hat [die Zeit vor *dem Versuch*^{i}] gut verbracht, *der*^{i} ihn berühmt
            machen sollte
            he has [the time before the attempt] well spent which him famous
            to-make was
            'He has spent well the time before the attempt that was to make
            him famous'

c. * Man hat [den Überbringer *des Befehls*] heftig beschimpft, [*den Platz zu verlassen*][18]

one has [the deliverer of the order] severely scolded [the square to clear]

'they have severely scolded the deliverer of the order to clear the square'

d. * Er hat [die Zeit vor *dem Versuch*] gut verbracht, [*über Wasser zu wandeln*]

he has [the time before the attempt] well spent [on water to walk]

'He has spent well the time before the attempt to walk on water'

(5)   a.   Mehr Leute sind hier, als in diesem kleinen Dorf wohnen

more people are here, than in this little village live

'More people are here than are living in this little village'

b. * Der Umgang mit mehr Leuten ist anstrengend, als in diesem kleinen Dorf wohnen

the relation with more people is straining than in this little village live

'Relations with more people than are living in this little village are straining'

In sum: extraposition out of DPs reveals a c-command-based dependency constraint for comparatives. Second, argument clauses and relative clauses precede comparative clauses. So, the conclusion is unavoidable that these clauses must be within the same domain as (or a smaller one than) a comparative clause. Consequently, extraposed clauses cannot be assumed to be adjoined at the right-hand side, above the VP, since then they would not remain in the c-command domain of VP-internal material.

A PF movement account predicts that clausal constituents are postponed indiscriminately. There should not be any *syntactic* restriction for PF 'extraposition' since as a PF operation, it is motivated only by exonerating the PF routines (prosodic organization) and the working memory. However, the above discussion highlighted clearly syntactic constraints. There is a locality constraint: argument clauses must not leave the NP domain, relative clauses may. There is a linearization constraint: a relative clause precedes other extraposed clauses. These restrictions are a challenge, both for approaches in terms of reconstruction, and for PF accounts. These accounts have no way of differentiating between

---

[18] The sentence is grammatical, of course, in the unextraposed variant:

(i)   Man hat [den Überbringer *des Befehls den Platz zu verlassen*] heftig beschimpft.

syntactically differentiated clause functions, since these properties are obviously not PF properties. Of course, proponents may adduce ad hoc restrictions, without explanatory plausibility, though, since the system predicts a different outcome.

5.3.6   Missing extraction site

Extraposition of argument clauses in German comes in two variants. One is the variant with a pronominal antecedent of the extraposed clause, namely *es* (it), or its amalgamated form in PPs, namely *da* (there). The other variant is extraposition without a pronominal correlate. This is true for object clauses as well as for subject clauses or prepositional objects.

(1)   a. Sie hat (*es*) ihr[i] nicht gesagt, dass Clara*[i] schwanger ist
             she did (it) her not tell that Clara pregnant is

         b. Mir ist (*es*) aufgefallen, dass sie schwanger ist
             me has (it) struck that she pregnant is

         c. Man hat ihn (*darüber*) informiert, dass sie schwanger ist
             one has him (*it*-about) informed that she pregnant is

Literal reconstruction proper would be an insufficient solution for the re-establishment of c-command relations. This is easy to see if one compares the two types of extraposition, namely extraposition with and without a pronominal antecedent of the extraposed clause. The c-command dependent relations, as for instance the principle-C effect in (1a), do not differ, but reconstruction cannot be at work because the presence of the pronominal antecedent of the extraposed clause would block reconstruction (see 2). Reconstruction on LF would not help either, since the reconstruction site marked by *es* is higher than the position of the binder in (2).

Bennis (1986) argued that the so-called pronominal correlate, and not the clause, *is* the argument of the verb. The clause just supplies the referential content for the pronoun, as in a right-dislocation configuration. If Bennis is right, the pronoun is not an expletive, it is the argument. Note that (1a–c) remain perfect if the clause is omitted. This shows that the pronominal may represent a propositional argument.

Empirically, reconstruction is dispensable. First, if an extraposed clause could be reconstructed into the position of *es*, this reconstruction position should be a possible position for a non-extraposed clause, which is not the case. The presence of *es* destroys the acceptability. Without the pronoun, the non-extraposed clause is acceptable, with a slightly marginal status, though, since extraposition is strongly preferred. But even if reconstruction is deferred to LF, the binding data would not follow immediately since in (2), there is no binding conflict, because the pronoun does not c-command *Max*.

(2)   Sie hat [(*es) [dass sie auf Max[i] böse ist]] ihm[i] nicht gesagt
       she has [(it) that she at Max furious is] him not told
       'She has not told him that she is furious with Max'

Second, for English, the consequence of reconstruction would have to be that extraposed subject clauses with a pronominal antecedent in 'spec-I' become barriers for extraction just like non-extraposed clauses. But this is not correct, as the well-known contrast in (3a,b) demonstrates:

(3)   a.   * Who[i] would [to have dinner with e[i]] be fun for you?

       b.   Who[i] would it be fun for you [to have dinner with e[i]]?

       c.   Mit wem[i] würde ?(es) dich freuen [dort e[i] zu dinieren]
             with whom would (it) you please [there to dine]
             'With whom would it please you to dine there?'

The extraposed clause in (3b,c) is – given that it is VP internal – transparent for extraction whereas the same clause in the spec position of a functional head is non-transparent (3a). This difference would be obliterated under reconstruction on LF in English. The fact that there are extraposed clauses that are transparent for extraction is the crucial evidence. Of course, there are non-transparent clauses as well, since there are additional conditions, like the 'bridge' property. A transparent clause is an argument clause of a *bridge* verb. The very same clause in the very same position is opaque for extraction in German and English if the verb is not a bridge verb.

Only for psych verbs does the pronominal subject, as in (3c), not block extraction. This is mysterious, since in other cases (see 4b,c), the presence of the correlate strongly deteriorates the extraction possibility.

(4)   a.   Sie hat (es) prophezeit, dass du ihn daran erkennen wirst
             she has (it) prophesied that you him that-by recognize will
             'She has prophesied that you will recognize him by that'

       b.   Woran hat sie (*es) prophezeit, dass du ihn erkennen wirst?
             what-by has she (it) prophesied that you him recognize will
             'What has she prophesied that you will him recognize by?'

       c.   Woran wurde (*es) dir prophezeit, dass du ihn erkennen würdest
             what-by was (it) (to) you prophesied that you him recognize will
             'What was it prophesied to you that you will him recognize by?'

Extraction out of an extraposed object or subject clause is impossible if there is a pronominal object that serves as the antecedent for the extraposed clause. This indicates that the antecedent pronoun, that is the subject of the psych verb in (3c), has a status that differs from the status of a transitive subject. The grammatical reason for this difference is not completely understood, however. The differences between (3c) and (4b,c) with respect to the presence/absence of *es* (it) as a blocking factor seem to be an effect of the argument status of psych-verb subjects rather than a general property of subjects. If it were merely a property of unergative subjects, passivization as in (4c) should not block extraction.

   Note once more that the extraposed clause precedes a comparative clause, both in the variant with *es* and in the variant without. This confirms that there is no difference in the extraposition site with and without a pronominal antecedent.

(5)   dass er (es) mehr Leuten übel nahm, dass sie gelacht hatten, als ich kannte
       that he (it) more people amiss took that they laughed had than I knew
       'that he took it amiss with more people than I knew that they had laughed'

Let us sum up. The theoretical impact is this: c-command-sensitive dependency relations between an element in the VP and one in the extraposed clause cannot be checked by reconstruction (or, in terms of the Minimalist Program, on the copy) because, in surface structure, there is no reconstruction site (or copy) if the extraposed clause depends on a pronominal antecedent. Nevertheless the dependency relations are identical for clauses with and without copy.

5.3.7   Split antecedents in coordinated structures

   A movement account of extraposition is unable to handle a relative clause that relates to split antecedents. In English, as well as in German coordinated structures, an extraposed relative clause may be dependent on an antecedent set that does not map on a single constituent of the clause. This was originally noted by Perlmutter and Ross (1970) and re-addressed by Gazdar (1981):

(1)   a. [John saw a man^i] and [Mary saw a woman^j] who$^{i \& j}$ *were* wanted by
          the police   (Perlmutter and Ross 1970: 128)

       b. [A man came in] and [a woman went out] who knew *each other*
          very well   (Gazdar 1981: 178f.)

       c. [Ein Mann kam herein] und [eine Frau ging hinaus], *die einander*
          sehr ähnelten
          [a man came in] and [a woman went out] who each-other very-much
          resembled

       d. [Ein Mann kam herein] und [eine Frau ging hinaus]. *Die/Sie* ähnelten
          einander sehr
          [a man came in] and [a woman went out]. These/they resembled each-
          other very-much

Obviously, the relative clause cannot be a clause extraposed by movement because it would not have a unique source position. Neither of the conjuncts can be the source because the DP in each conjunct is singular, but the relative clause refers to a plural antecedent. This behaviour is compatible with the pronominal status of the relative pronoun, however. It resembles the behaviour of demonstrative or personal pronouns (as illustrated in example 1d).

For a movement account, the split antecedent cases are embarrassing. For a base-generation plus construal approach, the possibility of split antecedents is expected. This is a familiar property of pronominal construal. (2a) is a case of overt pronominal construal. In (2b), the covert pronominal subject of the infinitival clause is controlled by split antecedents. This is another case of pronominal construal with split antecedents.

(2)   a. Er^i hat ihr^j erzählt, dass man das von ihnen$^{i\,\&\,j}$ erwarte
          he has her told that one this of them expects
          'He has told her that this is expected of them'
       b. Er^i hat ihr^j vorgeschlagen [PRO$^{i\,\&\,j}$ einander$^{i\,\&\,j}$ zu vertrauen]
          he has her proposed each-other to trust
          'He has proposed to her that they trust each other'

Note that only pronominals, but not anaphors, allow split antecedents. The anaphor *einander* (each other) in (2b) is uniquely bound by the covert subject. Being co-referent with the binder means in this case that the split construal is transferred to the anaphor as an instance of regular binding from its antecedent.

5.3.8   *Extraposition by movement over- and undergenerates*

Adjunction by movement is a source of *overgeneration*. First, it does not provide an account for the *order restrictions* for sentences with multiple extraposition. If extraposition is cyclic movement, one would expect that the extraposed clauses mirror the relative base order. This is not the case, however. The cyclically derived order (1a) is ungrammatical.

(1)   a. * Ich habe jeden^i gefragt, was er gesehen habe, [der^i dabei war]
             'I have asked everyone what he has observed [who was present]'
       b. Ich habe jeden^i gefragt, [der^i dabei war], was er gesehen habe
             'I have asked everyone [who was present] what he has observed'

What is crucial is not so much that (1b) is grammatical, but that the ungrammatical order in (1a) cannot be blocked. Cyclical movement and merger would produce (1a). This embarrassing pattern also holds for NP-dependent, extraposed clauses (as discussed in section 5.2 above).

The precedence property of relative clauses is sometimes overlooked and misinterpreted. In Wiltschko's (1997: 385) view, sentence (2a), with the object scrambled across the subject, testifies to a *nesting* dependency as the result of successive extraposition. But what she fails to appreciate is that the order among the extraposed clauses does not change when the scrambled arguments in (2a) are put back into their base order, as in (2b).

(2)   a. (?) weil das Argument ein Mann[i] präsentiert hat, der[i] niemals irrt, dass Bier gesund ist
'since the argument a man presented who never errs that beer is healthy'

b.   weil ein Mann[i] das Argument präsentiert hat, der[i] niemals irrt, dass Bier gesund ist
since the argument a man presented has, who never errs, that beer healthy is
'since a man who never errs that has presented the argument that beer is healthy'

In a movement account, a nesting dependency is expected. In reality, however, the dependency is often an intersecting one and the predicted order, namely the nesting dependency, is unacceptable.[19] This is overgeneration. The system generates a structure that is unacceptable.

The cases of *undergeneration* are less easy to identify. The diagnostics requires a closer look at the implementation of the movement operation. Let us for the sake of illustration entertain a very liberal approach towards adjunction so that undergeneration is unlikely to arise, as for instance Müller's (1996: 225), who allows right-adjunction to any kind of XP. Ingeniously, Müller (1997: 195f.) devises a derivational loophole for removing the prime problem of an adjunction analysis, namely the opacity for extraction in the adjoined position. At least in an OV language, a right-adjoined phrase is not in the directional licensing domain of the lexical head. But, nevertheless, extraposed argument clauses are not opaque for extraction. Müller's proposal is this: first extraction, then extraposition by adjunction of the clause to a phrase not lower[20] than the target position of the extracted element. Let us examine now briefly the empirical appropriateness of this technical account. It will turn out that it does not pass empirical testing. Here is an example.

Take any clause that obligatorily depends on a c-commanding antecedent. Embed it in a wh-clause whose wh-element is extracted out of another embedded

---

[19]   The placement of extraposed relative clauses is a clear case. If a subject-related relative clause and an object clause are extraposed, the predicted nesting order would be object clause before relative clause. This order, however, is unacceptable.

[20]   Otherwise, the strict cycle condition would be violated.

clause. Then extrapose both clauses. If the clause with the wh-trace precedes the other extraposed clause, it cannot be in a position adjoined higher. Consequently, the dependent clause that follows the clause with the wh-trace must be equally high or higher. Finally, you provide evidence that the dependency between this clause and its antecedent holds on the surface structure and cannot be checked under reconstruction. What you have gained then is an argument against extraposition by adjunction plus reconstruction.

An example of an obligatorily dependent clause is, for instance, a comparative clause (3a), since it obligatorily depends on a comparative. Comparative clauses must not be wh-moved since the dependency cannot be checked under reconstruction (3b). Having prepared the ground, as announced above, we are going to inspect (3c).

(3)   a.   dass sie lauter^i [als^i alle anderen] gesungen hat [als^i alle anderen]
             that she louder [than anyone else] sung has [than anyone else]

        b.   * [Als^i alle anderen]$_j$ hat sie lauter^i e$_j$ gesungen
             [than anyone else] has she louder sung

        c.   Wem$_j$ hast du behauptet, öfter^i e$_j$ versucht zu haben, das zu erklären,
             [als^i mir]
             whom have you claimed more-often tried to have this to explain
             [than me]
             'Whom did you claim to have more often tried to explain this to
             than me?'

        d.   dass du [öfter [als mir]] wem etwas zu erklären versucht zu haben
             behauptet hast
             that you [more-often [than me]] whom something to explain tried
             to have claimed have
             'That you have claimed to have more often tried to explain some-
             thing to someone than to me'

The extraposed comparative phrase depends on the comparative phrase in the embedded infinitival complement clause. This comparative is represented by an adverbial that modifies the VP head by *versuchen* (try). Given the dependency, the extraposition site of the comparative phrase must be within the c-command domain of the comparative. However, this domain is a proper subdomain of the matrix clause. Crucially, the extraposed infinitival clause headed by *erklären* (explain) precedes the comparative. Consequently, it cannot be adjoined higher than the comparative clause. But, and here comes the contradiction for Müller's account, the trace of the fronted wh-element is in the object position of the embedded, extraposed clause. The contradiction is this: if wh-movement of the interrogative precedes extraposition, wh-movement targets a higher cycle (i.e. the root clause) than extraposition of the comparative (i.e. the embedded clause). So, the object clause must have been extraposed before the comparative clause, otherwise it could not precede. Both instances of extraposition therefore target a lower cycle, contrary to Müller's claim. In an account like Müller's, (3c) cannot be derived since it would inescapably violate the principle of the cycle, contrary to his claim.

Note that this kind of derivational account – first move the lower X, then move the (containing) higher Y – is weaker than a representational approach. In a representational approach, a linguistic expression is assigned its structure instantaneously. There is no possibility of 'first transparent' and 'later opaque'. A domain is either transparent or opaque. So, a representational account is a stronger account. It does not allow the extra degrees of freedom one could gain in the movement account by inventing various shifting options.

5.3.9   VP topicalization and stranded adjuncts

There is an embarrassing dissonance between evidence from binding and evidence from movement for the assignment of the constituent structure to complex VPs, as Pesetsky (1995) points out. Why does *extraposed* material not behave like *adjoined* material under VP topicalization? Binding data support an analysis in which adjuncts are embedded in the VP; topicalization data however are captured best with a right-adjunction structure. These findings are obviously incompatible.

Standard arguments for a *layered* structure of English VPs with adverbials adjoined *on the right* draw on the behaviour under VP topicalization. Pesetsky (1995: 230), for instance, uses the standard line of argumentation with the following data. In (1a), the VP plus its adjuncts are topicalized, while they are stranded in portions in (1b) and (1c). This is apparently captured by a structure in which adverbials, but not arguments (1d) are merged with the VP on the right-hand side.

(1)   a.   … and [[[give the book to them] in the garden] on Tuesday] he did
       b.   … and [[give the book to them] in the garden] he did *on Tuesday*
       c.   … and [give the book to them] he did *in the garden on Tuesday*
       d.   * … and [give the book] he did *to them* in the garden on Tuesday

By the same token one would expect the advocates of the adjunction hypothesis for German to be able to produce analogous data. But the evidence for adjunction provided by VP topicalization is negative. The following examples (see 2a,b) illustrate a contrast between extraposed argument clauses and non-argumental clauses (in this case a relative clause). Argument clauses may be extraposed, but VP topicalization must not strand them (see 2c vs 2d). This is unexpected under the adjunction hypothesis. If they were adjoined to the VP as a consequence of extraposition they would end up outside the VP proper and therefore they ought to be strandable if the VP is topicalized. But argument clauses must not be stranded.

(2) a. dass sie den Befehl^i erteilt hat, {den Platz zu räumen; den^i keiner befolgte}

that she the order given has {the square to clear; that nobody followed}

'that she has given the order {to clear the square; that nobody followed}'

b. [$_{VP}$ Den Befehl^i erteilt, {den^i keiner befolgte; den Platz zu räumen;}] hat sie

[the order given {that nobody followed; the square to clear}] has she

c. [$_{VP}$ Den Befehl^i erteilt] hat sie, {den^i keiner befolgte/*den Platz zu räumen}

[the order given] has she {that nobody followed/*the square to clear}

d. wenn sie den Befehl erteilt, den man erwartet, den Platz zu räumen

if she the order gives, that one expects, the square to clear

e. */??[Den Befehl^i erteilt] hat sie nicht, den^i man erwartet hatte, den Platz zu räumen

[the order given] has she not, that one expected had, the square to clear

f. [$_{VP}$ Den Befehl^i erteilt, den Platz zu räumen], hat sie nicht, den^i man erwartet hatte

[the order given the square to clear] has she not, that one expected had

The immediate reaction to this fact is easy to guess, but misleading: one might think that the difference is as simple as Reinhart's (1980, 1983) claim that argument clauses are attached closer to their base position than non-argumental clauses. But this cannot be entirely correct. As emphasized above (noted first in Haider 1992/2000), extraposed relative clauses precede extraposed argument clauses (2d). Therefore it is impossible that extraposed argument clauses are adjoined lower than extraposed relative clauses.

The facts seem paradoxical: an extraposed relative clause or an argument clause (2a) may be pied-piped by VP topicalization (2b). Alternatively, a relative clause may be stranded; an argument clause must not (2c). An extraposed argument clause follows an extraposed relative clause (2d). But, and this is the paradoxical part, a relative clause must not be stranded if an argument clause has been extraposed although the argument clause follows the strandable relative clause (2e). On the other hand, the extraposed argument clause may be attached to the topicalized VP (2f) although in the extraposed version the relative clause would intervene.

Would 'right node raising' of the complement clause (see Brody's objection discussed in section 5.2) promise a way out? It would not. In the above example (2), the base positions of the extraposed clauses are uncontroversially DP internal. So, if extraposition is the result of movement, the two clauses must be extraposed out of the DP.

In the DP-internal position the order is an inverse one. The argument clause precedes the relative clause. This cannot be verified by simple inspection, though, since the DP is an extraposition site, too. So, we cannot be sure whether (3a) or (3e) is the base order. But the split-DP construction (3b,c) shows that the argument clause cannot be stranded if the relative clause is not stranded (3c). This indicates that the argument clause is more deeply embedded than the relative clause. Hence, in (3d), the argument clause must be in an extraposed position.

(3)   a.   Der Befehl^i, den Platz zu räumen, den^i sie erteilte
the order the square to clear that she gave
'The order to clear the square, that she gave'

b.   Befehle^i, den Platz zu räumen, gibt es keine, die^i sie erteilte
orders the square to clear, are there none, that she gave

c. * Befehle^i, die^i sie erteilte, gibt es keine, den Platz zu räumen
orders that she gave are there none the square to clear
'There are no orders that she gave to clear the square'

d.   [Befehle^i, den Platz zu räumen]$_{DP}$ gibt es keine, die^i sie erteilte,
orders the square to clear are there none that she gave
'There are no orders to clear the square that she gave'

e.   [Der Befehl^i, den^i sie erteilte, den Platz zu räumen]$_{DP}$
the order that she gave the square to clear

Let us assume now that we first extrapose the more deeply embedded argument clause and then the relative clause in order not to violate the strict cycle. The interim result will be the wrong order (4a). So we have to somehow get the argument clause to the clause final position in (4b).

(4)   a. * wenn sie den Befehl erteilt, den Platz zu räumen, den man erwartet
if she the order gives the square to clear that one expects
'If she gives the order to clear the square that one expects'[21]

---

[21] Note that the English gloss does not involve extraposition at all: 'if she gives [the order to clear the square that one expects]'

b.   wenn sie den Befehl erteilt, den man erwartet, den Platz zu räumen
if she the order gives that one expects the square to clear
'If she gives the order that one expects to clear the square'

But note that the argument clause is in a 'frozen' position. First, there is no obvious reason why it should move, except for the sake of getting the desired order. Second, movement of a phrase from the postverbal, clause-final, position is ill formed, as can be seen in a clear case like topicalization.

As for (5a), topicalization of the extraposed clause is clearly unacceptable. But you might object that there could be an intervening factor. After all, the topicalized clause would have been fronted across the DP it depends on. This is likely to provoke a crossing violation. So let us look at (5b), a topicalized V2 clause. This example needs some background information, however.

V2 complements (5c), unlike a C°-introduced complement (5d), are banned from clause-internal positions (5c). Topicalization, therefore, would have to start from the extraposed position, as in (5f). But, the result (5b) is ill formed. Hence, it is safe to conclude that moving a phrase from the postverbal position (to the clause-initial position) is ungrammatical. As for (5e), topicalization starts from the internal position (5d).

(5)   a. * [Über Wasser zu wandeln]$_i$ hat er [einen Versuch (e$_i$)] angekündigt e$_i$
over water to walk has he [an attempt] announced

b.*/?? [Sie sei krank] hat man schon lange vermutet e$_i$
[she is ill] has one already for-a-long-time presumed

c. * Man hat schon lange [sie sei krank] vermutet
one has already for-a-long-time [she is ill] presumed

d. (?) Man hat schon lange [dass sie krank sei] vermutet
one has already for-a-long-time [that she ill is] presumed

e. [Dass sie krank sei] hat man schon lange e$_i$ vermutet
[that she ill is] has one already for-a-long-time presumed

f. Man hat schon lange vermutet [sie sei krank]
one has already for-a-long-time presumed [she is ill]

What these considerations imply is that there is neither a trigger nor a licit derivation for the order of the extraposed clauses in (4b). This is a non-trivial challenge for a movement account of extraposition.

A solution for the incompatibility paradox has been suggested by Phillips (2003). It is a representational approach with incremental structure assignment. In Phillips's parsing-based account, syntactic structures are built incrementally from left to right, i.e. in the order in which the terminal elements are pronounced (see Phillips 2003, section 1). So, a constituency test may refer to only those strings that are constituents at the point in the incremental derivation when the test applies (= Phillips's prediction 1). Contradictions between constituency tests can arise only when the tests apply at different stages in the derivation (= prediction 2). The following example (6a) serves to illustrate how the apparent conflict between the assumption of a right-branching VP and the evidence from VP topicalization, notably the well-formedness of (6b,c) are reconciled under this approach. The examples in (6) illustrate Pesetsky's paradox of the mismatch between structures for binding and structures for VP extraction.

(6)   a. He will [give$_i$ books [e$_i$ to them^j [e$_i$ in the garden [e$_i$ on each^j other's birthday]]]]

b. and [give books to them^j] he did in the garden on each^j other's birthday

c. and [give books to them^j in the garden] he did on each^j other's birthday

d. [$_{IP}$ [$_{VP}$ Give books to them] [$_{IP}$ he [$_{I'}$ did # ^{22}

e. [$_{IP}$ [$_{VP}$ Give books to them [[$_{IP}$ he [$_{I'}$ did [$_{VP}$ *give books to them* #

f. Give books to them^j he did *give books to them^j* in the garden on each^j other's birthday

In (6a), the minimal constituent that contains the main verb is the constituent that contains everything that is within the VP because the verb c-commands everything to its right in a right-branching VP, as indicated by the bracketing in (6a). It is a VP-shell structure, with the verb as the head of the lowest V-projection. The anaphor *each other* is bound correctly by the c-commanding antecedent.

The crucial phases of the structure assignment of (6b) are given in (6d–f): (6d) shows the structure at the point in the structure assignment when the structure for both the fronted VP material, and the subject plus the auxiliary have been projected. Note that the fronted VP in this structure is a well-formed VP constituent.

(6e) is the result of copying the VP into its underlying position, in which theta-role assignment is possible. Finally, in (6f) the stranded PPs are added to, that is structurally integrated into, the reconstructed VP. 'This creates a structure in which the anaphor in the second PP is appropriately c-commanded by its antecedent. It also has the effect of destroying the constituency of the copied VP, but this is unproblematic, because the chain was created by constituent copying at the

---

^{22} The '#' sign denotes the point which the parser has arrived at in the given portion of the parse.

point at which it was created' (Phillips 2003, section 4.2). The resulting structure
for (6b) is a cascading structure, as in (6a). This example is representative of
apparent constituency conflicts that arise when partial VP fronting is used as a
constituency test.[23]

Once this approach has been fully explored and shown to be correct, the discrepancy between the results from c-command-sensitive relations and the results
from movement tests will have vanished. The convergent structure is a right-
branching VP. What Phillips suggests as a solution for the binding paradox provides a solution for the extraposition paradox, too.

The problem was this: topicalized VPs with extraposed material are ill formed
if they are reconstructed into the position of the extraction site. PP objects, for
instance, may be extraposed (7c). (7a) is the result of topicalization of a VP with
an extraposed PP. However, a VP with extraposition is ungrammatical in the base
position (see 7b). So there is no well-formed constituent to start with.

(7)   a.   [Gesprochen *mit allen*] hat er nicht mehr
             [spoken to everyone] has he not any more
       b.   * dass er nicht mehr [gesprochen *mit allen*] *hat*
             that he not any more [spoken to everyone] has
       c.   dass er nicht mehr gesprochen *hat* [*mit allen*]
             that he not any more spoken has [to everyone]

A potential excuse that could be raised for the missing base order (7b) is V-raising:
could it not be the case that the order (7b) does not occur because of obligatory
V-raising? In this case, the verbs would end up head-adjoined to the finite verb in
the higher VP or, for other implementations, in a functional head to the left of the
VP. But this is an untenable excuse. If this was the case, (8c) would be predicted
to be grammatical, which it is not. In (8a), the extraposed relative clause is clause
final. (8b) shows that the fronted VP is a possible extraposition site, too. If this
VP is reconstructed in its base position and the verb has raised, the extraposed
relative clause would end up in between the second DP and the sequence of verbs
at the end. This position is ungrammatical (8c), however. So, raising cannot be the
intervening factor.

(8)   a.   dass er *jenen* etwas gegeben hat, *die ihn darum gebeten haben*
             that he those something given has, who him for-it asked have

       b.   [*Jenen* etwas gegeben *die ihn darum gebeten haben*] hat er immer
             [those something given who him for-it asked have] has he always

---

[23] A similar problem with German VP topicalization and its incongruent reconstruction is
discussed in chapter 7, section 7.4.1.

    c. * dass er *jenen* etwas e$_i$ *die ihn darum gebeten haben* [gegeben hat]$_i$

(hypothetical structure)

        that he those something who him for-it asked have [given has]

        'That he has given something to those who have asked him for it'

What this indicates, too, is that the 'copy' of the topicalized VP is not necessarily identical with the topicalized VP. Otherwise (7a) and (8b) would be ungrammatical. This is confirmed by the contrasts in (9), whose original observation is due to Freidin (1986) and Lebeaux (1988): a referential expression inside the complement of a fronted NP induces a principle-C violation when a coindexed NP c-commands the extraction site (9a,c).

(9)   a. * The remarkable proof of Fermat's^i conjecture he^i could not fit in the margin

        b. The remarkable conjecture in Fermat's^i book he^i did not expect to raise much interest

        c. * Den vollständigen Beweis von Fermats^i Vermutung konnte er^i nicht am Rand unterbringen

           the complete proof of Fermat's conjecture could he not at-the margin fit-in

        d. Den Druckfehler in Fermats^i Beweis hatte man ihm^i verheimlicht

           the misprint in Fermat's conjecture had one (from) him kept-secret

Phillips (2003, section 4.1.2) assumes that the 'copy' of the fronted constituent that is created in the theta position consists only of the lexical head and its complement.[24] Accordingly, the adjuncts in (9b) and (9d) are not part of the copy, whence the immunity of adjunct-contained elements against a principle-C effect. This cannot be entirely correct, however, since complement clauses of topicalized VPs do not trigger a principle-C violation:

(10)   a. [Erklärt, wie man Max^i helfen wolle]$_j$ hat man ihm^i nicht e$_j$

          explained how they Max help wanted have they him not

          'They did not explain to him how they wanted to help Max'

        b. [(So) geholfen, (wie Max^i das wollte)]$_j$ hat man ihm^i nicht e$_j$

          so helped as Max it wanted have they him not

          'They did not help him the way Max wanted it'

---

[24] Phillips assumes that NPs are left branching and that adjuncts are right adjoined to the NP. This is inconsequent. The N-projection is, just like the V-projection, a head-initial projection. The principles for the internal structure of a projection cannot be category specific. In Haider (1992, 1992/2000) it is argued that the complex N-projection just like any other complex head-initial projection consists of a right-branching shell structure (see the following section).

A possible solution of the reconstruction problem is suggested in Haider (1990): the copy is generated by reconstructing the head and projecting its unsaturated A-structure. Thus, the discrepancy between the structure of the fronted VP and the well-formedness requirements at the reconstruction site is captured: since the reconstructed VP is not identical with the fronted VP, the results of application of the well-formedness constraints are not identical.

In sum, the ordering paradox is a subcase of the reconstruction paradox of a fronted VP, and a family member of the family to which Pesetsky's paradox belongs. A radical, though not mainstream-acknowledged, approach is Phillips's incrementality hypothesis. The price for its acceptance is the acceptance of a representational implementation of structure generation. Since the predominant model is a strictly derivational one, the incrementality approach would be hard to integrate in this model, it seems.

5.3.10   Recapitulation and implications

Extraposition turns out to be a recalcitrant phenomenon for an adequate grammar-theoretic modelling. None of the three strategies (i.e. movement and reconstruction, PF movement, base generation plus construal) of modelling this phenomenon has been developed into a fully satisfactory account yet.

The *PF account* fails since it is not selective enough. If extraposition was just an instance of postponed spell-out of clause-like constituents for the sake of reducing the working memory load (or for some other PF-relevant reason; see Truckenbrodt 1995), this process should be blind for finer-grained grammatical subcategories. A clause is a clause for PF. But extraposition is *syntactically* constrained. A clear case is the contrast between DP-internal clauses. Argument clauses must stay within the DP domain, non-argument clauses may be extraposed to the right boundary of the matrix clause of the DP. Another case of syntactically checked access to the right edge is the discrimination among PPs (1). Prepositional arguments and preposition adjuncts extrapose easily in German, but directional (1b) and resultative PPs (1d) must not be extraposed. If extraposition were a mere working memory relief operation on PF, it should operate on phonological units and not discriminate them in terms of their syntactic functions.[25]

(1)   a.   Sie hat nicht gewartet *auf uns*
                 she has not waited for us

---

[25] Another case is the stranding of focus markers with extraposition, but not with topicalization. In German, focus markers like *nur* (only) must not be pied-piped by extraposition, whereas in English, they are (see the beginning of section 5.3.2).

b. * Morgen soll ich seinen Brief bringen *in dieses Haus*
   tomorrow shall I his letter bring in(to) this house

c.   Morgen soll ich den Dienst antreten *in diesem Haus*

(Thomas Mann)

   tomorrow shall I for work report in this house

d. * Kirke hat seine Begleiter gemacht *zu kleinen Schweinchen*
   Kirke has his companions made (in)to little pigs

Second, there are semantic effects that correlate with extraposition. If extraposition is merely a PF operation, it should not be able to produce scope differences as in (2).

(2)   a. Sie war mit nichts zufrieden
          she was with nothing content
          'There was nothing that she was content with'

       b. Sie war zufrieden mit nichts
          she was content with nothing
          'She was content without anything'

Let us turn now to the *movement plus reconstruction approach*. Among its empirically inadequate features there are at least the following ones:

- Uncaptured asymmetries between extraposition and uncontroversial instances of movement (e.g. topicalization, scrambling): extraposition does not respect relevant movement constraints (subject condition, adjunct condition).
- Binding data do not follow from reconstruction because of the independently established resistance against reconstruction of A'-moved *clausal* constituents.
- Phrases with focus particles may be *topicalized* but not *extraposed* (OV effect): extraposed elements do not behave like moved elements.
- Missing extraction sites: extraposed phrases occur even without extraction sites. This is immediately obvious for relative clauses with split antecedents.
- Split antecedents for relative clauses are the positive proof of at least one clear case for the inadequacy of a detachment-by-movement approach to extraposition.

If these obstacles turn out to be insurmountable, the only remaining option is the *base-generation option*. What this means is that the 'extraposed' elements are characterized as detached elements generated at distance to a their antecedents, if they have any, and related to the antecedent by a construal relation. (3a) depicts the movement option, (3b) is the base-generation option. The right edge area is characterized as an optional, low shell of the phrase that is the locus of elements in extraposition. Languages may differ with respect to the availability of this shell. Strict head-final languages, that is, languages without extraposition, do not admit this shell.

(3)   a. moved & adjoined   b. base generated & construed

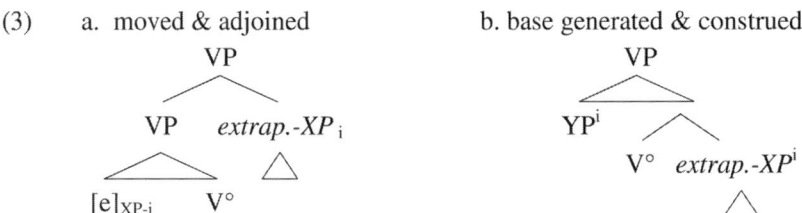

The base-generation option captures the binding data, since the extraposed elements are c-commanded by anything that precedes them. It is not subject to movement constraints but only to the specific construal rules, and these are known to transgress the locality domains of movement. The focus particle cases follow correctly from the directionality of the head (OV vs VO). Extraction sites are missing because there is no extraction.

So, what is unsatisfactory about base generation? First, we do not yet have a proper theoretical understanding of the structure of the right edge shell. Second, it obviously contains both selected elements (argument clauses, prepositional objects) as well as elements not selected by the head, namely all other extraposed material. We do not yet understand why the right edge does not discriminate and how the argument relations are managed, if arguments are base generated in the right edge. In sum, a theory of the structure of the lowest shell, if there is one, is wanting:

- What is the structure of the right edge ? – *Complement* s*ubtree with empty head* ?
- How are extraposed *arguments licensed* if they are base generated? What makes a phrase 'extraposable'?
- What determines the *relative order* of the extraposed phrases ?

5.4   Appendix: multiple shiftings to the left – Kayne (1994) and its extensions

The movement approach to extraposition has found yet another imple-mentation, in terms of Kayne's (1994) antisymmetry hypothesis. Extraposition is analysed as *stranding*, rather than movement to the right (Kayne 1994; Barbiers 2000: 189; Zwart 2000). There are two possible implementations. In Kayne's original version, the antecedent of the relative clause is moved to the left, and the relative clause is stranded. The second version is Zwart's (2000) proposal in terms of remnant movement of the stranded antecedent. First, move the relative clause to the left, and then front the VP containing the stranded antecedent to the left of the fronted relative clause. Both accounts are suboptimal, though.

In form of a slogan, these accounts read either as 'move the antecedent, and strand the relative clause' (1a), or 'move the extraposition candidate to the left, and then front the remnant phrase across the left-moved phrase' (1b):

(1)   a. $[_{XP} \ldots YP+RC]$ $\Rightarrow [YP_i \ldots [_{XP} \ldots e_i+RC]]$
        b. $[_{XP} \ldots YP+RC \ldots] \Rightarrow [RC_i \ldots [_{XP} \ldots YP+e_i \ldots]] \Rightarrow [[_{XP} \ldots YP+e_i \ldots]_j$
           $[\ldots [RC_i \ldots e_j]]]$

As for (1a), it is easy to see that no existing kind of movement is able to produce the desired result without violating grammatical constraints. If (1a), instantiated as in (2a), is derived by *A-movement*, this entails that A-movement must be able to split the relative clause from its antecedent by moving its antecedent. This movement is ungrammatical, however, as (2b) shows. A-movement of the DP plus stranding the relative clause is ungrammatical in a clear case like a passive. If, on the other hand, YP is fronted by *X'-movement*, a relative clause is predicted to be split off by X'-moving its antecedent. But this is ungrammatical, too, as topicalization in (2c) illustrates. Hence, there is no independently motivated way of fronting an antecedent of a relative clause and thereby stranding the relative clause:

(2)   a. I introduced someone$_j$ to her [e$_j$ [who$_i$ she already knew e$_i$]]
        b. * Someone$_j$ was [e$_j$ [who$_i$ she already knew e$_i$]] introduced to her
                                                    (A-mvt. of the target)
        c. * Nobody$_j$ would I [e$_j$ [who$_i$ she already knew e$_i$]] introduce to her
                                                    (A'-mvt. of the target)

Zwart (2000) suggests a different implementation: first, move the relative clause to the left, out of the DP, and then move the DP across the relative clause. The problems remain, however, both on the theoretical as well as on the empirical level.

On the theoretical level, *remnant VP fronting* is fronting to a spec position. Hence this fronted VP is turned into an opaque domain for extraction. The intriguing, though perfectly coherent, prediction would be this: you may wh-move an object only if there is no relative clause relating to this object. But the facts are disappointing for this grand forecast: (3d) is perfect, although it is predicted to be ungrammatical.

(3)   a. I introduced someone [whom she already knew] to her
        b. I [whom$_i$ she already knew e$_i$]$_j$ [introduced [someone$_i$ e$_j$] to her]

   c. I [introduced [[someone$_i$ e$_j$] to her]$_k$ [[whom$_i$ she already knew e$_i$]$_j$ e$_k$]]

   d. Who$_i$ did you [introduce [[e$_i$ e$_j$] to her]$_k$
      [[who$_i$ she already knew e$_i$]$_j$ e$_k$]]

In (3d), the wh-item is moved out of a phrase in a spec position. Hence, this is predicted to be ungrammatical. The evidence contradicts this prediction. (3d) is perfectly innocuous.

On the empirical level, a *remnant movement approach* overgenerates since it requires two independent processes, namely leftward movement and remnant fronting. Since extraposition is optional, remnant fronting is optional, and therefore leftward movement without subsequent extraposition is bound to produce completely ungrammatical expressions (4b):

(4)   a.   Er hat sie [[öfter [$_{PP}$ als ich]] angerufen]
           he has her [[more-often [than I] phoned]

       b. * Er hat sie [[$_{PP}$als ich]$_i$ [[öfter e$_i$] angerufen]]
           (= fronting the PP out of the adverbial)
           he has her [[than I] [[more-often] phoned]]

       c.   Er hat sie [[öfter e$_i$] angerufen] [$_{PP}$als ich]$_i$
           (= fronting the remnant VP across the PP)
           he has her [[more-often] phoned] [than I]

Finally, this approach misses a relevant generalization: as discussed above, movement to the left (topicalization, scrambling) is less restricted than 'movement' to the right. If extraposition is turned into a masked subcase of movement to the left, this difference remains unaccounted for. *Remnant movement* would have to operate differently for each of the phrases to be extraposed. But the constraints on extraposition are not constraints on the domain of the extraposition site; the constraints apply to the candidate for extraposition.

5.5   Summary

Extraposition is a ubiquitous but still insufficiently understood phenomenon. In this chapter, the popular, longstanding and commonsensical idea of movement to the right clausal periphery has been confronted with diverse counterevidence. For the time being, extraposition by movement to the right does not qualify as an empirically adequate account.

Extraposition as movement to the right lacks important properties of a movement phenomenon (violation of core constraints on movement), and the suggested implementations either overgenerate, or undergenerate, or suffer from both defects. So, either the movement approach is completely misguided in general (and the sun does not move, contrary to appearance) or there is a system of movements to the right whose properties have escaped an empirically successful and theoretically satisfactory modelling until now.

The alternative, that has been briefly described, is a non-derivational account. The phrases are generated in the right periphery and related to their respective antecedents by rules of construal. At present, this approach has not yet been worked out in sufficient detail.

A post-syntactic, PF movement account of extraposition (as a 'stylistic' rule, in older days' diction) is not adequate either. PF movement is not PF movement if it has to observe core syntactic constraints (on categories and functions of extraposition candidates), which it obviously does. It is not merely a 'heavy phrase' postponing operation but subject to specific syntactic rather than PF conditions.

This does not deny the advantage of extraposition for the organization of an utterance in production and perception. If extraposition was a PF phenomenon it should display the degree of a syntactic freedom that the distribution of clausal parentheses show (Haider 2005a).

6

Case: a nominative–accusative language with a four-way case paradigm

6.1 Introduction: on the morphosyntactics of the German case system

DPs are overtly case marked in German. This means that a DP is in a case relation to a case-assigning or case-checking element and that the case relation is morphologically realized at various positions in the DP. Morphological case is principally spelled out on the determiner, on the head of the attributive phrase (adjective or participle) and on the head noun. However, the inflectional paradigms for case are not always morphologically overt or biunique. That is, in some instances, especially in the paradigms for nominal heads, there may be no overt morphological sign for a given case, and, second, there is no one-to-one relation between a morphological sign and a given case relation. This is true for instance for neuter nouns, as in the case of the noun *Beispiel* (example) in (1). There is no morphological distinction between accusative and nominative or dative on the neuter noun. Only genitive is marked on the noun (1b); in most cases, the article codes the case (1b,c), and the head of the modifier phrase agrees.

(1)   a. *das* [für diesen Zweck geeignet*e*] Beispiel   (NOM/ACC)
           the [for this purpose suitable] example

        b. *des* [für diesen Zweck geeignet*en*] Beispiel*s*   (GEN)

        c. *dem* [für diesen Zweck geeignet*en*] Beispiel   (DAT)

What you see in (1) are merely morphologically different forms in the three positions mentioned above. The form of the determiner differs, the agreement inflection on the adjectival head differs, and the form of the head noun differs, but there is no unique form per case. The morphological case paradigms for nouns and adjectives are highly overlapping, that is, the same form occurs with more than one case relation. Only determiners, like the definite article in (2), and personal pronouns (3) signal the respective cases in a morphologically differentiated set of forms, though not without syncretisms.

(2)

	masc.	*fem.*	*neut.*	*plural*
NOM.	der	die	das	die
ACC.	den	die	das	die
DAT.	dem	der	dem	den
GEN.	des	der	des	der

(3)

	masc.	*fem.*	*neut.*	*plural*
NOM.	er (he)	sie (she)	es (it)	sie (they)
ACC.	ihn	sie	es	sie
DAT.	ihm	ihr	ihm	ihnen
GEN.	seiner	ihrer	seines	ihrer

As the paradigms (2) and (3) show, dative and genitive are marked with different forms in masculine and neuter and in plural. Nominative and accusative have systematically different forms only in one gender, namely masculine.

In German, case is assigned only to nominal categories and it is morphologically spelled out on nominal heads (pronouns, heads of DPs and NPs) and on heads that agree with a noun (adjectival and participial heads of attributes). Case gets transferred by agreement to the head of attributive APs. Note that in Germanic OV languages, only attributive APs agree, predicative APs do not. More will have to be said on case matching between an argument and a nominal predicate in the next section. Having briefly dwelled upon case licensees, let us turn to case licensers.

Which elements are case licensers in German? In principle, any one of the major lexical category heads ($V°$, $P°$, $A°$, $N°$) is a case licenser.[1] In addition, a functional relation is required for nominative assignment.

---

[1] The viewpoint taken here is mainly descriptive. Theoretically it is close to the theory in Chomsky's Principles & Parameters model. Current versions of Generative Grammar assume that case is a functional feature checked in a functional spec position. So, case licensing entails raising the (DP with the) feature to the respective position. This approach is inadequate for German, if it implies that DPs overtly move to case positions. See the discussion on the opacity of phrases in spec positions in chapter 1.

(4)

Table 6.1 *Case-licensing heads in German*

heads	*structural* (= alternating) case	*lexical* (= invariant) case
V°	accusative	dative, genitive
N°	genitive	–
P°	*accusative ??*[2] ⇒ ⇒	dative, genitive
A°	– [3]	dative, genitive
Agr°[+fin.]	nominative	–
Agr°[-fin.]	zero (PRO)	–

Table 6.1 summarizes the German case system that will be discussed in the following paragraphs. The distinction between *alternating* and *invariant* cases is motivated by facts like the following. As a consequence of relation changing processes that eliminate the subject argument (e.g. passive), accusative changes to nominative on the very same argument, but dative and genitive do not change in the corresponding contexts:

(5) a. Wurde der Kandidat /*den Kandidaten unterstützt ?
         was the candidate-NOM /the candidate-ACC supported

     b. Wurde dem Kandidaten /*der Kandidat geholfen?
         was the candidate-DAT / the candidate-NOM helped

Obligatory switch from accusative to nominative in (5a) illustrates the dependency of accusative licensing on nominative licensing. This dependency is often referred to as 'Burzio's generalization' and will be discussed in the following section.

[2] The question marks question accusative licensing: licensing of a structural accusative by P° differs from V°-licensed ones: (i) P° does not normally select a sentential complement in German (unlike in Scandinavian), but a verb selects a clause as direct object; (ii) accusative licensing is dependent on nominative licensing in clauses, but not in PPs. What would be the external argument of P°, given that structural accusative is licit only in the context of another, externally case checked argument (Burzio's generalization)? In sum, a P°-dependent accusative in German does not behave like a V°-dependent one.

[3] In German, there are no transitive adjectives. There is no subclass of adjectives with an accusative *object*. The accusative found with a small number of adjectives is an *adverbial* one (e.g. for measure expressions).

    (i)   Es wiegt einen Zentner und kostet nur einen Euro
          it weighs a hundredweight-ACC and costs only one euro-ACC

    Expressions like *jemanden los sein* (someone rid be – 'be rid of someone') appear to involve an adjective. However, this is a lexicalized combination with a copula. In the independent, attributive usage, it is ungrammatical: *die mich lose Freundin* (the me rid friend – 'the girl friend that got rid of me').

Why is genitive listed as a structural case with nouns as licensers but as an invariant one if licensed by V or A? Genitive objects of nouns correspond to accusative objects of verbs. This can be verified easily if we compare a verb and its nominalized infinitive:

(6)   a. den Lift benützen
            the-ACC elevator use
            'use the elevator'

        b. das Benützen des Lifts
            the use the elevator-GEN
            'the using of the elevator'

Not only is the genitive object in the NP in (6b) the argument that corresponds to the accusative object in the VP in (6a); nouns do not tolerate invariantly case-specified arguments at all. This becomes evident if we consider the nominalized infinitives of verbs with dative or genitive arguments, as in (7a,b) respectively.

(7)   a. das Gratulieren (*dem Sieger)
            the congratulate(ing) the winner-DAT
            'the congratulating of the winner'

        b. das Gedenken (*der vergangenen Zeiten)
            the commemorate(ing) the past times-GEN
            'the commemorating of the past times'

Objects of nouns receive genitive and they must be structurally case-licensed. Arguments with lexical case, even if it is a genitive object of a verb, are not admitted. The starred genitive in (7b) is the genitive object of the verb *gedenken* (commemorate) in the nominalized form. Although it is a genitive, it is ill formed as a complement of a DP, because it is an invariant genitive, that is, a genitive specified in the argument structure of the verb. Nouns combine only with structurally cased arguments. These are unspecified for a lexical case and receive the case that is licensed in the particular structural environment the argument appears in.

Prepositions license all cases except a nominative. The particular case a preposition licenses is a lexical property of the given preposition. The majority of German prepositions license either dative or accusative. Here are some examples:

(8)   a. mit dir   —   ohne dich
            with you-DAT   —   without you-ACC

        b. von dir   —   für dich
            of you-DAT   —   for you-ACC

        c. wegen deiner   —   innerhalb des Gebäudes
            because-of you-GEN   —   within the building-GEN

There is a class of prepositions that seems to license either accusative or dative. In fact, this alternation correlates with a precise meaning difference, namely the difference between locational and directional. In English, this difference is lexicalized for some prepositions (e.g. *in* vs *into*; *on* vs *onto*). In German, the two functions are differentiated by the case requirement of the prepositions.

(9)   a. auf den Berg   hinter den Berg   directional
          on(to) the mountain-ACC   behind the mountain-ACC

       b. auf dem Berg   hinter dem Berg   locational

          on the mountain-DAT   behind the mountain-DAT

The prepositions in (9a,b) are ambiguous. They come with an alternative lexical-conceptual content (locational vs directional) and the concomitant case licensing property. It is not the meaning of the preposition that directly determines its case licensing property, though. The meaning only discriminates the two variants.

If the meaning did directly determine the case, any directionally interpreted preposition would require accusative. This is not true, however. The preposition *zu* assigns only dative, in contrast with *in* in (10b), and this is not in conflict with the directional meaning in (10a). *Zu* (to) as a local preposition is directional only, while the prepositions with alternating case have a concomitant alternating interpretation.

(10)   a. Sie transportierte es *zu* mir /*mich
          she transported it to me-DAT /*ACC

       b. Sie transportierte es *im* Haus / *in* das Haus
          she transported it in-the house-DAT / into the house-ACC

Whether the correlation between the particular case licensing property and the corresponding lexical-conceptual structure is just a lexical idiosyncrasy or the reflex of a more principled relation is unclear at present. In other words, we do not know whether it is an accident or a grammatical necessity that these prepositions license the cases they license. We do not know whether a grammar in which dative correlated with directional and accusative with locational meaning would or would not be a possible human grammar.

Let us now briefly touch upon a theoretical issue indicated by the question marks in table 6.1 in (4), for P°. Does the differentiation between structural and invariant case make sense for prepositions? In other words, is the accusative licensed by a preposition the same kind of case as the accusative licensed by the verb? It could well be that the difference between structural and lexical cases for arguments makes sense only for heads with more than a single argument. In other words, verbs and nouns but not prepositions may be *transitive* vs *intransitive*, but for heads that invariably select a single argument this distinction is immaterial. What kind of empirical evidence could be helpful for clarifying this issue? Here are some facts about German that are potentially relevant.

In German, embedded sentences can be linked to arguments with *structural* case, but not to a dative argument.[4] There are no verbs whose dative argument could be represented by a sentential argument.[5] If a prepositional accusative was a structural case, we might expect these prepositions to take a sentential argument. This is contrary to the facts, however. Unlike the Scandinavian languages, German does not allow a clause as the complement of a preposition in prepositional objects:

(11)   * Ich bestehe [$_{PP}$ auf [$_{CP}$ dass du kommst]]
        I insist [on [that you come]]

The ungrammaticality of the English gloss shows that structural case cannot be a sufficient condition for clausal objects, otherwise English would tolerate sentential complements of prepositions, since English does not have invariant cases at all.

There are only two German prepositions that allow a sentential complement, but their case licensing properties are not exclusively accusative, as one might expect. *Ohne* (without) licenses an accusative (12b), but *anstatt* (instead) licenses a genitive (12a).

(12)   a. [$_{PP}$ anstatt [$_{CP}$ dass sie arbeitete]]
        instead-of [that she worked]
        'instead of working'

        b. [$_{PP}$ ohne [$_{CP}$ dass etwas passierte]]
        without [that something happened]

Another piece of evidence comes from case matching between an argument and the kind of predicative phrases illustrated in (13). German allows a mismatch, with a dative instead of a matching accusative, but only if the accusative is prepositional, and crucially not if the accusative is licensed by V°:

(13)   a. für eine Weltregierung, als das / dem Endziel   (Leirbukt 1978: 3)
        for a world government-ACC as the-ACC / the-DAT ultimate-goal

---

[4] This was noted first by Fanselow (1985).
[5] Astonishingly, however, arguments that require genitive for a DP object may be represented by a clause. So, the restriction is a restriction against dative, not against non-structural case in general.

   (i)   Ich bin mir (dessen) bewusst, dass es so ist
          I am myself (it-GEN) conscious, that this so is – 'I am aware that it is so'
   (ii)   Jemand hat ihn (dessen) beschuldigt, dass er sich nicht um seine Kinder kümmere
          someone has him (it-GEN) accused that he himself not for his children cares
          'someone has accused him of not taking care of his children'

b. für Österreich, als den / dem schwächeren Partner

(Leirbukt 1978: 4)

for Austria-ACC as the-ACC / the-DAT weaker partner

c. Österreich, als den /*dem schwächeren Partner unterstützen

Austria-ACC as the-ACC /*the-DAT weaker partner support

'support Austria as the weaker partner'

Van Riemsdijk (1983) suggested the following interpretation. Dative is the default case if the target of predication is an oblique case relation, that is, a non-structural case. In this situation, either the case is copied onto the predicate or the predicate gets dative case. This predicts that genitives can be combined with dative on the predicate. That this is the case, indeed, is illustrated by (14), from Lawrenz (1993: 114), who quotes various examples of this kind:

(14)   trotz eines wenig begabten Mannes als politischem Berater
        despite a little gifted man-GEN as political adviser-DAT

The contrast between (13b) and (13c) with respect to the admissibility of dative is robust. So, if van Riemsdijk's interpretation is correct, the accusative on a verbal object and the accusative on the complement of a preposition are different syntactic entities in terms of case licensing.

Let us turn now to adjectives. Like verbs, adjectives may provide more than a single object argument, but the majority of adjectives combine with a single object only. Unlike in English, adjectives can take nominal complements in German. The reason becomes obvious, once we look at the case of the complements. It is either dative or genitive, but there are no adjectives with accusative arguments (see footnote 3). In other words, there are no transitive adjectives. Since English does not have lexical cases, the transitivity gap for adjectives completely deprives adjectives of the possibility of nominal complementation. Here are some examples for adjectival complementation:

(15)   a. ein [ihr angenehmer] Vorschlag
           a [(to) her-DAT agreeable] proposal
           'a proposal that is agreeable to her'

        b. ein [des Minimalismus kundiger] Syntaktiker
           a [(of) the minimalism-GEN experienced] syntactician
           'a syntactician that is experienced in minimalism'

        c. ein [dem Gegner an Kraft überlegener] Kontrahent
           a [(to) the adversary-DAT in power superior] rival
           'a rival that is superior in power to the adversary'

    d. ein [sich seiner Sache sicherer] Redner
      a [himself-DAT (about) his cause-GEN sure] speaker
      'a speaker who is sure about his cause'

As for transitivity, it is instructive to compare *adjectival* with *participial* constructions. Participles of verbs can be used as adnominal attributes. The participle, like the adjective, agrees with the head noun. If the verb is transitive, the *present participial* construction will contain an accusative object, as in (16a). But, as illustrated in (16b), participial phrases with an accusative object cannot be used predicatively.

(16)   a.   ein [diese Frage untersuchender] Linguist
           a [this question-ACC examining] linguist

        b. * Ein Linguist ist diese Frage untersuchend
           a linguist is this question examining

Particularly instructive in this respect is the behaviour of psych verbs. The participles of psych verbs apparently can be used predicatively, but only *without* an object (17). This predicative usage of a present participle is apparent insofar as these participial forms only look like participles. They are adjectives by morphological conversion, that is, they are re-categorized as adjectives. That this is so becomes clear from the fact that participles in general cannot be used predicatively in German, irrespective of their argument structure (18). What these participials-turned-into-adjectives show is that adjectives do not tolerate an accusative object.

(17)   a. Die Frage ist (*ihn) sehr irritierend / quälend
          the question is (to him-ACC) very irritating / agonizing-ADJECTIVE

        b. die [ihn sehr irritierende] Frage
          the [him-ACC very irritating-PARTICIPLE+AGR] question

In (17a), *irritierend* is used as a predicative *adjective*. Its adjectival status is the result of morphological *conversion* of a verbal category (participle) into an adjective as the result of word formation.[6] In general, a participle cannot be used in predicative constructions with a copula in German, irrespective of transitivity (16b, 18b). As adjectives, they obey the argument format of adjectives and this leaves no room for a second argument[7] with structural case.

---

[6] This conversion is found mostly with verbs that denote a mental state: *bezaubernd* (enchanting), *erhebend* (edifying), *nervend* (making nervous), *störend* (disturbing), *schmerzend* (hurting), ...

[7] The first argument is the subject. In the copula construction, the adjectival head provides the arguments.

(18)   a.   ein schlafender Hund
              a sleeping dog

        b.   * Der Hund ist schlafend
              the dog is sleeping

In (18b) and in (16b), the predicate is a participle. In (17a) it is an adjective converted from a participle. Independent evidence for its adjectival status is shown by the fact that although comparative is possible[8] for this form, if the comparative is chosen, a direct object is not allowed.[9] This follows from the adjectival property: adjectives allow a comparative, but disallow a direct object.

Next, let me now briefly introduce the nominative. It is a special case. As the case of an *argument*, it requires agreement with the finite verb. In the absence of a finite verb, there is no nominative *argument*, and if there is a nominative argument in a clause, then there is a finite verb, too, which the nominative phrase agrees with in person and number. This correlation does not hold for non-arguments: in certain contexts, nominative seems to be a default case for non-arguments. This is true for 'hanging topics' (19a), or predicative DPs in an infinitival copula construction (19b), or predicative DPs in an apposition construction (19b).

(19)   a.   Der Nominativ[i], für den[i] gelten andere Regeln
              the nominative-NOM, for this-ACC apply different rules

        b.   Es ist nicht leicht, [PRO ein weiser Mann zu werden / sein]
              it is not easy [a wise man-NOM to become / be]
              'It is not easy to be / become a wise man'

        c.   Die Charakterisierung dieses Mannes als ein gefährliches Subjekt
              the characterization (of) this man-GEN as a dangerous fellow-NOM

In a left-dislocation construction (19a), the left-dislocated DP may either match the case of the argument it is co-referenced with (by means of a resumptive demonstrative within the clause), or it may be nominative, as in (19a). Note that the left-dislocated phrase is technically speaking not an argument. The argument is the demonstrative pronoun that functions as a resumptive.

---

[8] Example: Der Lärm ist (*uns) störender als der Geruch
              the noise is (us) more-disturbing than the smell

[9] Adjectives are unaccusative in German and copula constructions are unaccusative, too. If these two facts are combined, the correlation appears that the unaccusative format of the adjectives as theta-provider matches the format of the copula as the theta position manager in the clause. Note that the auxiliary *be* in English is not generally restricted to unaccusative contexts. In the copular and in the passive construction it is, but not in the combination with an *-ing*-suffixed verb.

The predicative DP in (19b) is a predicative nominative in a copula construction within an infinitival clause. The subject of the copula construction is the phonetically silent pronominal subject of an infinitival clause. Obviously, there is no finite verb to agree with, but nevertheless there is a non-argumental DP with nominative case.

In (19c), the nominative is the predicate of the appositive *as*-construction. It is predicated over the genitive complement of the noun. Again, this is a conntext without an agreeing finite verb, and the nominative-cased DP is a non-argument.

These examples may suffice for demonstrating that the tight correlation between nominative and an agreement relation with a finite verb only holds for arguments, but not for non-arguments. At present, it is open what the exact case mechanism for the other contexts as in (19) is. The notion 'default case' is not sufficient. It simply means that nominative is spelled out on a non-argument DP in the absence of a case licensing element. Obviously, this requires extra measures for avoiding overgeneration.

Let us now examine infinitival clauses. They provide another instance of a non-argumental nominative. The subject of an infinitival clause, namely PRO, is a subject in camouflage, and the widely accepted grammatical reason for its morphological invisibility is the unavailability of receiving case. But, appositions to this subject get nominative case:

(20)   a. die Absicht der Männer [PRO sich *einer nach dem anderen* krank zu erklären]
        the intention (of) the men-GEN [oneself *one*-NOM *after the other* sick to declare]
        'the men's intention to declare themselves sick one after the other'

        b. der Traum (des Mannes) [PRO als *erster Mensch* den Mars zu betreten]
        the dream (of) the man-GEN [*as first human-being*-NOM the mars to set-foot-on]

The case of the predicative DPs in (20a,b) is nominative, but the silent subject in each of the sentential infinitives is allegedly caseless, otherwise it would get lexicalized. Given the option of a default nominative, what blocks a default nominative on the subject of an infinitival clause? It is the subject–verb agreement. The subject is an argument of the infinitival verb. The verb is inflected for infinitive by a prefixed *zu*, but it cannot be inflected for agreement. If agreement between a lexical subject and the inflected verb is mandatory, a lexical subject would produce an agreement clash. It would provide specified agreement features but they could not be spelled out properly on the inflected verb. A morphologically silent subject avoids this clash.

6.2   Case assignment regularities

6.2.1   The nominative–accusative dependency

This section focuses on generalizations about case licensing and the particular settings of case licensing in German. Let us start with the nominative–accusative dependency, often referred to as 'Burzio's generalization' (BG). In Burzio's (1986) account, BG relates θ-assignment to the subject with the potential of the verb to assign structural case.[10] From a theoretical perspective, reference to theta-assignment seems to be dispensable, however. What BG describes is a dependency of accusative licensing: in a NOM–ACC-system, ACC-licensing on an argument is dependent on a structural case being licensed by a superordinate element on a co-argument. In other words, accusative is the second option and it is applied only once the first option has been exploited. In a finite clause, this is nominative, licensed by finiteness features (see Haider 1984a: 72 and 88; 1985: 13 and 30; Marantz 1991). BG can, and in fact must, be reformulated as a generalization about the licensing of structural cases. [11]

The German data sample in (1) illustrates the core effect described by BG: accusative (as in 1a) cannot be licensed unless the licensing of nominative has applied (as in 1c). This leaves nominative as the only option for the internal argument in (1b). Dative, a lexical, not a structural case, remains unaffected, as (1d) exemplifies.

(1)   a.   * Wurde ihm *den Fehler* vergeben?
             was him-DAT the mistake-ACC forgiven?

        b.   Wurde ihm *der Fehler* vergeben?
             was him-DAT the mistake-NOM forgiven?
             'Was he forgiven the mistake?'

        c.   Hat man ihm *den Fehler* vergeben?
             has one-NOM him-DAT the mistake-ACC forgiven?
             'Has one forgiven him the mistake?'

---

[10] The original formulation of Burzio's generalization is this: $\theta_s \leftrightarrow$ ACC (Burzio 1986: 185). 'All and only the verbs that can assign θ-role to the subject can assign (accusative) case to an object' (Burzio 1986: 178).

[11] The conceptual difficulty of the original version was obvious from the beginning: BG correlates two independent sets of conditions in a triggering configuration, namely θ-marking and case licensing. Even if BG was descriptively adequate, one would have to ask oneself how to derive this cross-modular constraint: BG as a primitive principle of grammar would contradict a basic assumption of the modular organization. A subrule of one module (i.e. theta marking of subject) would have to interfere directly with a subrule of another system (i.e. case licensing by V° or a functional head). Some empirical difficulties for the original formulation of BG (pointed out in Haider 1984a, 2000c) are discussed below.

d. Wurde *ihm* vergeben?
   was him-DAT forgiven?

The relevant condition can be characterized in a simplified form as follows: if two case licensing options are applicable alternatively, the case system has to provide a principled choice. In (1a,b), the object is in principle accessible for accusative licensing by the verb as well as for the (VP-internal) licensing of nominative by agreement on the verb. This licensing indeterminacy applies only to structural case. Lexical case is predetermined. The principle in question is a priority principle for external case licensing: the external licensing option must be exploited first.

Structural cases are the cases of arguments that are not prespecified for a specific case in the lexical entry. Their case is contextually realized (as accusative or nominative, or, in DP-internal positions as genitive). Let us start with English as a language without inherent case for verbal arguments. There are three alternative licensing relations for the very same argument, depending on the syntactic environment, namely nominative (2a), accusative (2b) and PRO (2c). For the latter, Chomsky and Lasnik (1995) suggested *zero case* as licensing relation. (2d) is an example with multiple licensing of accusative. All arguments in (2d) are arguments of *forgive*, and for each accusative, there is a unique licensing element, on the assumption that the licensing of accusative is effected by a $V°$-element.

(2)   a. *She* smiles
        b. [Make [*her* smile]]
        c. [PRO to smile] ...
        d. [Make [*her* [forgive$_i$ [*him* [[$_V°$ e]$_i$ *everything*]]]]] [12]

Nominative and zero case in (2a) and (2c), respectively, are licensed *functionally*, accusative is licensed *categorically* (2b), that is, by the higher $V°$. Functional licensing is licensing by functional features (like tense and/or agreement). Categorical licensing is licensing by a suitable lexical category in a local environment. In (2d), all occurrences of accusative are categorically licensed by a $V°$-head, one of which is an empty $V°$ in a VP-shell structure.[13] Functional licensing is not necessarily constrained to a spec-head configuration. Relevant empirical evidence for the need of a relational implementation of functional licensing comes from German: as pointed out by Haider (1984a), a topicalized VP may contain a nominative (3a,b), and a nominative DP may follow a co-argument in the neutral and canonical order (3c,d):

---

[12] The structure is a VP-shell structure. In Chomskyan terminology, the verb has raised to the vP-shell.

[13] In Chomskyan terminology, the case assigner for the indirect object is 'little v'.

(3)   a. [Gespenster begegnet] sind mir hier schon oft
          [ghosts-NOM come-across] are me here already often
          'Already often I have come across ghosts here'

       b. [Ein Linguist gelehrt] hat hier noch nie
          [a linguist-NOM taught] has here never ever

       c. dass auch Professoren manchmal Fehler unterlaufen
          that even (to) professors-DAT sometimes failures-NOM happen

       d. wenn wem was erklärt wurde
          if (to) whom-DAT what-NOM explained was
          'if something was explained to someone'

This is not a peculiarity of German. VP-internal nominatives are by no means a rare phenomenon. They are found in OV languages like German or Dutch, but also in VO languages, as in Icelandic (Yip, Maling and Jackendoff 1987).

6.2.2   *Non-structural case – lexical or inherent?*

Standard P&P case theory (Chomsky 1981) distinguishes two types of case, namely structural and non-structural. The structural cases include nominative and accusative, while the non-structural cases (customarily referred to as lexical or inherent) comprise dative, lexical accusative, and – for ergative systems – also ergative case (e.g. Mahajan 1989; Nash 1996; Woolford 1993, 1997).

The principal division of cases into structural and non-structural has been uncontroversial, but there is some disagreement in the literature as to which individual cases belong to which type. In particular, it has been argued that the more regular and predictable instances of the dative (and/or the ergative case in morphological ergative languages) must be filed as structural case, because of the predictability (e.g. Czepluch 1988; Uriagereka 1992; Wunderlich 1997; Blume 1998a). However, as Woolford (2006) and Vogel and Steinbach (1998) argue in detail for German, the impression that these datives are instances of structural cases does not stand the test, once the evidence is checked systematically and on a broad enough basis.

Let us now review some German data. Dative or genitive is not sensitive to BG and these cases do not share the properties of structural cases in other respects, either: passive does not trigger a case change. They do not change under exceptional case marking, and they do not alternate with a zero form in clausal infinitives.

Once more we have to compare the two sets of case relations, namely the structural and the inherent ones in each of these three contexts, namely (i) the nominative–accusative dependency (1), (ii) the alternation between (a derived) nominative and PRO (2), and (iii) the exceptional accusative on an argument that would be nominative in a finite clause (3).

The examples in (1) illustrate the passive effect with the combination of an auxiliary with a *zu*-marked infinitive, for the sake of variation, since it behaves completely parallel to the passive with participle plus auxiliary (*werden* – be, *sein* – be as copula). (1a) is the active version, with the auxiliary *haben* (have). (1b) is the passive version, with a switch of accusative to nominative. (1c), the version with accusative, is ungrammatical.

The verb in (1d,e) is a verb with a dative object. (1d) shows that a switch from dative to nominative is ungrammatical. The dative stays dative (1e). This indicates that a dative unlike an accusative is not dependent on the presence of an externally case-marked element.

(1) a. Jetzt haben wir diesen Fall zu prüfen
         now have we this case-ACC to check
         'Now we have to check this case'

    b. Jetzt ist dieser Fall zu prüfen
        now is this case-NOM to check
        'Now this case is to be checked'

    c. * Jetzt ist diesen Fall zu prüfen
         now is this case-ACC to check

    d. * Jetzt ist dieser Hinweis zu folgen
         now is this hint-NOM to follow
         'Now this hint is to be followed'

    e. Jetzt ist diesem Hinweis zu folgen
        now this hint-DAT is to follow
        'Now this hint is to be followed'

Nominative in a finite clause corresponds to the zero cased, silent subject in an infinitival clause. The two verbs in (2a,b) are synonymous, but *beglückwünschen* (wish good luck) is transitive, whereas the loan verb *gratulieren* (congratulate) requires a *dative* object. In the passive version (2a), the accusative switches to the external variant, which is the zero form in an infinitival clause. (2b) is ungrammatical. The dative object cannot change its case. Since it does not, the clause remains without a subject argument, and this is ungrammatical for sentential infinitives. The PRO subject is obligatory and must be assigned a theta role. It is the theta role of the argument that would surface as nominative if the clause was finite.

(2) a. Er hatte gehofft, [PRO dafür beglückwünscht zu werden]
        he had hoped [it-for congratulated to be]

b. * Er hatte gehofft, [PRO (ihm) dafür gratuliert zu werden]
   he had hoped [PRO (him)-DAT it-for congratulated to be]
   'He had hoped be congratulated for it'

c. * Er hatte gehofft, [PRO dafür gratuliert zu werden]
   he had hoped [PRO it-for congratulated to be]
   'He had hoped be congratulated for it'

As in English, German perception verbs take either a sentential complement or an infinitival one. In the latter case, the subject is 'exceptionally case marked' (ECM construction). This means that the subject of the lower verb receives object case from the higher verb.

In German, passive is dispreferred in ECM constructions. The example (3) confronts an intransitive verb (3a) with one of the rare 'impersonal' verbs of German (3b). '*Grauen*' (dread) has a single argument and the case of this argument is dative. As observed originally by Reis (1976), a dative argument resists the switch into an ECM accusative. It would stay dative in a construction that assigns accusative, whence the clash that results in ungrammaticality.

(3)   a.   Man sah ihn-ACC weinen
             one saw him weep

       b. * Man sah ihn-ACC / ihm-DAT grauen
             one saw him dread

What the data just reviewed demonstrate is a bipartition of the German case relations into two groups, namely the structure-dependent ones and the invariant ones. This difference can be captured in various ways, depending on the grammar model. The Principles & Parameters model (Chomsky 1981; for German case: Haider 1984a), provided the distinction of *structural* vs *lexical case*. Lexical case means that the specific case is specified in the lexical argument structure in combination with the argument format. A structural case is underspecified. Its morphological outcome is determined by the context in which the argument is licensed. So it can end up as nominative (if it is the subject in a finite clause), as accusative (as a subject in an ECM construction, or as the second structural argument, that is, the transitive object), or as zero (in an infinitival clause).

The term 'lexical case' should not be equated with idiosyncratic case. A lexical case is for many verbs a predictable case. For the majority of double object verbs, the indirect object is a dative. On the other hand, the dative is not predictable for the class of verbs with a single object that require a dative object rather than an accusative one. The verbs may even be synonymous (4a) or near synonyms (4b), but they nevertheless differ in their object selection property:

(4)

	ACC-object selection		DAT-object selection
a.	beglückwünschen (congratulate)	vs	gratulieren (congratulate)
b.	unterstützen (support)	vs	helfen (help)
c.	verfolgen (track)	vs	folgen (follow)
d.	beschädigen (damage)	vs	schaden (harm)
e.	widerlegen (refute)	vs	widersprechen (oppose)

The fact that dative is predictable for double object verbs does not contradict the assumption that it is a lexically specified case and hence an invariant case. It is predictable on the level of the lexical argument structure and inherent case is determined on that level.

In German there are three morphologically different ways of specifying the licensing relation for an object in the argument structure. First, the argument may be unspecified for a specific case in the lexical argument structure. This is what we refer to as a structural case relation. Second, it may be specified for a specific case. This is the lexical case, and it is invariant. Third, the argument may be lexically determined as a category with a specific case licenser. This is what we are used to calling a prepositional object. The preposition is determined by the selecting verb. The preposition is semantically vacuous, but it is a case licenser. Prepositional objects are truly idiosyncratic with respect to the choice of the preposition. This is easy to verify cross-linguistically. More often than not, the preposition in a given language does not match its translational counterpart in the other language.

(5)   a. trust *in*   vs   vertrauen *auf* (on)
        b. depend *on*   vs   abhängen *von* (of)
        c. arrive *at*   vs   gelangen *zu* (to)

What we need for predicting the case of the second object of a double object verb is at least a general restriction on the format of the lexical argument structure (see also Czepluch 1988).

(6)   Case licensing within a given syntactic structure is a biunique relation: a head cannot license more than one instance of a case type (i.e. structural case,[14] invariant case, or prepositional case) and for each case instance, there is a unique licensing head.

[14] German has only very few verbs with *two* accusative objects (cf. (i)). Passive ((ii) vs (iii)) shows that the two arguments are not equivalent. Only one of the two objects, namely the direct object, receives nominative:

If a verb cannot license more than a single instance of a case type, we can predict for a double object verb in German that its two objects will belong to different case types. What we cannot predict in each case is the particular setting of the case relation.

(7)   a. jemandem etwas verkaufen
            (to) someone-DAT something-ACC sell

        b. etwas an jemandem verkaufen
            something-ACC to someone sell

        c. jemandem mit etwas drohen   intransitive
            someone-DAT with something threaten

        d. jemanden mit etwas bedrohen   transitive
            someone-ACC with something threaten

        e. etwas jemandem aussetzen
            something-ACC (to) someone-DAT expose

The pattern (7a) is frequent in German. This means that there are many verbs that instantiate this pattern. These are most often verbs with an experiencer, source or goal role for the dative and a theme role for the accusative. The pattern (7a,b) resembles the so-called dative alternation in English. But in German, the apparent alternation between dative and an *an*-PP (to-PP) is limited to a much smaller class of verbs than in English or Dutch. (7c,d) illustrates the combination of a DP and a PP object. In (7c) the DP object is lexically cased, in (7d) it is structurally cased. (7e) is an example for a class of verbs with a dative object following an accusative object in the base order. It is a specimen of a small class of verbs with the dative as the lower-ranked argument. In English and Dutch, the corresponding verbs code this relation with a prepositional object. It typically denotes source or goal relations.

What the verbs in (7) illustrate are various combinations of case relations: structural case combined with lexical case (7a,e), structural case combined with prepositional case (7d), and lexical case combined with prepositional case (7c). The descriptive generalization behind the impression that the dative in (7a) is predictable is this: if a structurally cased argument is combined with a higher-ranked object, this object argument is specified for dative. Genitive objects or prepositional

(i)   Jemand fragt ihn die Vokabel ab
         someone checks him-acc the vocabulary-acc off
         'Someone tests him on the vocabulary'
(ii)   Er wurde die Vokabel abgefragt
         he-nom was the vocabulary-acc off-checked
         'he was tested on vocabulary'
(iii)   * Die Vokabel wurden ihn abgefragt
         the vocabulary-nom was him-ACC off-checked

objects are lower ranked, that is, they are merged first, and in terms of linearization they follow an accusative object. This generalization covers the big class of dative–accusative verbs (8a), as well as the unaccusative dative–nominative class (8b), and it is not contradicted by the small class of accusative–dative verbs like (7e).

(8)   a. *erklären* (explain), *geben* (give), *stiften* (donate), *untersagen* (forbid), *verzeihen* (forgive), *zeigen* (show), …

        b. *auffallen* (sth. strike someone), *einfallen* (occur to someone), *erscheinen* (appear to someone), *zustoßen* (happen to someone), …

Scholars who want to demonstrate that the dative on ditransitive experiencer/goal verbs in German is a structural case point to the apparent dative–nominative shift in the so-called recipient passive in (9). Wunderlich (1997) and Czepluch (1988) both emphasize that the dative of experiencers/goals must be a structural case because of its regularity, and refer to the recipient passive to strengthen that argument. Blume (1998) argues that even goals of single object verbs such as *congratulate* must be structural because of their regularity. These scholars justly object to confounding the regular dative of experiencers/goals with the truly idiosyncratic cases, but the evidence they base their claims on is not evidence for a structural case. It is evidence for distinguishing two types of lexical case, namely a regular one and an idiosyncratic one.

Woolford (2006) provides an insightful terminological distinction. She emphasizes the necessity of acknowledging two types of non-structural cases, namely an idiosyncratic lexical case ('lexical' in her terminology) and a regular and predictable one ('inherent' in her terminology):

> Case Theory must distinguish two kinds of non-structural Case, lexical and inherent. Lexical Case is idiosyncratic Case, which is lexically selected and licensed by individual verbs and prepositions. Inherent Case is more regular and predictable. Inherent Case is associated with θ-roles, but not directly with the many different small thematic roles, but rather with the larger thematic proto-roles that are mapped to distinct positions in syntax.
>
> The inherent Cases, although fairly regular and predictable, are nevertheless not structural Cases by any reliable diagnostic test; claims to the contrary stem from the fact that such diagnostic tests can produce misleading results in certain predictable situations in certain languages, because of interfering factors.

(Woolford 2006: 1)

Let us briefly evaluate the evidence from the German 'recipient passive'. This term refers to the combination of *kriegen* (get) or *bekommen* (receive) with a past participle, which is equivalent to the regular passive construction with the difference that the DP that remains dative in the regular construction appears as nominative in the recipient passive:

(9)   a. Gestern wurde jemandem ein Bein amputiert   passive
           yesterday was someone-DAT a leg-NOM amputated

        b. Gestern kriegte jemand ein Bein amputiert   'recipient' passive
           yesterday got someone-NOM a leg-ACC amputated

The gloss in (9b) suggests a parallel to the English *get*-passive. This is misleading because *kriegen/bekommen*, unlike *get*, are not standard passive auxiliaries. The combination with the participle of a monotransitive verb (10b) is ungrammatical, the restriction being that the participle must provide an experiencer/recipient argument (see also Abraham 1995: 206f.), which surfaces as nominative in this construction. (10c) is deviant with *kriegen*, but not with the regular passive auxiliary (10d), because the dative argument of *add* is a mere goal, and not a recipient.

(10)   a. I was/got fascinated by this topic

        b. Ich wurde/*kriegte fasziniert durch dieses Thema
            I was/got fascinated by this topic

        c. * Der Absatz kriegte etwas hinzugefügt
            the paragraph-NOM got something-ACC added

        d. Dem Absatz wurde etwas hinzugefügt
            the paragraph-DAT was something-NOM added
            'Something was added to the paragraph'

In the active construction, the subject argument of the recipient passive corresponds to a dative object of a ditransitive verb. The required argument structure of the selected verb matches the theta structure of *kriegen/bekommen* as main verbs. As main verbs, they are obligatorily transitive verbs with a theme object and a subject denoting the recipient (11a) or the experiencer (11b).

(11)   a. Er kriegte/bekam *(etwas) (von seinen Eltern)
           he got/received something from his parents

        b. Er kriegte/bekam große Angst
           he got/received big fear
           'He got very much afraid'

The passive effect in the recipient passive is the result of combining *kriegen/bekommen* (get, receive) as *semi-lexical* (quasi-auxiliary) verbs with a supine (past participle). Like the auxiliaries, *haben/sein* (have/be), the quasi-auxiliaries also combine with a *zu*-infinitive:

(12)   a. Du kriegst es nicht zu sehen/hören/fassen/kaufen
           you get it not to see/hear/grasp/buy
           'You do not manage to see/hear/grasp/buy it'

b. * Du kriegst es nicht zu beobachten/belauschen/verstehen/verkaufen
    you get it not to watch/listen in to/understand/sell
    'You do not manage to watch/listen in to/understand/sell it'

The theta role of the subject argument of the verbs in (12a), but not of the verbs in (12b), is a recipient role, whence the contrast in acceptability with agentive verbs in (12b). (12) is instructive for yet another reason, namely the absence of a passive effect. Compare (12) with the corresponding auxiliary constructions (13):

(13)   a. Sie hat mich instruiert
           she has me-ACC instructed
           'She has instructed me'

        b. Ich war instruiert   (copula + participle)
           I was instructed

        c. Ich wurde instruiert   (passive auxiliary + participle)
           I was instructed

        d. Sie hat mich zu instruieren
           she has me-ACC to instruct
           'She has to instruct me'

        e. Ich bin zu instruieren
           I am to instruct
           'I am to be instructed'

The combination of *haben* (have) with either a participle (13a) or an infinitive (13d) amounts to an active construction, while the combination (13b,e) with *sein* (be) yields a passive effect. (13c) is the regular passive construction with *werden* (become). In all these contexts (combination with a participle as well as with a *zu*-infinitive), we see the same effect, namely, that the combination with the unaccusative auxiliary (be) produces a passive effect. *Kriegen/bekommen* (get/receive) however, behave differently. The combination with the participle is passive (9b), the combination with the *zu*-infinitive is not (see 12a).

Why should this be so? If *kriegen* and *bekommen* are correctly described as passive quasi-auxiliaries, we expect them to work like passive auxiliaries also in the infinitive context, given the parallel with auxiliaries proper. But in the infinitive context, their function parallels *haben*, and not *sein* or *werden*. Of course, one could insist that *kriegen/bekommen* are passive quasi-auxiliaries only in the former context, and active quasi-auxiliaries in the latter. This would, however, merely rephrase what we see, without any further understanding.

The crucial property of *kriegen/bekommen* is their argument grid format. It is the format of a transitive verb with a theme role for the object and an experiencer role for the subject. It is this very property of the subject that qualifies them also for their secondary usage as quasi-auxiliaries in the contexts we see them. From a descriptive viewpoint, the auxiliaries inherit or filter the argument structure of the verb they select.

Have, as a transitive auxiliary, provides the full transitive argument format. *Be* in German has the format of an unaccusative verb. This does not provide room for a transitive subject argument. So, we find it as a tense auxiliary for unaccusative verbs and as an auxiliary that triggers a passive effect if combined with a transitive supine or infinitive form. *Kriegen/bekommen* as quasi-auxiliaries are transitive formats (like *haben*), but as quasi-auxiliaries they also restrict the thematic quality of the arguments they inherit (or filter). The subject argument must be a recipient. The passive effect with *kriegen/bekommen* is a result of this matching requirement (Haider 2001b; Woolford 2006).

In the *zu*-construction (12), *kriegen/bekommen* functions like *haben* (have), provided the subject argument matches the thematic restriction (recipient/ experiencer). In the construction with the participle (9b), the matching format of the participle excludes the subject argument of the participle (see Haider 2001b).

(14) a. bekommen, erhalten, kriegen: $<\underline{A}_{\text{Experiencer / Goal}}\ A_{\text{Theme}}>^{15}$
      get, receive, obtain[16]

  b. amputiert, geschenkt, gewidmet: $<[B_{\text{Agent}}],\ B[_{\text{Dat}}]_{\text{-Experiencer}},\ B_{\text{Theme}}>$
      amputated, presented, dedicated

  c. [amputiert bekommen] $<\underline{A}_{\text{Exp./Goal}}<[B_{\text{Agent}}], B[_{\text{Dat}}]_{\text{-Exp.}}, B_{\text{Theme}}>>$
      amputated get ('get amputated') $\Rightarrow$
      $<[B_{\text{Agent}}],\ \underline{A}_{\text{Exp. / Goal}} = B[_{\text{Dat}}]_{\text{-Exp.}},\ B_{\text{Theme}}>$

The quasi-auxiliaries (=semi-lexical verbs) in (14a) impose a format restriction for the thematic content they inherit from the selected participle. The restriction is this: the selected participle must provide a theta grid containing an experiencer/ goal argument and a theme argument. The participle of a ditransitive verb like those in (14b) provides the required content. The external argument (i.e. the agent in 14b) is blocked by participle formation.

(14c) illustrates the pooling of the argument structure in the verbal complex (see chapter 7.5.4): the theta grid of the selected participle replaces the respective theta slot of the selecting quasi-auxiliary (14c). When the imported theta grid is

---

[15] 'A' is a variable for 'argument'. An A in angled brackets is an implicit argument. An implicit argument is an argument of the argument grid that cannot be projected into the VP headed by the verb. The underlined $\underline{A}$ is the argument designated for external case licensing, that is, the candidate for nominative in the finite clause.

[16] The translation in the gloss applies to each of these verbs.

integrated, the two theta roles with identical thematic format are identified. This is the source of the apparent dative-to-nominative switch for the recipient passive. Its grammatical source is this: the semi-lexical verbs in (14a) provide a structural case for an experiencer/goal theta slot. This slot is identified with the indirect object of the selected participle (14c).

As for the combination of a semi-lexical verb of the type (14a) with a *zu*-infinitive (12), analogous considerations apply, with a different outcome, though. The difference stems from the function of *zu* (to). An infinitival marker *zu* (to) identifies and blocks the would-be-nominative argument (13e; 15a,b) .

(15)   a. Das ist zu beachten
            that is to consider
            'that is to be considered'

        b. Das bleibt zu klären
            that remains to solve
            'that remains to be solved'

Like *haben* (have) in (13d), the semi-lexical auxiliaries *bekommen/kriegen* provide a transitive format, and therefore the blocked argument of the selected infinitive gets re-instantiated in the pooled argument grid. As a consequence, the construction is active (16).

(16)   a. dass sie das zu essen kriegen
            that they this to eat get
            'that they get this to eat'

        b. dass sie das zu essen haben
            that they this to eat have
            'that they have to eat this' or 'that they have this for eating'

As mentioned at the beginning, the construction '*kriegen/bekommen* + participle' has received some attention because of the fact that it apparently makes a *dative* argument change into a nominative subject. Fanselow (1985, ch.10) proposed an account in terms of different case absorption properties of *werden* (accusative absorption) versus *kriegen* (dative absorption). This claim could be updated in terms of checking differences.

What the data discussed above suggest is that the 'recipient passive' does not compel us to reclassify dative as a structural case. Dative is an invariant case. The regularities for dative are regularities at the level of the lexical argument structure, or as Woolford (2006) suggests, at the level of case licensing of non-structural case, with different licensing properties for inherent dative and for lexical dative.

6.2.3   Case licensing and word order

In German, unlike English, case licensing does not presuppose unique structural positions for the licensees. This is particularly conspicuous for the licensing of nominative in unaccusative contexts like passive, that is, in contexts that require object to subject movement in English:

(1)   a. dass man ja Kindern Märchen erzählen muss
           that one-NOM PRT children-DAT fairy-tales-ACC tell must
           'that one must tell children fairy-tales'

       b. dass ja Kindern Märchen erzählt werden müssen
           that PRT children-DAT fairy-tales-NOM told be must

       c. [$_{VP}$ Märchen erzählt werden] mussten Kindern heute nicht
           [fairy-tales-NOM told be] must children-DAT today not

       d. [$_{VP}$ Märchen erzählen] muss man Kindern ja heute nicht
           [fairy-tales-ACC tell] must one children-DAT PRT today not

In German, passive has no effect on word order, as the comparison of (1a) and (1b) reveals. The nominative in (1b) gets licensed where the accusative gets licensed in (1a), namely in a VP-internal position. How can we assure ourselves that the nominative DP in (1b) is indeed in the same position as that accusative DP in (1a)? We have to consider the possibility that the nominative in (1b) could have been fronted, as in English, with the dative scrambled in front of the nominative. A first piece of evidence is VP-topicalization (1c). It confirms that the direct object plus the main verb can be fronted, irrespective of its grammatical function. (1d) is a VP-topicalization variant of (1a), corresponding to (1c).

Immediately supporting evidence comes from Dutch. In Dutch, unlike German, the relative order of arguments must not be changed by scrambling. In other words, an object cannot be scrambled across a preceding argument. Nevertheless, Dutch allows a nominative in-situ in the passive (2a,b), which is completely parallel to German. The following example (2a) is quoted from the Dutch standard grammar *ANS* (§ 22.5.6.2.).

(2)   a. Daarom werd de burgermeester het/een schilderij aangeboden
                                                                      Dutch
           therefore was-3.SG the mayor the/a painting-NOM-SG offered
           'Therefore the/a painting was offered to the mayor'

       b. Daarom werden de burgermeester schilderijen aangeboden
           therefore were-3.PL the mayor paintings-NOM-PL aangeboden
           'Therefore paintings were offered to the mayor'

    c. Daarom heeft men de burgermeester het/een schilderij aangeboden
      therefore has one-NOM the mayor the/a painting-ACC offered

Dutch, like English, distinguishes nominative and accusative only with pronouns, and the nominative agrees with the finite verb. If *a painting* in (2a) is replaced by a plural nominal, the verb agrees with the plural (2b). This indicates that the accusative in the active sentence (2c) switches into nominative in the passive variant (2a) in-situ, without movement to a structural subject position.

Note that this property of German and Dutch is not a peculiarity of West Germanic OV languages. Icelandic, too, allows VP-internal nominatives although it is a VO language. Example (3a) features a so-called quirky subject verb, with the dative in the structural subject position and a VP-internal nominative. In the corresponding German sentence, the dative precedes the nominative in the unmarked, that is, unscrambled word order.

(3)   a. að *henni/stelpunum* líkuðu hestarnir   *Icelandic*
        that her-DAT/girls-the-DAT liked-3.PL. horses-the-NOM
        'that she/the girls liked the horses'   (Sigurðsson 2004)

      b. dass *ihr/den Mädchen* die Pferde gefielen
        that her-DAT/the girls-DAT horses-NOM pleased
        'that the horses pleased her/the girls'

What the two languages have in common is this: the relative order of the arguments in the sentence directly reflects the ranking of the arguments in the lexical argument structure. Arguments are merged in the order of their ranking in the argument structure. The highest ranked argument will end up in the topmost argument position of the V-projection. In Icelandic, the top-most argument raises to the functional subject position. If the highest ranking argument is not the nominative, the result is a quirky subject construction. German does not have quirky subjects. This is not accidental. Quirky subjects are a VO phenomenon. For principled reasons, quirky subjects cannot come into being in an OV language since there is no functional subject position that requires to be lexicalized. A quirky subject is a non-nominative phrase in the functional subject position.

Dative–nominative orders in passive or with unaccusative verbs are but one facet of a more general property of case licensing. Nominative–dative and dative–nominative are possible basic orders, and so are dative–accusative and accusative–dative. What this shows once more is that there is no one-to-one correlation between a case form and a specific position in the sentence in German. In English and Dutch, the relative order between an indirect object and a direct object is constant. The indirect object precedes. In German, a dative object precedes an accusative for some verbs, but for other verbs – a minority class – the dative follows the accusative.

Verbs with accusative–dative order are verbs with a lexical dative, in Woolford's (2006) terminology. These relations require a morphologically coded dative. Hence, in English and Dutch, the corresponding verbs select a PP and this construction does not alternate with a 'dative' construction, that is, a double object construction in these languages. Note that the order in (4c) is a base order and not a result of scrambling.

(4)   a.   He exposed the sample to low temperatures

        b.   * He exposed low temperatures the sample

        c.   Er setzte die Probe tiefen Temperaturen aus
              he put the sample-ACC low temperatures-DAT out
              'He exposed the sample to low temperatures'

Let us recapitulate: in German, the case of a DP does not determine its position in the clause structure. In other words, case licensing in German is not a function of specific syntactic positions in the clause (see also Vogel and Steinbach 1998).

6.3   Case of non-arguments: adverbials and nominal predicates

6.3.1   Adverbial case

To a limited extent, German employs DPs also in adverbial functions. The case of an adverbial DP correlates with the type of its adverbial function. Cases recruited for adverbial functions are accusative, dative and genitive, as the following brief survey will exemplify. As in English, a DP denoting a time reference may be used as an adverbial. Its case is accusative in German:

(1)   Sie hat den ganzen Tag / die halbe Woche / letzten Monat gearbeitet
        she has the whole day-ACC / the half week-ACC / last month-ACC worked

As accusatives of non-arguments, these accusatives are not subject to the accusative–nominative dependency and consequently they are not affected by passive:

(2)   Den ganzen Tag/*der ganze Tag wurde gearbeitet
        the whole day-ACC / the whole day-NOM was worked
        'They worked the whole day'

In literary style, one still finds genitives in the function of temporal adverbials. While accusatives are used to specify time intervals for an ongoing activity, the genitives specify indefinite intervals for a reference point of an eventuality:

(3)   Er stand eines Sonntags / eines Tages / eines kalten Wintermorgens vor ihrer Tür
       he stood a Sunday-GEN / a day-GEN / a cold winter morning-GEN at her door
       'Once upon a Sunday / a day / a cold winter morning he stood at her door'

Another accusative adverbial function is the accusative for measures (weight, length), as in (4). In fact, the accusative for time *duration* in (1) could be seen as another instance of this:

(4)   a. Er wiegt eine Tonne
          he weighs a ton-ACC

       b. Er ist einen Meter lang
          he is one meter-ACC long

As for adverbial datives, it is in some cases difficult to draw a clear border line between argumental and adverbial status. So-called benefactive (i.e. 'for some-one's benefit/detriment') datives (5a) are usually filed as adverbial, but as Wegener (1990) argues, this dative function must be acknowledged as argumental since the recipient passive is applicable (5b,d):

(5)   a. Ich pflücke dir ein Edelweiß
          I pick you-DAT an Edelweiss

       b. Du kriegst ein Edelweiß gepflückt
          you-NOM get an Edelweiss picked

       c. Er wäscht dir das Auto
          He washes you-DAT the car

       d. Du kriegst das Auto gewaschen
          you-NOM get the car washed
          'You receive the car clean'

An uncontroversial instance of a non-argumental dative is the dative illustrated in (6). It is used only with a first person pronoun and conveys a vague empathic reinforcement of commands or wishes.

(6)   a. Seid mir gegrüßt!
          be me-DAT greeted

       b. Bleibt mir gesund!
          stay me-DAT healthy

The case regularity of a class of adverbial PPs – locational with dative, directional with accusative – has been introduced in section 6.1, example (9). The case difference is dependent on the semantics of the prepositional head. In other words, the prepositions involved are ambiguous. The different readings correspond to different case licensing properties of the given preposition. A higher verb is not involved.[17] This can be verified with NP-internal PPs. Nouns do not license any other case than genitive. So the dative or accusative selection (7) cannot be determined by the N-head. It is a function of the two related but semantically different prepositions *in*-DIR and *in*-LOC, with different case licensing requirements. English, in the gloss, shows that the prepositions for location and direction are different.

(7)   a. der Weg in den Wald
           the way in(to) the wood-ACC
           'the way that leads into the wood'

        b. der Weg in dem Wald
           the way in the wood-DAT
           'the way that is in the wood'

Let us finally raise a theoretical issue: what is the source of adverbial case? A simple answer is this: adverbial case is the morphological spell-out of a case feature that determines the adverbial function. Where does the case feature come from? It is an inherent property of nominal heads. In case languages, nominal heads have a case feature, and this feature needs to be licensed (checked). If it remains syntactically unchecked, it must be interpreted at the syntax–semantics interface, that is, it must have a direct connection to semantic interpretation. This is what we see with adverbial cases. The case is directly connected with a specific interpretation.

For English, Larson (1988) suggested an analysis for DP adverbials in terms of PPs with a silent preposition as case licenser (8a). This would allow subsuming adverbial case under the standard case licensing mechanism. German, however, does not justify this approach. Many overt prepositions for time adverbials license dative (8b), but the bare DP time adverbial is always marked accusative (8c).

---

[17] The fact that verbs that denote directional processes combine with a PP that licenses accusative (i), whereas locational verbs combine with dative PPs (ii), merely reflects the semantic selection property of a given verb and not its direct influence on PP-internal case relations:

(i)   Er tanzt in diesem Zimmer
        he dances in this room-DAT

(ii)   Er tanzt in dieses Zimmer
        he dances into this room-ACC

(8)   a. the performance (on) this Sunday evening

     b. die Aufführung an diesem Sonntag Abend / zu Weihnachten
       the performance on this Sunday evening-DAT / at Christmas-DAT

     c. die Aufführung diesen Sonntag Abend
       the performance this Sunday evening-ACC

This case difference makes the 'silent-PP' approach less attractive since the silent P° would have to be the silent variant of an overt P°. In this case, we would expect a dative in (8c), and not an accusative. An approach in terms of inherent adverbial case avoids this problem.

6.3.2   The case of nominal predicates

In finite clauses, a nominal predicate of a copula construction agrees with the subject in case, that is, both receive nominative (1a). This is not the complete picture, though, since the predicate is nominative in an infinitival clause as well (1b), without a nominative subject. Let us therefore complete the set of representative examples for copula constructions with nominal predicates (first presented in Haider 1984a):

(1)   a.   Er ist/wurde/blieb ein ehrlicher Politiker
           he-NOM is/became/remained an honest politician-NOM

     b.   Es ist unmöglich, [PRO ein ehrlicher Politiker zu werden/sein/ bleiben]
           it is impossible an honest politician-NOM to become/be/remain
           'It is impossible to become/be/remain an honest politician'

     c.   Die Umstände ließen ihn ein ehrlicher Politiker werden[18]
           the circumstances made him-ACC an honest politician-NOM become
           'The circumstances made him become an honest politician'

     d.   (?)Die Umstände ließen ihn einen ehrlichen Politiker werden[19]
           the circumstances made him-ACC an honest politician-ACC become

---

[18] Here is a 'professional' example, quoted from Stefan Zweig's novella *Marie Antoinette*:

    (i)   Lass mich dein guter Herold sein
       let me-ACC your good herald-NOM be
       'Let me be your good herald'

[19] A frequently heard instance of this construction is an idiom:

    (i)   Er lässt Gott einen lieben Mann sein
       he lets god-ACC a nice man-ACC be
       'He lets god be a nice man' = He takes life easy

In (1a), the predicate seems to match the case of the subject DP, namely nominative. The matching relation would fail in (1b), since the silent subject in the infinitival clause is not nominative, otherwise it ought to be replaceable by a lexical DP. (1c) is a blatant instance of mismatch. The subject is an ECM subject and the predicate DP is nominative. In (1d), however, the predicate DP matches the accusative of the DP it is predicated over. (1c) and (1d) are minimal pairs, and they are in free variation in German. How does the predicate in the examples in (1) receive (different) case?

Maling and Sprouse (1995) present a strong claim for the case of predicative nominals. They maintain that 'predicate NPs always receive case structurally' (1995: 167). In Icelandic, Swedish and German 'case features from a higher case-assigner are able to penetrate into the VP containing the predicate NP' (1995: 167) in order to assign nominative. What they fail to cover in their paper are the cases (1c,d), that are attested not only for German but also for Swedish. They base their claim on the cross-linguistic comparison of the patterns of (1a,b). The constructions (1c,d) are merely acknowledged in an appendix and declared as 'a topic for future research' (1995: 186).

The coexistence of the constructions (1c,d) is positive evidence for the existence of two alternative mechanisms for licensing the case of a predicative nominal. Furthermore, (1c) is covered neither by case matching nor by structural case assignment. At both occasions, the predicate would end up with accusative, as (1d) illustrates, but not with nominative. Where does the nominative come from in (1a,b,c)? A descriptive generalization that covers all three instances is this:

(2)   If a DP is predicated over a *subject*,
        a. it is licensed for nominative, or
        b. it may be case matched (see examples in (3)).

Let us review the constructions in (1) one after the other. In a finite clause, the subject is nominative and so is the predicate. This is covered by (2a) as well as by (2b). In both conditions, the result is nominative. In an infinitival clause the target of predication, the silent subject, is caseless. Hence the option (2b) cannot be applied. The predicate is nominative, according to (2a). In an ECM construction, both options are applicable. (2a) covers the nominative option, as in (1c). (1d) is the result of whatever principle is responsible for (2b).

Independent evidence for (2) and against a default case scenario comes from *as*-predication, as in (3). If the target of the predicate is an ECM accusative, nominative (3a) is an alternative option to case matching (3b). If the accusative is an object accusative, however, case matching is the only option (3c), and the nominative (3d) is ruled out. Analogously, a non-structural case is always matched (3e).

(3)   a.   Man sah/ließ ihn als erster aus dem Fenster springen
             one saw/let him-ACC as first-NOM out the window jump
             'They let him as the first one jump out of the window'

       b.   Man sah/ließ ihn als ersten aus dem Fenster springen
             one saw/let him-ACC as first-ACC out the window jump

       c.   Man pries ihn als den zweitbesten Syntaktiker
             one praised him-ACC as the second-best syntactician-ACC

       d. * Man pries ihn als der zweitbeste Syntaktiker
             one praised him-ACC as the second-best syntactician-NOM

       e.   Man gratulierte ihm als dem-dem /*der Syntaktiker des Jahres
             one congratulated him-DAT as [the syntactician of the year]-DAT /
             *NOM

If nominative was a default case for predicates, it should be available no matter what case and what grammatical function the target of predication bears. What we find instead is this: only if the target is a *subject* is nominative licensed, otherwise the predicate strictly matches the case of the target.

(2) is puzzling since it is not evident how to make it follow in a simple (or intricate) way from the principles of a case assignment system that correlates nominative licensing with specific conditions, like feature matching/checking by agreement. Furthermore, it is not limited to the domain of sentences. The very same pattern is found within attributive APs as shown in (4):

(4)   a.   Er erkannte den [als kreativer Syntaktiker sehr bekannten] Professor
             nicht
             he recognized the [as creative syntactician-NOM very famous] profes-
             sor-ACC not
             'He did not recognize the professor widely known as a creative
             syntactician'

       b.   Er erkannte den [ein kreativer Syntaktiker bleiben wollenden]
             Professor nicht
             he recognized the [a creative syntactician-NOM remain wanting] pro-
             fessor-ACC not
             'He did not recognize the professor wanting to remain a creative
             syntactician'

The nominative on the predicate is an instance of (2a). The target of predication is the silent AP-internal PRO subject. Hence nominative is the only option in (4).

Whatever source there is for the nominative on the predicate in the AP should not be different from the source of the predicate nominative in the clausal constructions. In both contexts – in an infinitival clause and in an attributive AP – the target of predication is a silent subject. If the source of the nominative (see Maling and Sprouse 1995: 169) is implemented in a style that relies too much on the clausal syntactic inventory (verbal tense or verbal agreement projections), the AP phenomena are likely to be neglected.

Let us recapitulate: the view that the morphological case of predicates in many languages is the result of a case-matching/agreement mechanism (see Maling and Sprouse 1995: 172, and literature cited there) is not fully adequate. It covers only the non-subject-related predicates. Predicates that relate to the subject present a more intricate and still not fully understood picture, namely a free alternation between matching case on the one hand and nominative licensing on the other hand.

6.4   Case in German is not 'positional'

In present day Generative Grammar, case checking is implemented as a positional function. The case feature of a case-bearing element is deemed to be checked in a positionally defined way, namely in the spec position of the respective case-checking head. So, the DP whose case feature needs to be checked has to move into the spec position of the case-checking functional head.[20] The empirical implications of this as a hypothesis with universal validity are clear and in conflict with the facts of German.

First, it is safe to assume that the cascade of case heads would be ordered and therefore it ought to strictly determine the sequence of cased, unscrambled DPs. This is at odds with the fact that in German the order of the arguments is determined by the lexical argument structure (whose structure is in part a function of the lexical-conceptual structure). So there are different base orders for different verb classes. There are verbs with NOM–DAT base order contrasting with verbs with DAT–NOM base order, and there are verbs with DAT–ACC base order contrasting with verbs with ACC–DAT base order. This is not a peculiarity of German, however. Virtually the same classes of verbs with the respective translational counterparts as members are found in Icelandic (see Kainhofer 2002 for details). In English and the continental Germanic languages, the loss of lexical case eliminated these classes in the diachronic development.

Second, if a cased DP was indeed in the spec of a functional head, anything preceding this DP would have to be in a higher functional spec or in a position

---

[20] We presuppose overt movement. The idea that there could be something like covert movement is just a way to make the theory irrefutable and therefore empirically void.

adjoined to a functional phrase. In any case, these phrases would inevitably be predicted to be opaque for extraction. As discussed in the chapter on scrambling (section 4.4.1), this is definitely not the case in German.

Third, the very same functional architecture would be needed not only in clausal but in any phrasal environment with case licensing potentials. Case-marked arguments occur not only in the functional extensions of VPs, but also within the DP domain (structural genitive) and within attributive APs (dative, oblique genitive). However, the domains differ with respect to the admissible cases. This is a function of the head of the domain. It would not be captured if each lexical domain could be extended with the same functional architecture for case checking.

Whenever the functional checking scenario has been adopted for German in the literature, it has been adopted because of its compatibility with the current version of Generative Grammar and not because of its superior coverage. Only Müller (1995) argued, based on detailed empirical evidence, for a positional account of the dative. His claim is that dative objects in German are raised from the VP base position to a surface A'-position at the left edge of the VP (Müller 1995: 183).

(1) $[DP_{DAT-i} [DP_{ACC} [e_i V°]]]$ (see Müller 1995: 197, ex. 20b)

The binding data that this claim is based on differentiate between the dative and the accusative object, but the only uncontroversial generalization is this: a reciprocal pronoun argument does not accept a *dative co-argument* as its antecedent (2a).[21]

(2)   a. * Ich habe den Gästen$_j^i$ einander^i e$_j$ vorgestellt
             I have the guests-DAT each-other-ACC introduced

         b. Ich habe die Gäste^i einander^i vorgestellt
             I have the guests-ACC each-other-DAT introduced
             'I have introduced the guests (to) each other'

Müller (1995: 212–14) argues that the ungrammaticality of (2a) is evidence for the raising account of the dative. If the dative in (2a) is analysed as raised to an A'-position across the reciprocal, it is not a licit antecedent, since its original position is lower than the reciprocal. In (2b), on the other hand, the accusative and the dative are in their base positions.

This account does not seem to be adequate, however, for the following reasons. First, it is in conflict with theoretical assumptions. Case licensing positions are A-positions and not A'-positions. This, however, would predict exactly the opposite, namely the grammaticality of (2a), since an A-moved dative would not be

---

[21] Note that this restriction does not hold for reciprocals inside a PP:

(i)   Ich habe den Gästen^i [von einander^i] erzählt
        I have the guests-DAT [about each-other] told

reconstructed. The English raising construction shows that an A-moved DP is a licit antecedent of an anaphor (3b). An A'-moved DP would not be a suitable binder, since A'-moved items are reconstructed for binding.

(3)   a. * It seemed to each[i] other [that the men[i] had not won the competition]

    b.   The men[j] seemed to each[i] other [e[j] to have not won the competition]

Second, there are empirical reasons, like scope data or data from wh-in-situ constructions. If (4a) has the derived structure indicated with the trace, it is predicted to be ambiguous with respect to the scope of the first quantifier (see chapter 4.3, property (v)). It can have wide scope, as the c-commanding quantifier or it can receive narrow scope since the second quantifier c-commands the trace of the first quantifier.

(4)   a. dass er mindestens einem Gast jedes Bild gezeigt hat
                                        (unambiguous: ∃∀)
        that he at-least one guest-DAT every picture-ACC showed

    b. dass er jedes Bild mindestens einem Gast gezeigt hat   (ambiguous)
        that he every picture-ACC at-least one guest-DAT showed

The contrast in (4a,b) follows from the standard base generation assumption of NOM–DAT–ACC for the class of verbs *zeigen* (show) belongs to, namely experiencer-theme verbs. The dative raising analysis would incorrectly predict exactly the inverse scope property.

    As for wh-in-situ, chapter 3 presents arguments that a wh-element in-situ in a functional spec position is ungrammatical. The target position of A'-raising a dative would have to be a functional spec position. Hence an in-situ wh-dative in German should be as deviant as an in-situ wh-subject in English. However, a dative wh is perfect in German (5).

(5)   a. Wer hat *wem* die Bilder gezeigt?
        who has whom-DAT the picture shown

    b. Was hat sie *wem* gezeigt?
        what has she whom-DAT shown

Why is (2a) deviant after all? An adequate descriptive generalization seems to be this: a structurally cased argument refuses a non-structurally cased argument as its binder. This is supported by independent observations[22] on

---

[22] Topic drop in German is another instance that separates nominative and accusative on the one hand and dative on the other:

Wo ist Max? (i) ø Habe ich soeben *zu dir geschickt*   (ii) * ø Habe ich *soeben den Weg gezeigt*

Where is Max?   ø-ACC have I just to you sent   ø-DAT have I just the way shown

case-based binding hierarchies (Fleischer 2006) and it is confirmed by data like the following:

(6)   a.   Sie hat den Leuten[i] von einander[i] erzählt
             she has the people-DAT of each-other-DAT told
             'She has told the people about each other'

        b. * Ich schien den Gästen[i] einander[i] zu kennen
             I seemed (to) the guests-DAT each-other-ACC to know
             'I seemed to the guests to know each other'

        c.   Die Gäste[i] schienen einander[i] zu kennen
             the guests-NOM seemed each-other-ACC to know
             'The guests seemed to know each other'

In (6a), the dative object binds a prepositional object, and the case of a prepositional argument is an oblique one and therefore binding is acceptable. (6b) is instructive because the dative is an argument of *scheinen* (seem) and higher in structure than the object of the infinitive, presumably also in Müller's system.[23] Nevertheless it is a bad binder, unlike the nominative subject in (6c).

What these considerations (typological findings, binding data from clustering constructions) indicate is this: the solution for the binding behaviour of datives is likely to be found in the difference between the two case types (structural vs invariant), rather than in a peculiar structural difference of datives. At least, this is the null hypothesis. This notwithstanding, there are persistent attempts to derive the contrast in the vein of Müller (1995), as for instance by Putnam (2005).

In sum, it is reasonable to continue assuming that a German dative object stays in its object base position just like any other object.

6.5   Summary

•   German has a four-way case system, with two structural and two invariant cases, with the following morphological realizations: structural case is spelled out as nominative, accusative, or zero (as the subject of infinitival clauses) in clausal domains, and as genitive within a nominal domain (i.e. on the complement of a noun). Dative and genitive are invariant cases in clausal domains. Accusative and dative arguments do not occur as the case of an argument selected by a noun, that is, they are not found inside NPs.

---

[23] When judging the validity of this datum you should bear in mind that the construction is an obligatorily clustering one and that the binder and the bindee are clause-mates (see chapter 7). Hence binding should be structurally perfect.

- Accusative–nominative dependency: structural accusative is the secondary option for a structural case. Its licensing is dependent on having
  exploited the *external* licensing option (nominative, zero). This dependency is customarily referred to as Burzio's generalization.[24]
- In German, any lexical head category (V°, N°, A°, P°) is a potential
  case licenser. Structural object case (accusative, adnominal genitive) is
  licensed only by members of a subset of lexical categories, namely V°
  and N°, respectively.
- Case licensing in German is not constrained to uniquely defined structural positions. Within the appropriate head domain, the word order is not
  determined by the case licensing requirements, but by the ranked lexical
  argument structure that determines the order of projection/merger.
- Nominal predicates with their accusative–nominative variation for subject-related predicates even in an infinitival clause or in ECM complements are a challenge for case theories. This property is not covered by
  contemporary models of case since the nominative is in these constructions neither positionally determined nor in an agreement relation.
- In sum, there is no immediate evidence and no compelling argument for
  the assumption that case is positionally tied to functional spec positions
  whose functional heads license the respective cases in German.

---

[24] But this correlation (Haider 1984a) is not Burzio's original generalization, since in his
version (Burzio 1986: 178), the availability of accusative is tied to the presence of a thematic subject (and not the realization of nominative).

7

Non-finite verbs and their constructions

German has three categories of non-finite verb forms, that combine with other verbs,[1] namely the *bare infinitive*, the *infinitive* with a *prefixed particle zu* (a cognate of English 'to'), and the *past participle*. Morphologically, the infinitive form is characterized by the suffix *-en*. The past participle is prefixed with *ge-*, except for verbs that are not stressed on the initial syllable (1c'), and suffixed with *-t* in the regular paradigm.[2]

(1)   a. such*en* – seek   a'. versteck*en* – hide   bare infinitive

       b. *zu* such*en* – to seek   b'. *zu* versteck*en* – to hide   zu + infinitive

       c. *ge*such*t* – sought   c'. versteck*t* – hidden   past participle

In English, there is good evidence for categorizing the particle 'to' as an independent functional head element rather than an inflectional particle prefixed to the verb. For instance, it is not required to be adjacent to the verb (2a), or it may precede conjoined verbs (2b).

(2)   a. He never had to *really* say much

       b. He seemed to [laugh and cry] at the same time

       c. Er schien gleichzeitig [zu lachen und *(zu) weinen]
          he seemed simultaneously [to laugh and to cry]

In German, *zu* must not be separated from the verb. Conjoined verbs (2c) require the *zu*-prefix on each conjunct.[3] This shows that conjoining two verbs must not exclude the infinitival prefix because it is a morphological part of each verb. *Zu*

---

[1] The present participle (verbal stem + *-end*, as e.g. *lesend–* 'reading') is used only as adverbial or as adnominal attribute.

[2] As in English, there is a huge class of morphologically irregular verbs. The verbs of the most extensive class are prefixed with *ge-*, but suffixed differently, namely with the ending *-en* (e.g. geblieb*en* – stayed, gesunk*en* – sunk, getrag*en* – carried, …). In addition there is a change in the stem vowel (e.g. s*i*nken – ges*u*nken). A smaller class is suffixed like the regular class, namely with *-t*, e.g. bringen (bring) – *ge*brach*t* (brought).

[3] Discussed first by Bech (1955).

has the properties of an affix, just like the participle prefix *ge-*. It is just a spelling convention that *zu* and the verb are spelled discontinuously. (3) illustrates the parallel distribution: the participial prefix (3b) attaches to the verb in just the same manner as the infinitival prefix (3c).

(3)   a. anfangen – begin (lit. on-catch)

       b. an*ge*fangen – begun

       c. an*zu*fangen – to begin

A more compelling piece of evidence has already been discussed in connection with the controversy on clause-final functional heads in chapter 2.1. If *zu* was a functional head, like the English *to*, it would be indicative of a *clause-final* functional head position. It has been pointed out that there are verbs that cannot leave their VP-internal head position, but they nevertheless may be used in the infinitive form with *zu*. This is a problem if *zu* is a functional head outside of the VP and if the infinitival verb would have to move to this position in order to merge with *zu* and end up in the required form of (1b).[4]

Moreover, movement out of the VP to a functional head position would be compatible with non-verbal material intervening. We would expect to find intervening material between the VP and the functional head position, as a mirror image situation of (2a), with the adverbial in between the VP and the preceding functional head. In German, extraposition targets the right VP boundary. So, extraposed material is predicted to precede a verb that is merged at a clause-final functional head position following the VP, but this is not the case.

A prepositional phrase may be optionally extraposed, as in (4a). (4b), a clause with a topicalized VP, shows that the right edge of a VP is an extraposition site. Therefore, if the infinitival verb must be raised to a clause-final functional head position in order to merge with *zu* in this position, an extraposed PP is predicted to be able to intervene. But this is not the case (4c). The extraposed PP follows the infinitival verb (4d).

(4)   a. dass er nicht gelernt haben muss *dafür*
           that he not learnt have must it-for
           'that he needed not learn for it'

       b. [$_{VP}$ gelernt haben *dafür*] muss er nicht
           learnt have it-for must he not

---

[4] Attempts to analyse *zu* as a functional head can be found in the literature: Stechow and Sternefeld (1988) try to analyse *zu* as a clause-final I° category; Wilder (1989) considers *zu* as clause-final C°.

   c. * ohne gelernt haben *dafür zu müssen*
       without learnt have it-for to must
       'without having to have learnt for it'

   d. ohne gelernt haben *zu müssen dafür*

The pattern with the infinitival verb in (4d) and the finite verb in (4a) is identical with respect to extraposition. The extraposed PP cannot intervene between the non-finite verbs and the finite verb in (4a). Neither finite nor infinitival verbs move to the right in German. So, *zu* cannot be analysed as the functional head in a clause-final functional head position that amalgamates with a raised verb.

7.1   Three types of infinitival construction in German

The three types are (i) the verbal cluster construction, (ii) the infinitival clause construction and (iii) the 'third construction'. The verbal cluster construction is obligatory whenever the dependent verb is a bare infinitive or a participle and the verbs appear in their respective selection environment, that is, in the clause-final position. For the *zu*-infinitive, clustering is obligatory for a small set of selecting verbs (e.g. epistemic verbs and a modal verb, namely *brauchen* – 'need'), and optional for a subset of control verbs. *Zu*-infinitives occur in all three constructions. Bare infinitives and participles are obligatorily clustering.

7.1.1   The cluster construction

The cluster construction is characterized by two qualities. The selecting verb and the infinitival verb form a syntactic unit (a verbal head–head cluster), and the construction is monosentential (*clause union*), that is, the infinitival verb does not project a clause, and arguably not even a verbal projection (if the cluster is considered base generated rather than derived).

Bech (1955) was the first syntactician who systematically analysed German infinitival constructions and the properties of the concomitant phenomenon of verbal clustering. He noted the *compactness* property characteristic of clustering: non-verbal elements must not intervene between the sequences of clause-final verbs. He coined the term 'verbal field' for the compact sequence of clustering verbs, and the term 'coherent infinitive' for the construction. Let us compare English and German in this respect. In English, and in fact in VO languages in general, V_1 and V_2 crucially are not required to be adjacent. Adverbials may intervene.[5]

---

[5] Norwegian is an exception. Intervening adverbs are not acceptable. The verb order, however, remains strict, unlike in OV Germanic cluster constructions (Nilsen 2003).

(1)   a. ... [$_{VP1}$ V$_1$ [$_{VP2}$ V$_2$ ....]]

  b. will [$_{VP1}$ have [*completely* [$_{VP2}$ finished ....]]]]

In German, the sequence of verbs in the verbal cluster is compact, that is, the verbs are strictly adjacent. This would not be expected at all if each verb is head of an independent VP (2a). The compactness property is indicative of a tighter syntactic organization. In combination with various other pieces of evidence to be reviewed below, this leads to the hypothesis[6] that the clause-final sequence of verbs in German is a separate constituent consisting of head-to-head adjoined verbs (2b), rather than the tail of a pile of stacked VPs, as in (2a). Note that the same considerations apply to Dutch.

(2)   a. ... [[[... beendet]$_{VP}$ worden]$_{VP}$ sein]$_{VP}$ (inappropriate structure!)
      finished been be
      'have been finished'

  b. ... [... [[beendet$_V$° worden$_V$°]$_V$° sein]$_V$°]$_{VP}$

If we take compactness as a preliminary diagnostic criterion for clustering, we identify the following combinations of verbal categories as *obligatorily* clustering:

  Obligatorily clustering verbs

(3)

	Dependent verb	*Selecting verb*	*Examples of selecting verbs*
a.	participle	auxiliary	*haben* – have, *sein* – be (PERFECT)
b.	participle	auxiliary	*werden* – be (PASSIVE)
c.	infinitive	auxiliary	*werden* – will (FUTURE TENSE)
d.	infinitive	modals	*können* – 'be-able-to', ...
e.	infinitive	causative	*lassen* – let, make
f.	infinitive	perception verbs	*sehen* – see, *hören* – hear, *fühlen* – feel
g.	infinitive	copula	*sein* – be, *bleiben* – remain
h.	zu-infinitive	modal	*brauchen* – need[7]
i.	zu-infinitive	auxiliary	*haben* – have, sein – be, *bleiben* – remain
j.	zu-infinitive	epistemic verbs	*scheinen* – seem, ...
k.	zu-infinitive	aspectual verbs	*beginnen* – begin, *anfangen* – start, *aufhören* – stop, ...

(3a) is the class of auxiliaries for perfect tense formation. They combine with a participle. Unaccusative verbs require 'be' as auxiliary. Passive is the result of combining a participle with the auxiliary *werden* (3b).

---

[6] First suggested by Evers (1975).

[7] *Brauchen* is a negative polarity item.

Future tense is coded by combining the auxiliary *werden* with a bare infinitive form (3c). Modals select a bare infinitive (3d), except for *brauchen* (need), which selects a *zu*-infinitive (3h).

The combination of the infinitive with the copula *be* (3g) yields the 'absentee' construction. This means that V + *be* is interpreted 'is absent because of doing V'.[8] The copula *bleiben* (remain) conveys the durative interpretation, but its use is restricted mainly to verbs denoting positions, like *stehen* (stand) or *liegen* (lie), as in *liegen bleiben* (remain lying).

Note that all categories of cluster-triggering verbs, with two 'exceptions', are verbs without thematically specified arguments or at least without a thematically specified subject (3j,k), as illustrated in (7). The two exceptions are (3e,f). Perception verbs are thematically specified and causatives have a thematically specified subject. As a consequence, they trigger an ECM[9] construction[10] (4):

(4)   dass sie *mich* ihn suchen lässt/sah
       that she-NOM me-ACC him-ACC seek lets/saw
       'that she makes/(lets)/saw me seek him'

The modal usage of auxiliaries in combination with a *zu*-infinitive (5c,d) produces an active–passive effect that is parallel to the active–passive effect in the combination of participle and auxiliary (5a,b). The active/passive effect is a function of the combination with an unaccusative auxiliary (*werden* – be/become, *sein* – be) in the 'passive' construction as opposed to a transitive auxiliary (*haben* – have) in the 'active' construction.

(5)   a. dass er den Fehler gefunden *hat*
          that he the mistake-ACC found has

       b. dass der Fehler gefunden *wurde/war*[11]
          that the mistake-NOM found was/was

---

[8] *Ich bin essen* (I am eat-INF) means 'I (am absent because I) am eating', *Sie ist einkaufen* (she is shop-INF) means 'She (is absent because she) is shopping', *Er war Milch holen* (he was milk fetch-INF) means 'He (was absent because he) was fetching milk'.

[9] ECM = exceptional case marking. The case of the infinitival subject is licensed by a transitive matrix verb or by a prepositional complementizer, as in the English *for-to* constructions.

[10] The German 'lassen' construction allows a morphologically uncoded passive variant:

(i)   Sie lässt mich die Tür öffnen
       she lets me the door open
(ii)   Sie lässt die Tür (von mir) öffnen
       she lets the door (by me) open ('She has the door opened by me')
For an analysis of this effect see Haider (2001a).

[11] The combination with the copula (*sein* – be) is the so-called adjectival passive in German.

    c. dass er den Fehler zu finden *hat*
       that he the mistake-ACC to find has
       'that he has to find the mistake'

    d. dass der Fehler zu finden *ist*[12]
       that the mistake-NOM to find is
       'that the mistake is to be found'

Haben/sein (have/be) in combination with a *zu*-infinitive (5c,d) get a modal interpretation (obligation, possibility) that is similar to the English counterparts: the combination with *haben* (have to) is interpreted as an obligation, the combination with *sein* (be to) is ambiguous. It can be interpreted as possibility or as obligation.

The counterparts of English subject raising verbs (seem, appear, etc.) are obligatorily clustering infinitival constructions in German. In addition to *scheinen* (seem) and *pflegen* (use to, tend to), there are semi-modal usages for at least two verbs that enter this construction, namely *versprechen* (promise) and *drohen* (threaten) in the reading that something is promising or threatening. In the other usage, these verbs are standard control verbs, that is, verbs with a sentential infinitival complement.

(6)   dass dem Mann die Zähne auszufallen drohten
         that the man-DAT the teeth out-to-fall threatened
         'that the man was in danger of losing his teeth'

Aspectual verbs are clustering as well. The aspectual usage of verbs like *anfangen* (begin) in (7a) differs from the usage as a control verb (7b). In the aspectual usage, the verb has a semi-auxiliary function without a specified thematic structure, similar to an English subject raising verb:

(7)   a. dass ihr schlecht zu werden anfing[13]/schien
          that her-DAT sick to become began/seemed
          'that she began/seemed to become sick'

      b. dass er sofort anfing/*schien, [PRO alle zu kritisieren]
          that he immediately began/seemed [all to criticize]
          'that he immediately started/*seemed to criticize all of them'

---

[12] Note that the English counterpart is not passive: *Am I to leave?* ≠ *Am I left?* Consequently, the 'be' contexts are not exclusively unaccusative in English, because of the aspectual construction 'be'+ V-ing.

[13] *Schlecht werden* (become sick) is in German a subjectless predicate, whose single argument is a dative. It is chosen here in order to make sure that this is a clustering construction and not a control construction, on the evidence that the matrix predicate remains subjectless.

This fairly simple set of circumstances gets complicated by the fact that this class of obligatorily clustering predicates is not the only class of clustering constructions. There is also a class of verbs that are *optionally* clustering. This is a subclass of control verbs that allow the clustering construction as an alternative to the clausal complementation construction.

Optionally clustering verbs are characterized as verbs that either select an infinitival clause as complement or enter the clustering construction. There is no construction-specific difference in meaning and the choice of the construction is free. In other words, the two construction options are truly optional variants. This has an implication for grammar theory: you cannot simultaneously adhere to the presently favoured maxim that there are no optional derivations on the one hand and *derive* one construction from the other, on the other hand.

As listed in table 7.1, there are not only verbal predicates that are optionally clustered but also adjectival ones. These adjectives are the counterparts of English *tough*-predicates. As will be shown below (11), the construction corresponding to the English *tough*-movement construction is a construction with verb clustering.

How can we reliably distinguish the clustering variant from the non-clustering one? We can take advantage of the fact that the clustering variant is compact. Hence, if we 'destroy' compactness, we ascertain that a given variant is the non-clustering variant. (8a) is structurally ambiguous, since it is compatible with clustering or with a sentential complement structure. Inserting an adverbial between the two verbs, as in (8b), eliminates a clustering analysis, since the two verbs are not adjacent, hence compactness would be violated.

Can we force the assignment of the clustering structure? Yes, topicalization of the verb cluster (8c) is compatible with a cluster analysis only. The topicalized verbs in (8b) are in a spec position. Hence they must be a constituent. However, they could not form a single constituent if the infinitival verb were the head verb of the infinitival complement clause, and the selecting verb was the main verb of the matrix clause. Hence we can be sure that (8b) is the sentential variant, (8c) the clustering variant, and that (8a) is structurally ambiguous since it is compatible with either analysis, as indicated in (9)

(8)   a. dass er niemanden zu stören beabsichtigt hat
          that he nobody to disturb intended has
          'that he has not intended to disturb anyone'

       b. dass er [$_{CP}$ niemanden zu stören] *wirklich* beabsichtigt hat
          that he [nobody to disturb] truly intended has
          'that he truly intended to disturb nobody'

Table 7.1 *Optionally clustering verbs*

	Dependent verb	Selecting predicate	Examples of selecting verbs
a.	*zu*-infinitive	control verb[14]	*erlauben* – permit, *hoffen* – hope, *vergessen* – forget, *versuchen* – try
b.	*zu*-infinitive	adjective	*einfach* – simple, *leicht* – easy, *schwer* – difficult, *unmöglich* – impossible

   c. [Zu stören beabsichtigt]$_{VC}$ hat er *wirklich* niemanden
     [to disturb intended] has he truly nobody
     'He truly did not intend to disturb anybody'

(9)   a. dass er [$_{CP}$ PRO niemanden zu stören] beabsichtigt hat
       that he [nobody to disturb] intended has

    b. dass er niemanden [[zu stören beabsichtigt]$_{VC}$ hat]$_{VC}$
      that he nobody [[to disturb intended] has]

As already noted by Bech (1955), (8a) is scope ambiguous with respect to the scope of the negative quantifier. It matches both the unambiguous reading of (8b), and the unambiguous reading of (8c). This is an immediate consequence of the structural ambiguity of (8a), illustrated in (9). In the sentential construction (8b, 9a), the scope domain of the negative quantifier is the embedded CP; in the clustering construction (8c, 9b), the scope domain of the negated quantifier is the matrix clause. The two different readings are paraphrased in (10).

(10)   a. He intended to *not* disturb anyone
    b. He did *not* intend to disturb anyone

The different scope domains are a reflex of the *clause union effect* of the clustering construction. The clustering construction has the properties of a simple sentence (monosentential), in contrast to the bi-sentential properties of the construction with the clausal infinitive construction. For a systematic review of the numerous phenomena that prove the clause union effect see section 7.5.

    As for *tough*-predicates, they either select a sentential infinitive (11a), or a clustering construction in German (11b,c). In the sentential infinitival

---

[14] The control verbs that optionally cluster are verbs that select the infinitival as a direct object (and not as a prepositional object or as a subject). In other words, the selected argument is the unmarked one.

construction (11a), the object of the infinitive is marked accusative. In the clustering construction (11b,c) it is nominative. This is the immediate consequence of the monosentential structure of the cluster construction.[15]

(11)   a.   dass [den Fehler zu finden] nicht schwierig war
              that the mistake-ACC to find not difficult was
              'that it was not difficult to find the mistake'

        b.   dass der Fehler nicht schwierig zu finden war
              that the mistake-NOM not difficult to find was
              'that the mistake was not difficult to find'

        c.   [Schwierig zu finden] war *der* Fehler nicht
              difficult to find was the mistake-NOM not

        d. * [Schwierig zu finden] war *den* Fehler nicht
              difficult to find was the mistake-ACC not

Topicalization (11c,d) clearly differentiates between the cluster construction (11c), and the clausal construction with the accusative object (11a). The clustering construction obeys compactness. (11d) is ungrammatical because the accusative is licit only in the sentential construction, and the verb cannot be removed out of the infinitival sentence. So (11d) is either ungrammatical because the verb has been removed out of the sentential complement, or because of the accusative (instead of the nominative) in the clustering construction.

    Note that the order of the infinitive and the *tough*-predicate differ in the clustering and the clausal construction, respectively. In the clustering construction (12a), the *infinitive* and the *copula* are adjacent, since they form a cluster. In the sentential construction (12b), the infinitival clause precedes the *tough*-predicate, and hence the infinitival verb precedes, too. This is the expected order for complements of adjectival predicates, since adjective phrases are head final, and therefore, the adjective and its preceding complement need not be adjacent. But, crucially, the verb and the adjective need not be adjacent. Topicalization (12c, 11d), eventually, confirms the existence of the cluster in (12a).

(12)   a.   dass der Fehler (nicht) leicht [[zu *finden*] *war*]
              that the mistake-NOM (not) easy [[to find] was]
              'that the mistake was (not) easy to find'

        b.   dass [*den* Fehler zu *finden*] (nicht) leicht *war*
              that [the mistake-ACC to find] (not) easy was

---

[15] Accusative cannot be assigned unless nominative has been assigned. If there is no subject argument as candidate for the nominative, the object is assigned nominative instead (see chapter 6).

c. [Zu finden gewesen] ist der Fehler/*den Fehler (nicht) *leicht*
   [to find been] is the mistake-NOM/the mistake-ACC (not) easy
   'To find the mistake was (not) easy'

Finally, there is a class of verbs that are *obligatorily non-clustering*. In other words, these verbs select clausal infinitival complements only and resist clustering. If one compares the class of clustering verbs and the class of non-clustering verbs, it turns out that the crucial property is a property of the argument structure of the selecting verb: the cluster variant is available only for the infinitival complement that represents the unmarked argument. The unmarked argument is the direct object. The direct object is an argument slot that is neither marked for a specific case requirement (i.e. inherent or prepositional case) nor marked for external case (i.e. marked as the unergative argument slot). According to this criterion, verbs with a nominal direct object in addition to the infinitival clause do not permit clustering (13a), nor do unergative verbs with a clausal subject (13b).

(13) a. Sie hat ihn [ihr zu helfen] gedrängt
          she has him-ACC [her-DAT to help] urged
          'She has urged him to help her'

      b. dass [ihr zu helfen] genügt hätte
          that [her to help] sufficed had
          'that it would have sufficed to help her'

      c. * [Zu helfen gedrängt] hat sie ihn ihr
          [to help urged] has she him her

      d. * [Zu helfen genügt] hätte ihr
          [to help sufficed] had her
          'It would have sufficed to help her'

As predicted, cluster topicalization is ungrammatical (13c,d), since clustering is not admitted for (13a,b), because the infinitival clause is not the unmarked argument. The argument in the argument grid of *drängen* (urge) that the infinitival clause is linked with is an oblique argument, namely a prepositional object.[16] In (13b), the infinitival clause is the unergative subject and hence not a (concealed) object, as in the case of ergative verbs: the clustering criterion predicts a minimal pair relation between unergative verbs that select an infinitival clause as (13b), and ergative verbs. For the latter, clustering is predicted to be an available option, because the infinitival clause represents the unmarked, internal argument of the

---

[16] If the object is not clausal, but nominal, a preposition is required:

(i)   Sie hat ihn *zu* etwas gedrängt
        she has him *at* something urged

verb. This is confirmed by verbs like *gelingen* (turn out well). (14b) illustrates the clustering variant, with the topicalized cluster. (14a) is the clausal variant.

(14)   a. dass ihr [es zu korrigieren] nicht gelungen ist
            that her-DAT [it to correct] not succeeded is
            'that she did not succeed in correcting it'

        b. [Zu korrigieren gelungen] ist es ihr nicht
            to correct succeeded is it her not
            'She did not succeed in correcting it'

7.1.2   The clausal infinitive construction

German infinitival clauses, as illustrated by (1a), are clauses with a non-dependent *zu*-infinitive[17] and an obligatory silent subject (i.e. PRO) that corresponds to the nominative subject in finite clauses (1b). In German, infinitival clauses do not allow a lexical complementizer and German does not allow infinitival wh-clauses (2),[18] which seems to indicate that the spec position of the complementizer is not available either. Finally, German does not allow an ECM construction with *zu*-infinitives (3b).

(1)   a. Es ist nicht nötig [PRO dagegen zu protestieren]
            it is not necessary [it-against to protest]
            'It is not necessary to protest against it'

        b. Es ist nicht nötig [dass man dagegen protestiert]
            it is not necessary [that one it-against protests]
            'It is not necessary that one protests against it'

In (1a), the silent PRO-subject receives a generic interpretation, as in English, since there is no referential antecedent in the matrix clause. It is interpreted like the generic indefinite in (1b). The sortal restriction is the same as in English. A potential referent for this kind of interpretation must be human.

---

[17] This means: the verb marked with *zu* is the verb that corresponds to the finite verb in the finite clause. It is not dependent on a cluster-mate verb. In a cluster, the *zu*-infinitive is selected, and hence locally dependent.

[18] Infinitival wh-constructions are possible only as bare infinitive constructions and only for a limited subset of all verbs that would select a finite indirect question, and they consist basically only of a wh-item and the verb:

(i)   Er weiß nicht, was tun
        he knows not, what do-INF ('He does not know what to do')

(ii)   *Er fragte (mich), wo es publizieren
        he asked (me), where it publish-INF ('He asks me where to publish it')

The absence of wh-infinitives in German still lacks an insightful account. It merely is a fact, and it is a problem for a straightforward CP analysis of the infinitival complement. See Wurmbrand (2001) for a proposal that waives a CP structure for clausal infinitives.

(2)   Er wusste nicht [wie mit ihr (*zu) sprechen]
        he knew not [how with her to talk]
        'He did not know how to talk to her'

Infinitival ECM constructions with the *zu*-marked infinitive are absent in German, but in this case, German is in good company with other languages.

(3)   a.   She expected him to accompany her

        b. * Sie erwartete ihn, sie zu begleiten
             she expected him her to accompany

        c.   Sie erwartete, dass er sie begleite
             she expected that he her accompanies

Unlike Dutch, German does not ban infinitival clauses from the clause-internal area (4a). Alternatively, as in Dutch, they may be extraposed (4b) or topicalized (4c). In Dutch, infinitival clauses are banned from the clause-internal region. Dutch uses the clustering construction instead. Dutch infinitival clauses are grammatical only in extraposed or topicalized positions. Hence, only German has the free alternation between a clausal infinitive construction and a clustering construction in the clause-internal base position.

(4)   a. Hoffentlich hat sie [ihn zu informieren] nicht vergessen
                                                          internal in-situ
           hopefully has she [him to inform] not forgotten
           'Hopefully, she has not forgotten to inform him'

        b. Hoffentlich hat sie nicht vergessen [ihn zu informieren]
                                                          extraposed clause
           hopefully has she not forgotten [him to inform]

        c. [Ihn zu informieren] hat sie hoffentlich nicht vergessen
                                                          topicalized clause
           [him to inform] has she hopefully not forgotten

        d. Hoffentlich hat sie ihn nicht [zu informieren vergessen]   clustering
           hopefully has she him not [to inform forgotten]

The matrix verb *vergessen* (forget) allows the clustering construction, but in (4a) the intervening negation particle separates the two verbs, hence the compactness property is not met, and so the clausal variant is the only admissible variant to be assigned to the word order in (4a). The clustering variant is possible with the order in (4d), and it is in fact required if negation is to be assigned wide scope (i.e. to not forget).

7.1.3   The third construction

This term was coined by den Besten and Rutten (1989) for constructions of a third kind, that is, constructions that are neither genuinely sentential nor genuinely clustering. A thorough analysis of this construction in German has been presented by Wöllstein-Leisten (2001). It is a construction mainly of colloquial German and other less norm-prone variants, as e.g. yellow press newspapers. It rarely occurs in literary texts (see Reis 2007: 39). Here are some examples:

(1)   a. weil er *heiliges Land* bereit war, für den Frieden aufzugeben[19]
           since he holy land ready was for peace to-abandon
           'since he was ready to abandon holy land for peace'

       b. Da habe ich *mich* angefangen, damit zu beschäftigen[20]
           there have I myself begun, it-with to keep-busy
           'There, I began to keep myself busy with it'

       c. dass *uns ein Staubsauger* versucht wurde aufzuschwätzen
           that us-DAT a vacuum-cleaner-NOM tried was to-talk-into-buying
           'that there was an attempt to talk us into buying a vacuum cleaner'

The examples in (1a,b) resemble the clausal construction, with an extraposed infinitival clause, but there shows up an element in the matrix clause that belongs to the embedded clause. In (1a,b), it is the direct object of the infinitival clause. In (1a) the direct object is an indefinite nominal phrase, in (1b) it is a reflexive pronoun. In (1c), both the direct object and the indirect object occur in the matrix clause.

The 'third construction' could be, and in fact usually is, analysed as long-distance scrambling from the extraposed clause into the matrix clause. However, this analysis is hard to maintain when looked at more closely. This analysis would not solve the problems it creates: if the 'third construction' were an instance of long-distance scrambling out of an extraposed CP, it is not clear why scrambling otherwise is clause bound. Second, this analysis does not cover immediately the generalization of Wöllstein-Leisten (2001) that the class of verbs that admits the third construction for their infinitival complement is a subclass of verbs that optionally admit a clustering construction. In her analysis, the third

[19] From a radio feature about Yitzhak Rabin, overheard by HH.
[20] From a radio interview with the author Stefan Heym, overheard by HH.

construction is a construction with an extraposed sub-clausal V-projection. Third, and fortunately, there is more immediate evidence for the non-sentential nature of the clause-final complement, namely long-distance passive which pre-supposes clustering.

For (1c) it is obvious that clause union must have applied. This becomes clear from the fact that the object of the infinitive (*ein Staubsauger*) appears in nominative case. This is the so-called 'long passive' that is characteristic only of (a subclass) of *optionally clustering* control verbs. Here are two more examples from, and tested by, Wöllstein-Leisten (2001: 311, 315)

(2) a. dass der Hund beschlossen wurde zu verkaufen

       (acceptance: 9 out of 11)[21]

   that the dog-NOM decided was to sell

   'that it was decided to sell the dog'

 b. ?? dass den Hund beschlossen wurde zu verkaufen

       (acceptance: 2 out of 11)

   that the dog-ACC decided was to sell

   'that it was decided to sell the dog'

 c. dass der Hund vergessen wurde zu füttern

       (acceptance: 9 out of 10)

   that the dog-NOM forgotten was to feed

   'that it was forgotten to feed the dog'

 d. ?? dass den Hund vergessen wurde zu füttern

       (acceptance: 1 out of 10)

   that the dog-ACC forgetten to feed

   'that it was forgotten to feed the dog'

Note that in these cases (2a,c), a scrambling analysis is bound to fail, without adding ad hoc measures to produce the case change. Scrambling never changes the grammatical relation of the scrambled item. Hence, a scrambling analysis predicts (2b,d) and rules out (2a,c). The clause union facts (nominative on the object, and other locality relations investigated by Wöllstein-Leisten) prove that the 'third construction' is a variant of the clause union construction. So, it is expected and predictable that the verbs that allow the third construction are a sub-set of the verbs that allow the clause union construction. The semi-modal usage

---

[21] Acceptance/rejection has been tested by Wöllstein-Leisten with a questionnaire that investigated four (cumulative) properties: (i) Is the construction acceptable at all? (ii) Is the nominative (on the infinitival subject) preferred? (iii) Is the accusative preferred? (iv) Are both, nominative or accusative, allowed as free variants?

of *drohen* (threaten) and *versprechen* (promise) alternatively allows the third construction[22] in place of the clustering construction (Reis 2007).

In short, the third construction arguably is a construction with a postverbal infinitival VP. In theoretical terms, this is a head-initial subtree in an otherwise head-final construction. The matrix verb selects an infinitival verbal projection, preferably a verbal cluster, but in case of the 'third construction' a (not fully saturated) infinitival V-projection. As a postverbal complement, it is not subject to the obligatory clustering requirement. Suffice it for the time being to remember that German infinitival constructions not only comprise clausal and clustering structures but that there is also a 'third construction', especially in spoken varieties of German (Reis 2007: 39).

7.2   The verbal cluster construction

The verbal cluster is a constituent consisting of the clause-final verbs (plus the particles of particle verbs). In German, the canonical order of the verbs in the cluster is head final. This means that the dependent verb precedes the verb it depends on (1). Dutch allows order variation, but it does not admit the German basic order as a grammatical variant in clusters with more than two verbs, cf. (2a) and (1). On the other hand, the order variants of the German cluster do not admit the Dutch order (2d), that is, the mirror image order of (1).

(1)   dass er nichts *gesehen haben kann*
       that he nothing seen have can
       'that he cannot have seen anything'

If we want to analyse the variation in (2) as movement effects, we have to know which order the movement operations take as input. (2c), for instance could be the result of moving the finite modal to the left edge of the cluster, if movement starts from a strictly head-final cluster structure (2a). On the other hand, (2b) could be derived by moving the participle one step to the left, if we think that the basic order of the cluster in Dutch is strictly head initial (2d).

(2)   a. * dat hij niets *gezien hebben kan*   *Dutch*
            that he nothing seen have can
            'that he cannot have seen anything'

---

[22] Here is an example:

(i)   weil bei Scheibbs ein Hang droht, die Leitung zu beschädigen
       since at Scheibbs a slope threatens the aqueduct to destroy

    b. dat hij niets gezien *kan* hebben

    c. dat hij niets *kan* gezien hebben

    d. dat hij niets *kan hebben* gezien   (*ANS* 1984: 1069)

Dutch and German contrast in another property of cluster syntax. Dutch allows separating the particle of a dependent particle verb in the cluster (3d,e). In German, a particle must not be isolated from the verb in the cluster (Kempen and Harbusch 2003).

    The relative order of the modal, the auxiliary and the lexical main verb in (3a–c) is identical with the order of the respective verbs in (2b–d). The difference is that the lexical main verb in (3) is a particle verb, and in Dutch the particle may be separated from the verb in the cluster. How could the variant particle order be derived? Either the verb moves and thereby strands the particle, or the particle moves away from the verb. What is the empirically adequate account? Particle stranding or particle shift?

(3)   a. dat ze deze liedjes **mee**gezongen *zouden hebben*   *Dutch*
            that they these songs together-sung should have
            'that they should have jointly sung these songs'

        b. dat ze deze liedjes *zouden* **mee**gezongen *hebben*

        c. dat ze deze liedjes *zouden hebben* **mee**gezongen

        d. dat ze deze liedjes **mee** *zouden hebben gezongen*

        e. dat ze deze liedjes *zouden* **mee** *hebben gezongen*

As for particle stranding, both in German and Dutch, particles of particle verbs get stranded when the finite verb is fronted. This shows that particle stranding is an available option in these languages. Stranding presupposes verb movement. For (3), this would entail that in (3d,e), the verb (i.e. the participle) has moved to the right and that the stranding position is a position that is in principle available for the participle. A comparison of (3a,b) and (3d,e), respectively, confirms that the stranding positions are indeed potential positions for the participle.

    Could particle shift be invoked instead as an alternative? This is unlikely because particle shift is not attested independently, either in the grammar of Dutch or in German. If the particle distribution in the cluster were an effect of particle shift, then particle shift would be a special property of the grammar of the cluster. The compactness property of the cluster includes particles. They must not be split off the cluster by intervening material in Dutch. Even a cluster-initial particle must be adjacent to the first verb of the cluster in Dutch.

    Let us turn now to a property of German cluster constructions that resembles the Dutch order variations. For certain combinations of governing and dependent verbs, German reorders the cluster. A frequent instance of reordering is the 'infinitive-instead-of-participle' construction (commonly referred to in German as *Ersatzinfinitiv*, in Dutch as 'IPP').[23]

Ersatzinfinitiv refers to the switch from the participial form to the bare infinitival form of the dependent verb (modal verb, perception verb, causative verb) when the (auxiliary) verb that governs the participial form precedes rather than follows the dependent verb. The trigger for this construction is avoiding the participle.[24]

For modal verbs, the use of the participial form has become obsolete: *dürfen* (may) – **gedurft*; *müssen* (must) – **gemusst*; *sollen* (shall) – **gesollt*. *Können* (can, be able to), *wollen* (want), and *mögen* (like), are used with the respective participial forms (*gekonnt, gewollt, gemocht*) as main verbs, but in the modal usage, the participial form is dispreferred (e.g. 4a).

The examples in (4) illustrate the *Ersatzinfinitiv* construction with the perfect tense auxiliary *haben* (have). The dependent modal verb changes from the participial form to the infinitive and the auxiliary that would govern the participial form, namely the perfect tense auxiliary is inverted.[25]

(4) a. dass er sie nicht *hat* fragen *können*   (instead of:
         that he her not has ask may-INF   ? fragen *gekonnt* hat [26]
         'that he has not been able to ask her'   ask may-PARTICIPLE has)

     b. dass er sie nicht *hat* zu fragen *brauchen*   (instead of:
         that he her not has to ask need-INF   ? zu fragen *gebraucht* hat
         'that he needed not to ask her'   to ask need-PARTICIPLE has)

---

[23] IPP is an abbreviation for *infinitivum pro participio*, which is Latin for: infinitive instead of participle.

[24] In the Austrian vernacular (notably in eastern varieties and especially in Viennese varieties), IPP is used without verb inversion. The participle is just replaced by the infinitive without any change in the order of verbs:

  (i)   dass er sie nicht fragen *können/müssen/lassen* hätte
         that he her not ask can/must/let had-SUBJUNCTIVE

[25] 'Inversion' is used here just as a descriptive term. Whether the derivation of the construction involves inversion as a syntactic operation (or whether it is base-generated) is a matter of dispute.

[26] Interestingly, the participle is accepted if the modal is used as a main verb in (Southern German) colloquial variants:

  (i)   Ich habe mal gemusst   (ii)   Er hat nicht gedurft
         I have once must   he had not be-allowed-to
         'I was in a must situation'   'He did not have the permission'

    c. dass er sie nicht *hat* fragen *lassen*   (instead of:
       that he her not has ask let-INF   ? fragen *gelassen* hat[27]
       'that he has not let her ask'   ask let-PARTICIPLE has)

The inversion construction is not limited to contexts of avoiding obsolete participles by replacing them with an infinitive form. The auxiliary (*werden*) for future tense and subjunctive allows the same distribution pattern, too. But there is no morphological effect or trigger on the dependent verb since this auxiliary selects a bare infinitive anyway.

(5)   a. dass er sie nicht *wird* fragen *können*   (instead of:
          that he her not shall ask be-able-to-INF   fragen *können* wird
          'that he shall not be-able-to ask her'   ask be-able-to-INF shall)

          b. dass er sie nicht *wird* zu fragen *brauchen* (instead of:
          that he her not shall to ask need-INF   zu fragen*brauchen* wird
          'that he shall not need to ask her'   to ask need-INF shall)

          c. dass er sie nicht *wird* fragen *lassen*   (instead of:
          that he her not shall ask let-INF   fragen *lassen* wird
          'that he shall not let her ask'   ask let-INF shall)

Both orders, the inverted one and the non-inverted one, are grammatical. The inverted one is preferred in the Northern varieties of standard German, the non-inverted order is the preferred order for Southern varieties of standard German.

    In general, the *Ersatzinfinitiv* inversion is not restricted to the finite auxiliary verbs, and it can be applied to more than one verb. In (6), the finite auxiliary *würde* (would) and the auxiliary that would govern the participle form on the modal *müssen* (must) in the non-inverted order are inverted. The resulting order for the inverted auxiliaries in (6a) is the partial mirror image of the base order (6b).

(6)   a. dass sie es *würde haben* bemerken müssen
          that she it would have notice must-INF
          'that she would have had to notice it'

          b. dass sie es bemerken *gemusst haben würde
          that she it notice must-PARTICIPLE have would-SUBJUNCTIVE
          'that she would have had to notice it'

---

[27] As Walter Huber has noted in his dissertation (1980), the participial form *gelassen* is acceptable in the *permissive* reading, but not in the *causative* reading of *lassen* (let):

    (ii)   dass sie ihn sitzen gelassen hat
          that she him sit let has
          'that she has let him sit' (idiomatic reading: she has left him)

The trigger is the modal. In the non-inverted order (6b), the modal is governed by the perfective auxiliary *haben* (have), which selects a participle form, which is obsolete for the modal. In order to invert the governing verb of the modal, namely *haben*, the auxiliary that governs *haben* must be inverted too.

The simple picture of the *Ersatzinfinitiv* construction sketched above (namely: invert the auxiliary and replace the participle by the infinitive) is more complicated, though. First, the inverted verb may target different positions. Second, full inversion lifts compactness, short inversion does not. In the above examples the inverted auxiliary precedes the entire cluster (*full inversion*). But the inversion may be shorter, as illustrated in (7).

(7)   a. ... für jemanden, der öffentlich in Stücke geschnitten *hätte* werden sollen[28]
          ... for someone, who in-public in pieces cut *had*-SUBJUNCTIVE been shall-INF
          'for someone, who ought to have been cut into pieces in public'

     b. ... sondern was gemacht *hätte* werden sollen[29]
          ... but what done *had*-SUBJUNCTIVE been shall-INF
          'but what should have been done'

     c. ob die Todesgefahr erkannt *hätte* werden müssen[30]
          whether the life-danger realized *had*-SUBJUNCTIVE been must-INF
          'whether the danger to life had to have been realized'

In (7), the inverted auxiliary follows the main verb. Another possibility would be an even shorter, that is, more local, inversion. The inverted verb may skip only the modal, as in (8), a variant of (7c).

(8)   ob die Todesgefahr erkannt werden *hätte* müssen
        whether the life-danger realized been *had*-SUBJUNCTIVE must-INF
        'whether the danger to life had to have been realized'

The variants (7) and (8), and the full inversion of the finite auxiliary as in (5) are free variants in standard German, with regional or individual preferences. The full inversion is apparently more frequent in Northern standard varieties, the 'intrusive' variants (7, 8) are more frequent in Southern standard varieties of German (see also Wurmbrand 2004).

Let us turn now to the compactness property. Full inversion (9a,c) lifts compactness in German (but not in Dutch). For the 'intrusive' inversion as in (7, 8), compactness holds. What this indicates is that full inversion targets a position

---

[28] German newspaper *Stuttgarter Zeitung*, 10 January 1989, p. 4.
[29] From the weekly magazine *Die Zeit* no. 52, 10 December 1985, p. 34.
[30] *Abendjournal*, 3 July 2001, Austrian radio feature.

outside the verbal cluster since non-verbal elements may intervene between the inverted auxiliary and the verbal cluster. This is a sharp contrast between German and Dutch. In Dutch, the sequence of verbs is compact under any order of the verbs. So, in Dutch, the domain of the order variation seems always to be identical with the cluster.

(9)   a.   dass er wird *nach Hause* gehen wollen   *German*
                that he will to home go want
                'that he will want to go home'

        b.   * dat hij zal *naar huis* willen gaan   *Dutch*
                that he will to home want go

        c.   dass er für sie nicht *hatte* die Firma am Leben halten wollen[31]
                                                                       German
                that he for her not *had* the company alive keep want-INF

        d.   * dat hij graag *wilde* kraanvogels fotograferen   *Dutch*
                that he with-delight wanted cranes photograph   (*ANS* 1984: 949)

The conclusion is obvious: in German, the inverted auxiliary in (9a,c) cannot be part of the cluster. This is reflected by the fact that non-verbal material may intervene between the fronted auxiliaries and the left edge of the original cluster. In Dutch, this is ungrammatical (9b). The clear contrast between German and Dutch in terms of admissible, non-verbal interveners is evidence for a structural difference in the cluster construction.

Let us finish the survey of facts on *Ersatzinfinitiv* reordering with a look at the range of verbs that participate: in German, it is a phenomenon restricted to a subset of auxiliaries, namely *haben* (perfective) and *werden* (future). Interestingly, the other perfective auxiliary, namely *sein* (be), and the passive auxiliary *werden* are excluded. German, in comparison to Dutch, is exceptional in this respect.

(10)   a.   dat hij het boek *is* komen halen   *Dutch*
                that he the book is come-INF fetch
                'that he has come to fetch the book'

        b.   * dass er das Buch *ist* holen (ge-)kommen   *German*
                that he the book is fetch come(-PARTICIPLE) /-INF
                'that he has come to fetch the book'

        c.   dat hij *is* blijven liggen   *Dutch*
                that he is remain lie
                'that he has remained lying (that he stayed in bed)'

---

[31] This is an excerpt from Thomas Mann's novel *Buddenbrooks. Verfall einer Familie.*

    d. * dass er *ist* liegen bleiben   *German*
        that he is lie remain
        'that he has remained lying (that he stayed in bed)'

    e.   dat hij is weggestuurd (geworden)   *Dutch*
        that he is away-sent (been)
        'that he has been sent away'

    f. * dass er ist weggeschickt worden/werden   *German*
        that he is away-sent been/be-INF

What these examples show is that an automatic IPP rule that fronts the finite auxiliary in the sequence $V_{Inf} + V_{Part.} + Aux_{Tense}$ would produce correct results only with perfective *haben* (have), but not with perfective *sein* (be). But note: all verbs that trigger the IPP construction (modals, causatives, perception verbs), select *haben* as auxiliary for the perfect tense. So, the exceptional behaviour of the other auxiliaries tends to be easily overlooked in the literature.

7.3   The infinitival clause

    German clausal infinitives are clauses with a *zu*-infinitive as superordinate verb and an obligatory subject. The subject is a phonetically *silent* pronominal, customarily referred to as PRO. Its interpretation is governed by the *control relation*. In (1), the superscripts indicate the control relation between a binder as antecedent and PRO as bindee.

(1)   a. Sie haben ihm[i] empfohlen [PRO[i] Alkohol zu meiden]
          they have him recommended [alcohol to avoid]

     b. Sie[i] haben ihm versprochen [PRO[i] Alkohol zu meiden]
          they have him promised [alcohol to avoid]

     c. Sie haben ihn[i] gebeten [PRO[i] den Raum verlassen zu wollen]
          they have him asked [the room leave to be-willing-to]
          'They have asked him to be willing to leave the room'

     d. Sie[i] haben ihn gebeten [PRO[i] den Raum verlassen zu dürfen]
          they have him asked [the room leave to be-allowed-to]
          'They have asked him to be allowed to leave the room'

Semantic factors determine the choice of the antecedent for the PRO subject. The 'minimal pair' (1c,d) is particularly instructive, since the matrix clause is identical, but the control relation is object control in (1c) and subject control in (1d). Obviously, the choice of the controller reflects the semantic compatibility of the selection requirement of the matrix verb and the semantics of the complement clause.

The PRO subject is *obligatory* and thematic, that is, it must be associated with a theta role provided by the verbal argument structure. The following examples illustrate this property. The embedded clause in (2a) is a subjectless finite clause. It is the passive construction of an intransitive verb. Since passive blocks the subject argument of the active construction, a passivized intransitive verb becomes subjectless. This is fine for a finite clause (2a), but ungrammatical for an infinitival clause (2b). In the infinitival clause in (2b), there is no theta role available for the PRO as the subject. The transitive verb *räuchern* (smoke), however, with the meaning of 'exposing something to smoke' in (2c) provides a thematic subject, namely the object argument promoted to the passive subject, whence the different grammaticality status of (2b) and (2c).

(2) a. Es ist angenehm, dass (hier) nicht geraucht wird
         it is pleasant that (here) not smoked is
         'It is pleasant that one does not smoke (here)'

     b. * Es ist angenehm, (hier) nicht geraucht zu werden
         it is pleasant (here) not smoked-INTRANSITIVE to be
         'It is pleasant that there is nobody smoking here'

     c. Es ist angenehm, (hier) nicht geräuchert zu werden
         it is pleasant (here) not smoked-TRANSITIVE to be
         'It is pleasant not to be smoke-dried here'

German provides direct evidence for the syntactic existence of the silent subject of an infinitival clause. In other words: there is direct and positive evidence that would not be directly covered if we assumed that an infinitival complement is just an infinitival VP, without a subject. This evidence comes from an appositive distributive marker.

(3) a. Sie hat die Männer gezwungen, *einer nach dem anderen* aus dem
         Fenster zu springen
         she has the men-ACC forced, one-NOM after the other out-of the window to jump
         'She has forced the men to jump out of the window one after the other'

     b. Sie hat die Männer *einen nach dem anderen* gezwungen, aus dem
         Fenster zu springen
         she has the men-ACC one-ACC after the other forced, out-of the window to jump
         'She has forced the men one after the other to jump out of the window'

The distributive expression in (3a) is nominative, and it is part of the extraposed infinitival clause. Accusative would be ungrammatical. In (3b), the distributive phrase is accusative and it is part of the matrix clause. Nominative would be ungrammatical. The case difference of the distributive phrases is a function of the case of the respective antecedents. The nominal head of the distributive matches the case of its overt antecedent. (3a) raises at least two questions: What is the antecedent of the distributive phrase in the infinitival clause, and what is the source of the nominative?

The answer is easy for the first question. The antecedent is the infinitival subject, namely PRO. Control provides it with the plural feature that the distributive phrase requires for its antecedent. The crucial point is that the distributive phrase requires an antecedent. So, for instance, a bare VP analysis of the infinitival complement as in LFG (*Lexical Functional Grammar*) would not provide a subject as an antecedent for the apposition. The antecedent would have to be the controller, that is, the object of the matrix clause. But this is an accusative DP, so the apposition would have to be accusative, contrary to the facts.

What is the source of the nominative? Either it is the case of the antecedent or it is a default case. The first option would imply that PRO has nominative case. This does not seem very attractive under the standard assumption that infinitival clauses do not allow a *lexical* subject for the very reason that no case is assigned to an individual subject, and a lexical subject obligatorily needs case. The second option would imply that the distributive phrase gets nominative as default case, in certain contexts. What are these contexts? The following examples provide a cue. A subject-related distributive may be assigned nominative, no matter what case the subject has. This covers the PRO subject of an infinitival clause as well as the accusative subject of a causative construction.[32]

(4)   a. Sie ließ uns einen/einer nach dem anderen aus dem Fenster springen
          she let us-ACC one-ACC/one-NOM after the other out-of the window
          jump

---

[32] Analogously, the case of the predicative DP in the causative construction shows the same alternation:

   (i)   Lass mich dein guter Herold sein
          let me-ACC your good herald-NOM be
          'Let me be your good herald'

   (ii)   Wir lassen Gott einen guten Mann sein
          we let god-ACC a nice man-ACC be
          'We let god be a nice man'

    b. Sie ließ die Männer uns einen/*einer nach dem anderen aus dem
       Saloon werfen
       she let the men us-ACC one-ACC/one-NOM after the other out-of the
       saloon throw
       'She let the men throw us one after the other out of the saloon'

In (4a), the antecedent of the apposition is the subject argument of *springen*
(jump), and the apposition may be accusative or nominative. Accusative is the
result of applying the 'copy rule', nominative is the result of the 'subject rule'.
(4b) shows that an apposition with the object as antecedent must match the case
of the object.

    Let us return now to the interpretation of the silent subject. In German, as in
English, the dependent interpretation ('controlled' PRO) is obligatory. The control relation cannot be waived. In other words, the generic interpretation of PRO
is ruled out if control is possible, as in (5b), even if the matrix verb would accept
a complement with a generic subject (*man* – one) as in the case of the finite object
clause (5a).

(5)   a. Er^i hofft, dass er^i/man die Lösung finden wird
         he hopes that he/one the solution find will

     b. Er^i hofft, PRO^i/*PRO^{Generic} die Lösung zu finden
         he hopes to find the solution

In German, the controller may be an implicit argument, as in the case of a passivized subject control verb (6a,b), or it may be the implicit argument of a verb with
an optional accusative or dative object in case of object control (6c). Passivizing
a matrix verb with an implicit argument as controller does not affect the control
relation (6d).[33]

(6)   a. Gestern wurde versucht/verabsäumt, eine Lösung zu finden
         yesterday was tried/failed a solution to find
         'Yesterday, an attempt/failure of finding a solution was made'

---

[33] This contrasts with the situation in English. In German, neither Visser's nor Bach's
generalization holds. *Bach's generalization* (Bach 1979) captures the fact that in
English, controllers that are direct objects themselves must be structurally represented
(i). *Visser's generalization* states the analogous requirement for subjects: a controlling
subject argument must be structurally present as a subject (ii) in English.

  (i)   He asked *(someone) [to close the window]
  (ii)   * I was promised (by her) [to be invited]

  (i′)   Er bat (jemanden) [das Fenster zu schließen]
  (ii′)   Mir wurde (von ihr) versprochen [eingeladen zu werden]
          me-DAT was (by her) promised [invited to be]

b. Gestern wurde uns damit gedroht, die Polizei zu rufen
   yesterday was us-DAT it-with threatened, the police to call
   'Yesterday, they threatened us with calling the police'

c. Sie hat (uns) gebeten/befohlen, die Tür zu versperren
   she has (us) asked/ordered the door to lock
   'She has asked/ordered (us) to lock the door'

d. Gestern wurde gebeten/befohlen, die Tür zu versperren
   yesterday was asked/ordered the door to lock
   'Yesterday, it was asked/ordered to lock the door'

(6a) illustrates the passive of subject control verbs without a nominal object. (6b) is the passive of a subject control verb with a dative object. (6c) exemplifies verbs with optional objects as controllers. The object of *bitten* (ask) is accusative, the object of *befehlen* (order) is dative. Passivizing the verbs of (6c) has no influence on the construal of control, as illustrated in (6d).

Having reviewed some properties of the silent subject of infinitival clauses, let us return to a structural issue mentioned in the introductory section, namely the absence of infinitival wh-clauses in German. In an infinitival clause, there is no room for wh-moved elements in a spec C position. Since interrogative constructions are just an instance of wh-movement constructions, we have to expect that the ban should apply to other instances of wh-movement constructions as well, namely relative clauses. This is the case, as illustrated in (7b). The construction (7c), however, looks as if an infinitival relative clause might be involved.

(7)   a.   This is the man who to ask

       b. * Das ist der Mann, *den zu fragen*

       c.   Das ist der Mann, *den zu fragen* ich beabsichtigt habe
             this is the man who to ask I intended have

But (7c) is not compelling. An infinitival relative clause would come into play only in a pied-piping analysis, as indicated in (8a). This is not the only available analysis, however. (7c) can be analysed as regular wh-movement in combination with a scrambled infinitival clause, as indicated in (8b).

(8)   a. Das ist der Mann, $[_{CP}$ [den zu fragen]$_i$ [e$_C$° [ich e$_i$ beabsichtigt habe]]]

       b. Das ist der Mann, $[_{CP}$ den$_i$ [e$_C$° [[e$_i$ zu fragen]$_j$ ich e$_j$ beabsichtigt habe]]]

(8b) is independently motivated by the fact that the same kind of structure is found with wh-movement in interrogative constructions. In the case of main clause interrogative constructions (9a,b), it is easy to verify that a wh-phrase is moved out of the scrambled infinitival clause because the finite verb in $C°$ intervenes between the scrambled infinitive clause and the target position in the matrix Comp.

(9c) contains an embedded version of (9b). The movement is string vacuous because there is no complementizer. The embedded wh-clause in (9c) is word by word identical with the relative clause in (9d).[34]

(9)   a. Welchen Mann$_i$ hat [e$_i$ zu befragen]$_j$ denn jeder e$_j$ beabsichtigt?
      which man has [to question] PRT everyone intended
      'Which man has everyone intended to question?'

      b. Womit$_i$ hat [sie e$_i$ zu beeindrucken]$_j$ denn jeder e$_j$ versucht?
      what-with has [her to impress] PRT everyone tried
      'With what has everyone tried to impress her?'

      c. Wir wissen [womit$_i$ [e$_C$° [sie e$_i$ zu beeindrucken] jeder versucht hat]]
      we know [what-with [her to impress] everybody tried has]
      'We know with what everybody has tried to impress her'

      d. manches [womit$_i$ [e$_C$° [sie e$_i$ zu beeindrucken] jeder versucht hat]]
      some-things [what-with [her to impress] everybody tried has]
      'Something that everyone has tried to impress her with'

The absence of genuine infinitival wh-clauses in German is puzzling since the assumed CP structure would provide room for wh-movement, in principle. The grammatical source of this property is not yet sufficiently understood and still enigmatic. If we assume a CP structure for infinitival clauses, the theory captures the clausal distribution and the cross-linguistic parallels among the control constructions. We have to ban wh-infinitivals, however, in order to avoid overgeneration. If, on the other hand, we assume that infinitival clauses are not CPs, but maybe only TPs, then we are able to correctly predict that there are no wh-variants, but we would be confronted with serious counterevidence. First, and foremost, we would be left without an answer for the fact that German does not allow ECM infinitives with *zu*. In a TP analysis, we would expect German to abound with ECM infinitives as counterparts to English sentential infinitives since the TP complements are turned into ECM constructions once the matrix verb is transitive. The detailed comparison of the German and English infinitival complementation structures in the following section surveys the properties contrasting English (VO) and German (OV) that ought to be captured by any empirically adequate model.

---

[34] German uses wh-pronouns in relative clauses when the antecedent is a neuter quantifier, and in free relatives. The default relative pronouns in German are formally identical with the demonstrative pronouns.

7.4   Comparing and contrasting English with German infinitival constructions

In English, the categories of infinitival complements correspond to the projection categories of the verb projection and its functional extensions, that is, at least VP (1), TP (formerly IP) as in (2), and CP.

(1)   a. It will/could [$_{VP}$ be [$_{VP}$ raining cats and dogs]]

     b. He has [$_{VP}$ been [$_{VP}$ criticized by nearly everyone]]

     c. They made/let [$_{VP}$ me laugh]

     d. I saw/heard [$_{VP}$ her laugh]

First, it is uncontroversial for English that modals select a bare infinitive as the head of the complement VP (e.g. *be* in 1a). Causative verbs (1c) and perception verbs (1d) arguably select the same category, and in addition, these verbs provide a structural case licensing context for the subject of the complement (ECM context). The auxiliaries used in tense formation and in passive formation select a participle (1b).

Second, it is uncontroversial for English that there are verbs that select an infinitival complement that is bigger than a VP, but smaller than a CP. And, as in the case of bare VP complementation, there is both a raising variant and an ECM variant.

The so-called subject-raising predicates are a category of heads that select a functional projection, but this functional projection is not a CP. Formerly, this category was called IP. The category label is not the main concern here. What we merely need to acknowledge is this: there is a class of verbs that select a functional projection headed by *to*, and this functional head selects an infinitival VP. The typical candidates of this class are epistemic predicates, like the verbs in (2a) or the adjectives in (2b). The subject of the infinitival predicate is raised to the subject position of the matrix.

(2)   a. She$_i$ seemed/appeared [$_{TP}$ e$_i$ [$_{I'}$ to [understand the problem]]]

     b. She$_i$ is likely/probable [$_{TP}$ e$_i$ [$_{I'}$ to [understand the problem]]]

The ECM variant of IP complementation is on the one hand found with exceptional[35] verbs like *believe* (3a), that exclusively select an IP infinitive complement, and on the other hand with verbs that optionally select this category, as alternative to an infinitival CP complement (3bc):

---

[35] *Believe* is exceptional since in other languages (Germanic, Romance) the semantic counterparts are control verbs.

(3)   a. We sincerely believed [$_{IP}$ him to become an excellent candidate]

ECM variant

   b. We expected [$_{IP}$ him to become an excellent candidate]

ECM variant

   c. He^i expected [$_{CP}$ PRO^i to become an excellent candidate]   CP variant

Note that the passive of a transitive ECM verb like *believe* or *expect* produces a derived format that is identical with the format of a raising predicate, that is, a predicate that selects an IP complement and does not provide a subject argument of its own. So, the passive variant of (3a,b) in (4) has the same format as the basic format of the verbs in (2):

(4)   He$_i$ is believed/expected [$_{IP}$ e$_i$ [$_{I'}$ to [be an excellent candidate]]]

Let us briefly assume a comparative perspective. In English, the availability of an IP as a separate functional layer in the clause structure makes this category a possible candidate for an infinitival complement selected by the appropriate matrix predicate.

In German, there is no evidence for subject raising structures – in the sense of moving a subject from the VP-internal position to a functional subject position – that involve *zu*-marked infinitival complements, nor is there evidence for ECM structures with *zu*-marked infinitival complements. This set of facts follows immediately if the German clause structure does not provide a functional layer corresponding to the English IP, that is, a functional projection whose spec is the obligatory functional subject position.

Here are the differences, in a nutshell: first, an ECM construction with *zu*-marked infinitivals is completely absent in German. Second, the counterparts of the English raising predicates are obligatorily clustering predicates (verbs or adjectives) in a simple clause with a head-to-head-adjunction cluster (5).

The examples chosen for (5) are subjectless predicates. This is to demonstrate that there is no subject position involved, given that an IP complement would involve an obligatory subject position. (5a) features one of the few predicates in German whose sole argument is a dative, namely *übel*$_A$° (sick). (5a) has the same argument equipment as a *passivized* verb with a NOM–DAT argument format (5b).

(5)   a. dass bei dieser Überfahrt fast allen [$_{VC}$ übel zu werden gedroht hat]
      that on this passage nearly everybody-DAT [sick to become threatened has]
      'that on this passage, nearly everybody threatened to become sick'

b. dass damit den Leuten [$_{VC}$ geholfen zu werden/sein scheint]
   that it-with the people-DAT [helped to become/be seems]
   'that people seem to have been helped with it'

Let us turn now to the fully clausal infinitivals. It is popular knowledge by now that English has at least four types of clausal infinitival constructions. One type is the familiar control construction, namely a CP with an empty C-shell (6a). The shell gets lexicalized once the clausal infinitive is a wh-clause (6b). In addition, there are clausal infinitive constructions with a prepositional complementizer, namely the *for-to* constructions (6c).

(6)   a. She prefers [$_{CP}$ C° [$_{TP}$ PRO to say so]]

        b. She does not know [what$_i$ C° [PRO to do e$_i$]]

        c. It is pleasant for the rich [$_{CP}$ for [$_{TP}$ the poor to do the hard work]]

Finally, and fourth, English has an infinitival construction with a puzzling property. This is the so-called *tough-movement* construction as in (7); see Culicover (1997: 205–8). The puzzling property is the fact that there is a gap that correlates with the matrix subject, but this relation cannot be an antecedent-gap relation created by movement since the gap is case marked. In the standard analysis, an empty operator is assumed to bind this gap. The 'O' in (7a,b) is the silent operator that binds the trace and is interpreted by means of construal with the matrix subject. But this solves only half of the problem since the matrix subject (7b) is left without a theta role, given that the matrix predicate does not assign one (7c). *Tough*-predicates semantically select a proposition, not an individual.

(7)   a. These violins^i are tough [O^i_j [PRO$_{ARB}$^{36} to play sonatas on e$_j$]]

        b. These violins^i are tough [$_{CP}$ O^i_j [PRO to believe [$_{CP/IP}$ you played sonatas on e$_j$]]]

        c. It is tough [$_{CP}$ PRO to play sonatas on these violins]

Note that the operator of the *tough*-construction may be in a long-distance relation to the embedded argument position (7b). This is a sharp contrast to the German construction. In German, the *tough*-predicates are merely adverbial modifiers in a clustering construction that is just a variant of the passivizing *sein* + *zu*-V°^{37} construction (be + to-V°). As illustrated in (8a), the combination of the *zu*-marked V° plus the copula is well formed in the absence of an adverbial modifier. The semantics of the adverbial, as in any case of adverbial modification, have to

---

[36] ARBitrary reference. The pronominal is interpreted generically, like German *man* or French *on*.

[37] Example: Ge.: *Das ist (leicht/nicht) zu verstehen* vs En.: That is *(easy /*not) to understand
       that is (*easy/not*) to understand

harmonize with the semantics of the construction; in this case, this is the modal reading ('possible') of the construction *sein* + *zu*-V° (be + to-V°).

(8)   a. dass ihm (nicht) (leicht/schwer/*absichtlich/*vergeblich) zu helfen ist
          that him-DAT (not) (easy/difficult/intentional/futile) to help is
          'that he is easy/difficult/intentional/futile to help'

      b. dass er (leicht/schwer/*absichtlich/*vergeblich) [zu finden
          (*anzunehmen)] war
          that he (easy/difficult/intentional/futile) [to find (to-assume)] was
          'that he was easy/difficult/intentional/futile (to assume) to be found'

      c. Es war leicht / schwer /??vergeblich /*absichtlich, [PRO anzunehmen,
          [PRO ihn dort finden zu können]]
          it was easy/difficult/futile/intentional [to-assume [him there find to
          be-able]
          'that it was easy/difficult/futile/intentional to assume to be able to
          find him there'

The complete absence of the long-distance variant (8b) in German clearly indicates that the construction in general is not an instance of a (long-distance) wh-type relation but rather a subinstance of the common 'Aux + *zu*-V°' construction in German, with the passive effect triggered by the combination with *sein* (be) rather than *have*. This construction crucially does not involve an embedded clausal complement. It is monoclausal and clustering, with the *tough*-predicate as an adverbial modifier. It cannot be successfully derived from the fully clausal control construction (8c).

7.4.1   The German infinitival constructions in comparison

Let us now review and compare the grammar of infinitival constructions in English with the corresponding constructions in German. In brief, German

- does not admit ECM *infinitives with zu*;
- does not show any indications of *subject-to-subject raising* in the sense that an obligatory subject position is targeted by the subjects of raising verb complements;[38]
- does not allow clausal *wh-infinitives* with a *zu*-infinitive;
- has, unlike English, and unlike other VO languages, but like the Germanic OV languages, *obligatory verb clustering* constructions.

---

[38] What appears to be a subject-to-subject raising construction in German, is a simple clause, with a *zu*-infinitive in a verbal cluster.

Is this set of differences an accidental ensemble or does it follow from a more basic difference in the make up of the respective grammars?

It is not accidental. First, clustering is a property of OV languages and absent in VO languages. Second, a VP-*external*, functional subject position is a characteristic and defining property of VO languages. It is this very functional projection that is the third infinitival category (IP), in addition to infinitival VP and CP complements. In OV languages, it seems that there are only clausal infinitival complements, but no IP or VP complements. IP is not a category of OV languages, and VP complements are replaced by the clustering construction. If there were an IP complement it would be turned into a clustering construction. A detailed explication of the analysis sketched here will be presented in section 7.5.2.

Let us now review the different types of German infinitival complements in terms of their syntactic categories: first, like English, and many other languages, German has *clausal infinitives* (control constructions), but unlike English, German has no subvariety with a lexical complementizer[39] (cf. the *for-to* construction), nor does German admit infinitival wh-clauses.

It is not clear what makes wh-infinitives unavailable in the German grammar.[40] So, for the time being, we are faced with the problem of overgeneration: if an infinitival clause is a CP, it ought to provide a spec position for wh-fronting. If, on the other hand, an infinitival clause was not a full CP in German, it would be transparent for case-checking and give rise to ECM constructions (1b) on a par

---

[39] Dutch employs *om* as an optional complementizer in control infinitives:

(i) Hij probeerde (om) te roken – 'He tried to smoke'

The complementizer has been recruited from its primary function as a complementizer for purpose clauses ('in-order-to'). With control infinitives, the complementizer *om* is semantically empty. Its presence or absence has no effect on the interpretation.

German *um* is restricted to final clauses. Arguably it is a preposition, like *ohne*. But unlike *ohne*, *um* is restricted to infinitival clauses:

(i)   Er ging [ohne [PRO zu grüßen]] – he went [without [to greet]] – 'He left without saying goodbye'
(ii)   Er ging [ohne [dass er grüßte]] – he went [without [that he greeted]] –'He left and did not say goodbye'
(iii) Er ging [um [PRO sie zu begrüßen]] – he went [in-order-to [her to greet]] – 'He left in order to welcome her'

[40] There are a few idiom-like wh-infinitives in German, but in any case they are infinitives without *zu*:

(i)   Ich weiß nicht [was (*zu) tun] – I know not [what (to) do] – 'I do not know what (to) do'

with the English ECM construction (1a). So, we would trade in a new case of overgeneration at the price of avoiding the first one.[41]

(1)   a.   I expect [$_{TP}$ this-ACC to follow from independent principles]

       b.   * Ich erwarte [$_{TP?}$ das-ACC aus unabhängigen Prinzipien zu folgen]

All subclausal infinitives in German are clustering constructions. This includes the cases corresponding to English VP complementation with auxiliaries and modals. But it crucially includes also the counterparts of English subject raising constructions. The adequate structure for (2b) is not (2c), but (2d).

(2)   a.   that he$_i$ seems [$_{TP}$ e$_i$ to tell us strange things]
       b.   dass er uns schräge Dinge zu erzählen scheint
             that he us queer things to tell seems
             'that he seems to tell us strange things'

       c.   * dass er$_i$ uns [$_{TP}$ e$_i$ schräge Dinge zu erzählen] (*manchmal*) scheint
             that he us queer things to tell (sometimes) seems
             'that he sometimes seems to tell us strange things'

       d.   dass er uns schräge Dinge [$_{VC}$ zu erzählen (*manchmal*) scheint]

First, (2c) is inadequate because infinitive constructions with epistemic verbs are obligatorily clustering. All clustering criteria discussed below are met by this construction. (2d) and (3) illustrate the compactness effect, for instance. Adverbs cannot be put at the position where they should appear given a structure like (2c). This is true of the semi-modal usage of control verbs, like *versprechen* (promise, look promising), or *drohen* (threaten), as well (see Reis 2007).

(3)   a.   dass die Reise interessant zu werden verspricht
             that the journey interesting to become promises
             'it looks promising that the journey will become interesting'

       b.   dass das Gebäude einzustürzen (*nicht/*unmittelbar) drohte
             that the building to-collapse (not/immediately) threatened
             'that the building did not immediately threaten to collapse'

Second, there is no evidence for subject raising. There is neither a requirement for a *lexical* subject (or an expletive) nor does the word order reveal a change in

---

[41] A third possibility that needs to be explored is this: the phonetically empty C° is specified as the head of an infinitival clause and this specification is incompatible with the spec-head agreement for a wh-feature that applies in embedded wh-clauses. This situation is the infinitival counterpart of the ban against V2 in embedded finite wh-clauses. The verbal features are incompatible with the wh-specification of the functional head.

the position of the subject. This behaviour is not surprising once it is realized that the construction is a clustering plus clause union construction, since in this case we expect exactly the same behaviour as in a simple clause without the epistemic verb. This is the case, indeed:

(4)   a.   dass ihm geholfen worden zu sein scheint
              that him-DAT helped become to be seems
              'that he seems to have been helped'

        b.   dass ihm geholfen worden ist
              that him-DAT helped become is
              'that he has been helped'

        c. * die Möglichkeit, [PRO (ihm) geholfen worden zu sein]
              the possibility [(him) helped become to be]
              'the possibility [to become helped]'

        d.   wenn wem die Zeit gekommen zu sein scheint
              if someone-DAT the time arrived to be seems
              'if it seems to someone to be the right time'

        e.   wenn (es) wem scheint, dass die Zeit gekommen ist
              if (it) someone-DAT seems that the time arrived has
              'if it seems to someone to be the right time'

(4a) is a subjectless infinitival construction parallel to the subjectless finite passive clause (4b). Note that in a truly clausal infinitive as in the control construction (4c), a subjectless infinitive construction is ungrammatical. In (4d), the nominative subject follows the dative object of the epistemic verb. The indefinite wh-pronoun is intentionally chosen because these pronouns do not scramble. This is a way to ensure that the order in (4d) is the canonical order and not deranged by scrambling. Since the dative object of the matrix verb precedes the subject of the infinitive, raising cannot have applied.

   Third, positive evidence, like scope data, tells us that the construction is a clause union construction and not a construction with an embedded functional projection. In the latter case, the functional constituent would be a c-command domain that constrains the scope of negation. The data tell a different story, however.

(5)   dass mir Syntaktiker diesen Umstand *nicht* zu würdigen scheinen
        that (to) me-DAT syntacticians this circumstance not to appreciate seem
        'it does *not* seem to me that syntacticians appreciate this circumstance'

The negation precedes the infinitive in (5). If this is a position embedded in the complement, the negation would not c-command the finite verb and would not – contrary to the facts – be able to serve as the sentence negation for the matrix clause. Similarly, since there is only a single domain for negation in the German clause, there is only room for a single sentence negation (6b,c). In English, there are two domains (6a). The italic instances of the negation particles in (6b,c) cannot be successfully interpreted as sentence negation but only as *constituent negations*.

(6)   a.   He did not seem to not have understood the question
       b. * Er schien *nicht* die Frage nicht verstanden zu haben

                                                     ('*' for sentence negation)
            he seemed not the question not understood to have
            'He did not seem to have not understood the question'

       c. * Er hat *nicht* die Frage nicht verstanden
            he has not the question not understood
            '*He did not have not understood the question' vs
            'It was not the question that he did not understand'

Let us turn now to the counterparts of English VP complements. In German, auxiliaries and modals are obligatorily clustering. The *potential* VP-status of the complement of a modal or auxiliary becomes visible only if a VP is topicalized.

(7)   a.   dass er mich nicht überrascht hat *mit dieser Frage*
            that he me not surprised has with this question
            'that he has not surprised me with this question'

       b.   dass er mich nicht überraschen könnte *mit dieser Frage*
            that he me not surprise could with this question

       c. * dass er mich nicht überrascht *mit dieser Frage* hat
            that he me not surprised with this question has

       d. * dass er mich nicht überraschen *mit dieser Frage* könnte
            that he me not surprise with this question could

       e.   [Überrascht *mit dieser Frage*]$_i$ hat$_j$ er mich nicht e$_i$ e$_j$
            [surprised with this question] has he me not

       f.   [Überraschen *mit dieser Frage*]$_i$ könnte$_j$ er mich nicht e$_i$ e$_j$
            [surprise with this question] could he me not

The examples (7a,b) illustrate the fact that extraposed material follows the clause-final verb. Crucially, it must not intervene and thereby split the verb cluster. (7c,d) are counterexamples for any account that assumes that the finite verb in German moves to a higher functional projection to the right, since in this case, the lower VP would be an extraposition site. That the right edge of VPs is a site for placing extraposed material becomes clear from (7e,f). Topicalized VPs are compatible with extraposition. But note that *reconstructing* the topicalized VPs into their extraction sites would produce the ungrammatical orders (7c,d), and so would be the copy in a copy theory of movement. What does this teach us?

At least we have to acknowledge that the topicalized constituent is not a simple copy of the phrase in the base position. So, do not trust topicalization as a test for the structure of the topicalized phrase *in its base* position. The topicalized phrase *is* a constituent, but its shape is not necessarily identical with the shape admissible in the base position (Haider 1990). From a descriptive point of view, the patterns in (7) show that clustering is obligatory for the VP *in the base* position. More generally, stacked VPs are obligatorily replaced by a single VP with a cluster. But this obligatory clustering requirement does not apply across distant dependencies as in (7e), that is, it does not apply under reconstruction.

There are at least two different theoretical implementations of these observations, namely a *derivational* one and a *representational* one. The *derivational* implementation option has to implement topicalization prior to cluster formation in the derivation. The serious problem with this option is obvious: topicalization is an unbounded movement process that targets at least the top spec position of its clause. Cluster formation is a local process confined to the 'bottom' of the clause. So, the indicated order of the derivation obviously violates the cyclic application of the rules of derivation. For (8), this would amount to first moving an embedded VP out of the local clausal domain to the top-spec position of the matrix clause and then returning to the embedded clause in order to apply cluster formation. This is not acceptable in any derivational grammar.

(8)   a. [Begeistert (gewesen) über diesen Vorschlag]$_i$ glaubte man [dass alle e$_i$ waren]
           [enthusiastic (been) about this proposal] believe one [that all were]
           'People believed that they all were enthusiastic about this proposal'

       b. Man glaubte [dass alle *begeistert (gewesen)* (**über diesen Vorschlag*) waren]
           one believed that all enthusiastic (been) (about this proposal) were
           'People believed that they all have been enthusiastic about this proposal'

The fronted VP in (8a) is a VP with a cluster (*begeistert gewesen*) and an extra-posed PP. The VP is in an antecedent gap relation to the embedded clause. As illustrated by (8b), the fronted VP cannot have an exact copy in the gap position because there is no extraposition site preceding the finite auxiliary. Cluster formation cannot take place after fronting since the cluster site is a proper subcycle.

The other option is a *representational* one with antecedent-trace matching in terms of a *type relation* rather than in terms of a strict *copy relation*. What follows is but a sketch of this idea. A moved phrase is the antecedent of a gap. So, an A'-moved V-projection is ultimately related to a trace in a base position. As a V-projection in a spec position, the structure is just that of a well-formed V-projection, that is, a V^n-category (see appendix at the end of this section for other cases of 'submaximal fronting'). If we admit that the variable n may be treated as *underspecified*, it is free to range from 'zero' to 'maximal'. In this way, it is possible to capture the antecedent-trace 'mismatch' by modelling the 'mismatch' as a *type relation* rather than a *token relation*.

(9)   a. $[_{V^n}$ Überrascht mit dieser Frage$]_i$ hat$_j$ er mich nicht $[_{VC} [_{V^n} e_i] e_j]$
           [surprised with this question] has he me not

       b. $[_{V^n}$ Mich überrascht mit dieser Frage$]_i$ hat$_j$ er nicht $[_{VC} [_{V^n} e_i] e_j]$
           [me surprised with this question] has he not

In the 'trace' position, the empty V^n is interpreted as V with a (partially) unsaturated argument grid. For (9a), this is the argument grid of a transitive verb, for (9b) it is the argument grid of an intransitive verb, since the direct object and the prepositional object are saturated in the fronted V^n already.

In the spec C position, the V^n-projection must fulfil the requirements of a phrasal V-projection, whereas in the trace position it must fulfil the requirements of an element in the cluster, that is, as a $V°$. Since the trace is *atomic*, a V^n-trace is always equivalent to $V°$ as an atomic element. On the other hand, the trace guarantees that the portion of the argument structure of the verbal head that is not satisfied within the topicalized constituent is transferred via the trace into the argument pool of the cluster. A copy approach to movement would fail since it requires that the structure in the target position and the structure in the base position are identical.

The following table summarizes the verb classes presented in this chapter. It makes clear that the grammar of German basically provides two types of constructions, namely the clustering construction and the clausal construction. Crucially, German does not employ IP complements (or, in present day diction, TP) or any other functional category in between CP and VP.

Table 7.2 *Synopsis of the types and forms of infinitival complementation in English and German*

Verb type	German		English	
	Category	Form	Category	Form
Tense and aspectual auxiliaries (*haben, sein, werden*)	clustering V°	bare infinitive past participle	VP	bare infinitive past participle *-ing*-form
Modal verbs (*dürfen, müssen, können, …*)	clustering V°	bare infinitive	VP	bare infinitive
Causative verbs (*lassen, machen*)	clustering V°	bare infinitive	VP	bare infinitive
Perception verbs (*sehen, hören, …*)	clustering V°	bare infinitive	VP	bare infinitive
Modal verb (*brauchen* – 'need')	clustering V°	*zu*-infinitive	IP	*to*-infinitive (e.g. 'ought')
Epistemic quasi-auxiliary verbs (*scheinen, pflegen, …*)	clustering V°	*zu*-infinitive	IP	*to*-infinitive
Semi-modal variants of control verbs (*drohen, versprechen, …*)	clustering V°	*zu*-infinitive	CP	*to*-infinitive
Aspectual quasi-auxiliaries[42]	clustering V°	*zu*-infinitive	IP	*to*-infinitive
ECM verbs with sub-clausal complement	not existing	not existing	IP	*to*-infinitive
Control verbs	CP	*zu*-infinitive	CP	*to*-infinitive
Optionally clustering control verbs	CP clustering V°	*zu*-infinitive	not existing	not existing
3rd construction control verbs	extraposed V-projection	*zu*-infinitive	not existing	not existing
3rd construction semi-modal variants[43]	extraposed V-projection	*zu*-infinitive	not existing	not existing

[42] Example: Ein Tief *kommt* über Österreich *zu liegen* (source: overheard, ORF weather forcast)
An (atmospheric) depression comes over Austria to lie
'A depression is going to stay over Austria'

[43] The semi-modal usage of verbs like *drohen* (threaten) and *versprechen* (promise) is constructed either as a clustering construction (i) or as a 'third construction' (ii), as argued in detail by Reis (2007).

(i)   [Einzustürzen gedroht] hat die Brücke unter der Last
[to-collapse threatened] has the bridge under the load
(ii)   dass die Brücke gedroht hat unter der Last einzustürzen
that the bridge threatened has under the load to-collapse

7.5 The grammar of clausal and clause union infinitival constructions

7.5.1 Recapitulation: the four types of infinitival constructions in German

The four infinitival constructions introduced above are the following ones: *clausal* infinitival construction, *obligatorily clustering* construction, the *optionally clustering* construction, and the so-called '*third* construction'. The optionally clustering construction is a *free* variation between the clausal infinitival construction (for the matrix verbs that permit it) and the clustering construction. In other words, an optionally clustering construction always has the clausal construction as a grammatical variant. Both constructions, plus the 'third construction', are constructions with the infinitival marker *zu* (to). The 'third construction' is a member of the same family, that is, it is a variant of the optionally clustering construction.

As for the constructional morphosyntax, the bare infinitive and the participle constructions are *obligatorily* clustering. Only the constructions with a *zu*-infinitive are responsible for the constructional varieties. Depending on the class of the superordinate verb, the construction with a *zu*-infinitive may be obligatorily clustering ('raising' verbs, as e.g. *scheinen* – seem), optionally clustering (control verbs, as e.g. *versuchen* – try), or obligatorily clausal (control verb, as e.g. factive verbs like *bedauern* – regret).

The particular challenge for the theoretical modelling of the grammar of optionally clustering infinitival constructions is the *clause union* property: the clustering variant is clearly monosentential, the clausal variant is clearly bisentential. A derivational scenario for capturing these constructions is faced with the problem that first, there is an undeniably *optional* variation between two well-formed clausal complement types, and second, in the clause union variant, any clausal boundary between the matrix clause and the infinitival complements apparently has disappeared.

For the current generative grammar theory, both properties are embarrassing. Optionality means untriggered derivational steps. From a meta-theoretical point of view, these steps are unnecessary since the clausal construction is perfectly well formed and the clause union construction does not add anything. There is no change in meaning. In many cases, the derivation would be string vacuous, that is, there is no word order change. What changes, though, is the clausal architecture and the grammatical constraints based thereupon. Radical clause union, on the other hand, cannot be achieved derivationally since derivations do not destroy or eliminate structures. In a representational approach, however, both variants can be generated independently, as two independent and convergent solutions for the string-to-structure mapping.

From the point of view of explanatory adequacy, it is important to realize that the clause union phenomena are OV-dependent phenomena.[44] We do not find them in VO languages.[45] So, the UG-based grammar machinery invoked for the derivation of clause union properties must be confined to the territories of OV systems, otherwise UG would be incorrectly characterized as admitting clustering and clause union in VO languages, too.

7.5.2   The clause union syndrome (CUS)

Clause union infinitivals, that is, the clustering variant of the clausal infinitival construction, differ from their clausal counterpart, that is, the control construction, in numerous properties. These constitute the reference set for the term in the title, namely the clause union syndrome. The source of these properties is, first, the fact that the clause union construction is monosentential while the control construction is bisentential. Clause-bound phenomena are sensitive to this difference since the presence or absence of a clausal boundary has an immediate impact for them. The second source is the cluster syntax. In the monosentential construction, the *zu*-infinitive and the selecting verbs are members of the same cluster. In the clausal complementation construction, however, the two crucial verbs belong to different clauses, and hence to different clusters.[46] This set of empirical circumstances is responsible for a predictable set of theoretical circumstances that is characteristic for each of the two constructions and for the empirical differences between them.

---

[44] 'OV' means strictly head-final languages, or at least languages with a head-final VP. It also includes *flexible OV* languages (see chapter 2). These are languages that combine the OV option (i.e. a head-final V projection) with the shell option that is needed for head-initial V-projections. Specimens of this type are Yiddish or Hungarian.

[45] The so-called restructuring of Romance infinitives is not a literal restructuring. It is *free alternation* between VP and CP complementation. Romance restructuring constructions are not compact (see appendix 7.7.3) and the verbs always appear in their canonical order (Cinque 2001). Germanic clusters are compact and allow for verb order variation.

[46] Gunnar Bech (1955) coined the term 'Verbalfeld' (verbal field) for the cluster and describes the difference between the 'coherent' (= monosentential) and 'incoherent' (bisentential) construction in terms of the verbal fields. What he failed to appreciate, though, is the fact that the incoherent construction is not identical with the extraposition variant. For him, incoherent is equated with clausal and postverbal, that is, extraposed clause. He apparently did not notice that the clausal infinitive is well-formed in the non-extraposed variant, too. The easily identifiable difference between the clausal variant and the clustering one is the compactness property. If there is an intervener, the construction must be clausal and cannot be the clustering one.

Table 7.3 lists sixteen properties in two columns, one for the clausal variant and one for the clustering variant. The detailed discussion of each property follows the table in the order of presentation. Note that this list is not considered to be exhaustive. Whatever phenomenon is sensitive either to clustering or to embedding will make a difference for the two constructions.

The sentence structure indicated in the second row of table 7.3 presupposes first, that clause union constructions are (underived) verb cluster structures, with the verb cluster as a complex verbal head, generated by syntactic head-to-head

Table 7.3 *Synopsis of the properties of infinitival clauses in comparison with clause union infinitivals*

clausal infinitivals	**clustering** (= *clause union*) infinitivals
[..... X [$_{CP}$ PRO ... Z ... *zu*-V°] (Y) V°]	[..... X ... Z ... [$_{V°}$ *zu*-V° (*Y$_{[-V°]}$) V°]]
(a) **Not compact**: *Y* may be non-verbal *Note*: Y is any material of the matrix clause that may intervene between an argument (clause) and the head verb, e.g. adverbials, negation *Note*: In Dutch, an infinitival clause in the midfield is ungrammatical. It must be either extraposed or topicalized.	(a) **Compact**: *Y* must be a verb of the cluster *Note*: Remnant-VP accounts fail because of this very property, since *remnant VPs* allow postverbal elements: 1. [Hingewiesen *darauf*] haben wir sie oft 2. *dass wir sie oft [hingewiesen *darauf* haben]
(b) Z may not *scramble* across X (*locality) 1.* dass ja mit dieser Frage$_i$ alle [$_{CP}$ e$_i$ ihn zu konfrontieren] sofort empfohlen haben that PRT with this question all [him to confront] immediately recommended have	(b) Z may *scramble* across X 2. dass ihn mit *dieser Frage*$_i$ alle e$_i$ sofort [$_{VC}$ zu konfrontieren empfohlen haben] *Note*: see also (k), for pronoun fronting
(c) *Extraposition* site for Z: embedded clause 1.* dass er [uns zu erklären] zweimal versuch that, [*wie Extraposition funktioniert*] that he [us to explain] twice tried has, [how extraposition works]	(c) *Extraposition* site for Z appears to be the matrix CP 2. dass er uns zweimal [$_{VC}$ zu erklären versuch hat] [*wie Extraposition funktioniert*] *Note*: The extraposition site is the *local* VP

Table 7.3 *(cont.)*

clausal infinitivals	**clustering** (= *clause union*) infinitivals
(d) If Z=*negation*: domain is the embedded CP 1. dass sie [ihm *nichts* zu verheim-lichen] ja beabsichtigte (*narrow scope only*) that she [(to) him nothing to keep-secret] PRT intended	(d) If Z=*negation*: domain is the matrix CP 2. dass sie ([ ) ihm ja *nichts* zu verhe-imlichen ( ]) beabsichtigte (*narrow /wide* scope) *Note*: sentence negation of the matrix by means of the negatively quantified object of the infinitive
(e) Two CPs, two domains of negation 1. dass *keinem* [sie *nicht* zu irritieren] gelang that no-one [she not to irritate] succeeded	(e) Single domain of negation (negation cancelling) 2. #[$_{VC}$ Zu irritieren gelungen] ist sie *keinem nicht*
(f) For Z a *quantifier*: domain in embedded CP see (d).	(f) For Z a *quantifier*: domain in matrix CP see (d).
(g) Two *time* domains (matrix/embedded CP) 1. dass er uns [*morgen* zu kommen] schon *gestern* versprochen hat that he us [tomorrow to come] already yesterday promised has	(g) Single *time* domain 2. #[Zu kommen versprochen] hat er uns *gestern* schon *morgen*
(h) PRO subject (in the embedded CP) 1. dass ihm^i [PRO^i sich^i zu befreien] (nicht) gelungen ist that him [himself to free] (not) succeeded has 'he did not succeed in freeing himself'	(h) no PRO subject (but theta identification in the VC) 2. *[Zu befreien gelungen] ist {sich^{*i} ihm^{*i} / ihm^{*i} sich^{*i} } (nicht) *Note*: In German, a reflexive does not readily accept a dative co-argument as binder (see (i) below, for *nominative*)
(i) If Z a reflexive, PRO is the local binder dass er^i [PRO^i sich^i zu befreien] (nicht) versuchte that he [himself to free] (not) tried	(i) If Z a reflexive, X may be the local binder 2. dass er^i sich^i (nicht) [zu befreien versuchte] *Note*: NOM is a licit antecedent, but not a DAT as in (h)2, above.
(j) If Z a pronoun, then free in infinitival CP 1. Max^i hat (uns^j)[PRO^j ihn^i zu zitieren] nicht erlaubt Max has (us) [him to quote] not permitted	(j) If Z a pronoun, then free in the matrix clause 2. [Zu zitieren erlaubt] hat Max^i /er^i ihn^{*i} (uns) nicht [to quote permitted] has Max/he him (us) not

Table 7.3 *(cont.)*

clausal infinitivals	**clustering** (= *clause union*) infinitivals
(k) If X and Z are pronouns: independent order 1. dass *er ihr* [$_{CP}$ *es* zu lesen] hätte erlauben müssen that he her-DAT [it-ACC to read] had permit must 'that he would have needed to permit her to read it'	(k) If X and Z are pronouns: dependent order (according to the template) dass *er es ihr* hätte [$_{VC}$ zu lesen erlauben müssen] that he it-ACC her-DAT had [to read permit must] *Note*: pronoun ordering template: NOM-ACC-DAT
(l) If Z is a direct object, matrix passive cannot affect Z 1. dass [ihn /*er zu reparieren] nicht versucht wurde that [him-ACC /*he-NOM to repair] not tried was	(l) If Z is a direct object of the infinitive, matrix passive may affect Z 2. dass *er* [$_{VC}$ zu reparieren versucht wurde] that he-NOM [to repair tried was] 2'. dass er [zu reparieren zu versuchen vergessen wurde] that he-NOM [to repair to try forgotten was]
(m) If Z is a direct object, its case is not affected by the matrix 1. dass *mir*^{j} [PRO^j ihn zu übersetzen] nicht gelang that me [it-ACC to translate] not succeeded	(m) If Z a direct object, it is NOM if matrix is *unaccusative* 2. dass *es* mir nicht [$_{VC}$ zu übersetzen gelang] that it-NOM me not [to translate succeeded]
(n) IPP: V$_{fin}$ does *not* precede the infinitival verb (see *hätte* in (k))	(n) IPP: V$_{fin}$ precedes the infinitival verb (see *hätte* in (k))
(o) [*zu*-V]$_{V°}$ cannot be topicalized 1. *Zu imponieren$_i$ hat er versucht [ihm damit e$_i$] to impress has he tried [him with-it] 1'. Damit$_i$ hat er versucht [ihm e$_i$ zu imponieren]	(o) [*zu*-V]$_{V°}$ may be topicalized 2. Zu imponieren$_i$ hat er ihm damit [$_{VC}$ e$_i$ versucht] *Note*: This pattern is characteristic of all VC constructions (with auxiliaries, modals, causative, etc.)
(p) nominalized VPs 1. [Dein [alle Deadlines verstreichen lassen]$_{VP}$]$_{DP}$ your [all deadlines expire let]	(p) nominalized verbal clusters 2. das [[Verstreichenlassen$_{V°}$]$_{N°}$] von Deadlines the [expire-let] of deadlines 2'. das Verstreichenlassenmüssen$_{N°}$ von Deadlines the expire-let-must of deadlines 'the having to let expire all deadlines'

merger.[47] Consequently, a clustering infinitival construction is monosentential. 'X' and 'Z' refer to arbitrary constituents that depend on the matrix verb and the infinitival verb, respectively. Second, it is assumed that the clausal variant is an embedded infinitival clause with a covert pronominal subject (PRO), subject to the standard control relation.

Property (a), namely *compactness*,[48] is the hallmark of all verb cluster constructions. In fact, compactness is characteristic of all complex predicates in German. Verb clusters are just one instance. Other instances are complex predicates consisting of a verb and a predicate with which the verbs (may) share an argument

(1)   a. dass dieser Satz [grammatisch (*nicht) ist]   copula + predicate
          that this sentence [grammatical (not) is]
          'that this sentence is not grammatical.'

       b. dass man diesen Satz [als grammatisch (*nicht) betrachtet]
                                                          verb + 'als'-predicate
          that one this sentence [as grammatical (not) regards]
          'that one does not regard this sentence as grammatical'

       c. dass man diesen Satz [grammatisch (*nicht) machen kann]
                                                          verb + result predicate
          that one this sentence [grammatical (not) make can]
          'that one cannot make this sentence grammatical'

Note that the ungrammaticality of the intervening negation in (1) is not a property of negation. Any other intervener, such as for instance an adverbial (e.g. *zwar* – 'in fact'), would produce the same ungrammaticality effect.

Compactness is a necessary property of clustering. In other contexts, German has no adjacency requirement for complements of verbs. In particular, an object

---

[47] Verbal clusters are *syntactic* head-to-head adjunction structures. Crucially, they are not complex verbs in the sense of morphological compounding. In German, there are verb–verb compounds, but they are easy to distinguish from verbal clusters (i), and nominalized clusters (ii), since compounding (iii) as a word formation operation does not involve inflectional material (neither the infinitival prefix *zu* nor the infinitival inflection -*en*):

   (i)   [*zu* frag*en* vergessen]$_{VC}$
          to ask forget
   (ii)   das [[Zu*frag*en vergessen]$_{VC}$]$_N$
          the to-ask-forget(ing)
   (ii)   [springreiten]$_V$° vs *[spring*en*reiten]
          jump-ride 'to show jump'

[48] In Dutch, the only interveners in the cluster are stranded elements of complex verbs (particles of particle verbs, predicates of predicate+verb complexes). German does not strand, whence the difference (see Haider 2003).

does not need to be adjacent to the verb in German. So, a clausal infinitival complement may be non-adjacent to the selecting verbal head. This accounts for the non-compact orders of a matrix verb and the verb in the infinitival clause.

Property (b) is a reflex of the *locality restriction on scrambling*. In German, scrambling is clause bound. So, if the clause union construction apparently allows scrambling of a complement of the infinitival verb across an argument of the matrix clause, this is not really scrambling out of a complement clause. It is scrambling within the same clause, since the two elements are clause mates in the clause union variant of infinitival complementation.

Property (c) is the locality constraint on *extraposition*. Extraposition is clause bound. What appears to be a violation of this locality restriction again is a clause union effect. The extraposition site for complements of the infinitival verb is the infinitival clause, or, if the verb is clustering, the matrix clause. If the clausal and the clustering variant are not distinct, it looks as if extraposition violates the locality restriction. But, in reality, locality is observed, if the infinitival construction is the clause union construction.

Property (d) is a domain effect at the syntax–semantics interface. The domain of negation is the simple clause as the linguistic representation of a proposition. If a negated element or a negation particle can serve as negator for the matrix clause, it cannot be embedded in an embedded clause. Hence (apparent) wide scope negation is an indicator of the clause union construction. This property was acknowledged already in G. Bech's (1955) profound study on infinitival constructions in German.

Property (e) is another aspect of the same condition. Each clause is a separate domain of negation. There are at least as many domains of negation as there are simple sentences. If the clause union construction is monosentential then there is only a single domain of negation in the infinitival clustering construction. Two instances of negation in a single clause amount either to double negation '(not(not P)) = P' (as a law of propositional logics) and the two negations cancel each other out (unless one of the two negations is phrasal negation[49]). If the complement is clausal, there is room for two negations, namely for one in the matrix and for the other one in the complement.

Property (f) is an indicator of the presence of the semantic side effects of an embedded clause as a semantic domain. C-command requirements restrict the domain of an operator to the domain of the simple clause. Negation is an operator element with this property (see also property (d)). But this is by no means the only element. Here is another case, namely adverbial quantifiers:

(2)   a. Er hat sie auch gestern *zweimal* zu küssen versucht   ambiguous
            he has her also yesterday two times to kiss tried
            'Yesterday too, he has tried to kiss her twice'

---

[49] Example: [Not bread] is missing, just butter to put on the bread.

b. Er hat [sie *zweimal* zu küssen] auch gestern versucht   '2 kisses'
   he has [her twice to kiss] also yesterday tried
   'Yesterday too, he has tried to kiss her twice'

c. [Zu küssen versucht] hat er sie *zweimal* auch gestern   '2 attempts'
   [to kiss tried] has he her twice also yesterday
   'Yesterday too, he has twice tried to kiss her'

Since (2a) allows two structural analyses, namely a sentential infinitival complement or a clause union construction, the scope of the frequency adverbial *zweimal*
(two times) corresponds to the alternative domains. The two readings are disambiguated once the syntactic contexts are disambiguated. (2b) only has the reading
with the scope of the frequency adverbial restricted to the embedded clause. (2c),
with the clustering construction signalled by the topicalized cluster, has the reading in which the frequency adverbial modifies the matrix predicate, that is, the
cluster with the matrix verb.

   Property (g) is a reflex of tense as a property of a simple clause. Temporal
adverbials are integrated into this local tense domain. So, if two temporal adverbials are incompatible because they contribute to situate the very same proposition in different and incompatible time intervals, the two adverbials cannot be
successfully integrated into the same simple clause. This accounts for the contrast
between the clausal and the clause union construction. The clause union variant
crashes if the clauses in the clausal construction are anchored in different time
intervals, while the clausal variant does not since each time adverbial has a different and independent integration domain.

   Property (h) highlights a core issue of the structural differences between biclausal
and monoclausal infinitival constructions. Only clausal infinitival constructions both
require and allow a covert subject, namely PRO. In the monosentential construction,
there is no clausal infinitival complement, hence there is no room for a covert subject.
The effect corresponding to the construal with PRO (i.e. the control relation) is the
identification of the argument identified by *zu* with the controlling argument as an
operation of pooling the arguments of the verbs in the verb cluster. This grammatical
device will be presented in more detail in the following subsection.

   The binding of anaphors (reflexive pronouns, reciprocals) discriminates between
control infinitivals and clustered ones if the antecedent of PRO is a dative. The
reason is twofold: first, reflexives and reciprocals do not accept a dative antecedent (3a). Second, the case of the accusative anaphor would change to nominative
in the clustering construction (see properties (l) and (m) below).

   In object control infinitive clauses, the dative controls the infinitival subject,
and this PRO subject is the antecedent of the reflexive or the reciprocal (3b). In the
cluster construction, however, the anaphor would have to be bound by the dative
directly, since there is no PRO as antecedent in a simple finite clause. Hence, the
clausal and the monoclausal infinitive constructions will differ precisely when a

dative control verb occurs in a clustering construction together with a reflexive or reciprocal. Topicalizing the cluster as in (3c) is a means of enforcing the clustering variant. Note that the deviance would be unexpected if a PRO subject was available in the clustering construction. The clustering construction will be deviant only for the reflexive and the reciprocal (3c), but not for an unbound object.

(3)   a. * dass ich den Leuten^i sich^i/einander^i vorstellte
            that I the people-DAT REFL/(to) each-other-ACC introduced
            'that I introduced the people to each other/themselves'

        c. dass den Leuten^i nicht gelungen ist, [PRO^i sich^i/einander^i
            vorzustellen]
            that the people-DAT not succeeded is [themselves/each-other
            to-introduce]
            'that the people did not succeed in introducing themselves/each
            other'

        d. [Vorzustellen gelungen]$_{VC}$ ist sie/*sich^i/*einander^i den Leuten^i nicht
            [to-introduce succeeded] is she/*herself/each-other the people-DAT
            not
            'that the people did not succeed in introducing her/themselves/each
            other'

There is an additional factor contributing to the strong deviance: in the mono-clausal construction, the direct object (anaphor) would have to surface as nominative (see properties (l) and (m) below), but anaphors do not have nominative forms in German.

Property (i) is just an implication of the binding requirements discussed with property (h). Given that the clustering infinitival does not provide a covert subject for control, the well formed binding in (4a) must be an instance of direct binding by the antecedent, that is, by the matrix subject. It is not mediated via control, as in the sentential construction (4b):

(4)   a. [Zu befreien versucht]$_{VC}$ haben sie^i sich^i/einander^i nicht
            [to free tried] have they themselves/each-other not
            'they have not tried to free themselves/each other'

        b. [[PRO^i sich^i/einander^i zu befreien] versucht]$_{VP}$ haben sie^i nicht
            [[themselves/each-other to free] tried] have they not
            'to free themselves/each other, they have not tried'

If (4a) is passivized, the anaphor as the direct object would have to be marked nominative. This is not possible for a reflexive or a reciprocal (see property (l)).

Property (j) is the counterpart of the local binding requirement for anaphors. It is the local *disjointness* requirement for pronominals. The prediction is evident: if the clustering construction is monosentential, pronouns within this domain must be disjoint in reference. So, the contrast between the clausal and the monoclausal variant will have an effect on the disjointness of personal pronominals. The data in (5) confirm this expectation.

(5a) is the standard case of long-distance construal of the embedded pronoun. Clustering, however, destroys binding. In the monoclausal (5b), co-reference would be a case of a locally bound pronoun, which is a binding violation. (5b) involves the same kind of deviance as (5c). Note that in a movement account of clause union, disjoint reference should not be at issue since A'-movement would not change the binding properties, as topicalization in (5d) illustrates.

(5)   a.   Klara^j hat ihm^i [PRO^i sie^j jederzeit anzurufen] erlaubt
            Klara has him [her at-any-time to-phone] permitted
            'Klara has him permitted to phone her at any time'

     b.   [Anzurufen erlaubt]$_{VC}$ hat Klara^j sie^{*j} ihm^i jederzeit
            [to-phone permitted] has Klara her him at-any-time
            'to phone her at any time, Klara has permitted him'

     c.   Klara^j hat sie^{*j} verletzt
            Klara has her injured
            'Klara has injured her'

     d.   (Nur) sie^j_i hat ihm Klara^j erlaubt [jederzeit e$_i$ anzurufen]
            (only) her has him Klara permitted [at-any-time to-phone]
            'Only her, Klara has permitted him to phone at any time'

Property (k) refers to the ordering template of pronouns (namely: NOM<ACC<DAT) within a simple sentence. If a clause boundary separates a series of adjacent pronouns, the template will apply to each clause separately. If the pronouns are clause mates, however, they will be ordered according to the template. This is exemplified by (6):

(6)   a.   dass *er ihr* [es zu erklären]$_{CP}$ (nicht) versucht hat
              that he-NOM her-DAT [it-ACC to explain] (not) tried has
              'that he has not tried to explain it to her'

     b.   [Zu erklären versucht]$_{VC}$ hat *er es ihr* (nicht)
              [to explain tried] has he-NOM it-ACC her-DAT (not)
              'Tried to explain it to her, he has (not)'

     c.   ?? [Zu erklären versucht]$_{VC}$ hat *er ihr es* (nicht)
              to explain tried has he-NOM her-DAT it-ACC (not)
              'Tried to explain it to her, he has (not)'

In (6a), the clausal construction, the accusative pronoun *es* is contained in the embedded clause and does not interfere with the ordering template of the matrix clause. In the clustering construction (6b,c), all pronouns are clause mates and they have to be ordered according to the template as in (6b), whence the deviance of (6c).

Property (l) is the so-called 'long-distance passive' first observed by Höhle (1978). That a 'long-distance passive' is just an instance of the regular clause-bound passive and not long distance at all becomes transparent once the clause union character of the construction is recognized. The passive subject in (7a) is the argument of the infinitival verb in the clause union construction. Syntactically it is therefore the regular object-turned-into-subject DP in the passive of a simple clause with a verbal cluster. In the clausal construction (7b), the object in the infinitival clause is not affected by passivizing the matrix verb, of course. It is the object of an infinitival verb within an infinitival clause.

(7)   a. [Einzuwerfen vergessen]$_{VC}$ wurde der-NOM /*den-ACC Brief nicht
            [to post forgotten] was the-NOM / the-ACC letter not
            'To post the letter was not forgotten'

        b. [Den-ACC/*der-NOM Brief einzuwerfen] wurde nicht vergessen
            [the-ACC/*the-NOM letter to post] was not forgotten
            'To post the letter was not forgotten'

But it is worth adding that the clause union passive is restricted (see Wöllstein-Leisten 2005). Not every verb that allows a clause union infinitive yields an acceptable clause union passive.[50] The nature of this restriction is not fully understood. That the clause union passive is not an automatic option admitted by UG is evident from the fact that Dutch does not allow a clause union passive although Dutch has the very same clause union property.

Property (m) is just another aspect of the phenomenon illustrated by the clause union passive. It is the reflex of the accusative-nominative dependency that is responsible for the object-to-subject case switch in the clause union passive. In the clause union construction (7a), matrix passive triggers the accusative-to-nominative switch on the direct object of the infinitive simply because the passive construction removes the original subject argument. This is an instance of the familiar accusative dependency as in (8a). In the clausal construction (7b, 8b), accusative is the only grammatical option. A'-movement as in (8b) does not affect case relations. The passivized verbal cluster is a derived unaccusative predicate. Hence, we also expect the same kind of case change for an unaccusative verb if it is part of a cluster. The facts confirm this expectation (8c). In the non-clustering variant (8d), nominative is ungrammatical.

---

[50] For instance, it is acceptable with *erlauben* (permit), *vergessen* (forget), *versuchen* (try) etc. but unacceptable with *beabsichtigen* (intend), *verstehen* (know), *wünschen* (wish) etc.

(8)   a. dass der/*den Brief eingeworfen wurde
           that the-NOM/*the-ACC letter-NOM posted was
           'that the letter was posted'

       b. Den/*der Brief_i wurde [e_i einzuwerfen] nicht vergessen
           the-ACC/*the-NOM letter-ACC was [to-post] not forgotten
           'To post the letter was not forgotten'

       c. Einzuwerfen gelungen ist mir der/*den Brief nicht
           to-post succeeded is me-DAT the-NOM/*the-ACC letter-NOM not
           'I did not succeed in posting the letter'

       d. dass mir [PRO den/*der Brief einzuwerfen] nicht gelungen ist
           that me-DAT [the-ACC /*the-NOM letter-ACC to-post] not succeeded is
           'that I did not succeed in posting the letter'

Property (n) is the *Ersatzinfinitiv* or IPP (*infinitivus pro participio*) phenomenon. It is a property of clustered verbs. Reordering the verbs in the cluster is restricted to cluster mate verbs and does not cross clausal boundaries. (9a) is the IPP construction in the matrix clause, with an embedded infinitival clause. (9b) is the clause union construction with IPP.

(9)   a. dass man [das zu analysieren]_{CP} (nicht) hätte [versuchen müssen]_{VC}
           that one [this to analyse] (not) had [try must]
           'that one would not have had to try to analyse this'

       b. dass man das nicht hätte [zu analysieren versuchen müssen]_{VC}
           that one this not had [to analyse try must]
           'that one would not have had to try to analyse it'

Property (o) highlights the fact that the main verb of a clause cannot be extracted out of the clause. This would be the case if the infinitival main verb of a clausal infinitive is topicalized, as in (10a). Here, the verb is extracted out of the extraposed infinitival clause. Extraction is possible for non-verbal constituents but not for the verb itself (10d). What is acceptable, though, is the topicalization of lower portions of a cluster, as in (10b). This is the reason for the minimal pair contrast between (10a) and (10c). In (10c), the topicalized verb is an element of the cluster, in (10a) it is the main verb of the clausal infinitive.

(10)   a. * Mitzuteilen_i hat er versucht [ihr etwas e_i]_{CP}
             to-tell has he tried [her something]
             'To tell her something, he has tried'

        b. Mitteilen_i wird_j er ihr etwas [e_i müssen e_j]_{VC}
             to-tell shall he her something [have-to]
             'Tell her something, he will have to'

c. Mitzuteilen$_i$ hat$_j$ er ihr etwas [e$_i$ versucht e$_j$]$_{VC}$
    to-tell has he her something [tried]
    'To tell her something he has tried'

d. Ihr$_i$ hat er versucht [PRO e$_i$ etwas mitzuteilen]
    her has he tried [something to-tell]
    'Her, he has tried to tell something'

Property p: nominalized verbal cluster. Finally, straightforward evidence for the existence of V-clustering is the nominalization of clusters. Nominalization is a word formation process and word formation is restricted to the level of the lexical categories, that is, the X° level. A verbal cluster is a head-to-head adjunction structure therefore a structure of category V°. Hence a cluster is eligible for a word formation process. A particular instance of such a word formation process is the deverbal nominalization by category conversion. In German, an infinitival verb can be freely converted into a noun. Analogously, a verbal cluster can be freely nominalized.

(11) a. [verstreichen]$_{V°}$ – [das Verstreichen]$_{DP}$[51]
          expire the expire(ing)

      b. [Deadlines [verstreichen lassen müssen]$_{VC}$]$_{VP}$
          [deadlines [expire let must]]

      c. das [Verstreichenlassen]$_{N°}$ der/von Deadlines
          the [letting-expire] the-GEN/of deadlines

      d. das [Verstreichenlassenmüssen]$_{N°}$ der/von Deadlines
          the [expire-let-must] the-GEN/of deadlines
          'the having to let the deadlines expire'

      e. * the let(ting) expire (of) deadlines

Since the cluster nominalization presupposes a cluster, and clusters are an OV phenomenon, cluster nominalization is absent in VO languages.

Intermediate summary and discussion: the sixteen syntactic characteristics listed above constitute substantive evidence for the syntactic differentiation

---

[51] V°(-cluster) nominalization must be distinguished from VP-nominalization. The latter is possible in English, too, of course. Thanks to Sam Featherston for providing example (iii). In German, NPs are head initial, VPs are head final. Hence it is easy to identify (i) as involving an NP, and (ii) as involving a VP.

(i)   das Verstreichenlassenmüssen der/von Deadlines (=11d) VC nominalization
(ii)   dein [die Deadlines verstreichen lassen müssen]$_{VP}$ VP nominalization
       your [the deadlines-ACC expire let must]
(iii) This [letting deadlines expire]$_{VP}$ gives the department a bad name.

between the clausal and the (optionally) clustering clause union variant of infinitival complements. These differences are a challenge, and their adequate coverage is a criterion of success for grammar theory. The clustering variant is monosentential, the clausal variant is bisentential. The *obligatorily* clustering infinitives pattern with the clustering variant of the *optionally* clustering ones. The crucial question is this, therefore: are the two constructions derivationally related or not? Current approaches try to provide a positive answer. In the author's opinion, the answer is no. The two constructions are independently base-generated, given that there are two convergent but independent constructional pathways.

The evidence for the monosentential syntactic organization of the clause structure is bipartite. First, there is clear evidence for a cluster. This is the compactness property and the IPP construction, that is, the verb order variation within the cluster. Second, there is a large class of phenomena that confirm the absence of a clausal boundary of an infinitival complement, that is, the clause union property. The evidence is sufficiently differentiated (scrambling; extraposition; domains of negation, tense and quantification; binding domain for pronominals and anaphors; ordering template for pronouns; matrix passive; topicalization) so that it leaves virtually no room for doubts on the monosentential status of the clustering construction.

The following subsection presents a brief synopsis of current approaches to modelling the clustering plus clause union phenomenon. It will turn out that the currently favoured toolkit of grammar theory does not provide the right kind of tool for handling clause union and clustering. The standard strategy is a derivational one. It seeks a way of deriving the clustering variant from the clausal variant by movement.

The first obstacle is *optionality*. Derivational accounts need triggers. But there is no trigger. The clausal variant is well formed and there is no need to convert it into a clustering variant.

The second obstacle is the *clause union property*. Derivations conserve the base relations. If a DP is moved out of its local domain, the chain of movement relates the moved item to its source of origin. Since A-movement is locally bound and does not cross clausal boundaries, the clause union properties cannot be captured by A-movement, that is, by moving elements of the infinitival control clause into the matrix clause. A'-movement, however, is not adequate either since A'-moved items are reconstructed for binding and scoping. But the clause union phenomena show that reconstruction is not at work. Movement approaches leave the clausal complement intact, so there is no clause union in the strict sense. Thus, these approaches have no easy way of accounting for the absence of an embedded clausal domain in clause union constructions.

The third obstacle is *compactness* of the cluster. Compactness is a property of the verb cluster, that follows immediately from a head-to-head merger structure. The derivational formation of a syntactic cluster, however, would require moving the verbal head out of a clausal constituent in order to form a minimal syntactic unit – namely the cluster – together with the matrix verb(s). This is a kind of head movement for which there is no independent evidence available. Another frequently suggested scenario is VP-evacuation followed by roll-up of the emptied VP(s). But in this scenario, there is no other way of guaranteeing compactness. Since there are full VP constituents involved, these constituents are each a possible target of extraposition. But extraposition destroys compactness. Most derivational accounts therefore fail to capture compactness and thereby fail to capture the essence of this construction. [52]

Fourth, current accounts do not reach the level of explanatory adequacy. They fail to provide an answer for the *grammatical motive* of this construction. Why should UG require or permit clustering and clause union clustering and why should these phenomena be OV-bound phenomena (see the following subsection)? The mechanisms suggested for handling clustering and clause union in current proposals could just as well apply in VO languages. But there is no VO language with clustering and clause union.[53]

7.5.3   How to derive clustering and clause union? V-clustering in grammar theory

The title question of this subsection is the most general way of asking how to adequately analyse the clustering and clause union construction. It subsumes at least the following sub-issues:

- What is the descriptively and explanatorily adequate way of modelling the *clause union syndrome* (CUS)?
- Why should this constructional freedom be restricted to OV languages, given the fact that the universal tool kit of grammar theory put into operation in current analyses could apply to VO structures in like manner?

---

[52] This approach is pursued by Koopman and Szabolcsi (2000). In order to avoid massive overgeneration, they are obliged to invoke numerous ad hoc filter devices to enforce compactness by filtering out non-compact orders.

[53] Romance 'restructuring' is not clustering (cf. Cinque 2001). It is a transparency phenomenon due to the free alternation between VP and CP complementation. Romance restructuring constructions are not compact and the verbs are always in their canonical order. Germanic clusters are compact and allow for verb order variation (see appendix).

- Should grammar theory allow for a *perfectly optional* choice between clause union and sentential complementation? (Yes – but only if clause union is not to be characterized as a derivational continuation of the sentential infinitival construction.)

The predominant strategy of modelling the grammar of clustering has been a derivational one from the beginning. Clustering has been regarded as the result of syntactic processes that operate on clausal structures of verbal complementation. Various kinds of syntactic tools have been employed: verbs may raise out of their projection and adjoin to a higher verb or to a functional head;[54] or verbal projections are emptied by removing everything except the verbal head, before they are moved ('roll-up' hypothesis); or a given complement structure is restructured by means of 'reanalysis'. What these tools have in common is that they could be implemented in the grammar of any language. In other words, the various approaches remain silent on the following question: why is clustering absent in consistent VO languages and why should verbs cluster at all?

A descriptively adequate clustering theory should take a stand on the appropriateness of the generalization that clustering is closely correlated with head-final verbal projections (Haider 2003; Bobaljik 2004: 129). Head-initial languages do not cluster the verbs of stacked verbal projections, but in OV languages, stacked head-final projections generally seem to cluster. For clustering properties of OV languages of different language families, see Sells (1990) and Han *et al.* (2007) on Japanese and Korean.

The major theoretical challenge for derivational approaches to clustering is the compactness of the clusters, the clause union effects, and the verb order variations in the clusters. In the pioneering work of Evers (1975), compactness and clause union are captured by a combination of V°-movement (as a non-local process of V-to-V adjunction = V-raising) followed by massive 'tree pruning', that is, deletion of the clausal boundaries. Later, 'pruning' got replaced by 'reanalysis' at the cost of admitting two coexisting, distinct structural representations for a single clause (Haegeman and van Riemsdijk 1986). Pruning is a brute force way of obtaining clause union; reanalysis, on the other hand, merely stipulates clause union by admitting a bi-representational analysis, without independent evidence for this assumption.

A new family of derivational approaches has evolved under the premises of Kayne's antisymmetry theory. Versions of this approach have been proposed for Dutch and Hungarian (cf. Zwart 1995, 1996; Koopman and Szabolcsi 2000).

---

[54] This, plus a powerful pruning mechanism, is Arnold Evers's (1975) original concept of 'verb raising'.

However, neither the clause union properties nor the compactness of the cluster received a straightforward solution. Koopman and Szabolcsi suggest an analysis of clustering which makes use of only phrasal syntax and XP-movement. The clause-final series of Vs is derived by first evacuating the VPs and then moving the VPs that contain only their verbal heads to the left of the VP of the selecting verb. Compactness is enforced, but not accounted for, by stipulating a series of filters (for a review see section 2.3 of Williams 2004). What drives these movements in OV, but forbids them in VO, remains entirely unclear.

An immediate way of covering the clustering properties is one that assumes base-generating the cluster (see Steedman 1985; Haider 1993; Kathol 2000), at the cost of admitting two systems of argument satisfaction. One way is the standard way of linking (a variant of *functional application*), the other way is pooling and relating the arguments provided by the verbs in the cluster (a variant of *functional composition*). Note that there is a convergence of the latter approach with the reanalysis approach, but only in terms of the resulting surface structure constituency.

The problem with the biclausal structure as a starting point in a derivational analysis is this: in order to capture the properties of clustering, the biclausal structure conserved in the derivation (by antecedent-trace relations) must be ignored completely. In the reanalysis approach (Haegeman and van Riemsdijk 1986), it merely serves as a kind of d-structure that is non-derivationally augmented with a reanalysed representation that contains a cluster. In the purely derivational approaches, this is an embarrassment. Although the embedded clause structure would be present all the time in the clustering variant (since derivations do not destroy structures), it must be ignored completely. The base-generation approach, on the other hand, entails the absence and unavailability of a biclausal representation in the clause union variant, but, on the other hand, it must provide means for the direct generation of the cluster and for its function as a complex VP head. So each approach has its specific price. The empirical and theoretical question is just which analysis is worth its price.

Here is an illustrative sample of the positions held in the research literature:

(i)   Verb raising + reanalysis/restructuring (OV)
                    Evers (1975); Haegeman and van Riemsdijk (1986); and later
(ii)   VP evacuation (VO) + head-to-head verb raising   Zwart (1995)
(iii)   VP evacuation (VO) + remnant VP fronting   Haegeman (2001)
(iv)   VP evacuation (VO) + 'roll-up'   Koopman and Szabolcsi (2000)
(v)   Base-generated variant subcategorization (OV)   Wurmbrand (2001)
(vi)   Base-generated verbal cluster (OV) + *flip*
                    Haider (1991); Jacobs (1992); Haider (2003); Williams (2004)

'OV' and 'VO' refer to the assumed base order in the proposals above. 'OV' means that German or Dutch are languages whose V-projection is generated as a head-final projection. 'VO' means that already the 'OV' structures are taken to be the result of a derivation that starts with a base order configuration that is a VO one (= English auxiliary order, postverbal objects). This is what followers of Kayne (1994) take for granted, without compelling empirical evidence (see the discussion of OV- and VO-related properties in chapter 2).

For the sake of concreteness, the following two sentences will be used as model sentences for illustrating the respective derivations. Note that these sentences are examples of non-sentential, obligatorily clustering infinitive constructions.

(1)   a. dass ich Lisa anrufen müssen werde   *German*
           that I Lisa up-phone have-to shall
           'that I shall have to phone up Lisa'

       b. dat ik Lisa op zal moeten bellen   *Dutch*
           that I Lisa up shall have-to phone
           'that I shall have to phone up Lisa'

In the standard analysis, the phrase structures assumed for (1) are structures with VP complementation (2a), like in English. The structure given in (2a) is the base structure that will be changed into a structure with a verb cluster. Since the German cluster order often is identical with the base order, (2a) can be used as a base order illustration. In Dutch, the base order never is a possible surface order, if the cluster does not involve a participle but only infinitival verbs. (2b) is ungrammatical as a surface order.

(2)   a.   dass ich [[[Lisa anrufen]$_{VP}$ müssen]$_{VP}$ werde]$_{VP}$ *German*

       b. * dat ik Lisa opbellen moeten zal   *Dutch*
             that I Lisa up-phone have-to shall
             'that I shall have to phone up Lisa'

In a VO-to-OV analysis *pace* Kayne, (1b) is taken to be derived from a base structure like (3a), which is identical with a VO structure as in English (3b):

(3)   a. dat ik [$_{VP}$ zal [$_{VP}$ moeten [$_{VP}$ opbellen Lisa]]]   *Dutch*

       b. that I [$_{VP}$ shall [$_{VP}$ have-to [$_{VP}$ up-phone Lisa]]]

In order to derive the surface structure (1b), obviously the object must be fronted, and the particle must get into a position preceding the verbs, too. Object fronting is not exotic, but particle fronting would be. Particles do not move; they are stranded. In Haider (2003) it is argued that the particle in (1b) is optionally stranded by locally flipping the sister constituents in the cluster, starting from the strictly OV order.

Note that in Dutch, infinitival clauses are banned from the midfield. This would mean that only non-clausal objects are fronted in the process of deriving the OV order. But for the clause union construction, the infinitival clause would have to be emptied by moving all elements out of the clause, way up into the midfield of the matrix clause (except for a clausal object). The most deeply embedded clause would have to be first evacuated into its matrix clause, and then this infinitival matrix is evacuated into the next higher matrix clause. Let us briefly check on this in German, and analyse (4a):

(4)   a. dass sie es hätten zu analysieren versuchen müssen
           that they it would-have to analyse try had-to
           'that they would have had to try to analyse it'

       b. dass sie [$_{VP}$hätten [$_{VP}$müssen[$_{VP}$versuchen [$_{CP}$ zu analysieren es]]]]
                                                                    alleged base order

       c. dass sie [$_{VP}$hätten [$_{VP}$müssen [[$_{CP}$ zu analysieren es]$_i$ [$_{VP}$versuchen e$_i$]]]]

       d. dass sie [$_{VP}$hätten [[[$_{CP}$zu analysieren es]$_i$ [$_{VP}$versuchen e$_i$]]$_j$ [$_{VP}$müssen e$_j$]]]

       e. dass sie es$_k$ [$_{VP}$hätten [[[$_{CP}$zu analysieren e$_k$]$_i$ [$_{VP}$versuchen e$_i$]]$_j$ [$_{VP}$müssen e$_j$]]]

The roll-up of the infinitival complements (clause, VPs) plus the long-distance extraction of the object of the infinitival clause (*es*) produces the required word order for (4a). But this surely does not produce the right kind of structure. First, the clause structure of the infinitival clause remains unaffected. Hence it provides an extraposition site, destroying compactness. Second, the evacuation of the clause (i.e. removal of any non-verbal material by shifting it to the matrix) is both unmotivated and insufficient. It does not capture the clause union properties since the movement is a variant of A'-movement and hence it would be reconstructed for binding, scoping, etc. In short, the analysis sketched above is a grammar-theoretical emergency measure rather than an insightful account.

What the advocates of these machineries fail to provide an answer for is the question as to why a language should bother at all with clause union. The cardinal question is the quest for a better understanding of the rationale of this ubiquitous option in OV grammars and its absence in VO systems. What the literature provides are technical proposals of how to patch up 'ordinary' grammars in order to enable them to capture the 'weird' clustering phenomena.

In the following paragraphs, the strategies offered in the literature will once more be briefly evaluated with respect to their success in capturing the grammatical properties of the clustering phenomena listed above.

(i) Verb raising plus restructuring (previously 'pruning') (Evers 1975; Haegeman and van Riemsdijk 1986)

In Evers's original proposal (1975), clustering and clause union are the result of two independent processes, namely 'verb raising' (5a), as right adjunction of the embedded verb to the selecting verb of the matrix, plus deletion of the headless structure ('pruning'). Pruning (5b) cuts out the VP headed by the raised verb and all higher projections above the VP. The result is clause union.

(5)   a. * dat ik [$_{VP}$ [$_{VP}$ [$_{VP}$Lisa [op bellen]] moeten] zal]   *Dutch*
              ⇒ iterative head-to-head adjunction
          that I Lisa up-phone have-to shall

       b.   dat ik [$_{VP}$ [$_{VP}$ [$_{VP}$Lisa [op ~~bellen~~]] ~~moeten+bellen~~] [$_V$° zal [$_V$° moeten
          bellen]]]   ⇒ *restructuring* (pruning)

       c.   dat ik [$_{VP}$Lisa [op] e$_i$] [$_V$° zal [$_V$° moeten bellen]$_i$]
          'that I shall have to phone up Lisa'

Since pruning is structure deletion and structure deletion is too powerful a mechanism for a grammar of human languages because it wipes out structure generated in the derivation of a clause (recoverability problem),[55] Haegeman and van Riemsdijk (1986) replaced pruning by 'restructuring' which in fact amounts to the simultaneous assignment of a *double* and *incongruent* phrase structure, namely the assignment of the clausal complement structure plus the assignment of a cluster structure within a simple clause.

Why this secondary structure should have the properties it has to have and why a double structure is admitted by UG, but only for clause union infinitivals, is an unresolved issue. The pruning and the restructuring approach both remain silent on the trigger question, on the descriptive as well as the meta-theoretical level. A trigger on the descriptive level is a grammar-internal mechanism that starts the machinery in the presence of a particular feature or structural context. On the meta-grammatical level, 'triggering' means an understanding as to why these processes should be embodied in particular grammars.

(ii) VP evacuation (VO) plus verb raising   (Zwart 1995)

According to Zwart (1995: 2), 'the word order variation in Continental West Germanic verb clusters results from two different movement processes: 1. *adjunction* of an infinitival verb to a modal verb (X°-movement); 2. raising of a *participle*

---

[55] Note: restructuring would have to delete not only VPs but also CPs, and any functional projections in between in order to account for clause union in verb-raising variants of control constructions.

to the spec position of an auxiliary verb (XP-movement)'. The reason for this differentiation is the fact that the participle + auxiliary order is variable, that is, both the German order (6b) and the inverted order (6a) are grammatical. For infinitives, only the 'inverted' order (6a), that is, selecting auxiliary before selected infinitive, is grammatical.

(6)   a. ...dat Jan kan werken   *Dutch*
           that Jan can work-INF

        b. ...dat Jan gewerkt heeft
           that Jan worked-PARTICIPLE has

Here is the derivation for the model sentence. Since Zwart presupposes a VO base structure, the derivation starts from a structure identical with a corresponding English sentence:

(7)   a. dat ik [$_{VP}$ zal [$_{VP}$ moeten [$_{VP}$ bellen op Lisa]]]   *Dutch*
           that I shall have-to phone up Lisa
                                   ⇒ iterative head-to-head adjunction

        b. dat ik [$_{VP}$ zal moeten bellen [$_{VP}$ ~~moeten bellen~~ [$_{VP}$ ~~bellen~~ op Lisa]]]
                                   ⇒ particle movement

        c. dat ik [op$_i$ [$_{VP}$ zal moeten bellen [$_{VP}$ ~~moeten bellen~~ [$_{VP}$ ~~bellen~~
           e$_i$ Lisa]]]]   ⇒ object shift

        d. dat ik [Lisa$_j$ [op$_i$ [$_{VP}$ zal moeten bellen [$_{VP}$ ~~moeten bellen~~ [$_{VP}$ ~~bellen~~
           e$_i$ e$_j$]]]]]

Let us evaluate this implementation. First, it is wanting an answer to the trigger question for VO vs OV. Second, it overgenerates (sec 8) if participle fronting is implemented as *XP*-fronting, because of disrespecting compactness. The fronted XP is a VP and the VP is an extraposition site, in Dutch as well as in German. But, no extraposed material may intervene between any two verbs in the cluster, neither in Dutch nor in German.

(8)   * dass ich [[*erklärt, warum das nicht stimmen kann*] *habe*]   *German*
           that I [[explained why this not correct-be can] have]
           'that I have explained why this cannot be correct'

Third, the derivation has to take care of particle stranding since in OV languages, a particle precedes the verb unless it is stranded by verb movement. 'Particle movement' would be an ad hoc operation since particles do not move. In VO languages with particle stranding, there are different particle positions (which are in fact the different stranding positions corresponding to the different verb positions in the VP shell structure), but in an OV language, the particle position is invariant, and it is the position immediately preceding the verb (cluster). In Dutch, particles may be stranded within the cluster, but the positions are positions where a particle verb may independently appear (Haider 2003). This is illustrated in (9) compared with (10). For each non-final verb position in the cluster (9b,c,d) there is a variant with a stranded particle at this position and the main verb to the right.

(9) a. [zou [kunnen [hebben *meegezongen*]]]   *Dutch*
         would be-able-to have together-sung

     b. [zou [kunnen [*meegezongen* hebben]]]

     c. [zou *meegezongen* kunnen hebben]

     d. [*meegezongen* zou kunnen hebben]

(10) a.   zou kunnen *mee* hebben *gezongen*   (stranding variant of 9b)

     b.   zou *mee* kunnen hebben *gezongen*   (stranding variant of 9c)

     c.   *mee* zou kunnen hebben *gezongen*   (stranding variant of 9d)

     d. * [*gezongen* [zou [kunnen [*mee* [hebben]]]]]

It is a robust fact that the particle must not follow the verb it belongs to in the cluster (10d). So, the stranding variants must be the result of local *rightward* movement of the verb in the cluster (see Haider 2003). Moreover, there cannot be any leftward movement producing stranding in the cluster, since in this case, (10d) would have to be grammatical. In the clear case of leftward movement, namely V2, the particle is stranded.

Fourth, head movement accounts for clause union fail for the clustering variants of control infinitivals since this would require long-distance head movement. This is not only an unwanted property of head movement but it is clearly ungrammatical if applied to clausal infinitives: XP extraction out of extraposed clausal infinitive is grammatical, but not for verbal heads (see **Property o** in section 7.5.2).

(iii) VP evacuation (VO) + remnant VP fronting   (Haegeman 2001)

Another proposal takes clustering to be derivable from a VO base structure with the (finite) verb moved to a functional head position to the left, and the remnant VP fronted to its spec. But the derivation of our model sentence in (11) again reveals a serious problem. If the object and the particle remain in the VP and the VP is fronted, the particle ends up in the wrong position, namely preceding the object. The object cannot be moved any further because the fronted VP is opaque for movement, being a moved phrase in a functional spec position. So we might try the following derivation (11a–d). (11e) is an original illustration of Haegeman's.

(11)   a. dat ik [$_{VP}$ zal [$_{VP}$ moeten [$_{VP}$ bellen op Lisa]]]   *Dutch* 'base order'
                                                                        $\Rightarrow$ V-movement

    b. dat ik [zal$_i$ [moeten$_j$ [bellen$_k$ [e$_i$ [e$_j$ [e$_k$ op Lisa]]]]]] $\Rightarrow$ Object-shift

    c. dat ik [Lisa$_m$ [zal$_i$ [moeten$_j$ [bellen$_k$ [e$_i$ [e$_j$ [e$_k$ op e$_m$]]]]]]]]
                                                                        $\Rightarrow$ VP-fronting

    d. dat ik [Lisa$_m$ [[e$_i$ [e$_j$ [e$_k$ op e$_m$]]]$_q$ [zal$_i$ [moeten$_j$ [bellen$_k$ e$_q$]]]]]
                                                                        Dutch surface order

    e. da [Valère [$_{FP}$ [$_{XP}$ ... [$_{AgrOP}$ [$_{VP}$ t_{su} [t_v en us]]]] [$_F$ kuopt] t_{xp}]]
                                                                        Westflemish
        that Valère a house buys   (Haegeman 2001: 214)
        'that Valère buys a house'

Obviously, this derivation is faulty. In order to get the particle in the right order, we first have to move out the object to a higher spec position (spec-AO?) and then move the emptied VP. But this movement must target a lower position and therefore it violates the principle of cyclic application. Note finally that each of the verbs individually moves to higher F-positions. So the problem of how to account for the *variable* orders is ignored. Finally, compactness is unaccounted for. It is a fact of VO grammars that non-verbal material may intervene between any of the V-projections involved.[56] So, in this style of derivation, there is ample room for interveners, each of which will produce an order that violates compactness.

(iv) VP evacuation (VO) plus multiple fronting
                                            (cf. Koopman and Szabolcsi 2000)

While in Haegeman's proposal, the moved VP is stripped of its verbal head, Koopman and Szabolcsi (2000: 156–8) propose to move the VP once all non-verbal elements have been evacuated. This proposal trails Kayne's (1994) postulate that OV orders are derived from VO structures by (unmotivated) movement of all non-verbal material out of the VP to positions on the left ('evacuation'). With this premise as a starting point, the verb order variation is characterized as an iterated process of pied-piping VP-fronting (referred to as 'roll-up').

(12)   a. dat ik [$_{VP}$ zal [$_{VP}$ moeten [$_{VP}$ bellen op Lisa]]]
                                                    $\Rightarrow$ evacuation of the particle
    b. dat ik [op$_i$ [$_{VP}$ zal [$_{VP}$ moeten [$_{VP}$ bellen e$_i$ Lisa]]]]
                                                    $\Rightarrow$ evacuation of the object

---

[56] Here is my favourite example from Quirk *et al.* (1986: § 8.20, p. 495) with an adverbial in each slot:

    (i)   The new theory *certainly* may *possibly* have *indeed* been *badly* formulated

c. dat ik [Lisa$_j$ [op$_i$ [$_{VP}$ zal [$_{VP}$ moeten [$_{VP}$ bellen e$_i$ e$_j$]]]]]

d. dat ik [$_{RefP}$ Lisa [$_{AgrS}$ [$_{PredP}$ op zal] [[$_{CP}$ moeten] [[$_{CP}$ bellen]
[–]]]]]]]]]]]]]]]]]]]]]]]]]]]]]]][57]

For the particular Dutch sentence, (12c) would suffice for deriving the desired word order. The structure actually proposed is (12d). In the end it is more complicated, however, because the theory is intended to cover clustering in general, based on the evidence from Dutch and Hungarian. So let us apply this theory to German, and in particular to our model sentence (13a). Again, the VO structure (13b) is the starting point, according to the 'OV is derived from VO' maxim. First we have to move the lowest VP to the spec of the next higher one (13c). Then we take this resulting complex VP and front it to the spec of the matrix VP (13d).

(13)   a. dass ich Lisa anrufen müssen werde   target
             that I Lisa up-phone have-to shall

         b. dass ich [$_{VP}$ werde [$_{VP}$ müssen [$_{VP}$ rufen-an Lisa]]]
                                                            alleged VO base order
             that I [shall [have-to [phone up Lisa]]]

         c. dass ich [$_{VP}$ werde [[$_{VP}$ rufen an Lisa]$_i$ [$_{VP}$ müssen e$_i$]]]
                                                            ⇐ VP-fronting

         d. dass ich [[[$_{VP}$ rufen an Lisa]$_i$ [$_{VP}$ müssen e$_i$]]$_j$ [$_{VP}$ werde e$_j$]]
                                                            ⇐ VP-fronting

(13d) is not the target order (13a) yet. The particle and the object are still intervening. They must be moved to the left. In the roll-up construction, they are captured in the spec of the spec of a VP, since the first VP has been moved to a spec position, and then it is moved to the next higher spec. The spec (of a spec) is an opaque domain for extraction. So they could only be fronted to the spec of their mother VP. This would not suffice, however, since in the clustering construction, the object of the infinitive may scramble just as in a simple clause, that is, the object must be able to precede the matrix subject. Note that evacuating the VP before the roll-up operation would run into problems with the cyclic application of rules since roll-up targets lower positions than fronting an object to a higher functional projection.

The shortcomings of this approach are easy to list (for a more detailed assessment, see Williams 2004: 188–200). First, it has no way of enforcing compactness, since the roll-up of VPs and higher functional projections, up to CP, allows at each

---

[57] This is a sketch of the original derivation. Be aware that the number of closing brackets for (12d) is *thirty*, and that the tree spreads over three pages. Note: This is not meant to be a counterargument in itself, but merely the reason why I did not bother filling in the '[–]' portion in (12d).

step for extraposition. The authors acknowledge this problem and suggest *filters* (Koopman and Szabolcsi 2000: 193–4) for filtering out the non-compact structures. But having to resort to filters is a syntactic capitulation in the face of the overgeneration of a system. Evidently, an overgenerating system is empirically inadequate and filters are just an ad hoc patch-up device. Filters are obviously the price one has to pay if one honestly insists that clustering is the result of phrasal movement.

The approach remains silent on the typological issue and it has no straight-forward account of the fact that the clustering variants come with a pool of verb order variations. Finally, the model lacks a motivation for the complex derivational machinery. Why should a grammar insist on roll-up if the input to the machinery is grammatically well-formed already? An understanding of the grammatical motivation is indispensable for a reasonable insight into this area of grammar.

Since this model is developed in order to capture the data of Dutch and Hungarian, a word on Hungarian is due here for the interested reader. From the perspective of English (or any other VO language), clustering constructions like those of West Germanic OV languages appear to be out of the ordinary. However, clustering is not a peculiarity of West Germanic. A non-Indo-European language like Hungarian displays clustering properties with virtually the same classes of verbs and with strikingly similar syntactic effects.

Consistently head-initial languages (i.e. VO languages and VSO languages) do not cluster nor do they reorder non-finite verbs of stacked verbal projections. Hence, a proper understanding of clustering and cluster reordering requires an insightful modelling of the grammatical causality between being head final on the one hand and clustering on the other hand. Hungarian is no exception to this generalization. Hungarian is clustering and it is surely not a standard VO language, contrary to the present day assumptions (see É. Kiss and van Riemsdijk 2004). According to É. Kiss (1987) and literature cited there, the Hungarian VP is 'non configurational'. As noted in the introductory section of the book, 'typologists do tend to classify Hungarian as an OV language on the basis of various properties' (É. Kiss 1987: 36). In fact, a language like Hungarian is neither OV nor VO. It arguably is, like Yiddish and like the Slavic languages, a language with flexible directionality for at least the V° head. So it is a language with optional V-movement in the VP and thus combines the structural properties of OV and VO (see Haider and Rosengren 2003; Haider 2005b).

(v) Base-generating phrasal complements, from VP to CP

(Wurmbrand 2001)

Wurmbrand (2001) tries to capture the difference between *obligatorily* clause union (= monosentential) and *optionally* clause union complements (plus an additional differentiation in terms of clause union properties) by category differences for the infinitival complements, and the respective selection requirement of the selecting verbs. In principle, this is what we are familiar with from English. In English, infinitival constructions may be VP (e.g. perception verbs) or IP (ECM and subject raising constructions) or CP complements (control infinitive), and there are verbs (e.g. *expect*, *want*, etc.) with an optional choice for the phrasal category of the complement.

(14)   a. She[i] expected [$_{CP}$ PRO[i] to meet me there]
        b. She expected [$_{IP}$ me to meet her there]

Wurmbrand (2001) replaces the biclausal vs monoclausal distinction by a four-fold one. This fourfold distinction reflects a fourfold differentiation of base-generated structure above the VP: functional restructuring infinitives are VPs with the matrix verb in a functional projection (Mod, Aux, etc.); the other infinitives have lexical matrix predicates that embed either just VPs ('restructuring' infinitives) or vPs/TPs ('reduced non-restructuring' infinitives) or CPs ('non-restructuring' infinitives): see table 7.4 below. Her notion of 'restructuring' is a purely allusive one. With this term, she refers to the classes of constructions discussed in restructuring approaches. For a detailed evaluation of this model and its shortcomings, see Reis and Sternefeld (2004). Here, just a few general properties will be highlighted.

First, like the other models, this approach leaves us without an answer to the trigger question for VO vs OV. It could just as well be implemented in a VO grammar. Second, it has no way of capturing compactness since all infinitival complements are phrasal, with a VP as the smallest complement category. But, as emphasized excessively, a VP is an extraposition site. So, extraposed material would be allowed to disrupt compactness (15b). This issue is not addressed at all in the monograph.

Third, it does not provide a principled account for the verb order variation in the cluster (because in this analysis there is no cluster). Fourth, scope properties do not follow unless special covert movement is assumed. Fifth, it would not rule out subjectless infinitival complements on structural grounds since 'capital VPs' (that is, subjectless V-projections, with the subject in the 'little' vP) are admitted as clause union variants of control verbs (16).

(15)   a. weil der/den Brief einzuwerfen vergessen wurde, der hier liegt
            since the-NOM / the-ACC letter in-to-put forgotten was, that here lies
            'since it was forgotten to post the letter that is lying here'

        b. weil *der/den Brief einzuwerfen, *der hier liegt*, vergessen wurde
            since *the-NOM / the-ACC letter in-to-put, that here lies, forgotten
            was

Table 7.4 *Categories of infinitival complementation according to Wurmbrand (2001)*

A. *functional* restructuring		VP (Mod., Aux., etc)	
B. lexical restructuring	a. restructuring	VP V	*versuchen* (try)
	b. reduced non-restructuring	{vPs, TPs} V	*hoffen* (hope)
	c. non-restructuring	CP V	*bedauern* (regret)

(15a) can be structured ambiguously, either as *clausal* (ACC-object), or a *clustering* (ACC-to-NOM). (15b) allows only a clausal embedding because of the extraposed relative clause that intervenes. And in this case, the clause union variant with the nominative on the object of the infinitive is ungrammatical.

(16) a. Es ist möglich, dass getanzt wird
          it is possible, that danced is
          'It is possible that there is dancing'

      b. Es ist möglich, geliebt/*getanzt zu werden
          it is possible loved/danced to be
          'It is possible to be loved/danced'

      c. dass beachtet/*getanzt zu werden versucht wurde
          that noticed/danced to be tried was
          'that one tried to be noticed/danced'

An infinitival clause requires an argumental subject (and so does its cluster variant). If the cluster variant is – as Wurmbrand assumes – analysed as a base-generated VP *without subject* (note: this is in violation of the projection principle if the subject is considered to be an argument of the verb), the contrast in (16c) must be derived from an obligatory control property. But there is no PRO subject available in the structure (since it is a VP without subject).

(vi) Base-generated V° cluster
           (Haider 1991; Jacobs 1992; Haider 2003; Williams 2002, 2004)

   The facts of West Germanic infinitival complementation call for a theory that provides at least two radically different kinds of structures. One kind of structure is the familiar bisentential structure with the infinitive phrase as a clausal complement. The other kind of structure is the structure required for the monosentential cluster construction. The standard theory does not yet provide adequate tools for capturing these circumstances since it has been tailored to the needs of VO-type structures.

The preceding discussion showed that at present, none of the various derivational accounts is able to pass reasonable criteria of descriptive and explanatory adequacy. The main stumbling block is the syntax of the cluster: the cluster is a compact unit, but it allows for verb order variation within this unit, and it correlates with a wide range of clause union properties. Derivational approaches fail to capture the clause union properties because derivations conserve the sentential base structure. So, ad hoc mechanisms have to be invoked. Furthermore, derivational mechanisms fail to capture the compactness properties. Again, ad hoc means like complex filters are introduced. This just underlines the basic failure. The system itself, without ad hoc interventions, would not guarantee the well formed outcome.

In the base-generation approach, the clustering variant is analysed as a separate syntactic structure, not as a derivationally produced variant. The variation between clausal and clustering constructions is a variation of two alternative options of projecting an infinitival construction. The grammar provides a clausal structure, and alternatively, there is the cluster option. This is an obligatory structure for some infinitival constructions (bare infinitives, participles) and an optional choice for others.

The cluster is a compact constituent of verbal heads and co-predicates[58] because it is a construction *with head-to-head merger* ($X°$ adjunction structure).[59] In terms of theta management, the cluster is a complex predicate, that is, a syntactically complex head structure with – in principle – more than one theta-providing head. So, we need novel means of theta management for the cluster. These means have to be conservative, however. For a trivial cluster, that is a single verb, the mechanism is the standard theta discharge mechanism. For a complex predicate we have to find out how the argument structures of the verbs in the cluster are pooled, and how they map onto the format of a single verb, so that the argument structure of the cluster can be dealt with just like the argument structure of a simple verb in a simple clause.

---

[58] 'Co-predicates' refer to secondary predicates (result predicates, directional predicates, etc. in the form of particles, adjectives or PPs) that form a complex predicate with the verb, with the same argument-sharing/pooling properties as the verbal 'co-predicates' in the cluster:

   (i)   Sie hat mich [hinaus/gesund gelacht]
          she has me [out-of/healthy laughed]
          'She laughed me out of (some place)/made me healthy by laughing'
   (ii)   Sie wird es [fallen lassen]
          she will it [drop let]

[59] This is not a bizarre property of verbs. In standard analyses of clitic placement, the series of clitics adjoined for instance to the finite verb in its functional head position form a cluster.

We have to distinguish two cases. The first case is the trivial case. There is only one verb with a specified argument structure (theta grid) in the cluster, namely the lexical main verb, and all other verbs are auxiliaries or quasi-auxiliaries (modals, epistemic verbs, etc.). So, the theta grid of the cluster will be identical with the theta grid of the main verb. The complicated case is the second one. There is more than one verb in the cluster with a specified theta grid. In this case the theta grids must be pooled and integrated. For a more detailed exposition of the technical implementation see Haider (2001a).

From a technical point of view, pooling the arguments of the verbs into a single grid amounts to *functional composition* (prior to *functional application*). For implementations of functional composition in other models of grammar for modelling verb clustering (HPSG or Categorial Grammar) see Kathol (2000) or Steedman (1985).

Note that it is the *syntax* (cluster formation based on verbal dependency relations implemented as morphosyntactic selection relations) that *constrains* the applicability of clustering and thereby the applicability of functional composition (see appendix 7.7.2). Otherwise, functional composition would be too powerful a tool.

(17) provides an illustrative sketch. The source of the illustration is a handout of Wolfgang Sternefeld from 2002, with the title 'Recipes for preparing the verbal dumpling'.

(17)

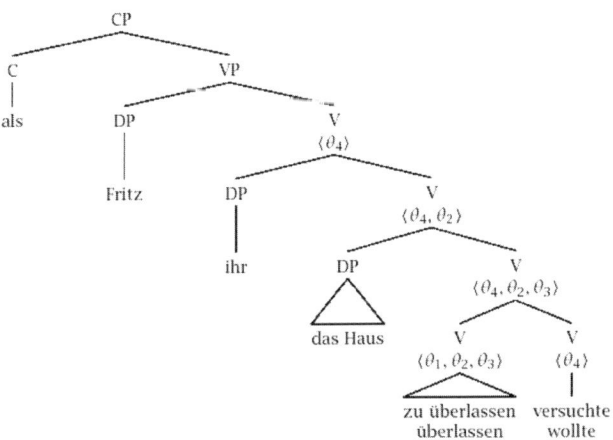

when Fritz (to) her the house (to) leave tried / (to) leave wanted
'when Fritz tried/wanted to leave the house to her'

The verbs in the cluster *pool* their arguments:

- The argument grid of the dependent verb replaces the object slot of the argument grid of the selecting verb (*grid importation*).
- The argument grid is *integrated*: the controlled argument is identified with the controller. Identifier: *zu* (to). This is possible only for the *unmarked structural argument*. Hence it is grammatical with the DO of control verbs.
- The result is an argument grid for the cluster.

Note that passivizing the cluster construction produces a nominative on the object of the embedded verb, since this is the object argument of the cluster.

7.5.4   *The grammatical causality of clustering: an OV phenomenon*

The clustering constructions raise several non-trivial questions for an adequate grammar-theoretic coverage and modelling. *First*, what is the grammar-theoretic motivation for the existence of cluster constructions instead of stacked V-projections? *Second*, why is clustering correlated with head-final projections?[60] *Third*, why is clustering obligatory in some contexts (bare infinitival and participle selection) and optional in others (clausal infinitival construction in German)?

Let us start with the first two questions and compare the structures found in German with auxiliary plus main verb combinations in VO. In English, as mentioned earlier, there is good evidence for stacked VPs (1a), whereas in German, the evidence points to the conclusion that the verbs are clustering (1c) rather than projecting separate VPs (1b).

(1)   a. $[_{VP} V_1 [_{VP} V_2 [_{VP} V_3 \ldots]]]$ VO order (English)
    b. $[_{VP} [_{VP} [_{VP \ldots} V_3] V_2] V_1]$ OV order (German)
    c. $[_{VP} \ldots [_{V}°[_{V}° V_3 V_2] V_1]]$ OV order (German)

A look at the bracketed representations in (1) provides a first cue for a critical structural factor. In (1a), but crucially not in (1b), the left-to-right order corresponds with the top-to-bottom organization of the phrase. (1a) is a syntactic

---

[60] Contrary to Koopman and Szabolcsi's claim (2000), Hungarian should be analysed as a VO language, with DP fronting into pre-VP topic and focus positions. As for the verbal complex formation, the obligatory order of verb and particle (namely V + particle, e.g. be (*in*) menni (*go-inf*) vs *menni be; see Koopman and Szabolcsi 2000:16f.) is evidence for an OV base order. In VO, particles follow the position of the verb. The possible reorderings are the result of two processes: (i) fronting of the finite verb, and (ii) optional reordering in the verbal complex of the Dutch type, that is left adjunction.

structure that is friendly to a parser (see chapter 1).[61] In a right-branching structure (1a), the parser can unambiguously identify the top-most node of the projection after encountering the first element of the projection, namely V_1. (1b), the left-branching structure, is not parser friendly, however. In order to determine the root node, or alternatively, in order to open the appropriate number of brackets, the parser would have to guess the depth of embedding of the element the constituent starts with. General top-down information on the possible structure of a VP will not help guessing because the number of auxiliaries is not context dependent. Structure (1b) is a case of centre embedding as the result of stacking instances of the same category, namely VP. This is known to be an extremely parser unfriendly data structure.

Here is the clue for clustering. The clustering construction, instead of stacked phrasal complements, narrows down the domain of structural uncertainty from an unbounded phrasal domain (e.g. stacked VPs) to a local domain, namely the verbal cluster. When the parser meets V_1 and cannot decide whether this is the main verb or not, the domain of uncertainty is small and local.

These considerations suggest an answer to the first question: clustering constructions enhance parser friendliness for head-final projections. So, if UG requires clustering instead of stacking VPs, this is a way to guarantee grammar–parser fit. It does not yet answer the second question, however. Parser friendliness is not sufficient for establishing a grammar-driven condition. If there is a context of obligatory clustering there must be a *grammatical* principle that enforces clustering. Parser friendliness by itself is a performance property and would not be strong enough to yield obligatoriness. Only in the perspective of cognitive evolution of grammars could parser friendliness have been a driving force in the selection of UG principles. A UG principle to this extent has been proposed in Haider (1992/2000) and in later work, namely the BBC.

BBC (*basic branching constraint*): projection-internal branching nodes of the (functionally or lexically extended) projection line *follow* their sister node.

The BBC as a principle of UG forbids right-branching basic projections and their functional or lexical extensions. Therefore, the BBC rules out a structure like (1b) if the VP nodes belong to an *extended projection* of a VP.

An extended projection is either a *functionally extended projection* or a *lexically extended projection*. The functional extension is the cascade of functional projections on top of the lexical projections targeted by overt head movement of

---

[61] The data-to-parser fit is optimal if the parser – a left corner parser – can simultaneously operate bottom up and top down, that is, with continuous data processing (bottom up) plus grammar guidance (top-down information on possible structures). This presupposes right-branching structures.

the head of the lexical projection. The lexical extension is a cascade of selected lexical projections whose pooled lexical features are equivalent to the feature format of a single verb. This amounts to the following situation: the verbs in the stacked VP do not introduce arguments, or else the arguments are pooled. The verbs are related by morphosyntactic government relations and argument merger. There is only one verb that introduces an event variable. These conditions single out auxiliary and modal verbs (no argument structure, no event variable), and verbs of perception, if the event variable is not instantiated.[62] These are obligatorily clustering verbs in German. The types of obligatorily clustering verbs are listed in (2) and illustrated in (3), in the respective order:

(2)   a. V° governs bare infinitival V°:
          werden (future tense aux.), modals, causative verbs.[63]

       b. V° governs past participle V°:
          werden (passive aux.); *haben, sein* (perfect tense aux.)

       c. V° governs bare infinitival *zu*+V°:
          scheinen (seem); *haben, sein* (deontic)

(3)   a. dass sie ihn *fragen* wird/kann/ließ
          that she him ask will/can/let

       b. dass er *gestoppt* wurde/hat
          that he stopped was/has

       c. dass er *zu stoppen* scheint/hat/ist
          that he to stop seems/has/is
          'that he seems/has to stop' / 'that he is to be stopped'

Having briefly sketched the necessary background, we can return to the question under discussion, namely: why is clustering in the relevant contexts obligatory in German and Dutch (and other OV languages)? The answer is this: clustering is

---

[62] Note that the well-known peculiarity of infinitival perception verb constructions, namely, the direct perception quality, is a consequence of a single event variable:

   (i) Ich hörte, dass er sein Büro verließ
       I heard that he his office left   (indirect or direct perception)
       'I heard that he left his office'
   (ii) Ich hörte ihn sein Büro verlassen
       I heard him his office leave   (direct perception only)
       'I heard him leave his office'

[63] Perception verbs and *lassen* (let) cluster obligatorily, but they do *not obligatorily* yield a passive effect. This means the subject of the infinitival is not obligatorily inactivated, which implies that the cluster is either not base generated or that the ECM construction that these verbs instantiate is the result of an exceptional argument pooling (see Lee-Schoenfeld (2007) for a derivational way of deriving this result).

obligatory in an extended V-projection because BBC rules out VP-stacking for head-final projections:

(4)   a. * $[_{VP} [_{VP} [_{VP \dots} V_3] V_2] V_1]$ OV   order with stacked VPs

       b. $[_{VP} V_1 [_{VP} V_2 [_{VP} V_3 \dots]]]$ VO (cf. English)

       c. $[_{VP} \dots [_{V}°[_{V}° V_3 V_2] V_1]]$ OV order with clustering

(4a) is ruled out by the BBC. It forbids a *right* daughter for nodes on the main projection line of a projection. (4b), a head-initial (extended) projection is well formed with respect to the BBC: there are no left brackets adjacent to each other. This is just another way of expressing the fact that there are no right daughters of nodes on the main projection line. The right daughter is always a node of the projection line (or, in other words, the target of merger).

(4c) is the grammatical alternative for (4a) that does not violate the BBC. The projection line of the VP starts with the highest V° node. It is the projection line of a simple VP. This is the answer to the third question raised at the beginning of this subsection.

Let us summarize and recapitulate the main points by means of the tree diagrams in (5).[64] They are intentionally drawn in horizontal layers in order to make clear the various depth of embeddings in terms of layers. (5a) is a stack of V-projections in a head-initial projection. It respects the BBC and it is therefore parser friendly. Once the parser reaches V_1 in the input, it can project the top VP node, proceed to the next item and instantiate the next VP, and so forth. Compare this with (5b), the structure of stacked VPs in a head-final projection (that is excluded by UG). The essential difference is immediately obvious, namely the difference in the depth of embedding: before the parser can reach the head node of the top VP (i.e. V_3) it must have parsed all dependent subtrees of the top VP plus all embedded VPs. This is the burden of centre-embedded structures.

(5)

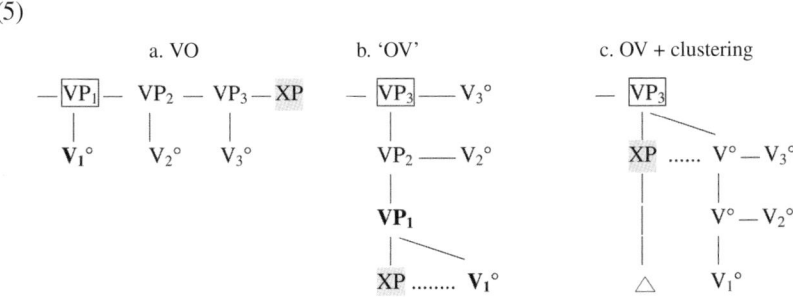

---

[64] Note that the indices of the verbs just refer to the relative order in the input, not to the dependency relations. V_1 is the first verb in the input. In VO, this is the highest one, in OV this is the lowest one.

In addition to the bottom-up parsing problem raised by (5b), there is also a top-down problem: in (5a), the parser can postulate the top node once it reaches the first element of the top projection. In (5b), however, it would have to guess how many verbs there will be in order to be able to decide how many V-projections need to be projected once 'XP' is reached.

The V-projection with the cluster (5c) reduces the potential VP-stacks considerably. The structural complexity is shifted from the phrasal projections to the V-cluster. But this is a local domain, which makes backtracking easy.

These considerations indicate that clustering contributes to parser friendliness. This notwithstanding, the grammatical causality of clustering is the BBC, not the enhancement of parsing. In other words, it is a UG property that facilitates parsing. Parsing functionality comes into play only in a cognitive evolutionary perspective: UG guarantees parser-friendly structures because parser friendliness is a selection criterion in the cognitive evolution of linguistic processing functions that produced UG as one of its results.

(5c) is still not the optimal solution, though, since it involves a residue of left-branching structures. The optimal structure would be a completely right-branching cluster as in (6). This is the Dutch solution of the problem. In Dutch, the verbs do not only cluster (as in 5c) but they are reordered in the cluster. The resulting structure is a fully right-branching one (6):

(6)   Dutch with the 'inverted' cluster

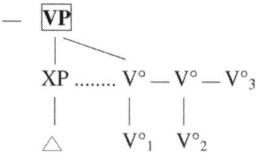

What remains to be accounted for is the third question. Why is clustering optional for sentential infinitival constructions in German? The trivial answer is this: in German, but not in Dutch, sentential arguments are grammatical in clause-internal positions. Hence, there are two possibilities of structuring infinitival complements in German. In Dutch, non-extraposed or non-fronted infinitival clauses are ungrammatical. Hence clustering appears to be obligatory. The non-trivial answer, namely the answer that would uncover the grammatical causality of this contrast between German and Dutch, I am not able to unravel at the present stage of grammatical wisdom.

Finally, the above reasoning leads to the prediction that clustering is OV specific and that it is not expected to apply in a VO language. VO languages happen to provide already parser-friendly stacked VPs, as (7) illustrates:

(7) $[_{VP1} V_1^\circ [_{VP2} V_2^\circ [_{VP3} V_3^\circ ....]]]$

Clustering applied to (7) would not improve but rather reduce parser friendliness because the cluster itself turns out as a subconstituent that introduces a left-branching structure into the VP projection and thereby violates the BBC: a base-generated cluster variant of (7) would look like (8). Because of the clustering of the verbs, the complement XP becomes a *right* sister of a *branching node* of the projection line of the VP and this is in violation of the BBC.

(8) $[_{VP1} [V_1^\circ [V_2^\circ V_3^\circ]]]_V^\circ XP]$

In sum, clustering is a structural option of grammars that provide head-final verb projections. It is a way for UG to guarantee parser friendliness. Clustering reduces the look-ahead domain for parsing from the unbounded domains of stacked VPs and higher projections to the local domain of a head-to-head adjunction cluster.

VO languages do not cluster, and the reason for this is their being VO. First, VO languages do not cluster because the non-clustered structure is a perfect, *right-branching* structure (7). Stacking of VPs and its functional projections yield (extraposition-like) structures with the complex complement on the right-hand side. Second, they do not cluster because clustering would *introduce a left-branching* structure, namely (8).

7.6   Summary

German has two major classes of infinitival constructions, namely the clausal one (control infinitivals) and the clustering construction. In addition, mainly in colloquial German, there is a 'third construction'. A standard analysis for the 'third construction' is still wanting. Competing alternatives for the third construction are on the one hand clausal extraposition plus non-standard, non-local scrambling, and on the other hand VP extraposition (restricted to infinitival VPs).

Clustering is a property characteristic of OV, that is, a head-final verbal projection:

- OV languages employ V° clusters instead of centre-embedded, stacked (extended) verbal projections.
- Typical for Germanic clusters is word order variation in the cluster. This is a correlate of the fact that the finite verb in Germanic languages

always moves (V2 property). Word order variation in the cluster is absent in strict OV languages like Japanese or Korean because of the absence of verb movement in general.

- Clustering as an alternative to embedded infinitival clauses is a 'free ride' option for the independently available clustering construction (whence the perfect optionality).

- V°-clustering (i.e. *head-to-head merger*) as an alternative to a phrasal projection is constrained by the mechanism of argument management in the cluster constituent.[65]

- VO languages do not cluster for principled reasons.

Starting with Evers's verb raising proposal in the mid 1970s, numerous derivational scenarios have been devised for capturing the clustering and clause union properties. None of these approaches has reached the level of descriptive or explanatory adequacy. Some of them fail to capture core generalizations (e.g. compactness), some of them have introduced too powerful derivational devices and are therefore faced with overgeneration.

This failure becomes understandable if it turns out to be correct that clustering and clause union is the property of a separate construction that is not derivationally related to phrasal complementation. It is a genuine option of OV systems that has been overlooked hitherto in the VO-biased approaches.

7.7   Appendices

7.7.1   Appendix 1 Remnant VP fronting vs fronting of submaximal head-final projections

Claim: remnant movement, originally suggested by den Besten and Webelhuth (1990) as analysis for partial VP fronting is dispensable. In a bare phrase structure system, subconstituents may be moved, unless this movement incurs violations (e.g. crossing violations by fronting a subconstituent with a trace across the antecedent of the trace).

In present day grammar theory, it is taken for granted that topicalized phrases are maximal projections. Consequently, what appears to be a topicalized subprojection of a VP or an AP is deemed to be a complete VP with subconstituents removed before fronting the VP or the maximal AP, respectively ('remnant topicalization').

---

[65] For an implementation of this construction in a HPSG (= Head-driven phrase structure grammar) framework, see Hinrichs and Nakazawa (1989, 1994).

(1)   a. [$_{VP}$ e_i e_j Vorenthalten] haben sie wem$_i$ was$_j$
            withheld have they someone-DAT something-ACC
            'They have withheld something from someone'

        b. [$_{VP}$ e_i Was vorenthalten] haben sie wem$_i$

The 'remnant fronting' analysis (1a) presupposes first, a string vacuous process of removing items out of the VP ('pseudo-scrambling') prior to fronting, and second, an amnesty for the crossing-violation configuration, since the antecedents of the pseudo-scrambled items do not c-command their respective traces. Note that the objects in (1) are items (namely wh-pronouns construed as indefinite pronouns) that do not scramble. So, pseudo-scrambling cannot be subsumed under the regular scrambling option.

   Note further that Dutch does not allow scrambling of arguments. In other words, changing the base order of arguments in the midfield is ungrammatical in Dutch. Nevertheless, Dutch allows fronting of the verb without its object (2).

(2)   a. (Hij heeft de rekening gevraagd, maar) [betalen$_i$ zal hij de rekening
            niet e_i]   *Dutch*
            (*he has for the bill asked, but*) [pay will he the bill not]

        b. [$_{VP}$ e_j betalen]$_i$ zal$_k$ hij [de rekening$_j$ [niet [e_i e_k]]]

If (2b) is considered to be the appropriate structure for (2a), the object must have left the VP. In this case, however, it is unclear how genuine scrambling could be ruled out. If the direct object may be fronted out of the VP in (2b) it could just as well be fronted out of a double object VP. The result would be genuine scrambling. But this is ungrammatical in Dutch. So, the assumption of remnant topicalization for cases like (2a) in Dutch runs into problems of overgeneration.

   Remnant topicalization is needed for head-final projections only, namely VP and AP (3) in German. Head-initial projections do not produce this phenomenon. So, remnant topicalization appears to be a speciality of OV, given the fact that English and the Scandinavian languages are strictly head initial, and that Dutch does not permit scrambling (and *a fortiori* should not allow pseudo-scrambling). As for (3c), be aware that genitive objects do not scramble, so, as in the case of indefinite wh-pronouns in (1), this is another case in which pseudo-scrambling would differ from regular scrambling in German.

(3)   a. [$_{AP}$ Sich seiner Sache sicher] war in diesem Fall keiner
            [himself (of) his cause-GEN sure] was in this case nobody
            'In this case, nobody was sure about his cause'

        b. [$_{AP}$ e_i Seiner Sache sicher]$_k$ war sich$_i$ in diesem Fall keiner e_k

        c. [$_{AP}$ e_i e_j Sicher]$_k$ war sich$_i$ in diesem Fall seiner Sache$_j$ keiner e_k

Why does remnant topicalization not apply to head-initial VPs? The answer that is normally presented cannot be entirely correct. It is this: there would be no way of evacuating the VP. In fact, however, there is a way, and it is a standard one. The objects are moved out of the VP to functional spec positions. Hence, there is an emptied VP that could be topicalized.

(4)   a.   ... and [$_{VP(?)}$ shown the document to the police]$_i$ he has indeed e$_i$

        b. * ... and [$_{VP}$ shown e$_j$ e$_k$]$_i$ he has indeed the document$_j$ to the police$_k$ e$_i$

In order to rule out (4b), it is necessary to implement the requirement that the verb has to move to the functional head position of the respective specs. This would radically empty the VP and make it invisible for topicalization.

Another, but non-derivational account of the ungrammaticality of (4b) is this: head-initial VPs are projections with the verb in a c-commanding position in a shell-structure (5). So, any constituent that contains the verb, necessarily contains the subtrees c-commanded by the verb. There is no way of topicalizing a 'remnant' of the VP in (5) without simultaneously topicalizing the subtree that contains the trace of the verb and the two arguments.

(5)   [$_{VP}$ V$^\circ_i$ [XP [e$_i$ [YP]]]]

The situation is completely different in head-final projections. There are well formed subtrees that contain just the verb, or the verb and an argument, excluding another, higher argument as the XP in (6).

(6)   [$_{VP}$ XP [$_{V'}$ YP [V$^\circ$]]]

In (6), there are three candidates for the fronting of an entire V^n constituent, namely for n = V$^\circ$, n = V', and n = V^{max}. Note that there is a crucial difference in the structural status of V$^\circ$ in (5) and (6). In (5), the status of V$^\circ$ is that of a head, related to a lower head position in a chain. In (6), V$^\circ$ is a head, too, but at the same time it is a proper subconstituent of the VP, namely the foot of the phrase. The V$^\circ$ in (5) is not the foot, it is the head-item displaced from the foot position. If fronting applies to minimally complete subtrees, V$^\circ$ is a proper subconstituent in (6) but not in (5). Analogously, V + XP would not constitute a minimally complete subtree in (5), but YP + V does constitute a minimally complete subtree.

This accounts for the difference between head-initial and head-final constituents, and therefore it accounts for the absence of remnant topicalization in head-initial contexts. VO languages do not topicalize subtrees, but OV languages do. The fact that English is the model language of present day grammar theory and the fact that English does not allow remnant topicalization invites the narrow and bold generalization that universally, subconstituents cannot be topicalized. But this generalization may turn out to be too narrow, once the facts from OV languages are judged from a less biased perspective.

Here is the alternative to remnant topicalization. It is what it appears to be, namely the topicalization of an X^n constituent, maximal or submaximal, with the appropriate well-formedness restrictions applied:

(7)   a. $[_{V^n}$ Vorenthalten$]_k$ haben sie wem was e_k
            withheld have they someone-DAT something-ACC
            'They have withheld something from someone'

        b. $[_{V^n}$ Was vorenthalten$]_k$ haben sie wem e_k

        c. $[_{V^n}$ Wem was vorenthalten$]_k$ haben sie e_k

The topicalized constituents in (7a–c) are well-formed V-headed constituents, each related to their respective trace position. The trace is in each case a verbal trace that heads the clause-final V-projection. It transmits the unsaturated argument grid. In (7a), all arguments need to be saturated in the midfield. In (7b) the direct object is saturated in the topicalized V-projection. In (7c), only the subject argument is left to be saturated.

This approach captures the OV/VO difference. In head-initial constituents, a subconstituent contains the trace of the head element whose surface position is in a higher shell. So, a crossing violation forbids fronting the subconstituent.

7.7.2   Appendix 2 'Control' in the cluster: zu *as identifier of the external argument position*

Claim: *zu* (to) is the identifier of the subject argument in an infinitival construction.

A crucial difference between the clausal (1a) and the clause union infinitive construction (1b) is the syntactic presence of a PRO subject in the first case, and the absence of PRO in the latter case. Nevertheless, the interpretation of a sentence remains the same, independent of its construction type. Hence, what corresponds to the control relation in the clause union infinitive construction and how is it implemented?

The answer is this: in the cluster construction (1b), the argument that is linked to the PRO subject in the clausal construction (1a) is identified with its controller already in the pooled argument grid (1c). Control is compensated by direct identification of the controller in the pooled argument structure (1c). This presupposes that the subject argument of the selected infinitival verb is not projected, but blocked.

(1)   a. dass sie^i [PRO^i zu gewinnen]$_{CP}$ hofft
            that she [to win] hopes
            'that she hopes to win'

        b. dass sie [zu gewinnen hofft]$_{VC}$

        c. [zu gewinnen hoffen]$_{VC}$: <AG$_g$, TH$_h$, [AG$_h$=AG$_g$] >

Here is the blocking mechanism. It is a function of the infinitival marker *zu*. It has
an operator function that applies on the interface level between argument structure and its projection onto phrase structure. Two facts confirm this.

Fact 1: an infinitival '*zu* V°', dependent on a control verb, obligatorily requires
an external argument which is represented by PRO (2a). If the infinitival verb
does not provide an external argument (2b), the construction is ungrammatical.
This is also true for the clause union construction (2c) but it is not true for a finite
clause (2d).

(2)   a. Sie hat gehofft [PRO dafür gelobt zu werden]
            she has hoped [it-for praised to be]
            'She has hoped to be praised for it'

        b. * Sie hat gehofft [getanzt zu werden]
            she has hoped [danced to be]
            'she has hoped that there will be dancing'

        c. * [Getanzt zu werden gehofft] hat sie bei dieser Musik nicht
            [danced to be hoped] has she with this music not
            'She has not hoped that there would be dancing with this music'

        d. Sie hat gehofft, [dass bei dieser Musik getanzt werde]
            she has hoped [that with this music danced is]
            'She has hoped that there will be dancing with this music'

In other words, in German, infinitival clauses (2a), unlike finite ones (2d), must
not be subjectless. If we take *zu* to be an identifier of the external argument, *zu*
(as in 2b) must not operate vacuously. It must identify a controllable argument
(whence: ungrammaticality of subjectless clausal infinitives).

Fact 2: *zu* in the participial construction blocks the *primary* external argument
(Haider 1984a,b).

   The infinitive of a verb, both the bare infinitive and the infinitive with the
marker *zu*, can be used as a participle in German. In this case, the verb form is
suffixed with adjectival agreement suffixes and is usually called 'present participle'. A crucial feature of the effect of *zu* becomes evident, once we compare the
construction with *zu* (3b) with the construction without (3a):

(3)   a. ein [den Fall akribisch *analysierender*] Syntaktiker
       a [the case-ACC meticulously analyse+AGR] syntactician
       'a syntactician meticulously analysing the case'

       b. ein [(von uns) akribisch ***zu** analysierender*] Fall
       a [(by us) meticulously ***to** analyse+AGR*] case
       'a case to be meticulously analysed by us'

The construction with *zu* induces a passive effect (3b). Only if *zu* is dependent on a clausal functional head does it license PRO. In a non-clausal environment, it identifies the external argument in the grid, and thereby blocks it, in the absence of a functional projection or a higher selecting verb. This is the case in (3b) and it explains the passive effect in the *zu*-V° + 'have/be' construction (4). The only difference between (3a) and (3b) is the presence/absence of *zu*. Hence, this must be the causal factor.

Note that in a finite clause, the passive effect with the *zu*-participle appears and disappears in the same context of auxiliaries as the passive effect with the past participle. An unaccusative auxiliary (4b, 4b') yields a passive effect, a transitive one yields the full argument structure (4a, 4a'). This effect follows from obligatory clustering:[66] the format of an unaccusative verb is incompatible with a transitive subject argument. An unaccusative auxiliary, i.e. *sein* (be), has the unspecified argument format of an unaccusative verb. Hence it will not combine with a transitive subject argument.

(4)   a. Er *hat* uns *zu instruieren*   a'. Er *hat* uns *instruiert*
          he has us to instruct   he has us instructed
          'He has to instruct us'   'He has instructed us'

       b. Wir *sind* (von ihm)   b'. Wir *sind/werden* (von ihm)
          zu instruieren   *instruiert*
          we are (by him) to instruct   we are/get (by him) instructed
          'We are to be instructed (by him)'   'We are instructed by him'

In (4b, 4b'), the governing auxiliary verb in the cluster is an *ergative* one. Hence its format has no room for a transitive subject argument, whence the passive effect in (4b, 4b'). What the comparison of the passive construction and the clustering construction for infinitives with *zu* shows is that the subject of the infinitive is blocked in each of the two constructions.

---

[66] Of course, clustering is only a sufficient but not a necessary condition, since the very same effect applies in VO languages too, if passive is coded by means of the combination of a blocking participle and an auxiliary (cf. English, or Romance languages). Apparently, the argument structure of the dependent verb is inherited by the auxiliary and its format filters the arguments that are to be inherited.

What these facts illustrate is this: the infinitival marker *zu* is directly related to the syntactic presence/absence of the infinitival subject. In a clause, the infinitival's functional head identifies the infinitival subject that *zu* is related to. In non-clausal contexts (cluster internal) the infinitival marker is subcategorized by a selecting verb in the cluster. The particle *zu* (to) is an operator on the A-structure. It identifies the subject argument of the infinitival verb with the controlling argument of the selecting verb. This identification in the pooled argument grid of the cluster is the equivalent of control in clausal infinitivals, with one essential structural difference: identification saturates the argument slot and it is not projected. Hence there is no PRO subject in non-sentential infinitival constructions.

Note finally that so-called subject raising verbs like *scheinen* (seem) are minimal-pair-like counterparts of the auxiliaries. Like the auxiliaries they do not have a specified subject argument, but their argument structure format is the format of a transitive verb. So on the one hand, they combine with any type of argument structure and on the other hand, they do not require a subject argument. So (5) contrasts with (2c). As discussed above, this follows from the absence of the requirement of an obligatory functional subject in OV.

(5)   dass zu dieser Musik nicht [getanzt zu werden scheint]
       that with this music not danced to be seems
       'that it seems that there is no dancing with this music'

What is the crucial difference between (2b,c) and (5)? In (5), the matrix verb is a quasi-auxiliary, namely an epistemic verb. In (2b,c) it is a control verb. The control verb governs the *zu* and requires an argument for integration. An epistemic verb does not have a subject argument. It simply integrates a subject argument of the selected infinitive. If there is none, the resulting argument structure of the verb *scheinen* in German is like that of a passivized intransitive or that of one of a handful of subjectless verbs, as in (6):

(6)   a. dass ihm davor graute
          that him-DAT it-at dreads
          'that he dreads it'

       b. dass ihr dabei gruselte
          that her-DAT it-with creeps
          'that it gave her the creeps'

Kindly note: since German does not employ an obligatory functional subject position, the counterpart of English raising predicates do not involve subject raising as an instance of A-movement. The German construction is just a simple clause with an obligatorily clustering verb that selects a *zu*-infinitive.

7.7.3   Appendix 3 Restructuring in Italian versus clustering in German

Clustering is an OV property. This claim is compatible with the fact that VO languages allow for transparency phenomena, like the so-called 'restructuring' infinitival in Italian.

Claim: Italian 'restructuring' does not produce verbal clusters. Clear evidence for this is the absence of compactness, that is, the possibility of interveners.

In Italian, as described in Rizzi (1982), there are verbs that select an infinitival complement that is (optionally) open for *clitic climbing*, 'long' *NP-movement*, and transparent for *auxiliary selection*:

- modal verbs (e.g. *potere* 'can', *dovere* 'must', *volere* 'want', ...)
- aspectual verbs (e.g. *cominciare* 'to begin', *finire* 'to finish', *continuare* 'to continue', ...)
- motion verbs (e.g. *venire* 'to come', *andare* 'to go', *tornare* 'to come back', ...)

In Rizzi's original analysis, the term 'restructuring' was used for describing the optional transparency phenomena. This term suggests that there is a derivational relation between a clausal variant and a 'restructured' one and one might think that 'restructuring' in Italian and clustering in German or Dutch might be related phenomena, especially since the sets of verbs involved are largely intersecting.

But this apparent similarity is misleading. The 'restructuring variant' in Italian is just an alternatively available structure assignment. In other words: a class of verbs alternatively admits a sentential and a subsentential infinitival complement (Cinque 2001, 2002). The 'reconstruction' structure is the standard structure for auxiliaries (stacked V-projections in VO). There are clear differences between the Italian transparency phenomena and the clustering construction.

First, the Italian reconstruction constructions do *not* involve *cluster formation*. This is evident from several independent facts, namely the absence of the compactness properties, the strict canonical order without any variation, and the impossibility of cluster nominalization.

(1)   a. Pia lo vuole poter (*immediatamente*) comprare.
          Pia it-CL-ACC wants to be able to immediately buy
          'Pia wants to be able to buy it immediately'

       b. dass es Pia kaufen können (*aus Jux) wollte
          that it Pia buy be-able-to (for fun) wanted
          'that Pia wanted to be able to buy it just for fun'

In Italian, but not in German or Dutch, the verbs in the 'restructuring' construction may sandwich 'cluster-foreign' material (cf. Monachesi 1999).

Second, the Italian 'reconstruction' construction is *optional* (2), with obligatory side effects, though:

(i)   'bandwagon effect' for clitic climbing (3)
(ii)   monosentential structure (e.g. negation domain; as in 4) (Monachesi 1999).

Optional (clitic climbing)

(2)   a. Pia *lo* vuole poter comprare
        b. Pia vuole poter*lo* comprare
        c. Pia vuole poter comprar*lo*

It appears as if clitic climbing is perfectly optional. Is this optionality a property of clitic climbing or a property of structure assignment? It is the latter, since clitics have to be treated alike ('bandwagon effect'). It is not possible, for instance, if there is more than a single clitic, to treat them differently and raise only one, and not the other.

'Bandwagon' effect *(no split clitics)*

(3)   a. *Te lo* voglio dare c.   * *Ti* voglio dar*lo*
           you it want (I) give
           'I want to give it to you'

        b. Voglio dar*telo* d.   * *Lo* voglio dar*te*

Clitics have to be treated equally, that is, they are cliticized to the same target although there may be in principle more than one available target (cf. 2). This effect is not captured by an optional clitic climbing rule since this would individually apply to each clitic. It is captured if the domain of clitic climbing is a function of the chosen category for the infinitival complement. In this case the domain is the same for all clitics, hence their target is the same.

Monosentential – **No embedded negation domain** *in the 'reconstruction' case*

(4)   a. Paola vuole *non* comprar*lo* immediatamente
            Paola wants not buy-it immediately
            'Paola does not want to buy it immediately'

        b. * Paola *lo* vuole *non* comprare immediatamente
            Paola it wants not buy immediately
            'Paola does not want to buy it immediately'

Clitic climbing signals a monosentential structure. Hence this is incompatible with an embedded domain for sentential negation. Conversely, if negation signals a sentential domain, clitic climbing would be non-local and therefore ruled out.

(Apparent) ***non-local relation changing operations*** *(NP-movement)*

(5)   a. Queste case$_i$ si vogliono (poter) vendere e$_i$ a caro prezzo
            these houses themselves want (be-able-to) sell at high price
            'These houses want to sell at a high price'

       b. Dieser Wagen will/würde sich nicht reparieren lassen
            this-NOM car wants/would itself not fix let
            'This car would not be able to be fixed'

In the impersonal/middle variant, the combination of verb plus reflexive triggers ACC-to-NOM for the direct object of the verb. In (5), the reflexive combines with the matrix verb, but nevertheless the effect applies to an argument of the embedded verb. Once more, this is evidence for a transparency relation. In Italian, it is the transparency of the VP-complement in an ECM-like configuration like English (cf. (6)). In German, it is the transparency in the cluster:

(6)   a. I make [you believe this]
        b. You$_i$ are made [e$_i$ to believe this]
        c. I^i made myself^i believe this

The infinitival complement of *make* is transparent for case checking with respect to the case of the infinitival subject (6a), and it is transparent for A-movement (6b), as well as for local binding (6c).

    An alternation between a clausal infinitival complement and a VP complement is in most cases string vacuous in Italian, and it accounts for the apparent simultaneity of biclausal and monoclausal syntactic properties. However, this does not require a process of restructuring.

Bibliography

Abraham, Werner (1995) *Deutsche Syntax im Sprachenvergleich*, Tübingen: Narr.

Adger, David (1994) 'Functional head and interpretation', Doctoral dissertation, University of Edinburgh.

Alexiadou, Artemis and Elena Anagnostopoulou (1998) 'Parametrizing AGR: word order, V-movement and EPP-checking', *Natural Language and Linguistic Theory* 16: 491–539.

Alexiadou, Artemis and Gisbert Fanselow (2002) 'On the correlation between morphology and syntax: the case of V-to-I', in Jan-Wouter Zwart and Werner Abraham (eds.), *Studies in Comparative Germanic Syntax*, Amsterdam: John Benjamins, pp. 219–42.

ANS (1984) *Algemene Nederlandse Spraakkunst,* see Geerts, Guido, Walter Haeseryn, Jaap de Rooij and Maarten C. van den Toorn.

Aoun, Joseph and Yen-hui Audrey Li (1993) 'Scope and constituency', *Linguistic Inquiry* 20: 141–82.

Bach, Emmon (1979) 'Control in Montague Grammar', *Linguistic Inquiry* 10: 533–81.

Barbiers, Lambertus Christiaan Jozef (alias: Sjef) (2000) 'The right periphery in SOV languages: English and Dutch', in Peter Svenonius (ed.), *The derivation of VO and OV*, Amsterdam: John Benjamins, pp. 181–218.

Barnes, Michael (1987) 'Some remarks on subordinate-clause word order in Faroese', *Scripta Islandica* 38: 3–35.

Bausewein, Karin (1991) 'Haben kopflose Relativsätze tatsächlich keine Köpfe?' in Gisbert Fanselow and Sascha Felix (eds.), *Strukturen und Merkmale syntaktischer Kategorien*, Tübingen: Narr, pp. 144–58.

Bayer, Josef (1990) 'Directionality of government and logical form: a study of focusing particles and wh-scope', Habilitation thesis, University of Konstanz.

(1998) 'Final complementizers in hybrid languages', *Journal of Linguistics* 35: 233–71.

(2001) 'Two grammars in one: sentential complements and complementizers in Bengali and other South Asian languages', in Peri Bhaskararao and Karumuri V. Subbarao (eds.), *The yearbook of South Asian languages: Tokyo symposium on South Asian languages – contact, convergence and typology*, New Delhi: Sage Publications, pp. 11–36.

(2003) 'Non-nominative subjects in comparison', in Peri Bhaskararao and Karumuri V. Subbarao (eds.), *Non-nominative subjects*, Amsterdam: John Benjamins, pp. 49–76.

Bech, Gunnar (1955) *Studien über das deutsche verbum infinitum*, Copenhagen: Munksgaard. (Second unchanged edition (1983), introduced by Cathrine Fabricius-Hansen, Tübingen: Niemeyer.)

Beerman, Dorothee, David LeBlanc and Henk C. van Riemsdijk (eds.) (1997) *Rightward movement*, Amsterdam: John Benjamins [*Linguistics Today* 17].

Benincà, Paula and Cecilia Poletto (2004) 'Topic, focus and V2. Defining the CP sublayers', in Luigi Rizzi (ed.), *The structure of CP and IP. The cartography of syntactic structures*, vol. II, Oxford: Oxford University Press, pp. 52–75.

Bennis, Hans (1986) *Gaps and dummies*, Dordrecht: Foris.

Besten, Hans den (1985) 'Some remarks on the ergative hypothesis', in Werner Abraham (ed.), *Erklärende Syntax des Deutschen*, Tübingen: Narr, pp. 53–74.

Besten, Hans den and Jean Rutten (1989) 'On verb raising, extraposition, and free word order in Dutch', in Dany Jaspers, Wim G. Klooster, Yvan Putseys and Pieter A. M. Seuren (eds.), *Sentential complementation and the lexicon*, Dordrecht: Foris, pp. 41–56.

Besten, Hans den and Gert Webelhuth (1990) 'Stranding', in Günther Grewendorf and Wolfgang Sternefeld (eds.), *Scrambling and barriers*, Amsterdam: John Benjamins, pp. 77–92.

Bhatt, Rakesh M. (1999) *Verb movement and the syntax of Kashmiri*, Dordrecht: Kluwer.

Blume, Kerstin (1998) 'A contrastive analysis of interaction verbs with dative complements', *Linguistics* 36: 253–80.

Bobaljik, Jonathan David (2002) 'Realizing Germanic inflection: why morphology does not drive syntax', *Journal of Comparative Germanic Linguistics* 6: 129–67.

(2004) 'Clustering theories', in Katalin É. Kiss and Henk C. van Riemsdijk (eds.), pp. 121–45.

Bobaljik, Jonathan and Höskuldur Thráinsson (1998) 'Two heads aren't always better than one', *Syntax* 1: 37–71.

Bošković, Željko and Daiko Takahashi (1998) 'Scrambling and last resort', *Linguistic Inquiry* 29: 347–66.

Brandt, Margarethe, Marga Reis, Inger Rosengren and Ilse Zimmermann (1992) 'Satz, Satztyp und Illokution', in Inger Rosengren (ed.), *Satz und Illokution*, vol. I, Tübingen: Niemeyer [*Linguistische Arbeiten* 278], pp. 3–89.

Bresnan, Joan (1977) 'Variables in the theory of transformations. Part I: Bounded versus unbounded transformations', in Peter Culicover, Tom Wasow and Adrian Akmajian (eds.), *Formal Syntax*, New York, Academic Press, pp. 157–96.

Brody, Michael (2004) '"Roll-up" structures and morphological words', in Katalin É. Kiss and Henk C. van Riemsdijk (eds.), pp. 147–71.

Büring, Daniel (1997) *The meaning of topic and focus. The 59th Street Bridge accent*, London: Routledge.

(2001) 'Let's phrase it! – Focus, word order, and prosodic phrasing in German double object constructions', in Gereon Müller and Wolfgang Sternefeld (eds.), *Competition in syntax*, Berlin and New York: Mouton de Gruyter, pp. 1–37.

Büring, Daniel and Katharina Hartmann (1995) 'All right', in Uli Lutz and Jürgen Pafel (eds.), *On extraction and extraposition in German*, Amsterdam: John Benjamins [*Linguistics Today* 11], pp. 179–211.

(1997) 'Doing the right thing', *The Linguistic Review* 14: 1–42.

Burzio, Luigi (1986) *Italian Syntax: a government and binding approach*, Dordrecht: Reidel [*Studies in Natural Language and Linguistic Theory* 1].

Cardinaletti, Anna and Michal Starke (1999) 'The typology of structural deficiency: a case study of three classes of pronouns', in Henk C. van Riemsdijk (ed.), *Clitics in the languages of Europe*, Berlin: Mouton de Gruyter, pp. 145–233.

Cheng, Lisa Lai-shen (1997) *On the Typology of Wh-Questions*, New York: Garland.

Choi, Hye-Won (1999) *Optimizing structure in context. Scrambling and information structure*, Stanford, CA: CSLI Publications.

Chomsky, Noam (1973) 'Conditions on transformations', in Steven Anderson and Paul Kiparsky (eds.), *A Festschrift for Morris Halle*, New York: Holt, Rinehart and Winston, pp. 232–86.

(1977) 'On wh-movement', in Peter Culicover, Tom Wasow and Adrian Akmajian (eds.), *Formal syntax*, New York: Academic Press, pp. 71–132.

(1981) *Lectures on government and binding*, Dordrecht: Foris.

(1982) *Some concepts and consequences of the theory of government and binding*, Cambridge, MA: MIT Press.

(1986) *Barriers*, Cambridge MA: MIT Press.

(1991) 'Some notes on economy of derivation and representation', in Robert Freidin (ed.), *Principles and parameters in comparative grammar*, Cambridge, MA: MIT Press, pp. 417–54.

(1992) 'A Minimalist Program for linguistic theory', *MIT Occasional Papers in Linguistics* 1.

(1995) *The Minimalist Program*, Cambridge, MA: MIT Press.

Chomsky, Noam and Howard Lasnik (1995) 'Principles and parameters theory', in Joachim Jacobs, Arnim von Stechow, Wolfgang Sternefeld and Theo Vennemann (eds.), *Syntax: an international handbook of contemporary research*, Berlin: Mouton de Gruyter, pp. 506–69.

Cinque, Guglielmo (1999) *Adverbs and functional heads. A cross-linguistic perspective*, New York and Oxford: Oxford University Press.

(2001) 'Restructuring and the order of aspectual and root modal heads', in Guglielmo Cinque and Giampaolo Salvi (eds.), *Current studies in Italian syntax. Essays offered to Lorenzo Renzi*, Amsterdam: Elsevier, pp. 137–55.

(2002) 'A note on restructuring and quantifier climbing in French', *Linguistic Inquiry* 33: 617–36.

(2004) 'Restructuring and functional structure', in Adriana Belletti (ed.), *Structures and beyond. The cartography of syntactic structures*, vol. III, Oxford: Oxford University Press, pp. 132–91.

Collins, Chris (1997) *Local economy*, Cambridge, MA: MIT Press.

Collins, Chris and Höskuldur Thráinsson (1996) 'VP-internal structure and object shift in Icelandic', *Linguistic Inquiry* 27: 391–444.

Corver, Norbert and Henk C. van Riemsdijk (eds.) (1994) *Studies on scrambling*, Berlin: Mouton de Gruyter [*Studies in Generative Grammar* 41].

Corver, Norbert and Henk C. van Riemsdijk (1997) 'The position of the head and the domain of scrambling', in Bohumil Palek (ed.), *Typology: prototypes, item orderings and universals*, Prague, Acta Universitatis Carolinae Philologica, pp. 57–90.

Culicover, Peter W. (1997) *Principles & parameters. An introduction to syntactic theory*, Oxford: Oxford University Press.

Culicover, Peter W. and Michael S. Rochemont (1990) 'Extraposition and the complement principle', *Linguistic Inquiry* 21: 23–47.

Czepluch, Hartmut (1988) 'Case patterns in German: Some implications for the theory of abstract case', *McGill Working Papers in Linguistics*, Special issue on Comparative Germanic Syntax: 79–122.

Dehé, Nicole (2002) *Particle verbs in English*, Amsterdam: John Benjamins.

Deprez, Vivian (1994) 'Parameters of object movement', in Norbert Corver and Henk C. van Riemsdijk (eds.), pp. 101–52.

Diesing, Molly (1992) *Indefinites*, Cambridge, MA: MIT Press.

(1997) 'Yiddish VP order and the typology of object movement in Germanic', *Natural Language and Linguistic Theory* 15: 369–427.

(2001) 'Multiple questions in and about Yiddish', in Ji-Yung Kim and Adam Werle (eds.), *UMOP 25, The Proceedings of SULA 1 (The semantics of underrepresented languages in the Americas)*, University of Massachusetts, Amherst, 20–22 April 2001.

Dikken, Marcel den (1992) 'Particles', Doctoral dissertation, University of Leiden.

(1995) *Particles*, Oxford: Oxford University Press.

Dryer, Matthew S. (1988) 'Universals of negative position', in Michael Hammond, Edith Moravcsik and Jessica Wirth (eds.), *Studies in syntactic typology*, Amsterdam: John Benjamins, pp. 93–124.

Duden Grammatik der deutschen Gegenwartssprache (1966) *Der große Duden*, vol. IV, Mannheim: Bibliographisches Institut Dudenverlag (second augmented and corrected edition, adapted by Paul Grebe).

É. Kiss, Katalin (1987) *Configurationality in Hungarian*, Dordrecht: Reidel.

É. Kiss, Katalin and Henk C. van Riemsdijk (eds.) (2004) *Verb clusters. A study of Hungarian, German and Dutch*, Amsterdam: John Benjamins.

Evers, Arnold (1975) 'The transformational cycle in Dutch and German', Doctoral dissertation, University of Utrecht (distributed by the Indiana University Linguistics Club, Bloomington, Indiana).

Fanselow, Gisbert (1985) 'Deutsche Verbalprojektionen und die Frage der Universalität konfigurationaler Sprachen', Doctoral dissertation, University of Passau, Germany.

(1991) 'Minimale Syntax', Habilitation thesis, University of Passau, Germany [Published as: *Groninger Arbeiten zur Germanistischen Linguistik* 32, Rijksuniversiteit Groningen].

(1993) 'The return of the base generators', *Groninger Arbeiten zur Germanistischen Linguistik* 36: 1–74.

(1997) 'Minimal link effects in German (and other languages)', unpublished MS, University of Potsdam. (Related handout from 1996 at www.ling. uni-potsdam.de/~fanselow/mlc.htm).

(2001) 'Features, theta-roles, and free constituent order', *Linguistic Inquiry* 32: 405–37.

(2002) 'Quirky subjects and other specifiers', in Ingrid Kaufmann and Barbara Stiebels (eds.), *More than words*, Berlin: Akademie-Verlag [*Studia Grammatica* 53], pp. 227–50.

(2003) 'Free constituent order: a Minimalist interface account', *Folia Linguistica* 37: 191–231.

(2006) 'Partial wh-movement', in Martin Everaert and Henk C. van Riemsdijk (eds.), *Syncom – The syntax companion*, chapter 47, Oxford: Blackwell.

Fiengo, Robert (1980) *Surface structure*, Cambridge, MA: Harvard University Press.

Fleischer, Jürg (2006) 'Dative and indirect object in German dialects: evidence from relative clauses', in Daniel Hole, André Meinunger and Werner Abraham (eds.), *Datives and other cases: between argument structure and event structure*, Amsterdam: John Benjamins (*Studies in Language Companion Series* 75), pp. 213–38.

Fortmann, Christian (2007) 'Bewegungsresistente Verben', *Zeitschrift für Sprachwissenschaft* 26: 1–40.

Freidin, Robert (1986) 'Fundamental issues in the theory of binding', in Barbara Lust (ed.), *Studies in the acquisition of anaphora*, vol. I, Dordrecht: Reidel, pp. 151–81.

Frey, Werner (1993) *Syntaktische Bedingungen für die semantische Interpretation. Über Bindung, implizite Argumente und Skopus*, Berlin: Akademie-Verlag [*Studia Grammatica* 35].

(2004) 'A medial topic position for German', *Linguistische Berichte* 198: 153–90.

Frey, Werner and Karin Pittner (1998) 'Zur Positionierung von Adverbien', *Linguistische Berichte* 86: 489–534.

Fukui, Naoki (1993) 'Parameters and optionality', *Linguistic Inquiry* 24: 399–420.

Gazdar, Gerald (1981) 'Unbounded dependencies and coordinate structure', *Linguistic Inquiry* 12: 155–84.

Geerts, Guido, Walter Haeseryn, Jaap de Rooij and Maarten C. van den Toorn (1984) *Algemene Nederlandse Spraakkunst*, Groningen: Wolters-Noordhoff.

Grewendorf, Günther (2002) *Minimalistische Syntax*, Tübingen: UTB/Franke.

Grewendorf, Günther and Joachim Sabel (1999) 'Scrambling in German and Japanese: adjunction versus multiple specifiers', *Natural Language and Linguistic Theory* 8: 1–65.

Grewendorf, Günther and Wolfgang Sternefeld (1990) 'Scrambling theories', in Günther Grewendorf and Wolfgang Sternefeld (eds.), *Scrambling and barriers*, Amsterdam: John Benjamins, pp. 3–37.

Grohman, Kleanthes (2003) *Prolific domains. On the anti-locality of movement dependencies*, Amsterdam: John Benjamins.

Guéron, Jacqueline (1980) 'On the syntax and semantics of PP extraposition', *Linguistic Inquiry* 11: 637–78.

Haan, Germen de and Fred Weerman (1986) 'Finiteness and verb fronting in Frisian', in Hubert Haider and Martin Prinzhorn (eds.), *Verb second phenomena in Germanic languages*, Dordrecht: Foris, pp. 77–110.

Haegeman, Liliane (2001) 'Antisymmetry and verb-final order in West Flemish', *Journal of Comparative Germanic Linguistics* 3: 207–32.

Haegeman, Liliane and Henk C. van Riemsdijk (1986) 'Verb projection raising, scope, and the typology of rules affecting verbs', *Linguistic Inquiry* 17: 417–66.

Haider, Hubert (1983) 'Connectedness effects in German', *Groninger Arbeiten zur Germanistischen Linguistik* 23: 82–119.

(1984a) 'The case of German', in Jindřich Toman (ed.), *Studies in German Grammar*, Dordrecht: Foris, pp. 65–101.

(1984b) 'Was zu haben ist und was zu sein hat – Bemerkungen zum Infinitiv', *Papiere zur Linguistik* 30: 23–36.

(1985) 'A unified account of case and theta-marking – The case of German', *Papiere zur Linguistik* 32: 3–36.

(1986) 'Affect alpha', *Linguistic Inquiry* 17: 113–26.

(1989) 'Theta-tracking systems – evidence from German', in László Marácz and Pieter Muysken (eds.), *Configurationality: the Typology of Asymmetries*, Dordrecht: Foris, pp. 185–206.

(1990) 'Topicalization and other puzzles of German syntax', in Günther Grewendorf and Wolfgang Sternefeld (eds.), *Scrambling and barriers*, Amsterdam: John Benjamins, pp. 93–112.

(1991) 'Fakultativ kohärente Infinitkonstruktionen im Deutschen', *Working Papers of the Sonderforschungsbereich 340* (Universities of Stuttgart and Tübingen) 17. (Reprinted 1994 in Anita Steube and Gerhild Zybatow (eds.), *Zur Satzwertigkeit von Infinitiven und Small Clauses*, Tübingen: Niemeyer, pp. 75–106.)

(1992) 'Die Struktur der Nominalphrase – Lexikalische und funktionale Strukturen', in Ludger Hoffmann (ed.), *Deutsche Syntax. Ansichten und Aussichten*, Berlin: Mouton de Gruyter, pp. 304–33.

(1992/2000) 'Branching and discharge' (1992) *Working Papers of the Sonderforschungsbereich 340* (Universities of Stuttgart and Tübingen) 23: 1–31; (2000) in Peter Coopmans, Martin Everaert and Jane Grimshaw (eds.), *Lexical specification and insertion*, Amsterdam: John Benjamins [*Current Issues in Linguistic Theory* 197], pp. 135–64.

(1993) *Deutsche Syntax, generativ*, Tübingen: Narr.

(1995) 'Downright down to the right', in Uli Lutz and Jürgen Pafel (eds.), *On extraction and extraposition in German*, Amsterdam: John Benjamins [*Linguistics Today*], pp. 145–271.

(1996) 'Wenn die Semantik arbeitet, – und die Syntax sie gewähren läßt', in Gisela Harras and Manfred Bierwisch (eds.), *Wenn die Semantik arbeitet*, Tübingen: Niemeyer, pp. 7–27.

(1997a) 'Extraposition', in Dorothee Beerman, David LeBlanc and Henk C. van Riemsdijk (eds.) (1997), pp. 115–51.

(1997b) 'Projective economy. On the minimal functional structure of the German clause', in Werner Abraham and Elly van Gelderen (eds.), *German: syntactic problems – problematic syntax*, Tübingen: Niemeyer, pp. 83–103.

(1997c) 'Economy in syntax is projective economy', in Chris Wilder, Hans-Martin Gärtner and Manfred Bierwisch (eds.), *The role of economy principles in linguistic theory*, Berlin: Akademie-Verlag [*Studia Grammatica* 40], pp. 205–26.

(1997d) 'Precedence among predicates', *The Journal of Comparative Germanic Linguistics* 1: 3–41.

(1997e) 'Scrambling – Locality, economy, and directionality', in Shigeo Tonoike (ed.), *Scrambling*, Tokyo: Kurosio Publishers [*Linguistics Workshop Series* 5], pp. 61–91.

(2000a) 'Scrambling – What's the state of the art?' in Susan M. Powers and Cornelia Hamann (eds.), *The acquisition of scrambling and cliticization*, Dordrecht: Kluwer, pp. 19–40.

(2000b) 'Adverb placement – Convergence of structure and licensing', *Theoretical Linguistics* 26: 95–134.

(2000c) 'The license to license', in Eric Reuland (ed.), *Argument & case: explaining Burzio's generalization*, Amsterdam: John Benjamins, pp. 31–54.

(2000d) 'OV is more basic than VO', in Peter Svenonius (ed.), *The derivation of VO and OV*, Amsterdam: John Benjamins, pp. 45–67.

(2001a) 'Heads and selection', in Norbert Corver and Henk C. van Riemsdijk (eds.), *Semi-lexical categories*, Berlin: Mouton de Gruyter, pp. 67–96.

(2001b) 'How to stay accusative in Icelandic and Faroese', *Working Papers in Scandinavian Syntax* 68: 1–14.

(2001c) 'Prosodic signals for reconstructing the basic item order. On the interplay between structure and prosody', in Bohumil Palek and O. Fujimura (eds.), *Item order: its variety and linguistic and phonetic consequences*, Proceedings of International Linguistics and Phonetics Conference 2000, Charles University, Prague: The Karolinum Press, pp. 347–66.

(2003) 'V-Clustering and clause union – Causes and effects', in Pieter Seuren and Gerard Kempen (eds.), *Verb constructions in German and Dutch*, Amsterdam: John Benjamins, pp. 91–126.

(2004a) 'Pre- and postverbal adverbials in VO and OV', *Lingua* 114 (6): 779–807.

(2004b) 'The superiority conspiracy', in Arthur Stepanov, Gisbert Fanselow and Ralf Vogel (eds.), *The minimal link condition*, Berlin: Mouton de Gruyter, pp. 147–75.

(2005a) 'Parenthesen – Evidenz aus Bindungsverhältnissen', in Franz J. D'Avis (ed.), *Deutsche Syntax: Empirie und Theorie*, Göteborg: Acta Universitatis Gothoburgensis, pp. 281–93.

(2005b) 'How to turn German into Icelandic – and derive the VO-OV contrasts', *The Journal of Comparative Germanic Linguistics* 8: 1–53.

(2006) 'Mittelfeldphenomena', in Henk C. van Riemsdijk and Martin Everaert (eds.), *Syncom – The Syntax Companion*, chapter 43, Oxford: Blackwell.

Haider, Hubert, Sue Olsen and Sten Vikner (eds.) (1995) *Studies in comparative Germanic syntax*, Dordrecht: Kluwer.

Haider, Hubert and Inger Rosengren (1998) *Scrambling*, Lund: Germanistisches Institut, University of Lund [*Sprache und Pragmatik* 49].

(2003) 'Scrambling – non-triggered chain formation in OV languages', *Journal of Germanic Linguistics* 15: 203–67.

Han, Chung-Hye, Jeffrey Lidz and Julien Musolino (2007) 'V-Raising and grammar competition in Korean: evidence from negation and quantifier scope', *Linguistic Inquiry* 38: 1–47.

Hiemstra, Inge (1986) 'Some aspects of wh-questions in Frisian', *Nowele* 8: 97–110.

Hinrichs, Erhard W. and Tsuneko Nakazawa (1989) 'Flipped out: AUX in German', *Papers from the 25th Regional Meeting of the Chicago Linguistic Society*, Chicago, IL, pp. 193–202.

(1994) 'Linearizing AUXs in German verbal complexes', in John Nerbonne, Klaus Netter and Carl Pollard (eds.), *German in head-driven phrase structure grammar*, CSLI Lecture Notes 46, Stanford, CA: CSLI Publications, pp. 11–37.

Hoeksema, Jack (1988) 'A constraint on governors in the West Germanic verb cluster', in Martin Everaert, Arnold Evers, Riny Huybreghts and Mieke Trommelen (eds.), *Morphology and modularity: in honour of Henk Schultink*, Dordrecht: Foris, pp. 147–61.

Hoffman, Donald, D. (1998) *Visual intelligence. How we create what we see*, New York: W.W. Norton & Company.

Höhle, Tilman N. (1978) *Lexikalistische Syntax: Die Aktiv-Passiv-Relation und andere Infinitkonstruktionen im Deutschen*, Tübingen: Niemeyer.

(1982) 'Explikationen für "normale Betonung" und "normale Wortstellung" ', in Werner Abraham (ed.), *Satzglieder im Deutschen. Vorschläge zur syntaktischen, semantischen und pragmatischen Fundierung*, Tübingen: Narr [*Studien zur deutschen Grammatik* 15], pp. 75–153.

(1991) 'Projektionsstufen bei V-Projektionen', unpublished MS, University of Tübingen.

Holmberg, Anders (1999) 'Remarks on Holmberg's generalization', *Studia Linguistica* 53: 1–39.

Holmberg, Anders and Christer Platzack (1995) *The role of inflection in Scandinavian syntax*, Oxford: Oxford University Press.

Hoop, Helen de (1992) 'Case configuration and noun phrase interpretation', Doctoral dissertation, University of Groningen.

Hornstein, Norbert (1995) *Logical form. From GB to Minimalism*, Oxford: Blackwell.

Huang, James C.-T. (1982) 'Logical relations in Chinese and the theory of grammar', Doctoral dissertation, MIT.

Huber, Walter (1980) 'Infinitivkomplemente im Deutschen: Transformationsgrammatische Untersuchungen zum Verb "lassen" ', Doctoral dissertation, Freie Universität Berlin.

Iversen, Ragnvald (1918) *Syntaksen i Tromsø Bymaal*, Kristiania: Bymaals-Lagets Forlag.

Jacobs, Joachim (1982) *Syntax und Semantik der Negation im Deutschen*, Munich: Fink [*Studien zur theoretischen Linguistik* 1].

(1988) 'Fokus-Hintergrund-Gliederung und Grammatik', in Hans Altmann (ed.), *Intonationsforschungen*, Tübingen: Niemeyer [*Linguistische Arbeiten* 200], pp. 89–134.

(1992) 'Bewegung als Valenzvererbung – Teil I', *Linguistische Berichte* 148: 85–142.

(1997) 'I-Topikalisierung', *Linguistische Berichte* 168: 91–133.

Jacobson, Pauline (1987) 'Phrase structure, grammatical relations, and discontinuous constituents', in Geoffrey J. Huck and Almerindo E. Ojeda (eds.), *Discontinuous constituency*, New York: Academic Press [*Syntax & Semantics* 20], pp. 27–69.

Johnson, Kyle (1991) 'Object positions', *Natural Language and Linguistic Theory* 9: 577–636.

Kainhofer, Judith (2002) 'Monadische Akkusativ-Subjekt-Konstruktionen im Isländischen', Master thesis, University of Salzburg, Dept. of Linguistics.

Kathol, Andreas (2000) *Linear syntax*, Oxford: Oxford University Press.

Kayne, Richard (1981) 'ECP extensions', *Linguistic Inquiry* 12: 93–133.

(1983) 'Connectedness', *Linguistic Inquiry* 14: 223–49.

(1994) *The antisymmetry of syntax*, Cambridge, MA: MIT Press.

Kempen, Gerard and Karin Harbusch (2003) 'Dutch and German verb constructions in performance Grammar', in Pieter Seuren and Gerard Kempen (eds.), *Verb constructions in German and Dutch*, Amsterdam: John Benjamins, pp. 185–221.

Kerstens, Johan (1975) 'Over afgeleide structuur en de interpretatie van zinnen' [On derived structure and the interpretation of sentences], unpublished MS, University of Amsterdam [cited in R.G. Ruys (2001)].

Ko, Heejeong (2007) 'Asymmetries in scrambling and cyclic linearization', *Linguistic Inquiry* 39: 49–83.

Koeneman, Olaf (2000) 'The flexible nature of verb movement', Doctoral dissertation, University of Utrecht.

Koopman, Hilda (1995) 'On verbs that fail to undergo V-second', *Linguistic Inquiry* 26: 137–63.

Koopman, Hilda and Anna Szabolcsi (2000) *Verbal complexes*, Cambridge, MA: MIT Press.

Kratzer, Angelika (1984) 'On deriving differences between German and English', unpublished MS, Berlin, Technische Universität.

Kress, Bruno (1982) *Isländische Grammatik*, Leipzig: Verlag Enzyklopädie.

Kuthy, Cordula de (2000) 'Discontinuous NPs in German. A case study of the interaction of syntax, semantics, and pragmatics', Doctoral dissertation, Universität des Saarlandes, Saarbrücken.

Larson, Richard (1988) 'On the double object construction', *Linguistic Inquiry* 19: 335–91.

Lawrenz, Birgit (1993) *Apposition: Begriffsbestimmung und syntaktischer Status*, Tübingen: Narr [*Studien zur deutschen Grammatik* 44].

Lebeaux, David (1988) 'Language acquisition and the form of the grammar', Doctoral dissertation, Amherst, University of Massachusetts.

Lee-Schoenfeld, Vera (2007) *Beyond coherence. The syntax of opacity in German*, Amsterdam: John Benjamins.

Leirbukt, Odleif (1978) 'Über dativische Appositionen bei akkusativischem Bezugswort im Deutschen', *Linguistische Berichte* 55: 1–17.

Lenerz, Jürgen (1977) *Zur Abfolge nominaler Satzglieder im Deutschen*, Tübingen: Narr [*Studien zur deutschen Grammatik* 5].

Mahajan, Anoop (1989) 'Agreement and agreement phrases', *MIT Working Papers in Linguistics* 10: 217–52.

   (1994) 'Toward a unified theory of scrambling', in Norbert Corver and Henk C. van Riemsdijk (eds.) (1994), pp. 301–30.

Maling, Joan and Rex A. Sprouse (1995) 'Structural case, specifier head relations, and the case of predicative NPs', in Hubert Haider, Susan Olsen and Sten Vikner (eds.), *Studies in comparative Germanic syntax*, Dordrecht: Kluwer, pp. 167–86.

Marantz, Alec (1991) 'Case and licensing', *Proceedings of ESCOL* 8: 234–53.

McCawley, James and K. Momoi (1986) 'The constituent structure of -*te* complements', in Shige-Yuki Kuroda (ed.), *Working Papers from the first SDF Workshop in Japanese Syntax*, La Jolla: Dept. of Linguistics, UC San Diego, pp. 97–116.

Meinunger, André (2007) 'About object *es* in the German Vorfeld', *Linguistic Inquiry* 38: 553–63.

Miyagawa, Shigeru (1997) 'Against optional scrambling', *Linguistic Inquiry* 28: 1–25.

   (2001) 'The EPP, scrambling, and wh-in-situ', in Michael Kenstowicz (ed.), *Ken Hale – A life in linguistics*, Cambridge, MA: MIT Press, pp. 293–338.

Moltmann, Friederike (1990) 'Scrambling in German and the specificity effect', unpublished MS, Massachusetts Institute of Technology.

Monachesi, Paola (1999) *A lexical approach to Italian cliticization*, Stanford, CA: CSLI Publications [*CSLI lecture notes* 84].

Müller, Gereon (1995a) *A-bar syntax. A study in movement types*, Berlin: Mouton de Gruyter.

(1995b) 'On extraposition and extraction in German', in Uli Lutz and Jürgen Pafel (eds.), *On extraction and extraposition in German*, Amsterdam: John Benjamins [*Linguistics Today*], pp. 213–43.

(1996) 'Incomplete category fronting', Habilitation thesis, University of Tübingen [SfS-Report 01-96. Published 1997, Berlin: Mouton de Gruyter].

(1997) 'Extraposition as remnant movement', in Dorothee Beerman, David LeBlanc and Henk C. van Riemsdijk (eds.) (1997), pp. 215–46.

(1999) 'Optimality, markedness, and word order in German', *Linguistics* 37: 777–818.

(2000) *Elemente der optimalitätstheoretischen Syntax*, Tübingen: Staufenberg.

Müller, Gereon and Wolfgang Sternefeld (1993) 'Improper movement and unambiguous binding', *Linguistic Inquiry* 24: 461–507.

(1994) 'Scrambling as A-bar movement', in Norbert Corver and Henk C. van Riemsdijk (eds.) (1994), pp. 331–85.

Nash, Léa (1996) 'The internal ergative subject hypothesis', *NELS* 26: 195–209.

Neeleman, Ad (1994) 'Scrambling as a D-structure phenomenon', in Norbert Corver and Henk C. van Riemsdijk (eds.) (1994), pp. 387–429.

(1995) 'Complex predicates in Dutch and English', in Hubert Haider, Sue Olsen and Sten Vikner (eds.), *Studies in Comparative Germanic Syntax*, Dordrecht: Kluwer, pp. 219–40.

Neeleman, Ad and Fred Weerman (1999) *Flexible syntax – A theory of case and arguments*, Doctoral, Kluwer [*Studies in Natural Language and Linguistic Theory* 47].

Nilsen, Øystein (2003) 'Eliminating positions: syntax and semantics of sentence modification', Doctoral dissertation, University of Utrecht.

Önnerfors, Olaf (1997) *Verb-erst-Deklarativsätze. Grammatik und Pragmatik*, Stockholm: Almqvist & Wiksel International.

Pafel, Jürgen (1993) 'Scope and word order', in Joachim Jacobs, Arnim von Stechow, Wolfgang Sternefeld and Theo Vennemann (eds.), *Syntax: Ein internationales Handbuch zeitgenössischer Forschung*, Berlin: Mouton de Gruyter, pp. 867–80.

(1996) 'Die syntaktische und semantische Struktur von was-für-Phrasen', *Linguistische Berichte* 161: 37–67.

Pasch, Renate (1992) 'Überlegungen zur Syntax und semantischen Interpretation von w-Interrogativsätzen', *Deutsche Sprache* 3(19): 193–212.

Paul, Hermann (1919) *Deutsche Grammatik. Vol. III, part IV: Syntax*, Halle (Saale): Niemeyer.

Perlmutter, David M. and John Robert Ross (1970) 'Relative clauses with split antecedents', *Linguistic Inquiry* 1: 350.

Pesetsky, David (1987) 'Wh-in-situ: movement and unselective binding', in Eric Reuland and Alice ter Meulen (eds.), *The representation of (in)definiteness*, Cambridge, MA: MIT Press, pp. 98–129.

(1995) *Zero syntax: experiencers and cascades*, Cambridge MA: MIT Press.

(2000) *Phrasal movement and its kin*, Cambridge, MA: MIT Press.

Phillips, Colin (2003) 'Linear order and constituency', *Linguistic Inquiry* 34: 37–90.

Pittner, Karin (1995) 'The case of German relatives', *Linguistic Review* 12: 197–231.

Platzack, Christer (1986) 'Comp, Infl and Germanic Word Orders', in Lars Hellan and Kirsti Koch Kristensen (eds.), *Topics in Scandinavian Syntax*, Dordrecht: Reidel, pp. 185–234.

Poletto, Cecilia (2000) *The higher functional field: evidence from Northern Italian dialects*, New York and Oxford: Oxford University Press.

Pollock, Jean-Yves (1989) 'Verb movement, universal grammar, and the structure of IP', *Linguistic Inquiry* 20: 365–424.

Postal, Paul M. (1993) 'Parasitic gaps and the across-the-board phenomenon', *Linguistic Inquiry* 24: 735–54.

(2004) *Sceptical linguistic essays*, Oxford: Oxford University Press.

Putnam, Michael (2005) 'An anti-localistic account of why scrambled datives in German can't bind anaphors', *SKY Journal of Linguistics* 18: 287–309.

Quirk, Randolph, Sidney Greenbaum, Geoffrey N. Leech and Jan Svartvik (1985) *A comprehensive grammar of the English language*, 4th edition, London: Longman.

Reinhart, Tanya (1980) 'On the position of extraposed clauses', *Linguistic Inquiry* 11: 621–4.

(1983) *Anaphora and semantic interpretation*, London: Croom Helm.

(1995) 'Interface strategies', *OTS Working Paper*, Utrecht Institute of Linguistics (OTS), University of Utrecht.

(1998) 'Wh-in-situ in the framework of the Minimalist Program', *Natural Language Semantics* 6: 29–56.

Reis, Marga (1976) 'Reflexivierung in deutschen AcI-Konstruktionen. Ein transformationsgrammatisches Dilemma', *Papiere zur Linguistik* 9: 5–82.

(1987) 'Die Stellung der Verbargumente im Deutschen. Stilübungen zum Grammatik: Pragmatik-Verhältnis', in Inger Rosengren (ed.), *Sprache und Pragmatik*, [*Lunder germanistische Forschungen* 55], pp. 139–87.

(2000) 'On the parenthetical features of German *was ... w*-constructions and how to account for them', in Ulli Lutz, Gereon Müller and Arnim von Stechow (eds.), *Wh-scope-marking*, Amsterdam: John Benjamins, pp. 359–407.

(2002) 'Wh-Movement and integrated parenthetical constructions', in Jan Wouter Zwart and Werner Abraham (eds.), *Proceedings of the 15th Germanic Syntax Workshop*, Amsterdam: John Benjamins, pp. 3–40.

(2007) 'Modals, so-called semi-modals, and grammaticalization in German', *Interdisciplinary Journal for Germanic Linguistics and Semiotic Analysis* 12: 1–56.

Reis, Marga and Wolfgang Sternefeld (2004) 'Review article of S. Wurmbrand "Infinitives. Restructuring and clause structure"', *Linguistics* 42(2): 469–508.

Richards, Marc D. (2004) 'Object shift and scrambling in North and West Germanic: A case study in symmetrical syntax', Doctoral dissertation, University of Cambridge.

Richards, Marc D. and Theresa Biberauer (2005) 'Explaining Expl', in Marcel den Dikken and Christina Tortora (eds.), *The function of function words and functional categories*, Amsterdam: John Benjamins [*Linguistik Aktuell / Linguistics Today*, 78], pp. 115–54.

Riemsdijk, Henk C. van (1983) 'The case of German adjectives', in Frank Heny and Barry Richards (eds.), *Linguistic categories: auxiliaries and related puzzles*, vol. I, Dordrecht: Reidel, pp. 223–52.

(2006) 'Free relatives', in Henk C. van Riemsdijk and Martin Everaert (eds.), *Syncom – The Syntax Companion*, chapter 27, Oxford: Blackwell.

Riemsdijk, Henk C. van and Edwin Williams (1981) 'NP structure', *The Linguistic Review* 1: 171–217.

Rizzi, Luigi (1982) *Issues in Italian syntax*, Dordrecht: Foris.

    (1997) 'The fine structure of the left periphery', in Liliane Haegeman (ed.), *Elements of grammar. Handbook in Generative Syntax*, Dordrecht: Kluwer, pp. 281–337.

    (2004) (ed.) *The structure of CP and IP. The cartography of syntactic structures*, vols. I and II, Oxford: Oxford University Press.

Roberts, Ian (1997) 'Restructuring, head movement and locality', *Linguistic Inquiry* 28: 423–60.

Rohrbacher, Bernhard (1999) *Morphology-driven syntax. A theory of V to I raising and pro drop*, Amsterdam: John Benjamins [*Studies in Generative Linguistic Analysis* 4].

Rosengren, Inger (1993) 'Wahlfreiheit mit Konsequenzen – Scrambling, Topikalisierung und FHG im Dienste der Informationsstrukturierung', in Marga Reis (ed.), *Wortstellung und Informationsstruktur*, Tübingen: Niemeyer [*Linguistische Arbeiten* 306], pp. 251–312.

    (1994) 'Scrambling – was ist das?' in Brigitta Haftka (ed.), *Was determiniert Wortstellungsvariation?*, Opladen: Westdeutscher Verlag, pp. 85–196.

Ross, John (1967) 'Constraints on variables in syntax', PhD dissertation, Massachusetts Institute of Technology.

Ruys, E. G. (2001) 'Dutch scrambling and the strong–weak distinction', *The Journal of Comparative Germanic Linguistics* 4: 39–67.

Sabel, Joachim (2000) 'Das Verbstellungsproblem im Deutschen', *Deutsche Sprache* 28: 74–99.

    (2001) 'Wh-questions in Japanese: scrambling, reconstruction, and wh-movement', *Linguistic Analysis* 31: 1–41.

Saito, Mamoru (1994) 'Additional wh-effects and the adjunction site theory', *Journal of East Asian Linguistics* 3: 195–240.

Saito, Mamoru and Naoki Fukui (1998) 'Order in phrase structure and movement', *Linguistic Inquiry* 29: 439–74.

Sauerland, Uli (1999) 'Erasability and interpretation', *Syntax* 2: 161–88.

Schenner, Mathias (2004) 'Natürlichsprachliche Quantifikation und das Partitionierungsproblem', unpublished MA thesis, University of Salzburg.

Schulz, Dora and Heinz Griesbach (1970) *Grammatik der deutschen Sprache*, 8th edition, Munich: Hueber Verlag.

Sells, Peter (1990) 'VP in Japanese: evidence from -te complements', in Hajime Hoji (ed.), *Japanese / Korean Linguistics*, Stanford, CA: CSLI Publications, pp. 319–33.

Sigurðsson, Halldór Ármann (1989) 'Verbal syntax and case in Icelandic', Doctoral dissertation, University of Lund [Reprinted 1992 by Málvísindastofnun Háskóla Íslands].

    (2004) 'Icelandic non-nominative subjects', in Peri Bhaskararao and Karumuri V. Subbarao (eds.), *Non-nominative subjects*, Amsterdam: John Benjamins, pp. 137–59.

Skopeteas, Stavros and Gisbert Fanselow (2007) 'Effects of givenness and constraint on free word order', unpublished MS, University of Potsdam (to be published in Caroline Féry and Malte Zimmermann (eds.), *Information structure from different perspectives*).

Stechow, Arnim von and Wolfgang Sternefeld (1988) *Bausteine syntaktischen Wissens*, Opladen: Westdeutscher Verlag.

Steedman, Mark (1985) 'Dependency and coordination in the grammar of Dutch and English', *Language* 61: 523–68.

Sternefeld, Wolfgang (1985) 'Deutsch ohne grammatische Funktionen', *Linguistische Berichte* 99: 394–439.

(2006) *Syntax, eine morphologisch motivierte generative Beschreibung des Deutschen*, Tübingen: Stauffenburg Verlag.

(2007) *Syntax, eine morphologisch motivierte generative Beschreibung des Deutschen*, 2nd revised edition, Tübingen: Stauffenburg Verlag.

Stiebels, Barbara and Dieter Wunderlich (1994) 'Morphology feeds syntax: the case of particle verbs', *Linguistics* 32: 913–68.

Szabolcsi, Anna and Frans Zwarts (1993) 'Weak islands and an algebraic semantics for scope-taking', *Natural Language Semantics* 1: 235–85.

Thráinsson, Höskuldur (2001) 'Object shift and scrambling', in Mark Baltin and Chris Collins (eds.), *The handbook of contemporary syntactic theory*, Oxford: Blackwell, pp. 148–202.

Travis, Lisa (1991) 'Parameters of phrase structure and verb second phenomena', in Robert Freidin (ed.), *Principles and parameters in comparative grammar*, Cambridge, MA: MIT Press, pp. 339–64.

Trosterud, Trond (1989) 'The null subject parameter and the new mainland Scandinavian word order. A possible counterexample from a Norwegian dialect', in Jussi Niemi (ed.), *Papers from the eleventh Scandinavian conference on linguistics*, Joensuu [*Joensuun Ylioppilaskunnan Kirjakauppa* 1], pp. 87–100.

Truckenbrodt, Hubert (1995) 'Phonological phrases: their relation to syntax, focus, and prominence', Ph.D. dissertation, Massachusetts Institute of Technology.

Uriagereka, Juan (1993) 'The Syntax of Movement in Basque', in Joseph Lakarra and John Ortiz de Urbina (eds.), *Syntactic Theory and Basque Syntax, International Journal of Basque Linguistics and Philology*, XXVII, 417–45.

Vergnaud, Jean-Roger (1985) *Dépendances et niveaux de représentation en syntaxe*, Amsterdam: John Benjamins.

Vikner, Sten (1994) 'Scandinavian object shift and West Germanic scrambling', in Norbert Corver and Henk C. van Riemsdijk (eds.), pp. 487–517.

(1995) *Verb movement and expletive subjects in the Germanic Languages*, Oxford: Oxford University Press.

(1997) 'V°-to-I° movement and inflection for person in all tenses', in Liliane Haegeman (ed.), *The new comparative grammar*, London: Longman, pp. 189–213.

(2001) 'Verb movement variation in German and Optimality Theory', Habilitation thesis, University of Tübingen.

Vogel, Ralf and Markus Steinbach (1998) 'The dative – an oblique case', *Linguistische Berichte* 173: 65–90.

Wali, Kashi and Omkar N. Koul (1997) *Kashmiri. A cognitive-descriptive grammar*, London: Routledge.

Webelhuth, Gert (1992) *Principles and parameters of syntactic saturation*, Oxford: Oxford University Press.

Wegener, Heide (1990) 'Der Dativ – ein struktureller Kasus?' in Gisbert Fanselow and Sascha Felix (eds.), *Merkmale und Strukturen syntaktischer Kategorien*, Tübingen: Narr, pp. 70–103.

Wilder, Chris (1989) 'The syntax of German infinitives', Doctoral dissertation, University College, London.

Williams, Edwin (2002) *Representation theory*, Cambridge, MA: MIT Press.

(2004) 'The structure of clusters', in Katalin É. Kiss and Henk C. van Riemsdijk (eds.), pp. 173–201.

Wiltschko, Martina (1994) 'Extraposition in German', *Wiener Linguistische Gazette* 48–50: 1–30.

(1997) 'Extraposition, identification and precedence', in Dorothee Beerman, David LeBlanc and Henk C. van Riemsdijk (eds.), pp. 357–95.

(1998) 'Superiority in German', in Emily Curtis, James Lyle and Gabriel Webster (eds.), *Proceedings of WCCFL 16 University of Washington (1997)*, Stanford, CA: CSLI, pp. 431–46.

Wöllstein-Leisten, Angelika (2001) *Die Syntax der dritten Konstruktion*, Tübingen: Stauffenburg Verlag.

Woolford, Ellen (1993) 'Symmetric and asymmetric passives', *Natural Language and Linguistic Theory* 11: 679–728.

(1997) 'Four-way case systems: ergative, nominative, objective, and accusative', *Natural Language and Linguistic Theory* 15: 181–227.

(2006) 'Lexical case, inherent case, and argument structure', *Linguistic Inquiry* 37: 111–30.

Wunderlich, Dieter (1983) 'On the compositionality of German prefix verbs', in Rainer Bäuerle, Christoph Schwarze and Arnim von Stechow (eds.), *Meaning, use and interpretation of language*, Berlin: Mouton de Gruyter, pp. 452–65.

(1997) 'Cause and the structure of verbs', *Linguistic Inquiry* 28: 27–68.

Wurmbrand, Susanne (2001) *Infinitives: restructuring and clause structure*, Berlin: Mouton de Gruyter [*Studies in Generative Grammar* 55].

(2004) 'West Germanic verb clusters: the empirical domain' in Katalin É. Kiss and Henk C. van Riemsdijk (eds.) (2004), pp. 43–85.

Wyngaerd, Guido van den (1989) 'Object shift as an A-movement rule', *MIT Working papers in Linguistics* 11: 256–71.

Yip, Moira, Joan Maling and Ray Jackendoff (1987) 'Case in tiers', *Language* 63: 28–250.

Zaenen, Annie, Joan Maling and Hoskuldur Thráinsson (1985) 'Case and grammatical functions: the Icelandic passive', *Natural Language and Linguistic Theory* 3: 441–83.

Zwart, C. Jan-Wouter (1993) 'Dutch syntax. A minimalist approach', Doctoral dissertation, University of Groningen.

(1995) 'A note on verb clusters in the Stellingwerf dialect', in Marcel den Dikken and Kees Hengeveld (eds.), *Linguistics in the Netherlands*, Amsterdam: John Benjamins, pp. 215–26.

(1996) *Morphosyntax of verb movement. A minimalist approach to syntax of Dutch*, Dordrecht: Kluwer.

(2000) 'A head raising analysis of relative clauses in Dutch', in Artemis Alexiadou, Paul Law, André Meinunger and Chris Wilder (eds.), *The syntax of relative clauses*, Amsterdam: John Benjamins, pp. 349–85.

• The 'verb cluster homepage': http://wurmbrand.uconn.edu/research/Bibliographies/vs-bib.htm.

Index